P9-DWD-397

RAQUELA

A beautiful ninth-generation Sabra. Raised in a land as old as time amidst the growing violence between Arab and Jew. Coming to womanhood as the climactic struggle began, and a country rich with the heritage of two civilizations became drenched in the blood of both.

RAQUELA

A nurse amid the tragic suffering of British interment camps, and the savage horror of four wars. A midwife delivering by flashlight the babies of holocaust refugees. A passionate woman torn by desire for two men. A doctor's wife joining her husband in courage and dedication. A mother making the ultimate sacrifice of a beloved young son to war.

RAQUELA

A woman of fiery intelligence and tempestuous spirit whose life was a triumph over tragedy and disaster. A woman who will make you remember what greatness is all about.

"More than just the story of a woman . . . it is the saga of a people!"   —Dore Schary

"A moving story of love and loss, desperation and hope!"   —*Publishers Weekly*

Big Bestsellers from SIGNET

☐ **THE CRAZY LOVERS by Joyce Elbert.** (#E8917—$2.75)*

☐ **THE CRAZY LADIES by Joyce Elbert.** (#E8923—$2.75)

☐ **THE THREE OF US by Joyce Elbert.** (#E7323—$1.75)

☐ **THE HOUSE OF KINGSLEY MERRICK by Deborah Hill.**
(#E8918—$2.50)*

☐ **THIS IS THE HOUSE by Deborah Hill.** (#E8877—$2.50)

☐ **FOOLS DIE by Mario Puzo.** (#E8881—$3.50)

☐ **THE GODFATHER by Mario Puzo.** (#E8970—$2.75)

☐ **REAP THE BITTER WINDS by June Lund Shiplett.**
(#E8884—$2.25)*

☐ **THE RAGING WINDS OF HEAVEN by June Lund Shiplett.**
(#E8981—$2.25)

☐ **ASPEN INCIDENT by Tom Murphy.** (#J8889—$1.95)

☐ **LILY CIGAR by Tom Murphy.** (#E8810—$2.75)

☐ **BALLET! by Tom Murphy.** (#E8112—$2.25)

☐ **EYE OF THE NEEDLE by Ken Follett.** (#E8746—$2.95)

☐ **JO STERN by David Slavitt.** (#E8753—$1.95)*

☐ **DAYLIGHT MOON by Thomas Carney.** (#E8755—$1.95)*

* Price slightly higher in Canada

Buy them at your local bookstore or use this convenient coupon for ordering.

THE NEW AMERICAN LIBRARY, INC.,
P.O. Box 999, Bergenfield, New Jersey 07621

Please send me the SIGNET BOOKS I have checked above. I am enclosing
$_____ (please add 50¢ to this order to cover postage and handling).
Send check or money order—no cash or C.O.D.'s. Prices and numbers are
subject to change without notice.

Name _____

Address _____

City_____ State_____ Zip Code_____

Allow 4-6 weeks for delivery.
This offer is subject to withdrawal without notice.

RAQUELA

A Woman of Israel

Ruth Gruber

A SIGNET BOOK
NEW AMERICAN LIBRARY
TIMES MIRROR

NAL BOOKS ARE ALSO AVAILABLE AT DISCOUNTS IN BULK
QUANTITY FOR INDUSTRIAL OR SALES-PROMOTIONAL USE.
FOR DETAILS, WRITE TO PREMIUM MARKETING DIVISION,
NEW AMERICAN LIBRARY, INC., 1301 AVENUE OF THE
AMERICAS, NEW YORK, NEW YORK 10019.

Copyright © 1978 by Ruth Gruber

All rights reserved. This book, or parts thereof,
may not be reproduced in any form without
permission in writing from the publisher.
For information address Coward, McCann & Geoghegan, Inc.,
200 Madison Avenue, New York, New York 10016.

For permission to quote from copyrighted material, the author gratefully acknowledges Harper & Row Publishers, Inc. for excerpts on pages
327 and 328 from *Adventures of Mottel the Cantor's Son* by Sholom
Aleichem. Translated by Tamara Kahana. (Abelard-Schuman). Copyright 1953, by the children of Sholom Aleichem and Henry Schuman,
Inc. Reprinted by permission of Harper & Row Publishers, Inc.

Maps drawn by Mary Mietzelfeld

This is an authorized reprint of a hardcover edition
published by Coward, McCann & Geoghegan, Inc.
The hardcover edition was published simultaneously
in Canada by Longman Canada Limited, Toronto.

SIGNET TRADEMARK REG. U.S. PAT. OFF. AND FOREIGN COUNTRIES
REGISTERED TRADEMARK—MARCA REGISTRADA
HECHO EN CHICAGO, U.S.A.

SIGNET, SIGNET CLASSICS, MENTOR, PLUME AND MERIDIAN BOOKS
are published by The New American Library, Inc.,
1301 Avenue of the Americas, New York, New York 10019

First Signet Printing, November, 1979

3   4   5   6   7   8   9

PRINTED IN THE UNITED STATES OF AMERICA

To Henry

RAQUELA

A Woman of Israel

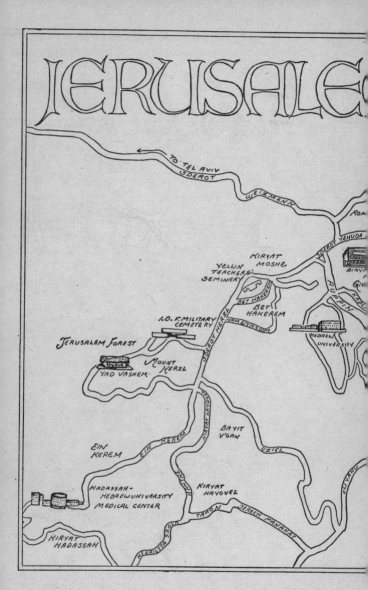

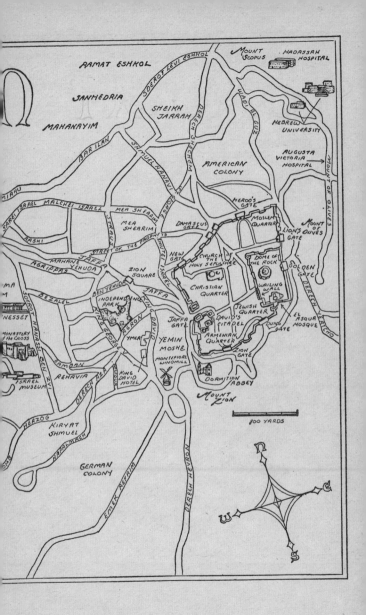

-⋖ Foreword ⋗-

A few years ago I flew to Israel on a quest: to find a woman—not Golda Meir, not a powerful world-renowned figure, but one whose life would define what it means to be a woman of Israel.

Having covered the story of Israel since its birth, as foreign correspondent for the New York *Herald Tribune*, I knew that every woman in Israel had a story; and when I began my search, I discovered that everyone with whom I talked, famous or obscure, had a candidate.

For countless hours, driving hundreds of miles up and down the country, I tracked down most of the candidates. I wanted a woman who had taken part in the so-called "illegal immigration" of Jewish survivors after World War II, fighting to enter Palestine; a woman who had been on the front lines in the four wars; a woman who had known in her own life the joy and agony of growing up in the biblical land, of being an Israeli.

In the end, It was Dr. Kalman J. Mann, the director general of the Hadassah-Hebrew University Medical Center, who said, "I think I have a candidate for you. She's a ninth-generation Jerusalemite. A nurse and midwife. She delivered most of the babies born to the illegal immigrants in the British camps in Athlit and Cyprus. She worked in the Hadassah Hospital during our wars. And was so beautiful that every man in Jerusalem wanted to marry her."

Five minutes after I met Raquela Prywes, in the King David Hotel in Jerusalem, I knew my search was over.

This, then, is her story.

For nine months my husband, Henry J. Rosner, and I lived in Jerusalem, first in the incomparable beauty of Mishkenot Sha'ananim, a writers' retreat facing the Old City, and then in all the places where Raquela had lived and worked; I wanted to capture a sense of place and time and history in the life story of a hitherto unknown but fascinating woman.

In the course of writing this book, I found that Raquela moved through so many levels of Israel's history, and her own life touched so many people, that to get the true measure of who she was and what she did, it was necessary to spend long hours interviewing not only her but also scores of others.

To all of them, I offer my deepest gratitude, for allowing me to share their memories and for giving me intimate and candid insights into Raquela's life, her character, and her relationships with her family, her friends, and the men she loved. Fuller acknowledgments are given at the end of the book.

I wish also to thank my friends Peggy Mann, Shira Cassel, and Dora Mae Gittler, for their invaluable criticism and help; John Geoghegan, my publisher; John Beaudoin, vice-president of the Reader's Digest Association; and Judith Wildman, my editor, whose enthusiasm spurred the book to completion.

And finally, I thank my husband, Henry J. Rosner, whose wisdom, perception, and love helped shape this book.

Ruth Gruber

~◄ Chapter One ►~

The handsome black-robed woman walked regally, carrying on her head a basket laden with eggs and freshly picked figs.

Five-year-old Raquela flung open the garden gate. Mama was already waiting in the little flagstone patio.

"*Salaam aleikum*, Aisha," Mama greeted her friend, in Arabic.

"*Salaam aleikum*, Mrs. Levy." Aisha lowered the basket from her head, easing it onto the stone floor as though it were filled with precious jewels. Mama brought out the shiny copper tray with demitasse cups filled with Turkish coffee.

Raquela stood, feet apart, in the center of the patio, an eager participant.

"Aisha"—Mama put down her cup—"I need the freshest eggs you have. My husband has the flu, and all he wants to eat is soft-boiled eggs."

Aisha drained the little cup. "Today I brought you eggs so fresh, this minute the chickens laid them."

"Then give me twenty-five. And I'll take a kilo of figs."

From her basket Aisha lifted a small wooden scale, measured the figs, and threw in an extra handful. "My present for your son Jacob. Because he gives me pine twigs from your garden for my cooking." She dropped her voice. "And because I love him."

"If your husband hears you love my son"—Mama's eyes were mischievous—"he will beat you up."

Raquela waited with familiar anticipation; it was a game they played every day.

Aisha smiled. "I won't tell my husband."

She bent to hug Raquela. "And you, little beauty, you will break many hearts in your time."

3

Raquela closed her eyes, letting Aisha wrap her in a cloak of musk and incense. She loved both these women, who could hardly have been less alike: Mama was tiny—barely five feet tall—with high-boned, Slavic cheeks, a delicate carved nose, and long chestnut hair radiant with sunlight. In her white blouse and pleated navy-blue skirt she looked like a young schoolteacher; she had, in fact, been teaching kindergarten when she married Raquela's father, her former teacher. Aisha, squatting on her heels, was exotic, mysterious, her body loosely robed in the voluminous Bedouin gown, her hair shrouded in a muslin shawl, her charcoal eyes burning inside the kohl lines she penciled around them.

The morning transaction was over. Aisha gathered up her basket and scales and disappeared down the street.

Early the next afternoon, Raquela was helping Mama pick flowers for the dinner table when the garden gate flew open.

Zayda, Mama's father, bolted in, the black coat-tails of his Hassidic garb flying behind him.

Mama dropped her shears. "What are you doing here on Friday afternoon before Shabbat?"

Zayda tried to catch his breath. He was slightly taller than Mama, with the same high Slavic cheekbones and the same sharp twinkling eyes. But today his eyes were different. Now they held fear.

Raquela had never seen him so excited. At home, in his threadbare cottage in a courtyard in the Mea Shearim quarter of Jerusalem, he was always bustling, laughing with Bubba, Mama's mother, singing Hassidic melodies, so happy even his beard seemed to bob with joy.

Now his beard was damp and sprinkled with perspiration.

"Trouble in Jerusalem," he panted. "I caught the bus to come up to warn you. I can stay only a few minutes—I must get home before Shabbat."

"But what happened?" Mama asked shakily.

"The Arabs are rioting in the Old City."

The panic in his voice sent Raquela hiding in Mama's skirt. Mama lifted her into her arms. "It's all right, child."

"I was praying at the Wailing Wall. I heard shouts and loud screams. So I ran down the street to see. There were maybe two thousand Arabs marching from the mosques.

Carrying banners like they carry on their holy days. Shouting 'Death to the Jews; there is no God but Allah; death to the Jews.' "

Zayda was frantic. "Don't waste a minute, Tova. Get your family together. Run."

Mama patted Raquela on the back reassuringly. "We have time. We're three miles away from the Old City."

"Three miles! You think up here, in Bet Hakerem, with your trees and your gardens and your playgrounds, you'll be safe? They can get here in an hour. Run, I tell you."

Raquela saw a shadow on the stone floor. Papa's six-foot-tall body filled the doorway.

"What's all the commotion?" His voice was raspy.

The August sun baked the patio, but Papa, wrapped in his burgundy winter bathrobe, was shivering.

"Nissim, you shouldn't be out of bed," Mama scolded. "with your fever, you'll catch pneumonia."

Papa stepped away from the door and towered over Zayda. "What terrible things bring you here before Shabbat?"

"Sick or not, Nissim"—Zayda shook his finger—"you must get the family to safety. Mobs of Arabs are leaving the Old City. They're fanning out in different directions, carrying guns and sticks. Some are already in Mea Shearim. Houses are burning. Who knows how many have been killed?"

"My mother?" Papa asked. "Do you have any word?"

Zayda shook his head.

Raquela shut her eyes, clinging to Mama. Were mobs of Arabs attacking her tall, beautiful grandmother?

"I don't know what parts of Jerusalem they're in now," Zayda said, his voice edged with hysteria. "We'll know soon enough."

"Is no one stopping them?" Papa demanded. "The British? The Haganah?"

The Jews of Palestine had formed small groups to defend themselves. They called themselves the Haganah—the Hebrew word for "self-defense."

"I saw some Haganah men with guns," Zayda said. "Wherever they appeared, the Arabs ran away. And I saw some British policemen on horseback chasing them. But they were only a handful; the Arabs are thousands. They must have been brought into Jerusalem from all over the country. Nissim, take the family and hide. Now I have to leave. It'll be sundown soon. If I can't get a bus, I'll have to run all the way home to Mea Shearim."

Zayda flew out of the garden gate.

"We have no time to waste," Papa said. "We must go straight to the Seminar." He looked out the gate, down Boulevard Street. "I see people running already. The news must be spreading fast. Ah, thank God, here are our boys."

Twelve-year-old Jacob and nine-year-old Yair entered the garden. Jacob was a runner for the Haganah. He looked at Papa. "You've heard?"

Papa nodded.

Jacob caught his breath. "We're expecting trouble from Deir Yassin and Ein Karem." These were nearby Arab villages. "I have five blocks; I have to tell the people to go to the Seminar immediately. I'll meet you up there."

Papa held Raquela's hand. Mama and Yair hurried out with the two baskets each family kept ready for just this emergency—one filled with clothing, the other with food. They ran down their street, then turned into the circle and raced up the Street of the Circle to the David Yellin Seminar, a teachers' seminary and school.

Raquela had watched the Seminar rise, like a romantic castle, on the highest hill. Not yet completed, it cut the sky, a huge bird of honey-colored stone with three arches in front and two long wings folded back. Someday there would be broad entrance stairs; now there was a concrete incline, and, inside, wooden planks formed a slanted runway from floor to floor.

Looking up at the parapets, Raquela saw two seventeen-year-old boys she knew, holding rifles, scanning the road for Arabs.

Grasping Papa's hand tightly, she ran up the concrete incline with Mama and Yair trailing with the two baskets and a pile of blankets. The building was already filling up with people as they mounted the wooden plank to the second floor.

The neighbors had long ago decided that if trouble came, the Seminar would be their sanctuary. Taking a lesson from the American pioneers, they had built it like a fortress. Here they could stand together and defend themselves. Each family's space had been carefully staked out according to the number of *balatas*—eight-inch-square

tiles—on the floor. Papa had been given space in the unfinished synagogue, where other families were already
camping in little clusters.

Mama spread some blankets on the tiles and bedded
Papa down. His tall, strong body was burning.

She took a swift survey of the narrow synagogue.
Arched windows with no glass, no protection. Cold *balatas*, cold tiles. Jerusalem days could be broiling in August,
but the nights were always cool, and sometimes freezing.

"I'm going home," Mama announced, "to get more
blankets and my warm featherbed quilt."

"Tova, don't go. It's too dangerous out there."

Raquela heard the anxiety in Papa's raspy throat.

"Don't worry, Nissim," Mama said. "I'll be careful."

Raquela clung to Mama's skirt. "Don't go, Mama.
Don't go."

"I must, child. Papa is sick. I don't want him getting
sicker, lying on that cold floor with the wind coming in at
night."

"I'll give him my sweater. Give him my blanket. I can
sleep on the tiles. Please, Mama, don't go."

"I've got to, Raquela. And I'll bring back your crayons
and your picture books."

Raquela stumbled down the wooden plank after Mama.
"Wait, Mama, don't go." She followed Mama toward the
door.

Papa called out, "Yair, go after Raquela. Get her
back."

Yair dragged her back into the fortress-school, weeping.

Within half an hour, Mama was back, carrying blankets
and the thick featherbed quilt. Through the open windows
they could see the sun beginning to sink behind the hills.
Mama took two small candlesticks from one of her baskets, set them firmly on the white cloth she had spread on
the tile floor, covered her eyes, and recited the Sabbath
prayer.

More candles were lit in the little campsites all over the
half-finished synagogue. The families joined in chanting
the love song to the Sabbath, the poem that Jews all over
the world would sing at dusk:

> O come, my friend, to meet the bride,
> O come and welcome the Sabbath queen.

The magic of Shabbat cast its familiar spell over the school. Raquela forgot the terror outside.

Shots rang out from the roof. A cascade of bullets rocked the building. Raquela dived under the blanket and squeezed herself into Papa's protective arms.

Instantly the women blew out the Sabbath candles. The sun was gone; the room was in total darkness. The families huddled together. Were they safe, even in their fortress-school?

Footsteps resounded on the wooden planks. The front door opened, and banged shut.

Mama whispered to Raquela, "Come, child. Get under the featherbed and try to sleep."

Raquela lay with her eyes shut, but she could not sleep. From a family group next to theirs, she heard a woman weeping, "Did we move up here to Bet Hakerem to be slaughtered?"

"Sh-sh"—Raquela could almost see Mama trying to calm the woman—"don't talk that way. We came here for our children, to get away from the crowded city, to give them good air and room to grow in."

"Good air!" the woman mocked. "Room to grow! They may never grow. We may all be killed."

Raquela lay under the warm quilt, frozen with fear.

Raanan Weitz, one of the seventeen-year-old sentries, entered the synagogue. He was carrying a rifle and a flashlight.

"We've driven them off," he announced.

Raquela, still awake, could hear little prayers of thanks going up around the room.

"We saw them from the roof," Raanan explained. "A whole gang of Arabs coming across the wadi from Deir Yassin."

Deir Yassin, an all-Arab village, was known to be a hotbed of fanatics. Playing on the rocks in Bet Hakerem, Raquela could look right across the riverbed to the Arab village she and her friends dreaded most.

Raanan tried to put the people's fears to rest. "We scared a whole bunch of them with our rifles, shooting from the roof. Then we ran down to make sure they hadn't penetrated Bet Hakerem. Sure enough, they had got into some of the gardens and were entering the houses."

Raquela listened, her heart beating wildly, as Raanan went on.

"When they saw us, they beat it back across the wadi to Deir Yassin. We're safe now. You can all go to sleep."

Saturday afternoon, flames lit the sky.

"Motza is burning!"

The words raced through the crowded halls. Everyone knew someone in Motza, the picturesque little resort village in the Hills of Judea.

An hour later, a young man entered the Seminar. He was taken immediately to Menachem Orshansky, a burly dark-mustached man who represented the Haganah in Bet Hakerem. The men and women of Bet Hakerem had not yet officially joined the Haganah. Orshansky, who had been an officer in the Russian army before the Revolution, had escaped from Russia, joined the Haganah, and now commanded the volunteers in Bet Hakerem's defense unit.

He called the people together in the auditorium. Papa, still feverish, insisted on going despite Mama's protests. The two hundred people—men, women, teenagers, toddlers, infants—assembled on the second floor. Raquela sat in Mama's lap.

Orshansky stood in front of the auditorium, lifting his hand for silence.

"We have a messenger from Haganah headquarters. They sent him to find out if Bet Hakerem needs help and to tell us what's happening in Jerusalem and Motza."

The young man, scholarly-looking with thick glasses, stood next to Orshansky. "Jerusalem is secure!" he said.

Relief swept through the room.

"We were lucky in Jerusalem. We had not only the British police, who really tried to quell the riot, but also the Haganah. And we had a group of Oxford students— Christians—who happened to be in the Holy Land. When they saw what was happening, they asked the police for guns. Those English students were incredible. They helped save Jerusalem."

"Thank God," Papa said, in a hushed voice, to Mama. "But if only we could find out if my mother is safe."

Raquela envisioned her grandmother, Señora Vavá, sitting on the windowsill, looking down at the Old City. Had Arab mobs bursting out of the Jaffa Gate broken into her grandmother's house, just outside the walls of the Old City, the way the Arabs of Deir Yassin had broken into Bet Hakerem? She felt numb. Señora Vavá had to be safe.

The people were murmuring, asking questions about what had happened in Jerusalem. Orshansky interrupted. "*Sheket*—quiet. Now we want to hear about Motza. Our messenger was there; let him tell you."

The bespectacled messenger began talking rapidly. Raquela tried to listen, though some of the words were unfamiliar to her.

"Yesterday, Friday morning, when the people of Motza heard about the riots in Jerusalem, a few of them said, 'Let's go to Jerusalem and ask the Haganah for protection.' But they didn't go. Do you know why?"

The people shook their heads in silence.

"The sheikh of Colonia, the Arab village next to Motza, came himself on horseback and swore by Allah that if any Arabs came up from Jerusalem and attacked them, he would return with his own Arabs and defend them. Were they not his good friends? Did they not buy all his fruits? The people of Motza were reassured."

Raquela saw Papa breathing hard.

The messenger's voice was the only sound in the crowded hall. "The Arabs did not come from Jerusalem. They came from Colonia. Yes, the sheikh himself was leading them. They knew all the houses. They broke down the doors. Murdering, looting, burning."

Raquela burrowed into Mama's body. Mama tried to stand up, and whispered, "Let's go back to the synagogue, Raquela." But Raquela seemed unable to move.

"They smashed their way into one of the rest homes, butchered the owner, his son, his two daughters, and two guests from Tel Aviv. One of them was Rabbi Solomon Schlacht, eighty-five years old."

A cry ruptured the hall. Raquela put her hands over her ears.

"Where were the British?" Papa called out.

"Where were the British?" Orshansky mocked. "Where are the British in Bet Hakerem? True, they were in Jerusalem. But they're still trying to be 'neutral.' They allow the Arabs to carry as many rifles as they want. We're arrested if they catch us with even a rusty old pistol."

Papa's breath seemed strangled. Cold sweat gathered on his forehead.

The Haganah messenger went on: "Word came to headquarters that Motza was burning. A group of us jumped into a car and drove up the mountain to the village. The

moment the Arabs saw our car, they fled down the ravines, carrying all the loot they had stolen. The minute they
see our guns, they run. They attack only defenseless Jews."
His voice changed. He spoke slower now. "We tried to put
out the fires. We went into the houses. Whole families were
dead." He paused, looking around the hall. "Do any of you
know the Makleff family?"

Raquela saw the look of horror in Mama's eyes.

"I do," Mama called out. "One of the girls was my
classmate; we taught together."

He looked straight at Mama. "The Makleff family have
been murdered. Only Moti, their nine-year-old son, is
alive. He hid under a bed and watched the massacre of his
father, his mother, and his entire family."*

All night in the darkness the families sat in their makeshift compounds, talking. What was happening in other
parts of Palestine? Were the Arabs rioting in the north?
The west? The desert?

This was the second serious riot. The first one had
started when a handful of Arab terrorists protested the
Balfour Declaration.

The Balfour Declaration! On November 2, 1917, as the
First World War I raged on, British prime minister Lloyd
George, grateful to the Jews for their part in the war and
sympathetic to the Zionist dream of a Jewish homeland,
authorized his foreign secretary, Arthur Balfour, to proclaim to the world, "His Majesty's Government views with
favour the establishment in Palestine of a national home
for the Jewish people."

The Balfour Declaration was celebrated with joy
throughout the Jewish world; the dream of returning to
the Promised Land, revived by the Viennese-Jewish play-
wright Theodor Herzl in the 1890s, was to be fulfilled.
Both Lloyd George and Arthur Balfour were deeply religious men, steeped in the Bible. According to Dr. Chaim
Weizmann, the distinguished scientist, statesman, and
leader, the two men "understood as a reality the concept
of the Return. It appealed to their tradition and faith."

The allies, meeting in San Remo, Italy, in 1920, had
confirmed the pledge given in the Balfour Declaration. In
the Middle East, once part of the Ottoman Empire, British

* In 1952, Moti Makleff became chief of staff of the Israel Army.

and French rulers replaced the Turks, and in 1922 Great Britain was given the "mandate" by the League of Nations to administer Palestine and establish the "national home for the Jewish people."

A small fringe of the Arab community went on a rampage, denouncing the Mandate. "There will be no Jewish homeland in Palestine!" they shouted. But they had little influence on the masses of Arabs who lived side by side with the Jews. For these Arabs the words "no Jewish homeland" had little meaning. Their own needs were crushing: to fight starvation, disease, blindness, to keep their babies alive. Under the Turkish rule there had been almost no medical care, and there were inadequate medical services under the British. Medical care came from their neighbors, the Jews, who were determined to wipe out the dread diseases and to keep Jews and Arabs alive.

Moreover, the Arab *fellahin* who worked for Jews in the towns and farms were paid the same wages as Jewish workers, often two or three times more than they received from Arab employers. The *effendis,* their cheap labor threatened, went into the coffeehouses and mosques to incite mobs of Arabs with the promise of rich loot if they killed the Jews. Still, most of the *fellahin* refused to join the mobs. And for a few years there was relative peace in the land.

Why, now, this second riot?

Sleeping fitfully under the quilt, Raquela heard voices around her. "Why should they attack us in Bet Hakerem?" Papa was saying, "We didn't steal this land. We bought it from the Greek patriarch of Saint Simeon Church, in Jerusalem. It was wasteland."

Papa had often told Raquela how Bet Hakerem had looked when he first saw it, seven years ago, in 1922—a barren mountain with not a single human living there, inhabited only by jackals and cratered with huge boulders bleached white in the sun. Jeremiah had walked on these hills.

The men in the blacked-out synagogue, now talking in whispers, were the very pioneers, teachers, scholars, poets, who had left their work in downtown Jerusalem each afternoon and tugged pickaxes three miles to these hills to break up the boulders and build their homes. Their dream was to make this newest outpost of Jerusalem like the Holy City of King David's day, when each man could sit beneath his fig tree in his own vineyard. Indeed, they named their colony Bet Hakerem, "house of the vineyard."

The house Papa built on his allotted two dunams, which equaled half an acre, was typical: a simple stucco cottage with a pink-tile roof, a porch in front, a small patio on the side, and a garden in which he planted the calla lilies he loved and a tree for each of his three children.

The little colony was surrounded by Arab villages, most of them friendly. The hostile ones, like Deir Yassin, were a few small groups within the Arab community.

Why, then, this new riot?

Sitting together on the floor of the synagogue, the people pieced together the events of the last few days. A week ago, they reminded one another, some two hundred boys and girls had come from Tel Aviv and marched to the Wailing Wall, raising the blue and white flag of Zion. It was to protest harassment by Arab agitators who for months had marched their camels and goats in front of the Wall; they had played cymbals and beat drums to drown out the prayers of the worshipers.

The young people from Tel Aviv had come to ask the British to do something—to make sure the Jews had their full right to the Wall. They demanded protection to pray before the holy place where Jews had prayed for two thousand years.

The Arabs had used the peaceful demonstration as their excuse; they spread rumors throughout the country: "The Jews have held a warlike demonstration against us." Arab newspapers carried the headlines PROTEST! COME TO JERUSALEM!, AND DO WHAT MUST BE DONE!

A week before, on Friday morning, August 16, a mob of Arab Moslems had left their mosques and begun marching and shouting. The people at the Wall heard them in time and fled through the streets of the Old City. The *shamus* remained at his post to guard the prayer books and the prayer shawls. The mob attacked him, tearing off his clothes and beating him. Then they ripped the prayer books, made a fire, and burned the holy books and the prayer shawls.

The next day, Shabbat, a young Jewish boy, retrieving his soccer ball in an Arab garden, was stabbed. The neighborhood erupted; Arabs and Jews were injured. A few days later, the young boy died. Thousands of Jews joined

the funeral cortège as the shocked parents walked beside
the body of their son.

The procession was moving down Jaffa Road when
gangs of Arabs broke into the Jewish quarter and attacked
the mourners. British and Arab policemen mounted on
horseback charged into the crowd, brandishing clubs, chasing people in all directions. The men carrying the boy's
body were beaten on the head, forced to put the body
down and to run from the police. Amid all the running
and beating and yelling, the body of the young boy was
left alone. Hours later, his family crept back through the
quiet streets to bury their son.

Sunday afternoon Orshansky called the people to return
to the auditorium.

"Raquela," Mama had said, "you go play with the other
children."

Most of the parents had decided to keep their children
out of the auditorium; yesterday's experience had given
too many of them nightmares.

Raquela and a handful of children played their favorite
game—racing up and down the wooden planks where
someday there would be stairs. But soon she grew tired of
the game and tiptoed to the back of the auditorium. She
saw Orshansky; his eyes were bloodshot, his mustache
bristled. She heard him lash out, "There is not one Jew
left in Hebron!"

"Impossible!" someone shouted.

Jews had lived in Hebron since the days when Abraham
had come and pitched his tent. Here David had reigned
for seven and one-half years before he made Jerusalem his
capital. Here the patriarchs Abraham, Isaac, and Jacob,
and their wives, Sarah, Rebecca, and Leah, were buried.
Hebron was one of the four sacred Jewish cities:
Jerusalem, Hebron, Safed, and Tiberias.

Orshansky rustled notes in his hands. "Headquarters has
just sent us the facts about Hebron. Many of us have relatives and friends there; you will know their names. You
know the pharmacist, Ben Zion Gershon. The man who
healed hundreds of Arabs. Sixty-five years old. On Shabbat, a gang of Arabs broke into his home. First they cut
off his nose and hands. Then they pierced his eyes. They
broke the skulls of three of his children, caught his oldest
daughter and raped her."

Raquela saw Mama sitting against the wall, her face white with horror.

Orshansky was bitter. "I'll read you one more. Someone all of us have heard of and whom many of us know—the chief Ashkenazic rabbi, Rav Jacob Joseph Slonim. They broke into the house of his oldest son, Eliezer Dan Slonim—the only Jew in Hebron the British allowed to have a gun for protection. The Arabs chopped his hand off before he could shoot. They killed him, his wife, and his five-year-old son. His wife's parents were visiting; her father was the chief rabbi of Zichron Yaakov. They were both killed."

The room seemed to grow suddenly dark.

"An eighty-year-old woman, Mrs. Paya Hillman,* the mother of a rabbi, lived in a room in the young Slonim's house. When they saw the Arabs butchering the Slonims, seventeen people huddled in one room to escape. The Arabs broke in. The old Mrs. Hillman fell to the floor and pretended she was dead. To test her, the Arabs cut her left arm from the elbow right through her hand. She lay there, not moving, not uttering a sound. The Arabs, convinced she was dead, then slaughtered the others and threw them on top of her. Finally, when all was silent in the house, she called out, 'Get off me. You're killing me.' Nobody moved. They were all dead. She lay there bleeding, her head bruised from the boots of the men they had thrown on top of her. Finally, a policeman entered the house and found her moaning. They took her to a hospital in Jerusalem."

"What about the rabbi?" Raquela heard Papa's voice. "Rav Slonim? Is he alive?"

"The Arab mob moved from young Slonim's house to his father's house across the road. They pushed open Rabbi Slonim's door, screaming, 'Kill the rabbi! Kill his family!' Suddenly the noise stopped. The rabbi's Arab landlord rode his horse up and down in front of the house, shouting to the mob, 'Over my dead body will you enter this house.' The rabbi was saved, with his wife and his eight-year-old daughter Rivka.† But he is a broken man."

---

* Mrs. Paya Hillman is the great-grandmother of Ambassador Chaim Herzog, Israel's delegate to the UN.

† Now Mrs. Yosef Burg, whose husband was minister of the interior in the Rabin government and minister of the interior and police in the Begin government.

"How many Jews were killed in Hebron?" a woman asked in an anguished voice.

"Sixty-six murdered," Orshansky said. "Fifty-eight wounded. Those are the figures we have so far." He paused. "You're wondering about the British. When the Arabs attacked, their war cry was '*Al dawlat ma'ana*—the government is with us.' " He looked around the room. The people were silent. "Finally the British officer in Hebron called for police to come in from Jerusalem. Twelve British police and twelve Royal Air Force men arrived. Just twenty-four additional men, and they were enough to drive the Arabs off. Now the police have rounded up not the Arabs but all the Jews of Hebron, more than six hundred, and locked them in the police station. For protection, they say."

"Where are the people now?" Josef Weitz, Ranaan's father, asked.

"Taken to Jerusalem. Forced to leave everything—books, jewels, family heirlooms—abandon everything to the Arabs. The British have told the Jews they will never again be allowed to live in Hebron."

Hebron! The word spread like brushfire through the room.

Orshansky's face contorted with anger. "If we need any proof to the world that we can rely only on the Haganah, these riots have shown it. Wherever the Haganah intervened, even with only two or three men, the mobs fled. There was no Haganah in Hebron. The Jews were afraid our men would provoke the Arabs. 'We've been living with Arabs for hundreds of years,' they said. 'They'll do us no harm. We go to one another's weddings and festivals. We treat their sick in our Hadassah clinic. They're our friends.'

"The Haganah didn't go to Hebron." Orshansky's words became a bitter lamentation. "No, we didn't go to Hebron. Look what happened!"

Raquela stole out of the auditorium and fled back to the security of her featherbed quilt. She kept hearing the words—*Hebron, Motza, Rabbi Slonim*—and seeing the Makleff boy in Motza. But *she* was the boy, hiding under the bed, watching Arab men cut off Mama's and Papa's heads.

Papa found her under the quilt, sobbing hysterically. He

lifted her and held her tightly. "We're safe here, my darling. What you heard—it's just a few bad Arabs. The Haganah knows how to make them run away."

Raquela's sobs began to subside.

Papa stroked her hair. "Most of the Arabs are good. Look at Aisha. She would never do these bad things."

Raquela lay in his arms, still trembling.

⚔ Chapter Two ⚔

September 1929

For two weeks the families lived inside the fortress-school.
Occasionally Mama slipped home to get a change of underwear for the children, but with the little grocery shop
closed, food soon ran out. Zayda came one morning, walking the three miles with baskets of fresh fruits and bread
and jars of chicken soup that Bubba had cooked. The
Haganah men guarding the highway to Bet Hakerem tried
to stop the little bearded man in black Hassidic garb, warning him of the dangers. He laughed. "God will protect
me."

The people in the unfinished synagogue crowded around
Mama and Papa. They shared not only the food but also
the news Zayda brought, for there was not a single telephone in all of Bet Hakerem.

Another day Zayda slipped past the Haganah lines and
brought the good news that he had made a special trip to
Señora Vavá's house. He had found her unharmed, concerned only about her children and her grandchildren.
Raquela ran into Zada's arms; her beautiful grandmother
was safe.

But the rest of his news was frightening. Safed had suffered a fate similar to that of Hebron: homes burned and
looted, synagogues vandalized, Bibles desecrated; forty-five
men, women, and children savagely murdered.

Mama let Raquela stay and listen to Zayda, but most of
the time when the news was bad, she sent her to play with
her kindergarten friends. Raquela raced and skipped and
slid down the wooden planks, and played hide-and-seek in
the unfinished classrooms. The days passed swiftly, but the
nights were long and dark, and the terror and the nightmares returned.

Finally, again on a Friday morning, Orshansky called

18

the people together. "We believe the riots are over." Papa, recovered from the flu, though still weak, helped Mama and the children gather up the blankets and baskets. The families went home.

Peace returned to Jerusalem.

But Raquela was scarred.

She no longer stood on the road, waiting for Papa to return from school; she no longer waved at the Arab men riding their donkeys back to their villages. Rumors grew among the children that Arab men were kidnapping pretty Jewish children.

They were home only a few days when Mama, standing on the front porch, saw Raquela twisting her mouth and crossing her eyes.

"What kind of faces are you making?" Mama called out.

"Sh-sh," Raquela whispered, running up to the porch. She pointed to the road. "Those Arab men—they steal little girls. I make these faces so I won't look beautiful."

Mama put her hands on her hips. "And who told you you're beautiful? You're not so pretty."

Raquela burst into tears. "Everybody says I'm pretty. Only you don't." Her voice choked. "Only you don't say I'm pretty."

"Look here," Mama said, "you're a healthy child. You're not pretty. No Arab is going to steal you."

Raquela tossed her head and entered the cottage. She went into Mama's bedroom, opened the door of the wardrobe, and studied her face in the mirror. She saw short blond hair curling around her forehead. She turned to look at her nose in profile. It was straight, like Mama's. She had Papa's dark Sephardic eyes and Mama's fair Russian skin.

She drew herself up; she was already taller than most of her friends in kindergarten. She hoped she would be tall, like Papa. Then, moving closer to the glass, she touched her face to the mirror and grimaced. No matter what mama said, she would twist her mouth and cross her eyes whenever she saw an Arab. She *was* beautiful, and it was better to be safe.

Saturday belonged to Papa's mother, Señora Vavá. Early Shabbat morning, Raquela strode happily between

Mama and Papa while Jacob and Yair sauntered ahead, up and down the myriad hills that made up Jerusalem, until they saw Mount Zion and the ramparts of the Old City.

Señora Vavá lived just outside the Old City, in the oldest quarter of new Jerusalem, Yemin Moshe. Her house was halfway up a hill of broad yellow-stone stairs, amid a cluster of gardens, olive trees, and sun-dappled stone houses topped by a white windmill.

She stood at the window, waving to the family; then she came to the door, greeted Papa and Mama and the two boys, and bent to kiss her favorite grandchild, Raquela.

Raquela, properly respectful, kissed her hand. *"Shalom,* Señora Vavá," she said. "Señora Vavá" was the Sephardic greeting; it meant, literally, "Mrs. Grandmother," a fitting tribute of courtesy for the elegant matriarch. Raquela, aware she was singled out, danced after her, inside the door.

The house smelled of Shabbat. The tile floors sparkled; the bright oriental carpets caught the sunlight; the burnished oak table was festive with a white lace cloth and brass candlesticks. Raquela licked her lips as she drank in the rich, varied Mideastern odors of hot *barakhas,* the little cakes her grandmother stuffed with meat or vegetables, and the special Shabbat stew Señora Vavá prepared on Friday and carried to the communal oven, a huge black cave in the side of the hill. The baker kept the oven steaming hot all Friday night, until Saturday noon. For no food could be cooked on Shabbat; the stew, its delicious medley of odors wafting through all the houses of Yemin Moshe, was uniquely Jewish, born of the proscription against doing any work on the Sabbath, the day of rest.

They seated themselves around the oak table.

"Señora Vavá," Raquela asked hesitantly, putting down her spoon, "were there Arab riots when you were a little girl?"

Her grandmother looked meaningfully at Mama, who nodded. "No, Raquela, we lived peacefully together inside the Old City; many of us lived next door to one another. Even though there were different quarters—the Jewish quarter, the Armenian quarter, the Greek quarter, the Moslem quarter—it didn't matter. We played games together, running and laughing through all the quarters; we were in and out of one another's houses all day long."

Señora Vavá smiled at her five-year-old granddaughter,

who basked in the warmth of the smile. Señora Vavá was a portrait in brown: her long, full dress was a rustle of brown silk, with tiny mother-of-pearl buttons from her high collar to her waist; a richly brocaded stole of brown damask woven with gold threads draped her shoulders; and a brown silk kerchief, which she knotted in front, Sephardic style, covered her long hair, which was blond, like Raquela's.

"Inside the Old City it was peaceful," she went on. "But outside there was danger. Gangs of Bedouins used to rob and even kill travelers coming up to Jerusalem for the holy days to pray at the Wailing Wall."

Raquela's eyes opened wide. The Wailing Wall! Why did they always seem to be killing people who wanted to pray at the Wall?

"Señora Vavá?" Yair spoke up.

"Yes, Yair?" Señora Vavá looked at him across the table. The children knew she carried the whole story of the family in her head.

"Abdullah—he's an Arab shepherd boy I meet sometimes when I play in the boulders—he says we had all these troubles, the Arabs killed all these people, because it was their country and they were here before us. But you always say our family is here three hundred years."

Señora Vavá looked serious. "You tell your friend Abdullah your great-great-great-great-great-great-great-grandfather came here in the year 1650."

"From Spain," Jacob added. At twelve, he was the intellectual of the family, following in Papa's footsteps.

"Yes," she said, and nodded to Jacob. "We left Spain in 1492. The same year Christopher Columbus discovered America. Then our family went to Italy, and from Italy they came to Jerusalem."

"But Abdullah says they were here before us," Yair persisted.

She was angry now; Raquela felt uneasy.

"What does your friend Abdullah mean, they were here before us? Abraham was here more than four thousand years ago. Thousands of years before Mohammed, who died, if I remember right, in 632 A.D."

The family sat around the table, silent. Señora Vavá's amethyst eyes were flashing.

"You, children"—she turned from Jacob and Yair to Raquela—"you are ninth-generation Jerusalemites. You

are as much part of this land as the rocks and boulders
you play on. Our family, and not only ours—hundreds of
families—have been here, making this land what it is. The
land of Israel.

"Your links go back even in your names." She looked at
Jacob, her first-born grandson. "You, Jacob Mordechai,
you were named not only for my husband, Jacob Mordechai, of blessed memory, but you were also named for a
long line of Jacob Mordechais. All rabbis." She repeated
the words, like a litany. "All rabbis. Spiritual men.
Guarding Jerusalem. Keeping it holy." Raquela had rarely
seen Señora Vavá so impassioned. Usually she was calm,
serene, with a little mysterious smile around her lips. Now
her lips were tight as she spoke. "One of the holiest of all
the rabbis was your grandfather; may he be a good petitioner for you. He was the right arm of the chief
Sephardic rabbi of the Old City. Everyone came to him.
He knew each person's problems; he knew their births and
their deaths, their troubles and their happiness. Only your
father broke the long line of rabbis. He became a
teacher." The smile returned. "Maybe it's just as well. It's
not so bad having a famous son who's head of the important Elementary School for Boys."

Raquela felt a surge of pride. She knew Papa was
special; now Señora Vavá, who carried so much in her
head, confirmed it.

Mama removed the empty plates and brought out the
barakhas. They finished the Shabbat lunch and moved to
the burgundy velvet sofa and the hard-backed chairs protected with lace antimacassars.

Señora Vavá sat in her favorite chair, near the window
overlooking the Old City. She called Raquela to sit on a
wicker stool at her feet.

"When I was a little girl, your age"—she leaned toward
Raquela—"the Old City was so crowded, the people were
so poor, they lived on top of one another in little rooms
like chicken coops. Then, maybe fifty years ago, the great
Sir Moses Montefiore came to Jerusalem in a golden coach
with his wife, Judith, and saw the misery and poverty.
And an American Jew, Judah Touro, who lived in a place
called New Orleans, left money for the poor of Jerusalem,
and with it they built these first houses outside the Old
City. Both these men were like us—Sephardic Jews."

She looked out the window. Raquela could almost see

the Montefiores riding in their golden coach through Jerusalem.

"They had to pay some of the families to move out," Señora Vavá said ruefully. "The people were afraid to leave the Old City, where the big gates, like the Jaffa Gate, were bolted shut every night. But not your grandfather. Not Rabbi Jacob Mordechai Levy. We moved on, in 1909—twenty years ago—to this very house. And we named our whole quarter Yemin Moshe—'the hand of Moses'—for the great Moses Montefiore." She shut her eyes. "We gave up the protection of the Old City so our children could live better. But these riots—who would have dreamt?" Her voice trailed off.

The afternoon sun fell in golden bars on the carpet.

The Sabbath was over.

Señora Vavá bade good-bye to the family and embraced her granddaughter. "When you come, I see my childhood all over again. I see myself in you. It is good you bear my name: Raquela."*

In the years that followed, tensions continued to build. Hitler came to power in 1933; a trickle of German Jews arrived in the Holy Land; by 1936, seventy thousand had found refuge in Palestine.

The Arab mufti of Jerusalem, Haj Amin el-Husseini, went on a new rampage to halt the immigration. Husseini was the most notorious terrorist in Palestine. In the early 1920s the British had appointed him "mufti of Jerusalem," the highest Moslem post in Palestine, reasoning that power and money would make him turn respectable, and amenable to British rule.

At first, it seemed the British had chosen well. The red-bearded, blue-eyed mufti abandoned his terrorist tactics until he was elected president of the Supreme Moslem Council. This post gave him control over the mosques, the courts, the schools, the cemeteries, and all Moslem religious funds in Palestine. Now he discarded his cloak of respectability; he used his money and power to win over the illiterate *fellahin,* and sought to terrorize not only the Jews but also the British, hoping to drive them all out of Palestine.

The mufti sent his cohorts to roam the highways and to

_____

* Sephardic Jews name their children for the living as well as for the dead.

rob trucks for more money to buy more guns. They murdered in the kibbutzim; they rioted in the towns.

The Haganah, still outlawed by the British, and unable to rely on the Mandatory Government, grew stronger. Many of the farm settlements became fortresses, like the Seminar. And the Seminar itself became the Haganah's secret training ground for the whole western slope of Jerusalem. Here, too, young men and women of eighteen, idealistic and courageous, were sworn into the Haganah.

Jacob Mordechai Levy, not yet nineteen, descended the side steps of the Seminar, into the basement. The light was dim. He could make out a long table and the shapes of three men. Someone took his hand and led him to the table, facing the men. Gradually his eyes adjusted to the darkness; at one end of the table he saw a Bible, at the other end a gun. He understood the symbolism. He was to defend the Book, the Land of the Book, and the People of the Book.

A slender, attractive young woman—whom he recognized in the shadows as a Haganah leader from the Zichron Moshe quarter—approached him.

"Jacob," she said, "stand up."

He rose and moved to the wall.

"Place your hand on the Bible," she said, "and repeat after me the oath of the Haganah."

Jacob repeated. . . . "I hereby swear that I will dedicate all my strength, and if necessary give my life, for the defense of my people and my homeland, for the freedom of the Land of Israel and the redemption of Zion."

Later, at home, Jacob called the family into the living room. "From now on," he said, "you must never ask me where I am going or where I have been. If the British or the Arabs capture me, they will surely come here and try to force information from you. They may even torture you."

Raquela flung her arms around her brother. But no words came from her throat.

Mama and Raquela entered the bus to go shopping downtown. Raquela could hardly sit still, anticipating her Bat Mitzvah, November 2, 1936. It was her twelfth birthday—her coming of age in the Jewish community. They were to spend the day buying her a white party dress, white pumps, and an assortment of cakes at the Patt Bakery.

The bus was crowded. Behind her she heard two women speaking Hebrew with German accents. The German Jews had added a new ingredient to the rich, polyglot Jewish population. They had brought with them, to the still-provincial Middle East, their industry, their skills, their sophistication, their European culture. Listening to the women, Raquela thought of Rafi Blumenfeld, at school. His father had been the leader of the Zionist organization in Germany and was now a power in the Jewish Agency. Going to Rafi's house was like taking a trip abroad for Raquela. The furniture was German Biedermeier, stately and elegant, unlike Mama's simple, unadorned sofa and chairs. The Blumenfelds had brought a large record collection with them, and Raquela and Rafi, both now studying violin, sat transfixed, as if they were in a Berlin living room, listening to Bach and Mozart.

"I always feel better"—one of the German women sounded fearful—"when we get past this part of Jerusalem." Raquela caught her anxiety: fear was a contagion, riots could break out any moment, anyplace.

They were driving through Romema. On the sidewalk Arab men with long black skirts sat on little stools in front of their shops and coffeehouses, smoking hubble-bubbles. Behind them were buildings of rose limestone in which Jews and Arabs lived together. The mukhtar of Romema had made a trip to America, where he had seen people from all parts of the world living peacefully together. He had made an unwritten covenant with the Jews and Arabs of Romema that they would never attack each other.

But he was anathema to the mufti Haj Amin el-Husseini. The mufti's terrorists beat him up so badly he was unable to walk for three months.

In a few more minutes they would be out of Romema. Only an empty field lay ahead of the bus. Then they would be in the Jewish quarter.

Suddenly two Arabs in red and white checkered *keffiyehs* leaped out of nowhere across the open field. They hurtled toward the bus and aimed their rifles into the windows.

Mama pushed Raquela to the floor. A bullet crashed through the window and over their heads. One of the German-Jewish women screamed, *"Gott in Himmel!* They've hit me."

Raquela's stomach turned over. Through the shattered window, she could hear the two Arabs cursing.

The bus swerved toward Jaffa Road.

A third Arab surfaced and hurled a hand grenade at the rear window. The bus shook crazily; people screamed. Raquela's head hit the legs of the seat in front of her, exploding with pain. Dizzy, she opened her eyes to hear the driver shout, "Look at that! The grenade ricocheted. It was supposed to kill us. It's killed him. His body is flying in all directions!"

Raquela lifted her head almost involuntarily to look through the jagged glass.

"Get down, Raquela," Mama called. "It's still not safe."

The driver raced on until he reached the Hadassah Hospital, on Rabbi Kook Street. The wounded were helped into the hospital. The German woman was carried on a stretcher. Raquela and Mama crossed over to the Street of the Prophets. Raquela's body shook; her knees were buckling.

She looked up at a stone building with a sign over the doorway:

J. PATT
BAKERY & PASTRY

The Patts lived right over the store; she hoped her friend Shula Patt was home, and she would get hold of herself telling Shula what had happened on the bus.

Inside the busy bakery, Shula's mother, standing behind the counter, greeted them.

Mrs. Patt was known all over Jerusalem; most of the poverty-ridden doctors from the Hadassah Hospital ate here. They paid her when they had money. When they had none, she smiled indulgently and gave them more food. *"Shalom,* Mrs. Levy. *Shalom,* Raquela," she greeted them. She was a statuesque Brunhild, with transparent fair skin and startlingly blue eyes.

"Shalom, Mrs. Patt," Mama said. "Did you hear all the excitement? The Arabs shot at our bus. Even threw a bomb at us."

The customers surrounded Mama, all talking at once. "Was anybody killed? How many were wounded? Who was on it? I'd better run home and make sure my children are safe."

Hearing the commotion, Mr. Patt opened a door in back of the bakeshop. Through the doorway Raquela could see the huge ovens and smell the hot loaves of bread. She began to feel less queasy.

"What's going on out here?" Mr. Patt asked. He wore a white baker's apron covered with flour. "What's all the racket?" He turned to his wife.

"They had a bomb on the bus," she told him.

Mama added quickly, "We had a marvelous driver. Without him, we might really be dead."

Mrs. Patt came around the counter and patted Raquela on the shoulder. "I'm sorry Shula isn't home. Never mind—I will take care of you myself. Both of you come into the tearoom. Mrs. Levy, I'm going to give you a glass of cognac. Your nerves must be shot."

"Just a glass of tea will be fine," Mama said.

The garden tearoom was a mass of white uniforms; young doctors and nurses from the Hadassah Hospital sat at little tables, eating sandwiches and cakes.

Raquela, sitting with Mama, looked furtively at the open yard behind the bakeshop. In the center of the yard was the cistern used to catch the precious rainwater. But this cistern had been emptied of its water. Shula had taken Raquela down the stepladder one day and shown her the underground cavern that stretched beneath the whole yard and the house. Every evening, Shula told her, twenty or thirty young Haganah men climbed down the ladder. They marched; they drilled; they learned to shoot rifles. And no one could hear them. For the Patt apartment was head-quarters for the Haganah High Command, and Jacob Patt, Shula's uncle, famous for his bravery, was Jerusalem commander.

Two men in mufti sat at the table next to theirs, sipping coffee. Jacob had taught her to observe closely. Yes, she could see a bulge near their back pockets.

When they finished their tea, Raquela and Mama returned to the bakeshop to make their selection for the Bat Mitzvah. Raquela studied the glass showcase, her mouth watering as she chose cheesecake, layer cake, a honey cake golden brown and flecked with almonds, English sponge cake, cookies, *mish-mish,* apricot pie, and her favorite, Mrs. Patt's apple strudel.

A bell rang. Mrs. Patt whispered, "It's the British. The bell is to warn us they're coming. The Haganah boys on the terrace must have seen them heading here. Just stand and talk to me as if nothing is happening."

Raquela saw the men with the bulging pockets dash in from the garden tearoom. Mrs. Patt grabbed their pistols, pushed open the back door where the bakers were kneeding dough for doughnuts, and tossed the guns into the pile of soft dough.

In seconds, the guns disappeared.

Back at her station behind the counter, she casually began writing up Mama's order. The glass door opened. Raquela's heart began thumping so loudly she was sure the two British policemen could hear it.

Afraid to lift her eyes, she saw their khaki shoes, their khaki socks, their khaki shorts. Coarse, curly brown hair covered their bony legs. She raised her eyes a little; each of them carried a club with a leather handle strapped to his wrist; attached to their khaki belts were black holsters. She tried to look calm, like Mrs. Patt and Mama.

"What can I do for you?" Mrs. Patt asked.

"We're sorry to trouble you, ma'am. But we have a search warrant," the taller policeman said.

"Search," Mrs. Patt said expansively. "Search wherever you want. But pray, may I ask, what are you searching for?"

The policemen cast their eyes around the bakeshop. "Mrs. Patt, you know very well what we are searching for."

"Please, gentlemen"—Mrs. Patt's voice was controlled— "I don't know what you're talking about, but go right ahead."

Raquela watched the two uniforms enter the garden tearoom. All the doctors were frisked. The law prohibiting Jews from carrying weapons was strictly enforced, and there were Jews languishing in jail, serving hard sentences, for carrying so much as a pocket knife. Arabs were almost never searched.

The only "weapons" the doctors had were stethoscopes. The policemen returned to the bakeshop and opened the back door to the bakery. Inside, the bakers were rolling the dough. Raquela thought her heart would burst right out of her body.

She saw the policemen approach the bakers. She sent a

silent message through the air: *Dear God, don't let them look in the dough. Please don't look in the dough.*

The policemen strode past the bakers' table to the icebox. Shula had once shown her how the Haganah concealed its guns in the upper half of the icebox, behind sacks of vegetables.

The policemen opened the lower half of the icebox, looked in, found nothing, and shut the door. They returned to the bakeshop. Raquela's heart dropped back into place.

"May I offer you gentlemen some cake?" Mrs. Patt smiled, never more gracious.

The policemen looked at the glass buffet. "You know how we fancy your cheesecake, Mrs. Patt," the shorter one said. "But we have no time. We have a few more places to search. We'll be back."

"You are always welcome," Mrs. Patt said. "Maybe you'll take a few cookies with you now? A little nourishment for the road."

"You're very kind. Don't mind if we do."

She stuffed two large bags with cake and cookies.

"Thank you, ma'am," the policeman said, smiling. "You're most generous indeed."

Raquela watched the two khaki-clad men, who had marched into the shop bristling and suspicious, walk out like pleased customers.

Mrs. Patt turned to Mama. "Now back to Raquela's Bat Mitzvah!"

The garden was set with long tables covered with Mama's white sheets and centerpieces of Papa's white calla lilies. Raquela and her brothers brought out bowls heaping with fresh fruit, platters of sliced tomatoes and cucumbers, cheese sandwiches, bottles of orange juice and *gazoz*—lemon-flavored soda—and trays stacked high with cakes still hot from the Patt Bakery.

Mama, putting the last touches of ferns on the table, looked up at Raquela, already several inches taller than she. Raquela saw tears form in Mama's eyes. "If only Zayda and Bubba could have lived to see this day," Mama said. "It's already over six years since they died, and I can't fill the hole they left in my life."

Raquela put down the glass bowl she was holding.

"They were always so happy." She looked beyond the

festooned garden, down the road Zayda had walked so often. "They worked so hard, yet they were always laughing. Sometimes I think, wherever they are, they're whirling around, dancing and singing their Hassidic songs. I still remember Zayda's stories. How excited he was when he came here from Russia, from his town, Vitebsk. When was it, Mama—about 1880? That's more than fifty years ago. He used to tell me how a good Hassid loves two things— the Torah and work. They both loved living so much; I can't think of them being dead."

Mama wiped her eyes. "We must hurry, child. This is no day to be sad."

Earlier in the morning, Mama had asked Raquela, "Would you like to invite Aisha? She'll be coming soon with her figs and eggs."

"Aisha! I don't know, Mama." The terror in the Seminar welled up.

"Maybe it's better not to ask her," Mama said. "It might not be too healthy for her if some of the ruffians in Ein Karem found out she had come to your Bat Mitzvah."

All afternoon the guests arrived, relatives from both sides of the family, Mama's Russian and Papa's Sephardic cousins and aunts and uncles, school friends and family friends from Jerusalem and from the towns in the north and the kibbutzim that had become Haganah sentinels.

Raquela, radiant in a white party dress with a ruffled collar, stood at the garden gate to welcome each guest. Soon the party was in full swing; some guests danced on the patio; others sat at the tables, eating the food and drinking orange juice and *gazoz*.

The accordionist struck up a *hora*. Mama and Papa joined hands with Raquela, and soon most of the guests were up, dancing in a circle, faster, faster, faster, until, laughing and damp with exhaustion, they stopped.

Now the musician began pumping a Russian melody. Mama danced alone, her slim, well-shaped legs flying over the patio floor. Like Bubba and Zayda, Mama could dance at any hour. She pulled Raquela and her school friends out to the floor for a polka or one of the Hassidic dances she had learned as a child.

The music changed. Señora Vavá, dressed, as always, in brown, with a necklace of three strands of seed pearls twined in her hair, rose from the table. Everyone moved to the side watching as she led Raquela into the center of the patio, the stately grandmother and the growing girl, delighted smiles on their faces, both holding their heads tilted ever so slightly back, both carrying their bodies gracefully yet regally straight, dancing a formal Spanish dance, the brown silk skirt swishing against the party dress, as if even the dresses were magically drawn to each other.

It was long past midnight when the music stopped and the guests began to depart. Señora Vavá bestowed her benediction on Raquela: "May you be as Rachel, your namesake in the Bible. May you be, like her, a mother in Israel." Raquela shut her eyes, her grandmother's fingers seemed to press the blessing into her forehead. "Be as Rachel . . ." "Raquela" was the Sephardic form of "Rachel."

Señora Vavá bent toward her. "Never forget, no matter what happens—more riots, more disasters—no matter what lies they tell about us. Never forget, Raquela, you are a ninth-generation Jerusalemite. Sephardic on your father's side, Ashkenazic on your mother's. You carry within you the two great streams of Jewish civilization. Never forget!"

-*✤ Chapter Three ✤*-

January 31, 1943

Snow rarely fell in Jerusalem: at most, once or twice a year.

Raquela jumped out of bed, on the last Sunday in January, to find snow swirling around her open bedroom window. She stood before it freezing as the wind raced toward her, ferrying white flakes in its wake.

Was the snow an omen: good, because it made all of Jerusalem, even its poorest alleys, beautiful? or evil, because the city, isolated on its mountains, was so vulnerable?

On the treacherous hairpin-curved roads, nothing moved. And Raquela was due at eight in the morning for her first day at the Hadassah–Henrietta Szold School of Nursing.

She closed the window, rubbed her hand over the frozen pane, and watched the uncertain daybreak. Was the city paralyzed already?

Swiftly, then, she pulled a woolen skirt and a sweater over her head. She glanced in the mirror as she brushed her long hair, now chestnut brown with hints of gold. In these six years since her Bat Mitzvah, she had grown tall, like Papa and Señora Vavá. She held the hairbrush motionless for a moment, mourning the beloved grandmother who had died just before World War II engulfed the Middle East.

How would Señora Vavá have reacted to my becoming a nurse? she wondered. *Be a mother in Israel.* . . . Was nursing wounded soldiers back to life—was that not being a mother in Israel?

She finished packing the clothes, checking them off the nursing school's list: six bras, six panties, six slips, six pa-

32

Beirut

LEBANON
(after 1947)

Tyre

• Damascus

• Kuneitra

Safad
T.berias

Haifa

SYRIA

Hadera
Netanya
Petah Tikva
Tel Aviv
Jaffa

Afula

Mediterranean Sea

Rechovot

Jerusalem

TRANSJORDAN

• Amman

Gaza

Hebron

Beersheba

• Kerak

Ma'an

PALESTINE
BRITISH MANDATE
1922 PARTITION

1947 U.N. RESOLUTION
☐ -JEWISH STATE
▨ -ARAB STATE
▦ -INTERNATIONAL
     ZONE

Sinai

• Aqaba

Mudawwara

Gulf of Aqaba

SAUDI ARABIA

0   62 Miles
0   100 Km

jamas—all labeled with her name—and one party dress and pumps.

Papa and Mama were waiting for her as she joined them at the dining table in the entrance foyer. Papa was quiet, a faraway look in his eyes. Mama, bustling back and forth to the kitchen, boiling coffee on her little *primus*—the one-burner kerosene stove—kept talking: "And remember, Raquela, if you don't like the school, if you don't like being a nurse, you can always come home."

"I'll be all right." Raquela downed the hot brew. "Don't worry, Mama."

"Just don't be ashamed. If you're not happy, just tell them you don't want to stay and you can—"

Raquela jumped up. "I'd better get going. Who knows if any buses will even be running in this snowstorm."

She scurried back to her bedroom and took a swift look at the simple iron bed, the books, the cut-out pictures on the wall. She said farewell to her childhood, picked up her suitcase, and ran out. At the table Papa still sat, deep in thought.

He stood up and embraced her. "May God go with you."

She stooped to kiss Mama. But Mama was putting on her winter coat. "I'm coming with you," Mama announced.

"Oh, no. I'm not a child, Mama. I'm eighteen years old."

"Of course you're not a child. Who in these black years can be a child anymore? I want to see with my own eyes where you'll be spending the next three years of your life."

Raquela was already putting her arms into her coat.

"Mama, please. I have to do this on my own."

Papa placed his arm on Mama's shoulder.

"Tova," he said gently. "Trust her."

Mama slowly took off her coat. "But put a scarf on your head. Don't catch a cold your first day."

Raquela smiled. "Good-bye, Mama."

She turned to go. The wind leaned against the door.

She pushed it open. Mama and Papa stood at the door, watching her crunch through the fallen snow to the bus stop.

The world was white and silent. She looked at her watch; it was exactly seven o'clock. One hour to reach Mount Scopus—if the buses ran. Through the white fog

she heard heavy tires skidding around the circle. She
gripped her suitcase; the omen was good.

Bus 8 heaved into sight, pulling up directly in front of
her. The driver stepped down to wipe the streaked windshield.

Raquela lugged the suitcase up the steep stairs, slid it
under the first seat and sat down next to the window. The
driver clung desperately to the steering wheel, as if he
were pinning the thick tires to the slippery road. Raquela
held tight.

They were out of Bet Hakerem now, entering Romema
from the west, its sidewalk coffeehouses deserted; then
they were winding through the Jewish quarters. In the
fresh snow, Mea Shearim looked like a winter *shtetl* in a
Chagall painting.

Downtown, on King George Street, she stepped out to
change buses. Luckily for her, Bus 9 pulled right up.

She slid her suitcase down the aisle. Bus 9 was jammed,
most of its passengers Arab men in white *keffiyehs*. They
watched her walk unsteadily until she found a seat at the
rear.

Huddled against the window, cold and uneasy, she
peered out as the bus skirted the walls of the Old City,
dropped some of the Arabs in East Jerusalem, then lumbered up the road to Sheikh Jarrah, now the most dangerous quarter in all Jerusalem.

Here were the stone palaces, high and majestic behind
stone fences, of the wealthiest Arab families, many of
them leaders in the Arab riots. Here was the villa of the
notorious terrorist leader, the mufti Haj Amin el-Husseini,
reviled and feared even by the other effendi families. But
the mufti was not home; he was in Berlin, creating a
Nazi-Arab axis, counseling with Hitler in his war office on
the fine art and science of killing Jews and conquering the
Middle East.

The bus stopped in Sheikh Jarrah; Raquela watched the
Arab men draw their *keffiyehs* across their faces until only
their eyes were visible. Then they lifted their long skirts
over their western-style brown shoes as they descended
into the snowstorm.

She tried to force herself to think of Aisha, but her
mind refused to relinquish the still-vivid memory of the
bus attack before her Bat Mitzvah, in 1936. For three
years those attacks had continued, increasing in violence

as the mufti's gangs plundered, attacked, murdered. Then, in 1939, the riots ended abruptly.

The mufti and his terrorists had achieved their goal: a spectacular capitulation from the British.

Nineteen thirty-nine: the year that Hitler sealed the borders of Germany; the year the Nazi dictator sent his Panzers blitzkrieging across Poland and Central Europe, trapping Jews, holding them for the kill; the year Great Britain issued its "White Paper."

The White Paper. Henceforth, for the next five years, the number of Jews permitted to enter Palestine would be cut drastically. Then, in 1944, no Jews at all would be allowed to enter. Jews could no longer buy any land in Palestine. Nor could they settle the land they already owned.

The Arab terrorists could afford to wait until 1944. For the White Paper meant the end of the British promise to establish a Jewish homeland. And, perhaps, with a few more riots, the extinction of the Jewish community in Palestine.

The bus was taking a long time unloading Arabs in Sheikh Jarrah. Raquela looked down at her hands. Sunburned. Callused. She smiled. Even her cheeks still felt the sun and wind of the last eight months working on a farm.

Like high-school graduates all over Palestine too young to join the army, she had volunteered for "national service." The farms were desperate for help. Fifty thousand Palestinian-Jewish men and women had joined the British army; one hundred thousand British troops were in Palestine. They needed food.

Mama and Papa had sent her off with their blessings when school ended the last day of June 1942. With her friend from school, Rena Geffen, who lived nearby, she traveled north to Tel Adashim, a *moshav,* a cooperative village in the center of the Jezreel Valley between Jewish Affulah and Arab Nazareth.

The young women could easily have been sisters: both tall, well shaped, with luminous dark eyes, they were two of the prettiest and most popular girls in the University High School. They were happy young women, open and ripe for adventure.

They had chosen Tel Adashim for their wartime service

because Papa had friends there whom Raquela had met as a child.

Tel Adashim had a pastoral air: barns filled with cows and horses, chicken coops, Caterpillar tractors, small stucco farmhouses with pink tile roofs, eucalyptus trees lining the unpaved roads. The main thoroughfare was aptly called the Mud Street.

The girls woke every morning at six and spent most of the day picking apples, pears, plums, and grapes, and corn for the cattle. They spent three days in *meshek*, three days in *neshek*. *Meshek* was farming; *neshek* was training in defense. The Haganah used the synagogue as headquarters; Raquela and Rena trained with the young sons and daughters of the moshav. They were taken into the fields and taught to use old World War I British and Italian rifles. They learned how to use clubs in hand-to-hand combat in case of Arab riots. They hid their guns in the underground "slicks" where the Haganah cached its firearms, away from the prying eyes of the British patrols.

Evenings they danced and sang and visited; they were the "sophisticated" city girls from Jerusalem, sharing their experiences with the girls on the farm.

After eight months they returned to Jerusalem, their national service completed.

In the living room in Bet Hakerem, Raquela confronted Mama and Papa. "I'd like to become a nurse so I can go to the front."

Mama reacted instantly. She was angry, dismayed. "What do you want to be a nurse for? Mess around with bedpans and sick people. All that blood. See people dying. Ugh! What does a girl with your talents want that for?"

Papa, who had been writing in his looseleaf diary, stood up from his desk and paced the room restlessly.

"We always thought," he said, "that you were going to be a teacher."

"Papa, I can't go to a teachers' seminary and take courses in education while boys are dying."

"Teaching is important, too," Papa said, "Even in wartime. Molding the minds of children is important for the future."

"There may be no future if Hitler wins and comes to Palestine. I've got to do something about the war. If not nursing, then let me join the ATS."

"The ATS!" Mama had burst into tears. "I have two

sons in the army. I don't sleep nights worrying about
Jacob and Yair. If you enter the army, too, there'll be no
place for me to put my head."

Raquela stared out of the snow-flecked window with relief; they had left Sheikh Jarrah. Looming ahead was the
highest mountain in the Holy City, Mount Scopus.

There it was. Set back from the highway, surrounded by
a pine grove, white, starkly beautiful: the Hadassah Hospital, a garden, the nursing school.

Somewhere she had read that Erich Mendelsohn, the
hospital's German-Jewish architect, had written that he
wanted to create something for eternity, something to fit
into the eternal hills of Jerusalem ". . . in the light of the
monumental austerity and serenity of the Bible."

It was indeed serene: a monumental building of long
white tiles that glistened like pristine marble; an open-
columned portico with three white cupolas—Mendelsohn's
trademark—topped the sweeping entrance.

The bus stopped opposite the nursing school. Raquela
descended and stared up at the three-story building. It,
too, was serene. Monumentally austere. She opened a glass
door. A buxom, motherly woman with ink-black hair and
lively dark eyes greeted her.

"*Shalom.* My goodness, your hand is freezing. Come in.
What is your name?"

Raquela introduced herself.

"And my name is Mrs. Hannah Simonson," the woman
said in a high but pleasing voice, leading her into the
foyer. "I'm the housemother. You're the first girl in our
special wartime class to arrive. Take your coat off. Here,
let me help you. My, you're soaking wet; we have to get
you warmed up."

Carefully, Raquela hung her wet coat on a rack and set
her suitcase beside it.

Her teeth were chattering. Was it nerves?

She followed the housemother through the entrance hall
into a luxuriant living room covered with Persian rugs.
Glass doors led to a garden patio; jutting into the room
was a grand piano, so highly polished Raquela could see
her face in it; and scattered in little intimate circles were
small tables and chairs catching the morning light through
lace-curtained windows.

Mrs. Simonson waved her toward one of the little circles. "Do sit down and warm up, Miss Levy."

Raquela perched herself at the edge of a chair while Mrs. Simonson shuffled around the room. "In a minute, I'll go fetch your mother," she said.

"My mother?" Raquela was bewildered.

Mrs. Simonson smiled; her pink cheeks rose above her lips like kneaded dough, dimpling. She shut her eyes when she smiled. "Not your real mother. Every freshman gets her own 'mother.' She's a second- or third-year student who shows you around and helps you adjust to your new home and the nursing school."

She went back to the foyer and called, "Judith, can you please come down."

Then she returned. "Now, while we're waiting, let me begin with some of the things you ought to know. The first six months are a trial period. You'll be on probation."

Probation. The word sounded ominous. *Six months' probation. I've got to make it,* she thought. *Prove to Mama and Papa they were wrong about nursing.*

Mama's angry words still pounded in her ears.

"But Mama," she had held out. "It's my way of fighting the war."

But how, living in Jerusalem, did one fight this war? Raquela had been caught, as were most Jews in Palestine, in a terrible dilemma.

In Europe, when the war broke out in 1939, England had been magnificent. She had been alone, saving Western civilization, her back against the wall, her cities bombed and burning, holding off Hitler's hordes.

France had collapsed. Belgium, Holland, and Luxembourg had been over-run. Mussolini had joined forces with Hitler. Denmark fell, then Norway. The list seemed endless. The United States had not yet entered the war. And Hitler was confiscating the manpower, the factories, and the resources for his war machine from all the countries he had conquered.

The gallant British had to be helped by every able-bodied Jewish man and woman in Palestine.

Yet in Palestine itself, the hated White Paper drastically restricting Jewish immigration had become the law of the land. The name itself, *White Paper,* became the enemy, and the Haganah fought it like an enemy.

To save Jews who could still escape from countries Hitler had not yet swallowed—the eastern half of Poland, Hungary, Rumania—the Haganah organized shiploads with hundreds of immigrants and beached them, under cover of night, on the coasts of Palestine. Safe at last from Hitler.

But the White Paper declared Jews "illegal." Incredibly, the British diverted sorely needed troops and patrol boats to halt the "illegals." It was an enigma. Britain was fighting on two fronts—the war against Hitler, in Europe, and the war Churchill later called the "sordid" war against the Jews, in Palestine.

The Jews were caught in a death struggle. Should they, too, fight on two fronts? *With* the British in Europe; *against* the British in Palestine?

David Ben-Gurion, the chairman of the Zionist Executive, solved the dilemma: "We shall fight the war as if there were no White Paper and we shall fight the White Paper as if there were no war."

Jacob and Yair, with tens of thousands of others, men and women, rushed to join the British forces to fight the Nazis.

But still the British tried to be "neutral."

Desperate for manpower, they agreed to let the Jews join—men in the regular forces and the RAF, women in the ATS (Auxiliary Territorial Service)—provided that for each Jewish volunteer there would be an Arab volunteer. One hundred thirty thousand Jewish men and women of military age volunteered. But so few Arabs came forward that in the end, until December, 1941, when the United States entered the war, the only allies the British Commonwealth had were the Jewish men and women of Palestine.

Mrs. Simonson was talking. "Miss Levy." She seemed aware Raquela's mind had wandered. "You may receive men visitors here in the lounge. No men are allowed above this first floor. And they must leave early. All lights in the dormitory must be out at ten P.M. And windows drawn with black muslin curtains for the blackout. Ah, here is your 'mother.'"

The door opened. Raquela looked up at a slender young woman in a blue and white student uniform, with a starched white cowl hiding her hair.

"I'm Judith Steiner." She extended a firm hand. "I'll show you your room."

Raquela gathered her coat and suitcase and followed her.

She's a third-year student, Raquela thought; that means she's two years older than I. But she seems old—really old. Why?

They were walking down a broad white corridor lighted by a bank of windows; green ferns spilled to the floor; miniature palm trees rose out of ceramic pots; ivy trailed up to the ceiling. Outside the snow fell on the garden; but the corridor was warm and friendly, hoarding sunshine.

They climbed a stairwell to the third floor and entered a dormitory bedroom. Two sofa beds flanked one wall; the other held two wardrobes, two desks with mirrors hanging over them, and two straight chairs.

"Your roommate is Debby Kahana," Judith said. "She's a term ahead of you."

Raquela looked at the shelves over Debby's bed, a mélange of knicknacks, books, and photos.

"I hope you'll like her," Judith went on. "She's a nice girl, but she seems to be having a hard time. We're not sure if something personal is troubling her or if she's just not studying enough. She's still on probation."

The ominous word again: "probation."

Raquela lifted her suitcase to a chair.

"Do you mind if I stay a few minutes while you unpack?" Judith asked.

"Not at all. Won't you sit down?"

Judith pulled up a chair.

"Watching you take your things out brings back memories of Czechoslovakia. Of my mother packing me up to go to Palestine in 1939. With ten hats."

Raquela turned from the closet. "Ten hats! What were you supposed to do in Palestine with ten hats?"

"Hitler didn't allow us to take out any money. Only clothes. So my mother gave me the best clothes we had in the house. Along with twelve pairs of shoes and four evening gowns!"

Raquela shook her head; her one party dress was already hanging in the closet.

"You couldn't take out any jewelry, not even the simplest school ring," Judith went on. "I won a prize as a

good student, a pretty gold ring. The Nazis at the border
yanked it off my finger."

"What a terrible experience," Raquela shuddered.
"Have you heard from your mother since the war began?"

Judith's blue eyes clouded over. "Not one word. Four
years, and not one word about my entire family."

Was that why she looked so much older than twenty?

Raquela spoke carefully. "It's so hard for me to know
what you've gone through. Except for one year on a moshav, I've never really been out of Jerusalem."

Judith stood up. "Do you know how lucky you are?"
Then, abruptly, she said, "I'd better go now."

Raquela stepped through the French doors to a small
circular balcony. She could see the hospital linked to the
nursing school by a graceful pergola running through the
garden. The snow was still falling. The omen was good.

Raquela turned back and went into the room. A young
woman stood eyeing her.

"I'm Debby. I guess you're my new roommate." She
was short, with red hair cropped like a boy's; freckles
fanned across her snub nose.

"How do you do?" Raquela extended her hand. "I'm
Raquela."

Debby gave her a limp handshake, then flopped on her
bed. "I'm exhausted. They work you to death here. They
expect you to learn anatomy, physiology, chemistry, phar-
macology, ethics, the principles and practice of nursing—
the whole history of nursing, from Florence Nightingale to
Hadassah. Lord only knows why I ever thought I could be
a nurse."

Raquela was startled by the outburst. "What made you
decide to become one?"

"I did it to please my boyfriend. He joined the British
army the minute they would take him. He's so patriotic, I
felt I had to become a nurse to show him I was patriotic,
too."

She pointed to a framed photograph dominating the
shelf over her bed. "That's him. His name is Carmi Eisenberg."

Raquela stepped toward the shelf; she saw a young man
with a brilliant smile, white teeth, light hair, light eyes,
and strong yet oddly sensitive features. He was in a British
uniform, his army cap perched at a jaunty angle.

"He looks like a movie star," Raquela said.

"He's handsome, all right," Debby acknowledged. "We're planning to get married when the war's over. He's one of those idealists, you know. Writes poetry and dreams about killing Nazis. He's going to save the Jewish people, single-handedly."

Raquela glanced up at the photo again, thinking that he was the handsomest man she'd ever seen.

It was four-thirty that afternoon when Raquela and the new student nurses were called down to the lounge for tea. They were all outfitted in the same uniforms: simple white probationers' caps on their hair and blue cotton dresses covered with white aprons crisscrossed in back. White stockings and shoes were war casualties; instead they wore heavy black oxfords and gray cotton stockings that bagged around the knees. They were the first stockings Raquela had ever worn.

Judith took her into the lounge, introducing her to little groups standing near the piano or sitting at the little tables. Raquela was awed into silence by their self-confidence.

A hush fell on the room; an attractive woman of medium height sailed in. "Mrs. Cantor," Judith breathed to Raquela, "the director."

Shulamit Cantor was a commanding vision in white, from her nurse's cap, nesting in a bower of magnificent white hair, her starched white uniform, down to her—war be damned—white stockings and shoes.

"Welcome," Mrs. Cantor said. "Welcome to the Hadassah–Henrietta Szold School of Nursing. You new girls came so covered with snow we're going to call you the 'Class of Snow Whites.'"

Raquela watched the animated woman, startlingly beautiful, her features small and delicately carved, yet authoritative even when she smiled.

"Maybe some of you had problems convincing your families to let you become nurses. . . ."

How did she know?

"Because of the war and the terrible shortage of nurses, we've created this special winter class," she said. "You've chosen a difficult profession. It's not going to be easy, but we will help you overcome the difficulties. You'll start with theory and practice; during the next three years, you will rotate in all the wards; you will learn every branch of medicine. Your practice at the hospital is a continuous learning program, and yet it must in no way interfere with our whole program of education. We keep tight discipline, and we expect you to give the best you have in you."

Raquela listened with a mixture of fear and respect. Mrs. Cantor sounded tough, stern, intimidating; yet beneath her starched exterior Raquela sensed something feminine and delicate.

"I'm not going to keep you much longer." The director looked across the lounge at the novices. "I want you to know—I believe there is not a nobler profession in the world than the one you have chosen. In these days we can either be soldiers or nurses. You have elected to become nurses, and so long as you devote yourselves, with your hearts and minds and bodies, you will have no problem in our school. And now"—she permitted herself a smile—"let me introduce Miss Bertha Landsmann, director of nursing services in our hospital. An American."

An almost doll-like woman, exquisitely dressed in a white silk uniform, stood up. She had bobbed white hair cut in a thatch of bangs over her brow.

"Hello, girls." She spoke Hebrew with a New York accent. "Welcome to Mount Scopus."

"And this is my first assistant, Mrs. Eyta Margolith. She will be one of your chief instructors." A dark-haired, middle-aged woman stood up, nodded warmly, and sat down.

"And now, young ladies"—Mrs. Cantor stepped aside with a wave of her hand—"help yourselves to tea and cake."

Raquela woke the next morning at five-forty-five, drew aside the blackout curtains, opened the French doors, and stepped out to the little white balcony.

The world had changed. The snow had disappeared. Pastel lines of orange and pink were penciled in the sky, lighting up the Hills of Moab in the distance, then the Dead Sea and, closest to her, the sand-locked hills of the Judean desert.

She had grown up in this city, yet there were times when the whole history of the land seemed to seep inside her skin.

The Hills of Moab. It was across this very desert that

Ruth, the Moabite, had come with Naomi to the Land of Israel . . . *whither thou goest.* . . .

Raquela looked at the Dead Sea, the lowest spot on the surface of the earth. Who had named it "Dead"? she wondered. No one in the Bible. It was alive, so full of minerals that Lot's wife, looking back from its shores, had turned into a pillar of salt.

She was part of this land, part of its history, part of all the generations that had built it.

Raquela closed the French doors and dressed in the blue uniform and probationer's cap. Hurrying down the back stairs, she entered the tunnel under the pergola that led to the hospital.

The dining room was crowded with doctors and nurses sitting at square tables. She took her turn in the cafeteria line, put a hard-boiled egg, a slice of rye bread and jam, and a cup of coffee on a hospital tray, and searched for Judith.

She found her sitting with two student nurses, joined them, and ate eagerly, impatient to begin the day.

She returned to the nursing school and entered a classroom, where she waited until the twenty newcomers in the Class of Snow Whites assembled. A senior nurse took over.

"Today, I'm going to teach you how to make beds," the nurse said. "Beds," she repeated. "Beds with tight corners. Proper folds. The first know-how in nursing is making beds properly."

For the next few hours, Raquela maneuvered among the white dunes of hospital sheets, tucking in corners, tightening the sheets until they were so taut she could have bounced on them and not left a wrinkle.

The students were getting tired. "Most of you look as if you're good sleepers," the senior nurse said. "But I can tell you—when I can't sleep, I count sheets instead of sheep."

Raquela heard the girls grumble: "This must be my punishment for never making a bed at home." "My mother spoiled me rotten; she made all the beds." "My father said I'd never make it as a nurse. I'll show him—but oh, my aching back."

Lunch. Rest. Classes at five in the afternoon. More beds. This time with dolls, life-size. Dolls to roll over while you changed the sheets. Dolls to sponge-bathe without drowning.

By nine o'clock, Raquela fell into her own bed; her arms were limp, her legs leaden. Within seconds, she was asleep. At midnight, she woke with a start. Mrs. Simonson flashed a light in her face.

"What is it? Is there trouble? A bomb attack?" Raquela shot out of bed.

Mrs. Simonson held her fingers to her lips. "It's just the nightly check. Go back to sleep."

A few days later, Judith came to her room. "Mrs. Cantor would like to see you."

"What does she want?"

Judith looked mysterious. "Let her tell you."

Raquela hurried down the stairs. Mrs. Cantor's office opened off the corridor opposite the ferns and potted palms.

"Come in, Miss Levy." Mrs. Cantor smiled expansively. "How would you like to go to a dance for the soldiers tonight? The Women's Committee for Soldiers asked me to send fifteen of my prettiest nurses."

Raquela blushed. "But I—I have classes tonight."

"You can get there after classes. Eight-thirty would be fine. It's at the Menorah Soldiers' Club. You can go there by bus with the other girls I'll be inviting."

Raquela raced up the stairs. She had never been inside the Soldiers' Club. She had never been to a formal dance before. Upstairs in her room she found Judith waiting, holding on her arm the four evening gowns her mother had packed in Czechoslovakia. Debby lay on her bed, watching.

"I thought one of these dresses might fit you," Judith said. "The women usually wear long gowns at those dances. Maybe some glamour helps the soldiers forget the war."

"You're very kind, but I can't borrow one of your dresses. What if something happened to it?"

Judith smiled. "I'm your 'mother.' Come on, let's see how they look. Try this one."

She handed Raquela a turquoise gown of shimmering satin. Raquela stepped into it, turning slowly in front of the mirror over the desk. Her skin looked golden against the turquoise; the skirt billowed out as she turned.

"Every soldier will flirt with you tonight," Judith said approvingly.

Debby bolted from her bed and stalked out of the room.

"What's bothering her, I wonder." Raquela turned to Judith.

"I think she's worried. Her probation period is almost up."

The Menorah Soldiers' Club was a low, one-story building set inside a garden gate. Two flags fluttered from the rooftop—the British Union Jack and the blue and white flag of Zion.

The nurses Mrs. Cantor had chosen stood shyly at the entrance door. Dance music drifted out to them. They looked at one another. Do you ring a bell? Do you just march in?

A committeewoman standing near the door spotted them. "We're so glad you came. And you all look beautiful. Come with me; we need help pouring tea."

They walked across the brilliantly lighted ballroom floor. Men and women in British uniforms milled around, some holding drinks in their hands, some talking animatedly, some wandering under the tinted photographs of King George, the reigning monarch, and Queen Elizabeth.

Long tables stacked with food lined the walls. Raquela, standing behind a buffet table, began pouring tea from an antique silver tea service.

In Europe, the front was exploding; here they were dancing, drinking, eating, squeezing in a few days of respite, away from the war.

Words floated to Raquela through the smoke-filled air: *Tobruk . . . El Alamein . . . North Africa . . . Italy.* Palestine had become not only British headquarters, with a network of army camps, training schools, and airfields, but also the favorite rest-and-recreation area for soldiers on leave.

Politely they took the teacups Raquela handed them, thanking her in all the accents of the Commonwealth, including those of Palestine.

A middle-aged major waited his turn at the table.

"May I give you some tea?" Raquela asked.

He shook his head. "Would you give me the honor of this dance?"

A committeewoman next to Raquela spoke up quickly. "Of course, dear. You go right ahead; I'll pour."

Soon they were fox-trotting on the crowded floor. In silence.

Finally he spoke. "I'm Major Thomas," he said. "From London."

"And I'm Miss Levy," she said, "from Jerusalem."

He concentrated his energies on his feet.

A tall blond second lieutenant tapped the major on the shoulder. "May I cut in?"

"Of course." The major handed Raquela over reluctantly.

She stared. She had seen this face every night. On Debby's shelf.

The fox-trot had changed to a Strauss waltz; the young lieutenant was holding her close, whirling her around the floor, smiling. The same movie-star smile.

"You don't know me," she said, "but I know *you*. You're Carmi Eisenberg."

"What are you, psychic?"

He stopped dancing in the middle of the floor.

"You're Debby's boyfriend," Raquela said. "She's my roommate."

His cheeks flushed. "I *was* her boyfriend."

"That's not what she told me. She said she and you—"

He interrupted. "It's over. We're finished. Believe me."

He put his arm around her and slowly began to dance again. "I didn't want to come tonight. I figured these committee ladies would all be like my mother's friends—all looking for a husband for their daughters."

"Had any good offers tonight?"

"I didn't give the ladies a chance. The minute I saw you, I said, 'This is for me.' "

Was he telling the truth? Then why did Debby keep his photo on her shelf?

He broke the silence. "You still haven't told me your name."

"Raquela Levy."

"Raquela! I've never heard that name before."

"It's Sephardic; it's the Spanish 'Raquel,' with a Russian diminutive. My father wanted to name me Balforia because I was born on Balfour Day. But my mother had promised to name me for my grandmother."

"Let's go down to the garden," he said impulsively, dancing her toward the back door of the ballroom. "It's too hard to talk with all this noise."

They walked down a short flight of stairs. The garden, filled with palms and fragrant winter-blooming flowers, lay in wartime darkness. The Jerusalem sky was deep blue and hung with silver stars.

"How did you know I was Debby's boyfriend? How did you recognize me?"

"Debby has your picture right next to her bed."

"If she has any illusions, it just means she refuses to face reality. We broke up a few weeks ago. It was all wrong. We just weren't meant for each other. You do believe me, don't you?"

"I don't think you lie." She said it without thinking, then realized that she wanted very much to believe it.

A wind blew through the palms. Carmi pulled off his British army jacket. "Here, put this on." He slipped it around her shoulders.

"If I were wounded—" He stopped short, drew back, and cupped her face in his hands. "If I woke up and saw a white uniform and your beautiful face, I would never want to get well. I'd want to have you take care of me forever."

Through the open door, they could hear the musicians strike up a tango. "La Paloma."

In his khaki shirt, he drew himself up in the stance of a flamenco dancer. He brought Raquela toward him, gracefully flung her away, then drew her back and kissed her.

She shut her eyes.

Her body ached with his nearness.

She wanted him to hold her, as no one had ever held her before—none of the boys in school, who took her walking through the quiet tree-lined streets of Bet Hakerem; none of the Haganah boys, Jacob's friends, who kissed her, brotherly-fashion, on her cheek.

She had never felt so intoxicated.

But what if he were lying about Debby? What if he were one of those soldiers she was always reading about. The kind who believed everything was fair in love and war. Live today, for tomorrow you may be . . .

The word "dead" had never frightened her before. She lived with it twenty-four hours a day, in the classrooms, in the textbooks, in the wards. Why now did it make her tremble? She had just met Carmi, yet already she felt a sense of loss clawing inside her.

Outside the garden, a jeep revved up its engine, patrolling the blacked-out streets.

"Raquela," Carmi whispered. "It's the most beautiful name in the world."

He drew her close. Inside, the musicians were still playing.

"Raquela," he said. "Raquela . . . Raquela . . . Raquela."

--⟞ Chapter Four ⟝--

February 1943

The next afternoon, the telephone rang down the dormitory hall. Raquela was called to the phone.

"Hello, Raquela." Her heart catapulted.

No one had ever spoken her name as he did. Carmi was talking urgently. "I've just got orders. My unit is leaving tomorrow."

"Tomorrow!" She heard the dismay in her own voice, and it startled her.

"I've got to see you before I leave."

"Of course. But I have classes until seven." Her mind was in turmoil. Should she cut school? "Will seven give us enough time?"

"I'll be there. Good-bye . . . Raquela."

She struggled through the afternoon classes. One of the senior doctors from the hospital was teaching anatomy, but she kept seeing Carmi's face, hearing him whisper in the dark flower-scented garden: *If I was wounded . . . and saw your face . . .*

Promptly at seven, Carmi appeared in the lounge. Raquela raced down the stairs to greet him. He stood near the grand piano in his British-army uniform, six feet tall, golden, burnished.

"I couldn't leave without seeing you." He took her hands in both of his. "Can we go somewhere, where we can be alone?"

"We can walk right here on Mount Scopus," she said, her heart still palpitating. "I'll go up and get a sweater. I'll be down in a few minutes."

In their room, Debby lay on her bed, her eyes shut. She opened them a slit, watching Raquela go to the closet and take out a white woolen sweater she had just finished knitting.

51

"Hm, going somewhere?" Debby asked. "Got a date?"

Raquela moved closer to Debby's bed.

"Debby"—she leaned toward her red-haired roommate —"is something worrying you?"

She nodded. "It's near the end of my probation. And you know how tough Mrs. Cantor is."

On the shelf over Debby's head, Carmi smiled down at both of them.

"Debby, I'd like to ask you something. Are you still seeing Carmi Eisenberg?"

Debby looked stunned. Without answering, she reached her arm up to the shelf, pulled down a textbook, and opened it.

Raquela persisted. "Are you still seeing him?"

"Sure," she said. But her voice sounded unsure to Raquela. "Look, you've got a date," Debby said. "And I'd better memorize this junk, or next thing you know I'll be kicked out. Then what'll Carmi say?"

Raquela was confused. Who was telling the truth?

She descended slowly to the lounge. "Sorry I took so long," she said.

Carmi took her arm. "You're here. That's what counts."

He opened the glass door and led her out of the school. "Let's walk to the university garden," he said.

Raquela walked with her eyes to the ground as they trudged along the narrow dirt ridge that led to the campus of the Hebrew University, some two hundred yards from the nursing school. Mount Scopus seemed to divide two worlds: on one side lay the Old City and new Jerusalem, rising on the hills; on the other, the Judean desert. Looking west, civilization, ancient and new; looking east, the strange untamed wilderness, and beyond the wilderness, Transjordan, Iraq. For six thousand miles eastward, this was the only university; and Hadassah, the only medical center.

Three Arab boys approached them, whipping their donkeys. The boys waved their hands and smiled at the attractive young couple in uniform, he in army brown, she in white with the little probationer's cap in the pompadour of her hair. The boys were probably on their way to Issawiya, a little Arab village that lay on the slope of a hill just below the hospital.

The Arabs of Issawiya were in and out of the hospital constantly, as workers and as patients. Even the three boys grinning appreciatively seemed familiar; Raquela was sure she had seen them often on the hospital grounds.

As the boys waved good-bye and descended the ridge eastward to Issawiya, their donkeys' bells seemed to be tolling peace on the biblical mountain, while Carmi was marching off to war.

Raquela clung to Carmi's arm, her body taut with excitement. But she was troubled by doubts and guilt.

Should she even be walking with him?

Ahead of them, the cupola of the great National Library loomed up; here and there lights shone in the buildings; a few students hurried past them; others strode like lovers, arm in arm.

They entered the pillared pergola linking the library with the tall Humanities building. They paused for a moment, looking through the open colonnades at the terraced garden below; then they made their way down the steps into the garden and gravitated toward a large circular bench, with an unobstructed view of the Old City.

Carmi took her in his arms and kissed her. The wind hurried through the Jerusalem pines.

She shivered, chilled and warm, exhilarated and uncertain. They sat on the bench, looking at the luminous panorama below them.

The Old City looked magical. The golden Dome of the Rock stood out like a jewel amid the spires and minarets and the battle walls that framed the ancient city where David had reigned and Solomon had built his temple. The sky darkened, suffusing the bustling courtyards and streets where Señora Vavá and all the generations of Papa's family had lived and loved and died.

Beyond the Old City, new Jerusalem rose up on the gentle hills in the west and the south—Bet Hakerem and its neighboring Jewish and Arab suburbs catching the last light in the sky.

"Carmi"—Raquela broke the spell—"I must know the truth."

"What truth? What greater truth is there than this sight we're looking at? I want to imprint it, like a woodcut, on my brain. From now on, no matter where they send me, every time I think of you, I will see you here, on Mount Scopus, looking down on the Old City."

"Carmi," she said, "Debby says you still see each other."

"It's not true. We haven't even spoken to each other for weeks."

"She told me you even plan to get married when the war is over."

Carmi turned his body toward her and put his hands on her shoulders.

"Now, listen to me, Raquela. Debby and I had it out. She's too jealous. I couldn't take it any more. She was always complaining that I didn't love her enough. Every time I sneezed, she thought it was an excuse not to see her. If I met an old schoolfriend on the street, she asked me if I had been in love with her, and maybe still was. I told her we were finished."

"But she's a bright girl. Why doesn't she believe you?"

"I don't know. Maybe it was something in her childhood. She lost her father when she was still living in Haifa and she was about five. I think she blames him for deserting her. I don't think she can trust any man. She's always looking for love—and then she can't accept it when it comes. She's bright, all right; but as I got to know her more, I knew our relationship was all wrong for both of us."

"I guess her pride is hurt," Raquela said slowly. "Maybe that's why she still keeps your photo on her shelf. It's very fashionable to have a boyfriend in the army."

He smiled. "Now you have one, too."

He embraced her again. She felt his strong slim body, his masculinity, his love, enveloping her.

"I'll be thinking of you every minute while I'm away," he whispered in her ear. "And I'll write you every single day."

He was crushing her against his uniform. "Wait for me, Raquela." He breathed the words. "I'll come back from the war. Wait for me."

She trembled in his arms.

"I'll wait, Carmi."

Silently, she added, "Carmi, stay alive!"

At lunch in the dining room the next day, Judith pulled up a chair beside Raquela.

"Debby's telling everyone you stole her boyfriend."

Raquela stopped eating. "What?"

"She says someone saw you kissing him last night."

"I'm going up to talk to her right now." Raquela ran out of the dining room.

Upstairs, Debby was tossing clothes into her bag. The shelves over her bed were bare.

Raquela's anger subsided. "You're leaving?" The guilt was back.

Without looking at her, Debby shouted, "I never want to see you—never—for the rest of my life."

Raquela tried to grab Debby's hand. "Please don't leave. Please. Is it because of Carmi?"

Debby shoved her aside. "Leave me alone."

"Please don't throw away your whole career."

"I hate you." Debby turned her rage on Raquela. "I hate you both!"

She stormed out of the room.

Raquela dragged herself to the French doors and slowly stepped out to the balcony. Tears welled in her eyes, blurring the Judean wilderness and the Dead Sea.

Judith's voice brought her back into the room.

"I just heard the news, Raquela."

Raquela brushed her cheek. "What news?"

"Debby's probationary period ended today. She failed all her exams. Mrs. Cantor told her she doesn't have the qualifications to be a nurse. She's been expelled."

Winter yielded unwillingly to spring, the winds of Mount Scopus howling their last farewell.

Carmi was somewhere in Egypt with the British Eighth Army. Raquela wrote him every day. In her spare time, she knit khaki gloves and mufflers and mailed them to him, care of a British-army post office.

His first letter took weeks to arrive. Raquela found it in the wooden honeycomb where the students received messages. She bounded up to her bedroom and slit open the blue airmailer.

DEAR RAQUELA:

We traveled 24 hours by train from home to get to this base. I'm covered with dust from head to foot. Dust and sand are everywhere—in the water, in the food, in our lungs.

To write you the truth, it's very hard to get used to camp life now that I've met you in Jerusalem. On the whole train ride, I thought about you every minute.

My soul is tied to yours.

Raquela shut her eyes. Slowly, she reread the line. *My soul is tied to yours*. She read on.

I love you, Raquela, with all my heart, and I will love you until I die.

May 1943

Carmi was back for a week's home leave.
Raquela was to meet him at seven. She pulled off her blue uniform, changed into a frilly white blouse and skirt, and flew down to wait in front of the building.
A cab drew up. Carmi stepped out in summer khaki, his face desert-burnished, his hair sun-bleached like corn.
He held her to him in the cab as they drove off to a café in Zion Square. They were too happy to talk.
A pianist, an accordionist, and a violinist were playing dance music as the couple entered. Jewish couples and young Arab men sat at little tables.
They chose a table far from the bandstand. Carmi gave the waiter their order: "Vermouth for the lady. I'll have a scotch."
He reached across the little table and took her hand. "Raquela, I dream of you every night. I walk through the camp and think only of you."
He lifted her hand to his lips and kissed it. "I've never loved anyone as I love you, Raquela."
She drew both his hands toward her, and placed her cheek against his warm palm. She heard herself say it aloud for the first time. "I love you, Carmi."
"Say it again, Raquela. So I will hear it when I'm back in the desert."
"I love you, Carmi."
The May day had been unseasonably and fiercely hot. Now the cool night wind blew off the hills of Jerusalem.
They danced waltzes; they sipped drinks; they held hands.
"You know, Carmi," Raquela said, "in a way we're still strangers. I don't know very much about you."
He smiled. "I can give it all to you in a few words. Born in Rehovoth. My father's a judge in Jerusalem. He

wanted me to study law, but I hate dead things. I love watching things grow. I finished agricultural high school in Pardess Hanna. And when I'm finished with the army, I want to be a farmer and marry you."

Raquela tried to visualize Carmi, resplendent now in uniform, as a farmer in blue kibbutz shorts, bending over his crops, driving a tractor. He looked like one of those posters that hung on the school walls—Sabras ploughing the fields, their faces toasted golden brown, tawny like the summer hills.

Suddenly she glanced at her watch. "Oh, my God, it's nearly ten o'clock. Mrs. Simonson will have my head."

"Won't she understand this is a special night for us?"

"She doesn't accept any excuses. I must go. I don't want to be expelled like—" She caught herself in time.

In the taxi Raquela tried to cheer up Carmi.

"Mrs. Simonson is really like a mother. She wakes us up in time to go on night duty, and while we're dressing, she prepares tea and sandwiches and cookies. When we come off the evening shift, she's still waiting up with something to eat and drink."

Raquela chuckled. "But her biggest problem is how to protect our purity. She doesn't even allow us to bring our brothers up to our rooms."

"Don't any of the girls cheat?" Carmi asked.

"Of course. Especially when they have a boyfriend in the army who's back on home leave. The girls fix their blankets to look as though they're sleeping. But they don't always get away with that. She puts her flashlight right on the bed."

"Did you fix your bed?" His voice sounded a little strange, as if he were testing her. "After all, you've got a boyfriend on home leave, too."

"I was too excited to think about it. I should have asked one of the girls to take my place." She laughed, still trying to amuse him. "We try to protect each other. Sometimes one girl is assigned to cover three beds. She gets in one bed, covers herself up to her chin, pretends to be asleep, and as soon as Mrs. Simonson checks her bed and room, she gets out, runs up the stairs, and gets into the next bed before Mrs. Simonson gets there."

A cloud seemed to pass over his face. "Do you cheat sometimes, too, Raquela?"

She shook her head as the cab made its way through
East Jerusalem. "I've never stayed out late."

"Never?" Raquela detected a slight edge of suspicion, as
he repeated, "Never?"

She felt a need to explain herself. "I'm an obedient,
law-abiding person, Carmi. I believe if you want something, you have to accept the rules. Right now, I want to
be a nurse more than anything in my life. And I don't
want to do a single thing that will make them throw me
out."

"Couldn't you stay out late just one night—for *me?*"

"I'm allowed to stay out one night until twelve-thirty.
Let's save that for the night before you have to go back."

"But there's a whole week before I go, Raquela. I want
to spend every minute with you."

"Carmi, I promise, I'll see you every single evening after my classes. But I'll have to get back each night before
ten—except the last night. I really must, Carmi. I don't
want to be expelled."

But Raquela was nearly expelled.

It was June 1943, a month before her probationary
period was to end. Mrs. Cantor sent for her.

She walked through the sun-splattered corridor and
opened the office door, half crazed with fear.

"Miss Levy, I'm very disappointed in you." Mrs. Cantor
sat behind her desk, her black eyes dark and troubled.

"We had high hopes for you when you started the program. Now I get reports that you come to classes unprepared; that you sit daydreaming; that you're not even
aware when you're called upon, as if you were somewhere
in Timbuktu. Have you anything to say for yourself?"

Raquela lowered her head. She would be thrown out in
disgrace. Like Debby. All her dreams of nursing wounded
soldiers would be smashed. Yet everything Mrs. Cantor
said, every charge she made, was true.

Raquela had been consumed with thoughts of Carmi.
She carried his love letters in her apron pocket, reading
them in classes, on duty in the wards, at night in bed, until
she knew every word by heart.

She was lonely for him, and her loneliness turned into
fear. Was he in danger? He had told her he was stationed
somewhere in Egypt. But where?

Since his last home leave, she had been studying maps.

The big push for Tunisia had started early in May. It was taking a heavy toll on British and American troops. The Allies seemed to move forward only to be pushed back as the Nazis regained the territory they had lost. Why was there so little news in the papers and on the radio? *Carmi, where are you,* she often heard herself cry out in the night.

Maybe her brother Jacob would know. Suffering from colitis, Jacob had been honorably discharged from the British army. He had rejoined the Haganah and become part of Shai, the Intelligence Unit.

Jacob revealed almost nothing to the family except that he had taken a new name to throw the British CID (Criminal Investigation Department) off his tracks. In the Jewish underground army, he called himself Absalom, for the legendary Absalom Feinberg, who had worked for the British against the Turks in World War I and had been murdered by the Bedouins.

At Shabbat lunch with the family, Raquela showed Jacob the coded post-office box on Carmi's censored airmail letters. Jacob quickly deciphered the code.

"He's stationed on the border of Egypt and Tripoli. He's in Battalion Two of the Palestine Buffs, the same unit I was in."

Jacob, short, exuberant, razor-sharp, could almost always make Raquela feel better, but today even Jacob could not stop the fears for Carmi that kept gnawing at her insides. Yair, too, was in Egypt, not with the Buffs but with the RAOC—the Royal Army Ordinance Corps.

"Do you think Carmi and Yair are in danger?" she asked.

"Every soldier faces danger. It's a fact of life and war, Raquela, and you have to live with it." He toyed with his teacup. "Probably the most dangerous assignments are the paratroopers'. The British are dropping our boys and girls behind the enemy lines in Europe. I can't tell you who they are; you may have gone to school with some of them. I can only tell you our Haganah boys and girls are making contact with the underground resistance. And we hope bringing some word of hope to the Jews that they're not alone, they're not forgotten."

"And the Jews, Jacob?" Papa asked sadly. "What news do you have that you *can* tell us?"

Jacob's face turned grim. "Extermination! So ghastly

even we can't believe the reports we get. We've seen Arab riots here. They're child's play compared to the stories our underground sources send us from Poland, Austria, Germany."

Raquela was unbelieving. "What can be worse than the way the Arabs raped women in Hebron and ripped out their stomachs?" The memory of their weeks in the Seminar could still shoot pains through her body.

Jacob clutched the arms of his chair, almost pulling himself up. "You're like all the rest, Raquela. Naive." He turned to Papa. "You too. Because you love the German language so much, you can't believe *das Land der Dichter und Denker*"—he spat the words out—"the land of poets and thinkers, could become a land of monsters and sadists."

Silence fell on the dining-room table.

Back at the nursing school Raquela's mind kept returning to Jacob's words: *extermination . . . Jewish parachutists making contact with the underground resistance . . . Hitler's hordes conquering Europe . . . maybe America . . . maybe the Middle East.*

Stay alive, Carmi.

The words were a drum beating in her head.

And now Mrs. Cantor was threatening her with expulsion.

"You have less than one month to buckle down, Miss Levy, and prove yourself. You may go now."

August 1943

The wartime Class of Snow Whites waited in the lounge as Mrs. Cantor, immaculate as an admiral, breezed into the room, her face wreathed in smiles.

"I am happy to tell you," she said to the twenty young women, "that you have all passed your six-month probation period."

Twenty young women pulled off their probationers' caps. Carefully, they lifted the starched white cowls and draped them over their hair. They looked like a pageant in a Renaissance painting.

This would be Raquela's headdress for the next two and a half years.

* * *

All the next year Raquela worked tirelessly in class and in the wards, her life punctuated by Carmi's home leaves—one week every three months.

By now thousands of Jewish men and women from Palestine were in the army, navy, and air force serving under the British flag in France, England, Greece, Crete, Ethiopia, Libya, Cyprus, and Iraq. They distinguished themselves in the battles of Tobruk and El Alamein, in the landings in Sicily and in Italy. The trail of the war was marked with many of their graves. Yet many were bitter and frustrated. They yearned to go as a unit, under their own flag, to fight Hitler.

Carmi's letters from Egypt told her of the restlessness among the troops.

> We're doing only guard duty and transport. You can almost feel the demoralization. Here are young idealistic boys and girls willing to sacrifice their lives to fight the murderers of our people, and we're stuck in this hot desert—no action, only boredom and monotony. When are they going to let us get to the front?

Finally, on the twentieth of September, 1944, the British War Office made an announcement which electrified the Jews of Palestine:

> H.M. Government have decided to accede to the request of the Jewish Agency for Palestine that a Jewish Brigade Group should be formed to take part in active operations.

A week later, on the twenty-eighth of September, Prime Minister Winston Churchill delivered a speech in the House of Commons that was carried by the BBC to every soldier in the desert and to every home in Palestine. Raquela heard it on the radio in the nursing school:

> I know there are vast numbers of Jews serving with our forces and the American forces throughout all the armies. But it seems to me indeed appropriate that a special Jewish unit, a special unit of that race which has suffered indescribable torments from the Nazis, should be represented as a distinct formation amongst the forces gathered for their final overthrow, and I

have no doubt they will not only take part in the struggle, but also in the occupation which will follow.

Carmi heard the news the morning after Rosh Hashanah. He wrote Raquela: "I volunteered the first day. Now at last we will fight Hitler as a unit under our own Jewish flag. I pray I will get home to see you before they ship us out to Italy."

He arrived in Jerusalem two days after his letter. He had two weeks' home leave.

Raquela managed to see him every evening after school. They walked; they sat in cafés; they danced at the officers' club; they went to the movies and the Philharmonic, clinging to each other.

The two weeks sped by.

Carmi was to leave early Sunday morning. They decided to spend his last night in Jerusalem, in the university garden on Mount Scopus, looking down at the Old City. The campus was empty; silence was their lone companion, a presence they could feel with their fingertips.

On the stone bench, he pressed her to him. "I want to marry you, Raquela, but I don't even dare ask you to become engaged to me until this is all over. If anything happens to me—"

She dug her head into his shoulder. She could feel the patch he wore so proudly on his left arm, with its blue and white stripes and gold star of David embroidered in the center. Below the patch, in a separate strip, were the words: JEWISH BRIGADE.

"You won't believe how I feel, Raquela," he said. "On the one hand, I'm so happy and excited that we have our own brigade, our own unit, our own flag; I can't wait to set foot on the soil of Europe—to get a chance to destroy Hitler before he destroys the world. On the other hand, I want desperately to come back to you."

"You must come back," she whispered.

A rustle in the garden startled them. A young intern approached. "Hello, Raquela."

Carmi dropped his arms abruptly.

"Hello, Shmuel," Raquela said. "I'd like you to meet my friend Carmi."

Shmuel extended his hand. Carmi shook it limply.

"Beautiful evening, isn't it?" Shmuel said, and walked away.

"Who's Shmuel?" Carmi demanded. His eyes followed the white-jacketed figure.

"Just a young doctor in the hospital."

"Is he in love with you?"

Raquela stared at Carmi in amazement. "In love with me? I hardly know him."

"I didn't like the way he looked at you."

Raquela moved away on the bench. "Carmi, are you jealous?"

"I'm sorry, Raquela. I can't help thinking every doctor in the hospital must be in love with you, you're so beautiful." He tried to embrace her.

"You didn't like it when Debby was jealous of you. Now are you accusing me? You've got no cause, Carmi."

"I can't help it, Raquela. In camp I went crazy in my bunk thinking somebody was kissing you."

"Well, you can put your mind to rest. Nobody's been kissing me except you." She knew she was in love with this man, but his unfounded jealousy troubled her.

It was after midnight when they walked along the ridge of Mount Scopus toward the nursing school.

At the door Carmi held her fiercely in his arms. "There's still so much to say," he said. "I don't know how long I'll be in Europe. I can't bear to say good-bye to you."

"Let's not say good-bye. I'll try to get permission to come to the railroad station tomorrow morning to see you off."

His arms dropped. "You mustn't come."

"Carmi!"

"Please, Raquela, don't come."

"But why? All my friends see their boyfriends off at the train."

"You must not come to the station." His voice had an edge of harshness she had never heard before.

She was silent, distraught. "You know a man," Papa had always said, "by his anger."

Finally she asked, "Don't you want to spend your last minutes in Jerusalem with me?"

"Don't come, please. Let's not talk about it anymore. Just know that I adore you, Raquela."

October 24, 1944

Dearest Raquela,

It is just thirty-six hours since we said good-bye. I walk around the camp like a lunatic, bereft of my senses. You wanted to come to the train Sunday morning to say good-bye; but I didn't want it. Don't be angry with me; you can't imagine the terrible scenes that take place at the railroad station—the weeping, kissing, hugging, and more weeping. I didn't want to make a spectacle of myself. It's not my style.

She stopped reading. Was that it—that he didn't want to make a spectacle of himself? Or was he afraid that she too might lose control? How could he know that she would never cry in public, not Señora Vavá's granddaughter.

She picked up the letter again.

On the train back from Jerusalem I relived every moment we spent together. I will love you forever. I will love you as long as I live. Is it true? Am I correct that you feel the same?

-✦ Chapter Five ✦-

November 5, 1944

The tile floors were sponged and flooded with pails of soapy water, the French doors flung open, the carpets whacked with wicker beaters on the terrace, the rooms aired, the beds changed.

Henrietta Szold was coming to the nursing school directly from the hospital. The legendary American woman who had founded Hadassah in America and helped build the hospital and the nursing school in Palestine was to convalesce after a near-fatal bout with pneumonia. Mount Scopus was to be her magic mountain.

The whole staff waited at the garden door. A frail woman with soft white hair walked slowly through the pergola, assisted by a doctor and two nurses.

"Welcome, Miss Szold." Mrs. Cantor stepped forward. "We've set up two rooms for you on the second floor, overlooking the Old City."

"You're very kind." She spoke slowly, in a low musical voice. "I hope I haven't inconvenienced anyone." Even her voice had dignity.

"Not at all," Mrs. Cantor assured her. "It is an honor to have you here."

Miss Szold's presence pervaded the school. For the next three months the staff and students seemed to focus on one thing—making their famous, gentle, undemanding patient comfortable.

Few visitors were allowed to see her in the nursing school, yet she mapped each waking hour. She read reports and publications and books; she answered much of her correspondence in her own neat, flowing handwriting.

Each morning, Raquela saw a tall handsome woman with raven hair enter Miss Szold's room. She was Emma Ehrlich, who had come in 1921 as a young woman from

Boston and started working immediately as Miss Szold's secretary. She was now her confidante.

"Since none of you can sail the Atlantic and visit me, because of the war," Miss Szold had written her family, in Baltimore, "Emma has become my sister, my friend, my mother."

Raquela soon discovered that to Emma, who knew her better than anyone in Palestine, Miss Szold was "a saint and a genius."

Another daily visitor was Miss Szold's beloved disciple Hans Beyth, director of Youth Aliyah, the Children's Migration. Since 1933 Youth Aliyah had been rescuing children from Hitler's Germany. Now, Germany and Europe were sealed; no one knew how many millions of children were in danger of annihilation—perhaps already annihilated.

Yet, despite the war and despite the White Paper, children were still being smuggled into Palestine—many of them filtering in across the northern frontiers, from Syria and Lebanon.

One day Raquela overheard Hans Beyth describing how these children had walked hundreds of miles, fleeing from Arab lands where there were Nazi sympathizers and where Jews were now in danger.

"How do you tell if these children are Arabs or Jews?" Miss Szold asked him.

"When they come to the border, I meet them," he answered, "and I begin by saying 'Sh'ma.' If they continue, 'Sh'ma Israel, Adonai Elohenu, Adonai Ehad—Hear, O Israel, the Lord our God, the Lord is One'—I know they're Jews, and we take them immediately to a Youth Aliyah village."

Miss Szold leaned back in the bed, and shut her eyes. She breathed a sigh of contentment. Of all her myriad activities, rescuing children during these war years was closest to her heart.

The student nurses were given two assignments. The first was the special privilege of arranging the flowers and tropical plants that admirers sent and cutting fresh flowers for her from the garden. The second assignment, a rotating one, was to change Miss Szold's sheets, their reward for the backbreaking hours they had spent learning to make beds properly.

The first time it was Raquela's turn to change the

sheets, she entered the room with trepidation. Would the distinguished patient be remote, austere? With no patience for a young admirer, or for small talk?

Miss Szold looked up from a book and smiled.

The room smelled of honeysuckle and roses. Miss Szold was in a frilly bed jacket, her long white hair brushed softly around her face. Pneumonia and a heart attack had left their mark. The gentle, compassionate face with huge brown eyes that Raquela had seen in newspaper photos was now sharper, lined. Only her hands were youthful, artistic, well cared for.

Silently Raquela moved about the room, replacing the flowers, helping Miss Szold out of bed, into a chair, changing her sheets, trying to fathom how this frail woman had become the first lady of Palestine.

In the next weeks Raquela learned some of her story. She had been born in Baltimore, Maryland, in 1860, at the outbreak of America's civil war. Her father, a rabbi from Hungary, treated her as the son he never had. He became her teacher, her guide, her mentor, instilling in her his spirituality, his scholarship, and his sense of the truth and beauty of Judaism. She became his secretary, his deputy rabbi, and his researcher. Many young men were attracted to the brilliant young woman, but when any of them came to the house in Baltimore, Henrietta would tell her sisters, "You take him off my hands; I'm busy."

When her father died, she moved to New York City with her mother and began to publish her father's papers. To understand them better, she applied for admission to the Jewish Theological Seminary, the first woman allowed to enroll. She was accepted on the condition that she would not become a rabbi.

She was at the seminary a short time when she met Dr. Louis Ginzberg, a newcomer from Germany, dark and bearded, like her father, and a great scholar, like her father. For Henrietta, it was love at first sight. She was in her early forties.

As she had worked with her father, so now she worked with the man she loved, translating his material from German into English, editing it, polishing it, giving it her felicitous touch. Each Saturday he came to the apartment on Riverside Drive for lunch, and evenings they walked along the Drive while he tried out his ideas and let her shape them into publishable form.

The first volumes of his *Legends of the Jews* acknowledged her role as translator and editor.

For her, at least, the relationship meant fulfillment, commitment, happiness. She once wrote, "Why should one expect that a woman great in intellect should not love greatly, too?"

Then, one summer, Dr. Ginzberg returned to Germany. Sitting in a synagogue, he looked up at the women's section in the balcony. An attractive young woman caught his eye. After the service he arranged to meet her, and soon he asked her two questions: are you interested in keeping house, and are you interested in having children? Her answer to both was yes.

He returned to New York and announced to Henrietta that he was engaged to a young German-Jewish woman.

Henrietta ended her relationship with Dr. Ginzberg abruptly.

Her mother, seeing her brokenhearted daughter grow depressed, suggested they go to Palestine. It was 1909. The two women, traveling through the Holy Land, were shocked by the neglected land, by the filth and poverty, by the women who died in childbirth, the infants decimated before they were one year old, the schoolchildren blinded by flies stuck to their white-filmed eyes.

Henrietta's pragmatic seventy-seven-year-old mother made a suggestion. "Here is work for you. You have a study group of ladies at home. Let your group do something for these children instead of talking, talking, talking."

They returned to America, where Henrietta organized her women. On February 24, 1912, they met in Temple Emanu-El in New York and created Hadassah. The meeting was held during the festival of Purim, and "Hadassah" was the Hebrew name for Queen Esther, who had saved the Jews. They took their motto from Jeremiah 8:22: *Arukhat bat ami*—"the healing of the daughter of my people."

Hadassah was to become the world's largest organization of Jewish women.

In 1920, at the age of sixty, when most women might retire, Henrietta Szold brought a team of American doctors and nurses to Palestine. They established hospitals all over the country; they opened outpatient clinics; they built laboratories attached to the hospitals. Miss Szold insisted that they must establish a school for nursing as an integral part of medical care. Her approach to teaching was, "Work and study, theory and practice: the two must go hand in hand. You must not stop studying because you work, and you must not stop working because you study."

Some of the established male doctors in Palestine looked upon her nursing school with contempt. Why did a nurse need to study for three years? A month of practice in a hospital should be sufficient. And why do women need to become so professional? We never had this under the Turks; we don't have it under the British. And no self-respecting Jewish mother will let her daughter leave home for three years.

Miss Szold was adamant. Her answer to her critics, delivered in her firm, carefully controlled voice, was, "You can't expect a girl to support herself honorably and earn a living unless she is trained professionally and on a professional standard. You cannot train a nurse in one month. Our school will be of the highest standards of nursing, and medicine in America."

And now here she was, convalescing in the nursing school she had built, cared for lovingly by the nurses whose professionalism she had fought for and secured.

Raquela helped her walk out of her room to the large rounded terrace at the front of the building. She settled her into a soft lounging chair, and watched her smiling with pleasure as she looked down at the Old City.

Work and study. The words kept ringing in Raquela's ears. Miss Szold had gone on, carving a legend as she pulled medicine in her adopted land into the twentieth century.

The Jewish leaders of Palestine recognized her impact and in 1927 chose her to be a member of the Zionist Executive. Three years later she was elected a member of the *Vaad Leumi* (National Council for Palestine) and was put in charge of social welfare. She revolutionized the social services as she had revolutionized medicine.

Then, in 1933, when Hitler came to power, she saw, long before most people were willing to accept the reality, that he was bent on extermination. Jews would be trapped and annihilated.

At seventy-five, she had gone to Hitler's Germany. "If we cannot save all the Jews," she cried, "let us at least save the children."

Youth Aliyah, first created by Recha Freier in Berlin, became Henrietta Szold's obsession and love. In Germany, she brought her organizational talents and skills to the Children's Migration, which would eventually bring thousands of children to Palestine. They were never called orphans, though most of their parents died in concentration camps.

Home in Palestine, rain or shine, winter or summer, Miss Szold drove from Jerusalem to Haifa. She stood on the dock to meet every ship and shake the hand of every parentless child she had rescued.

Around the world, people began calling her "the mother of ten thousand children."

She protested. "A child has only one mother," she said.

And sadly, she sometimes added, "I am not a mother."

How had she done it all—medicine, the nursing school, the hospital, Hadassah, the women's Zionist Organization of America, social welfare, Youth Aliyah?

Early one morning, Raquela, arranging an armful of flowers she had cut in the garden, worked up the courage to ask. She found Miss Szold sitting on the terrace, wrapped in a robe, with a blanket around her feet. In the early light, the Old City was sharply outlined, as if someone had taken a soft crayon and defined each building, the white granite tower of the Rockefeller Museum, the synagogues, the churches, the mosques, and even the embattlement walls. The houses inside the walls cast long early-morning shadows upon one another. Even the sky seemed to frame the Old City in pale blue with tints of pink and turquoise.

"Do I disturb you, Miss Szold?" Raquela asked.

Miss Szold turned her eyes away from the morning panorama and looked at Raquela. Her brown eyes seemed to Raquela to be filled with wisdom.

How should she begin? How could one ask a woman as important as Henrietta Szold how she had achieved so much, and still kept herself so carefully groomed, her hair always shining, her hands young?

In her last letter to Carmi—somewhere on the Italian front, fighting the Nazis—Raquela had told him of Miss Szold. "Someday," she wrote, "I'll ask her the questions that keep churning around in my brain."

This was the day.

"Miss Szold," she blurted out, "how did you do it?"

"Do what?" Miss Szold asked. Her soft white hair was combed in a precise center part, her well-formed lips drawn in a smile.

"Everything." Raquela tossed her head. If Miss Szold refused to answer, she would turn and race down the stairs. The words tumbled out. "I mean, I heard you got up before dawn, and worked eighteen hours a day, and did everything, and on Shabbat had open house in your room in Pension Romm on 11 Rambam Street, right across from the second windmill, the windmill that really works, not like the one at Yemin Moshe, where my grandmother lived. I mean—how did you do it?"

Raquela put her hands to her mouth. The questions were out now—not all, not the personal ones, the love affair with the scholar in New York. Did she feel about him the way Raquela felt about Carmi? They too had fallen in love at first sight. No, she would not ask questions that invaded her privacy.

"If you don't want to answer, if you don't feel like talking, it's all right. Really."

"I don't mind," Miss Szold said.

Raquela stood, waiting.

"The body is a machine through which we function," Miss Szold said. "Years and years ago, I decided I must keep the machine in good working order. A machine, like any tool, needs care every day. I knew if I didn't massage my hands every day, they would become twisted and gnarled like the hands of many women, and I would not be able to write, to keep up with my correspondence with my family and all my friends."

Raquela nodded silently. She had seen her writing in her room, or on the terrace, hours at a time.

"And your hair?" Raquela barely breathed the words. She had often watched Miss Szold brush her white hair forward, then back, then side to side.

"I had no time to go to beauty parlors," Miss Szold answered seriously. Perhaps the questions were not so trivial after all. "I brushed—and I still brush my hair one hundred strokes a day. I used to use a sturdy brush; now in the hospital, I use a baby brush and a fine comb. I've even stopped using soap these last months. Someone told me hair should be cared for the way you groom a horse or a dog. And I believe it."

Raquela was relaxing; Miss Szold had put her completely at ease. "Did you have a routine—one you stuck to every day?"

"Of course." She smiled again. "It's the only way to keep the machine well tooled. I got up at quarter to five every morning. Those first two hours of the day were mine. That's when I did my regular setting-up exercises, brushed my hair the hundred strokes, massaged my hands, took my bath, dressed and had my breakfast." She laughed a little. "Then I was ready for a day's work to begin."

Raquela felt a sudden impulse to bend down and kiss Miss Szold's cheek, but she didn't dare.

Some weeks later, at eleven o'clock on the morning of Tuesday, February 13, 1945, Miss Szold fell into a coma. That afternoon, she died as she had lived: quietly, with consummate dignity, and in the nursing school she had created and loved.

Months before, she had prepared her own shroud. That, too, was typical: to cause as little inconvenience as possible, she had told Emma Ehrlich where to find the shroud inside her wardrobe at home.

Cables were sent to her family in America, but the war in Europe made transportation impossible, and not one of them could come to her funeral.

Miss Szold's body, wrapped in the shroud, lay in state on the floor of the lounge. A navy-blue cloth covered her; two tall candelabra with lit tapers stood near her head. The white-cowled student nurses kept vigil, the honor guard whose leader had fallen.

Raquela's watch came at midnight. Silently she said farewell.

In the morning the heavens opened. "Even God is weeping," Judith said, wiping the tears from her eyes.

Thousands of mourners came to Mount Scopus. Solemnly, they stood in line in the pouring rain, then entered the school and filed past her body. Above the Hadassah Hospital, the flag of Zion, with its star of David, flew at half mast.

All through the dark morning the mourners came, and on into the early afternoon. At three o'clock the cantor intoned the memorial prayer. There were no speeches. In the somber, darkened lounge, Raquela leaned against the wall, surrounded by doctors and nurses; Emma Ehrlich, weeping as if her heart would break; Hans Beyth, his eyes rimmed with sorrow; Jewish, Arab, and British political leaders, paying their last respects.

Dr. Judah Magnes, the American-born president of the Hebrew University, recited the Kaddish, the prayer in praise of God.

Now the pallbearers carried Miss Szold up the road along the ridge of Mount Scopus to the university campus. Raquela walked with the student nurses in the procession of leaders and workers, of the famous and the obscure, and of thousands of Miss Szold's beloved Youth Aliyah children.

The heavens ceased weeping. The sky was a sheet of gray.

At the university the pallbearers gave up their burden. Miss Szold's body was placed in a hearse and carried to the sacred burial place on the Mount of Olives, where for thousands of years pious Jews had buried their dead.

The long endless procession approached the grave.

Tears formed in Raquela's eyes.

-—❧ *Chapter Six* ❧—

March 1945

Raquela was in the labor room, mopping the forehead of her sister-in-law, Meira, Jacob's wife.

Meira's soft, pretty face was chalky, her dark hair stringy and wet. A scream exploded; her body trembled. Then she lay back, exhausted.

"I've been here all night, Raquela," she said weakly. "What time is it?"

"Eight o'clock, Meira."

"My God, it's more than thirteen hours. How much longer, do you think?"

Raquela tried to comfort her. "It can't be too much longer. First babies are always the hardest. By the time you and Jacob have had—who knows—three, four, five, you'll be dropping them like a peasant in the fields."

She sounded more reassuring than she felt. She was worried; the water bag had burst. The contractions had started, then stopped. Started again. Then stopped. Meira was weak with fatigue. Raquela changed the wet gown.

Meira looked at Raquela gratefully. "I'd go out of my mind if you weren't here," she said with a sigh. "I'm so glad you could get out of your class."

Raquela chuckled. "I had to do a real selling job with Mrs. Margolith to do it. You know, she's Mrs. Cantor's top assistant, and she doesn't believe in third-year students' missing a single class."

Meira leaned back wearily. Raquela tried to make her laugh.

"Did I tell you what happened to me the other day with Miss Landsmann? She's the director of nursing services, an American, and she never learned Hebrew. She speaks to us in English with some Yiddish and a few Hebrew words. A few days ago she caught me, with another student, sun-

74

bathing on the terrace. She scolded us. 'Girls, don't stand
nekket on the balcony. Three policemen are standing over
there on the *kveesh* (road) *kooking* (looking) at you.'"

Meira laughed, holding her swollen belly.

She and Jacob had been married a little more than a
year, a simple wartime wedding with only a handful of
relatives present. Most of the young men in the two
families were at the front.

Raquela knew how Jacob adored his vivacious wife.
Searching for something to divert her, Raquela felt for a
letter in her apron pocket. "Would you like me to read
you Carmi's last letter? It's all about Italy when the Jewish
Brigade landed."

Meira tried to make herself comfortable. "Please read.
I'll try my best to listen."

"Stop me whenever you like." Raquela pulled the well-
worn letter out of her pocket. She began reading:

> "Wherever we go in Italy—in the areas our Allied
> forces have just begun liberating—the people come
> out on the road and stare at our trucks with the blue
> and white star of David. They wave, they shout greet-
> ings, they throw kisses at us, toss flowers as if even
> the trucks were human."

"I can almost see them," Meira whispered.
Raquela went on.

> "We keep looking for Jewish survivors. Tragically,
> most of the Jews of Italy have been deported or mas-
> sacred. But every now and then we meet a few who
> were hidden by kindly Christian neighbors. They
> come and put their heads on our trucks and weep.
> When we stop, some of them jump inside and em-
> brace us. Jews from Palestine! They can't believe
> we're real."

She looked up from the letter. Meira clutched her body
with her hands, as if to ward off an unbearable pain. "Go
on, Raquela. I'm listening. What an experience for our Sabras—to meet the survivors."

Raquela nodded. "I'm sure they'll never forget that first
moment—Sabras and survivors embracing. He goes on:

*   *   *

"The Germans' reaction to our Jewish Brigade is incredible. We listen to the Nazis on the radio; they sound as though they've gone berserk. They say, 'Churchill has let mad dogs loose on Europe.'"

"Any idea where he is?" Meira sat up. The pain had stopped again.

"Somewhere north of Rome, in the mountains. He describes what it's like in those hills:

"How cold it is. The winds howl like a hungry animal and the sound is like an unfinished symphony. Only Satan himself can conduct this orchestra.

"Whenever I leave my tent, I pull on everything I own, six layers of underwear, and then two sweaters. I can just about get my army jacket closed.

"We're fighting on two fronts—the first front is against the Nazis, and the second front is against nature. In the dark night the wind blows us around in all directions as if we were drunk. And the mud! Sometimes I think I'll never get the mud out of my boots or my pants."

She stopped reading. Meira lay with her eyes closed. "I'll skip this part," Raquela said.

She read the next paragraphs to herself; she knew them almost by heart.

I look at your picture (I always carry it in my left pocket, next to my heart; it's so comforting to have Raquela near me) and repeat to myself for the thousandth time, again and again and again. There is no question—I love the most beautiful and fantastic girl in the world.

I am only flesh and blood. The chambers of my heart are overflowing with the emotions I feel toward you.

Many kisses from the one who longs for you.

A white-jacketed doctor entered the room. Raquela jumped to her feet like a private confronted by the commanding general.

"And how are you this morning, Mrs. Levy?"

"Feeling better already now that I see you, Dr. Brzezin-ski." Meira straightened the sheet above her abdomen.

She introduced Raquela. "This is my sister-in-law, Raquela, Jacob's sister."

Dr. Brzezinski smiled at Raquela. "I remember you sitting in front of the window in my G-Y-and-O class. I had no idea you two were related."

Raquela was flustered. Dr. Aron Brzezinski, deputy chief of gynecology and obstetrics, had noticed her. He was not handsome. His face was round, and he wore thick dark-rimmed glasses. He was in his middle thirties, already slightly paunched and an inch shorter than she; yet he moved in an aura of warmth and compassion. She saw Meira looking at his kindly face as if his very presence would make her labor easier.

He examined Meira. "Not yet. I don't want to induce labor unless we have to."

Meira shut her eyes and began breathing deeply. In minutes she was asleep.

Dr. Brzezinski turned to Raquela. "Would you like to have some coffee with me? I'm going down to the cafeteria."

She looked at Meira. "Is it all right to leave her alone?"

"We'll take only a few minutes, and there is still plenty of time. I'll tell the nurse in the hall to look in on her."

The cafeteria was crowded. Raquela noticed the heads of some of the doctors and nurses turning to watch her as she strode self-consciously into the room. She smoothed her uniform and straightened her starched white cowl. What were they thinking?

He seemed oblivious as they stood in the cafeteria line, poured their own coffee, and made their way to a small table.

"Well, young lady," he began, "how do you like nursing?"

"I love it. I can't wait until next February to graduate and really dig in."

"That's good. I like to see enthusiasm in our young nurses; it bothers me when I see some who look at nursing as just another job."

They sipped their coffee slowly. Dr. Brzezinski leaned across the table and picked up her right hand.

"You have good strong hands," he said.

Raquela did not know how to react.

He went on, "They could be the hands of a surgeon. Or a musician. Do you play some instrument?"

"I played the violin. At one time I even considered becoming a professional violinist."

"And?" He lit a cigarette.

"I chose nursing over music, I guess because of the war."

He took the cigarette out of his mouth and flipped the ashes into a metal ashtray.

"I'm glad you made this choice, Raquela. May I call you Raquela?"

She felt flattered and uneasy.

Her hand dropped to her lap; Carmi's letter burned through her apron pocket. . . . *There is no question—I love the most beautiful and fantastic girl in the world.*

"Where did you disappear?" Meira asked.

"Dr. Brzezinski invited me for coffee."

Meira raised her eyebrows. "Really? That's nice. I think all the nurses around here are in love with him."

Raquela busied herself straightening the sheets.

Meira went on. "He has time for everybody. He sits beside you as if there's nobody else in the world. He comes in and reads me Sholom Aleichem stories. He always has *etzes*—advice—for everybody's problems. If there are six women in the ward and each one speaks a different language, he can shift from one language to the other. You should hear him—Yiddish, Polish, Russian, French, German, English. What did I forget? Oh, Hebrew, of course."

Raquela felt a cold sweat of guilt moisten the back of her uniform.

"Raquela, help me, help me!" Meira shrieked. "I think the baby's coming."

Raquela ran to the nurses' station. "Can you get Dr. Brzezinski right away?"

Within minutes he appeared.

He examined Meira, talking in a low voice, comforting, reassuring.

"You're ready," he said. "Fully dilated."

Meira smiled weakly.

Raquela and an orderly eased her onto a hospital cart and wheeled her into the delivery room. They put her on the delivery table, covered her with sheets and waited for Dr. Brzezinski.

A few minutes later he appeared in a green operating-room uniform and cap. He scrubbed up and pulled rubber gloves over his hands.

Raquela stood to the side, watching. Dr. Brzezinski was an artist, a sculptor, maneuvering, turning, molding. His capable hands were drawing life from her body.

A cry pierced the delivery room.

Meira had a son.

Each day, Raquela listened to the radio reports and clipped articles from the newspapers. The Jewish Brigade—part of the British Eighth Army—was now fighting with the Americans under General Mark Clark, Commander of the U.S. Fifth Army in Italy.

On the northern Italian front, along the river Senio, the Brigade was separated from the Nazis only by the river, which was no-man's-land. They faced a German parachute division and Panzer units on the northern bank and in the hills.

Raquela kept a scrapbook of eyewitness accounts by two Jerusalem correspondents, Ted Lurie, of the English-language Palestine *Post*, and Israel Finkelstein, of the Hebrew daily *Haaretz*. Lurie described the enemy artillery pounding in the background while the troops conducted a Passover Seder in a barn.

That Passover week was the worst thus far for the Brigade; it was typical of the Nazis to inflict their cruelest attacks during Jewish holidays. The Brigade, suffering its heaviest losses, buried its men in a small Jewish military cemetery in the Italian hills, under the star of David.

While the Nazis were being pushed back on the Italian front, Allied forces were racing across Europe. Liberating parts of Germany, Austria, and Poland, they came upon the concentration camps whose names no one had heard before: Dachau. Bergen-Belsen. Mauthausen. Treblinka. Theresienstadt. Oswieczim, which the Germans called Auschwitz.

Raquela read that tough, battle-hardened British and American generals wept when they entered the death camps. Strong American soldiers vomited and weak ones fainted when they saw and smelled the charred bodies and human bones inside huge ovens. They saw bodies piled on

top of one another, some naked, some in prison garb, half
eaten by lye, hastily tossed together by the retreating Nazis. They met cadaverous-looking survivors. They gave
them their rations and some died from the food their emaciated bodies could no longer accept. American GIs gave
the morphine syringe each front-line soldier carried to the
doctors and medics to alleviate the suffering of the half-
dead concentration-camp victims.

As Raquela cut and pasted the clippings, tears of anguish fell on the scrapbook. She felt anger. Disbelief. Even
animals had more humanity.

She was home on a Saturday evening with Mama and
Papa when they heard Moshe Sharett on the radio. Head
of the political department of the Jewish Agency, Sharett
had landed in Italy on April 14 to visit the Jewish troops.
Now, two weeks later, in carefully chosen, emotion-packed
words, he was reporting what he had seen:

"Thousands of our young men and women have gone
from Palestine to Italy, not as exiles, but as liberators. Not
as victims, but proud of their strength . . . in fulfillment
of a mission to fight shoulder to shoulder with the sons of
other nations against the foe of their people and all man-
kind."

Raquela felt a surge of pride. He was talking of Carmi.
She leaned forward, listening:

"For the first time since our exile, Jewish soldiers have
appeared on the field of battle as members of a nation
rooted in its homeland, and representing a distinct national
civilization."

"Good!" Papa hit his desk with his hand clenched.

"They appear as the messengers of the beginning of
their people's rebirth."

People's rebirth. The words had never had so much
meaning. After the war. After the obscene deaths. Now
the rebirth.

Carmi wrote constantly. He had been gone more than a
year and a half. She found him receding in her consciousness. She tried to hear his voice, to see his face, to feel his
presence. But it was as if she were walking in a fog.

"You have begun to write less and less," he complained
in his last letter. "Has anything happened? Are you sick?
We are still fighting our two wars. Nobody has to be jealous of me . . ."

She had stopped reading. How odd that he talked of jealousy. The memory of his jealousy in the university garden, when Shmuel, the young intern, had approached them, was like the taste of sand in her mouth.

How little we know each other, she thought. *Only his letters and those brief visits on home leave. Can one really know another human being this way?*

The traditional Friday-afternoon peace settled on Jerusalem. Offices and shops closed early. Men hurried home bearing flowers for their wives. The Shabbat crier, in a long black coat, walked through the city, blowing the *shofar*—the ram's horn—announcing the approach of the Sabbath. Men in silk caftans and round fur hats walked like kings to the synagogues; women, in their freshly scrubbed homes, lighted their candles.

Raquela, working the late-Friday shift on Mount Scopus, felt the Shabbat peace envelop the hospital. The wards were filled with flowers; on nighttables near their beds, the women patients blessed their candles; the men wrapped themselves in their prayer shawls and sang the Sabbath prayers.

She was at the nurses' station when Dr. Brzezinski approached. "Do you have time for another cup of coffee?"

She looked at the clock on the wall. Eleven P.M. "I'll be off duty in one hour, if you can wait, Dr. Brzezinski."

"I'll come back."

Using a little pocket mirror, she freshened her lips with lipstick, and rearranged the white cowl on her hair.

The nighttime hospital corridor was eerily quiet when Dr. Brzezinski returned, carrying a bouquet of flowers. "I picked them for you from the garden," he said.

"Thank you," she murmured.

"I'm sorry we can't have coffee," he said. "I've just been called on an emergency. Are you free tomorrow morning? We could go for a walk."

"I'm free," she said.

"I'll pick you up at the nursing school, say about ten."

The night passed slowly. She read; she chatted with her friend Rena Geffen, who had entered the nursing school a term behind her. But she could not discuss either Dr. Brzezinski or Carmi even with Rena. She was worried. She had read that the Brigade had crossed the river Senio, pushing back the German front. The Nazi parachute and Panzer Divisions were in retreat.

Was Carmi safe?

At last she fell asleep.

Dr. Brzezinski was waiting in the lounge the next morning as she entered. She had dressed carefully in a white summer blouse and a cotton skirt.

"Would you like to walk to the Old City?" he asked. "I see you're wearing walking shoes."

Did he guess that she had borrowed flat pumps so she would not be taller than he?

They set off, descending Mount Scopus, cutting across Sheikh Jarrah down to the crenellated walls surrounding the Old City. The hills were carpeted with spring flowers; gentle breezes blew from the Hills of Judea.

It was hard to believe in this Shabbat peace, that men were dying in Europe.

They entered the Old City through the huge vaulted Damascus Gate. The narrow streets were crowded. Jewish men in long black silk coats were hurrying toward the Western Wall to pray. In the Jewish quarter, children in holiday clothes strolled in the sun; synagogues rang with the sounds of men and women at prayer.

The Jewish shops and kiosks were shuttered for the Sabbath, but in the other quarters Moslems, whose Sabbath was on Friday, and Christians who shut their shops on Sunday, called to Raquela and Dr. Brzezinski, "Come inside . . . beautiful jewelry . . . you want rug? . . . copper tray . . . Turkish coffeepot? . . . Come in, don't cost you no money . . . looking is free . . ."

"Let's go into one of the shops and look." Dr. Brzezinski took her arm.

From a tray he chose a necklace of blue beads made of Hebron glass. He draped the necklace around Raquela's throat.

"But—but, Dr. Brzezinski. I—I—"

"No arguments, Raquela. I like what blue beads do for you."

She glanced at herself in the mirror on the counter. She saw red spots on her cheeks.

"I know a restaurant right outside the Damascus Gate that has the best fresh fish in Jerusalem," he said. "Let's go there and have some lunch. Are you a fish eater?"

"I eat everything, Dr. Brzezinski."

Just outside the Damascus Gate, on one of the main thoroughfares of East Jerusalem, they stopped in front of a small restaurant. Live fish swam in tanks inside the window.

"We can choose our own fish," he said, "and they'll cook it for us."

They chose St. Peter's fish, brought down from the Sea of Galilee, entered the little restaurant, and gave their order to the owner. A young Arab, probably the owner's son, showed them to a long family-style table. A few Arab men sat at another table, eating.

The smell of fish cooking made Raquela ravenous. The young waiter brought a plate heaped with hot *pitta* and an order of *humus,* a delicious paste of chickpeas. They devoured it and ordered more.

For the first time Raquela felt confident enough to ask Dr. Brzezinski about himself. She knew only that he was a bachelor; that he lived right in the hospital, in the bachelors' quarters, in the underground level of the maternity wing; and that he had come from Europe.

"A piaster for your thoughts, Raquela." He smiled indulgently.

"I was just about to ask you about yourself, Dr. Brzezinski."

"What would you like to know?"

"Where are you from?"

"I was born in Poland. In Lodz. I always knew I wanted to be a doctor. But a Jew couldn't study medicine in Poland. So my father sent me to Paris in 1928. I spent seven years in medicine at the Sorbonne. Then I came here, in 1935. I went directly to Tiberias."

"Of all places. Why would a young doctor fresh from Paris go to that tiny village?"

His round face broke into lines of laughter. "I had written my thesis at the Sorbonne on the healing powers of the waters of Tiberias on the Sea of Galilee. I wrote it only to please my father. He was a Zionist leader back home. So when I came here I thought I would go to Tiberias and start practicing. I was a real yokel. I found there was one doctor there already. He said to me, 'Young man, get out of here as fast as you can. I don't have enough bread myself. If you stay here, we'll both starve.' "

Raquela's laughter rippled through the restaurant. She was unconcerned that everyone turned to look at her. This man, gracefully dissecting the fish on his plate, was different from anyone she had known before. He had European charm, European manners, like a courtly gentleman in a Russian novel. She compared him to Carmi. Carmi was far more handsome than he. But Carmi was unworldly, immature, self-absorbed. Dr. Brzezinski could laugh at himself. Imagine a famous doctor calling himself a yokel.

Now he was serious. "You've never known what it is to live in the diaspora, in a country like Poland where you're hated for one crime—being a Jew."

He seemed to turn inward. "You Sabras," he said thoughtfully, "you're a new kind of Jew in the world." He looked at her, leaning across the table. "Maybe that's why you intrigue me so, Raquela."

"Your background intrigues me, too, Dr. Brzezinski. I'd like to know more."

He patted her hand. "You will. In time."

Lunch was over.

They walked back in the afternoon sun to Mount Scopus. The light was changing. The wind sang through her hair; she felt lighthearted and happy.

"May I ask your advice, Dr. Brzezinski?" The white hospital and nursing school loomed ahead on the crest of the hill.

"With pleasure. I have special hours when I become an *etza*-giver."

"What are your hours, Doctor?"

"Whenever you need me. I have *etzas* of all sizes for all seasons."

She laughed.

"So now, I'm the *rebbe*." He waved his arms expansively. "This is my courtyard. What is your petition, my child?"

"Mrs. Cantor called me into her office yesterday. She said they're starting a special course in midwifery. And even though I'm still a student nurse, I was chosen to be in the class. The rest are already graduate nurses. *Rebbe*, I'd like your advice."

He stroked his chin as if he had a long white beard. "As it is written, my daughter, you are a lover of life. And those who love life have a sacred duty to bring new lives into the world. Not only do I think you should take the course and become a midwife. But I will be happy to assist you in your first delivery."

"I really don't know what to say. Thank you. Thank you, Dr. Brzezinski."

"Call me Arik."

She stopped walking. "You really want me to—to call you Arik?"

"Yes, Raquela."

-- Chapter Seven --

May 8, 1945, morning

After a few weeks, Raquela was ready to perform her first delivery.

She had worked, studied, assisted the nurse-midwife-teacher, until she knew every stage of the delivery, every movement of the hands to ease a baby into the world.

"Call me," Arik had told her, "when you take your patient to the delivery room." He had gone even further. "I'll arrange it with your supervisor. I'll do the supervising myself."

At seven in the morning, Raquela, flattered and apprehensive, waited behind the desk at the nurses' station for the first pregnant woman to arrive. *Will she be young or old?* she wondered. *Fat or thin? Inexperienced—with her first baby—or someone who's had so many children she can give me lessons?*

The hospital corridor was empty and silent. She looked at the calendar on the wall. May 8, 1945. Four days earlier, General Mark Clark's Fifth Army, liberating northern Italy, had joined forces at the Brenner Pass with General Alexander C. Patch's Seventh Army, sweeping down from Austria. The next day, the remnants of the German army in Italy collapsed. The Nazi parachute division and the Panzer units fighting the Jewish Brigade surrendered.

She tried to picture Carmi with the victorious army. She could see the trucks, with the blue and white stripes and the star of David. She could see the liberated people tossing flowers, weeping with joy.

But her image of Carmi himself was wraithlike. Why?

Was it because Arik was two floors below, probably still asleep in his room? Was seeing him daily at the hospital, drinking coffee with him, letting him help her fold the hospital linen in pleats so they opened like an accordion—was his physical nearness making Carmi's image grow obscure?

Or was Carmi's immaturity the flaw, his jealousy the spoiler?

Two women approached the nurses' station, an older woman with a flowered kerchief in her hair leading a younger woman wearing a cotton smock over her pregnant body.

"Are we in the right place?" The older woman looked questioningly at Raquela's student uniform and white cowl. "My daughter—she's going to have a baby."

Raquela walked around the nurses' station. "Yes, this is the maternity wing. Do sit down." She offered them chairs and returned to the desk. "I'll need to get some information from you."

On a master chart she recorded the young woman's vital statistics. Name, Batya Ovadiah. Husband's name, Shimon. Address, Street of the Jews, in the Old City. Age, twenty-one (exactly my age, Raquela thought). Second pregnancy.

Despite her advanced pregnancy, Batya sat, poised like a dancer, with a braid of black hair, glowing olive skin, and soft, doelike eyes.

"That's all the information I need right now." Raquela took the chart. "Now come with me."

She turned to the older woman. "You can either wait here or go home and come back later."

"I'd better go home. We left Batya's little girl with a neighbor."

She kissed her daughter on the forehead. "I pray to God you will have an easy confinement. Papa must be in *shul* already, praying you will come home with a son. As for me, I just want you to come home with a live, healthy baby." She looked at Raquela. "Take good care of my daughter." She turned and left.

In the examining room Raquela handed her young patient a hospital gown and instructed her to undress and change. Step by step, detail by detail, Raquela followed the obstetrical procedure she had been taught.

She prepared Batya for delivery. Weighed her. Took her temperature. Pulse. Blood pressure. Urine. Recorded everything on the master chart. Any abnormality had to be watched like an enemy smoke signal. Urine and blood pressure, especially. A sign of albumen in the urine, or high blood pressure, could mean toxemia. Batya or her baby could die.

No albumen. Blood pressure normal.

While Batya lay on a bed, Raquela listened through her stethoscope to the baby's heartbeat. She nodded. The beat was strong and steady.

Now she prepped her, carefully shaving the black pubic hair that curled under her belly. An enema, and she was ready to examine Batya internally.

The bag of water had burst. The cervix had begun to dilate. There was a show of blood.

A pain convulsed Batya's body. She bit her lip, stifling a scream.

"You're ready for the labor room right now," Raquela said. She helped her off the bed and took Batya's arm as she waddled to the next room. There were empty beds; Raquela was grateful they had the room to themselves.

The pains now came fifteen minutes apart. Raquela timed them on the wall clock. The young woman, her forehead beaded with sweat, tried bravely to suppress her scream.

"You're doing fine, really fine, Batya."

She had no problem calling Batya by her first name. The intimacy of childbirth gave them a special relationship.

Between contractions, with Raquela sitting at her side, talking to her quietly, Batya seemed to have full confidence in her young midwife.

"Try to relax as much as you can between the pains," Raquela suggested.

An hour passed. Batya relaxed and began to talk. "I wish my husband were home. It's hard to have a baby when he's so far away."

"Where is he?"

"With the Jewish Brigade. I haven't heard from him for so long, I don't know if he's alive or dead."

Raquela jumped from her chair. She checked the baby's heartbeat again. Then Batya's pulse. Her blood pressure. The pains were coming closer. Ten minutes apart. Eight. Seven.

She examined her internally again.

It was still too soon to call Arik.

Five minutes apart. Four. Three.

"Just a little while longer," Raquela assured her.

Two minutes.

She examined her again.

She raced to the nurses' station and telephoned Arik.
She was breathless. "Arik, she's fully dilated! She's ready
to deliver!"

"I'll be up right away. I'll meet you in the delivery
room."

She found the orderly; they moved Batya to the large
delivery room and slid her onto the delivery table.

The early-morning sun rising over the Judean wilderness
entered through the windows, softening the white walls,
the white table, the white cabinets, the white bassinets, the
white sheets. Raquela pulled a long white apron over her
uniform and white rubber gloves over her scrubbed hands.
Then she covered each of Batya's legs, now firmly flexed
in the stirrups, with a tentlike white sheet. The entire area
around Batya, the theater in which she was to perform
and Raquela to direct, was sterile and white.

Dr. Brzezinski strode in, serene and confident in his surgeon's uniform, his hair covered by the surgeon's cap.

My *rebbe*, Raquela thought for a fleeting moment. The
best obstetrician in the hospital, taking precious time to be
with me. I must not make a single mistake.

He patted Batya comfortingly on the shoulder. Then he
walked to Raquela, who was standing at Batya's feet. In a
low voice that only Raquela could hear, he said, "You're
in command. I'm right here if you need me."

She braced herself. "Batya, listen carefully. I will tell
you exactly what to do."

Batya raised her body a little. "I'll try."

A moment later, a new contraction forced a scream that
seemed to come from inside the earth.

"Push!" Raquela commanded. "Push down. As if you're
going to have a bowel movement."

Batya pushed.

"Good. Now relax again."

Raquela saw that Batya had used up her breath in the
mammoth thrust.

"Now take another breath. A good one. Fill up your
lungs with air!"

Batya sucked in the air. The next pain came instantly.

"Push, Batya! Push! Push!"

With all the strength she could summon, Batya pushed
and bore down.

Raquela forgot Dr. Brzezinski was watching. For suddenly, mysteriously, what had been a small aperture in

Batya's body—the two small pink lips of the vagina's labia—parted easily. They were to become an exit.

Now Raquela saw it: the tiny wrinkled skull covered with a soft mat of black hair.

Like the crust of the earth opening.

Like the first day of Creation.

Raquela moved swiftly, almost instinctively, remembering what she had been taught and had observed. With her right hand she held the perineum—the soft pink tissue below the vagina—to prevent it from tearing, to spare Batya the pain of an episiotomy, of cutting and suturing the tissue.

With her left hand she went inside Batya's body to help ease out the baby's head. The head burst forward, face down. Batya no longer needed commands. Nature and Raquela were in control. Raquela cupped the baby's head in her left hand, still gripping the perineum with her right. Gently she helped rotate the baby's head to the right until it lay sideways on its face.

Now she lowered the head and, with a slow, steady pull, drew out the baby's upper shoulder. Then, continuing the slow and steady pull, she raised the baby's head, so that the lower shoulder emerged. She drew that one out.

Now something happened for which no teacher and no textbook had prepared her. The head and shoulders in Batya's body had acted like a cork. The moment they emerged, the rest of the amniotic fluid, in which the baby had been swimming, gushed forth. A geyser drenched Raquela from head to foot.

She shook the warm fluid from her body. There was no time to waste. She had never felt so competent, so completely in control.

With both hands she grasped the baby around its body and continued lifting it out. Wet and purplish red and trailing its white and blue-veined umbilical cord, the baby completed the long hazardous journey out of Batya's body, entering the strange new world. Crying out.

Raquela felt a surge of joy. "Batya," she called out, "You have a beautiful baby girl."

Batya lay back on the table and smiled with relief.

Moving swiftly, with a sterile diaper in her hand, Raquela drew out the shelf under the delivery table and covered it with the diaper and the baby, still attached to Batya through the cord.

With a tube Raquela sucked the amniotic fluid out of the baby's mouth. Now she clamped the umbilical cord in two places, and between the clamps she cut the cord.

Batya lifted her head. "Is everything all right?" she asked anxiously. "Is the baby normal?"

"Normal? A genius. She has five fingers on her hands," Raquela sang as she tied a name tag on the baby's wrist. "Five toes on each foot. You want her IQ, too?"

"No." Batya heaved a sigh. "As long as she's normal; that's all I want."

Raquela heard Dr. Brzezinski laugh. She would have liked to see his face, but she had no time. She was concentrating now on the new life, on the baby. She washed her with a warm sterile cloth, dried her, cleansed her eyes with cotton, and placed a drop of silver nitrate in each eye.

The baby was pink and healthy. She wrapped her in another cloth and lay her on Batya's flattened abdomen.

She had been taught to do that, to place the baby on its mother's abdomen. The ecstasy on Batya's face told her it was right. It was right that Batya should first feel the body she had carried inside her body for nine months, before she looked at it. Batya's eyes were shut, and her hands moved eloquently, caressing the baby that had grown from one single cell to billions of cells, with eyes that would see the world, and ears that would hear music, and a heart and a mind.

Raquela lifted the baby and placed it in a warm bassinet next to Batya. There was still work to be done. The placenta—the afterbirth that had transferred oxygen and life-giving nourishment from Batya to her baby—was still inside her uterus, and it was not moving.

Raquela massaged the uterus through the abdomen.

Ten minutes passed. Batya continued to bleed.

Silently, Raquela weighed her options. To wait? Turn to Arik for help? Continue massaging Batya's uterus, causing it to contract and expel the placenta? Squeeze the uterus in the cup of her hand and push the placenta down? Or ask that Batya be given anesthesia, then go into the uterus, seize the placenta, and draw it out?

She waited. More minutes ticked by. She continued massaging. The baby slept peacefully in the bassinet. Its ordeal was over. But not Batya's. Raquela looked across the room at Arik.

In a low, calm voice, she asked, "Still time, Doctor?"

Arik nodded. "A little."

Fifteen minutes.

Twenty minutes.

At last. The placenta was moving!

Raquela drew it out, rushed it to a table at her side and spread the huge sack on a towel. She examined it minutely, inch by inch, making sure no small pieces had broken off and remained inside Batya.

Now Raquela shouted joyfully, *"Mazal tov!"* Congratulations.

This too was hospital practice. To have congratulated her before the afterbirth was out and whole might bring bad luck.

Raquela lifted the baby and now for the first time placed her in Batya's arms.

The baby's eyes opened as though she wanted to see the face of this stranger in whose body she had swum and slept, and taken nourishment and warmth and shelter, and survived.

For Raquela this was the moment of poignancy, watching the mother and child.

Batya, lost in rapture, as if she were trying to fathom the mystery, stroked her baby's cheeks. She counted the fingers on each hand; then she freed the pink feet from the cloth and counted the toes, then back to the face, tracing the tiny nose, the rose-petal mouth.

Finally she whispered, "She is beautiful. Dear God, let Shimon come home alive and see his little daughter."

Arik walked to Batya; he put his hand on her arm as it encircled her baby.

"You were very good," he said. Then he looked down the delivery table to Raquela. "To say nothing of how skilled and brilliant your midwife was; you were so good that you can come back next year."

Arik's approval seemed to cement the circle around the two young women; they would never be strangers again.

Raquela was still working; she washed the remaining blood from the young mother's body and draped her in a clean white sheet.

"You rest here on the table for a while," she said, "and maybe sleep a little. I'll take your baby downstairs to the nursery. I'll bring her to you as soon as you're in your room."

She took the baby in her arms. Arik came and ran his

hand over the baby's forehead and the satin-soft skull. His gentleness and his genuine pleasure in touching the baby sent tremors through Raquela's skin.

They walked out of the room to the nursery. "I'm proud of you, Raquela. It was a perfect delivery." He stopped in the hallway, looked at her, and chuckled. "Even to the baptism."

She held the baby tighter and smiled. "Next time I'll wear a raincoat and boots."

--*Chapter Eight *--

May 8, 1945, 6 P.M.

"The evildoers now lie prostrate before us."
Winston Churchill's voice on the BBC rose and fell on
the hushed assemblage. The student nurses and teachers
stood at attention in the lounge, breathing, drinking, in-
haling Churchill's words: the war in the West was over.

From the House of Commons they heard the opening of
"God Save the King." Proudly they joined in the singing.
Then, as the BBC ended the broadcast, they sang their
own anthem, *Hatikvah*—"Song of Hope."

Raquela saw tears rolling down Judith's cheeks. She put
her arms around her.

"Maybe you'll hear something now, Judith. Maybe
you'll get some word about your family in
Czechoslovakia."

Judith wiped her eyes. "If only—if only they're alive.
It's six years since I saw them. And not one word."

Raquela looked around the lounge. Each woman was
alone with her thoughts. For each of them the victory had
a special private meaning. She knew which ones were waiting for their husbands, boyfriends, fathers, brothers, to
come home. For her the end of the war meant Carmi.
Now, in the mixture of joy and anxiety that filled the
room, Carmi's face seemed clearer, closer to her, than it
had for months. She saw the jaunty cap. The movie-star
smile. How soon would he hold her in his arms?

Mrs. Cantor was calling for attention. "We've just had a
phone call. We've all been invited to a victory celebration
in Augusta Victoria."

It seemed fitting to celebrate victory in the castlelike ed-
ifice the Germans had built after Kaiser Wilhelm II came
here, in 1898, and received Theodor Herzl. Now it was
one of the British-army headquarters.

The nurses changed into party dresses and drove across the ridge to Augusta Victoria, whose massive wings and tall tower filled the skyline between Mount Scopus and the Mount of Olives. Its formidable stone walls were lit up with lanterns. Flags and streamers waved in the night winds that came off the desert. In the great halls, army bands played. Raquela and the nurses joined the officers and soldiers. They ate sandwiches and brandy-filled English fruitcake. They waltzed and fox-trotted and jitterbugged. In long lines, shaking their hips and waving their index fingers in the air, they snaked up and down the long halls in the conga. They sang English and Hebrew songs and joked that the old German empress Augusta Victoria must be rolling in her grave. They toasted the king; they toasted the empire. And, silently, Raquela toasted Carmi, who would soon come home.

But Carmi did not come home.

The men of the Jewish Brigade were detained by the British in Europe. It was clear to everyone in Palestine that Whitehall feared that the demobilized soldiers might use their military skill to help Jewish survivors enter Palestine.

Raquela waited impatiently, joining the ranks of the other lonely women. The waiting during the postwar days seemed interminable.

The men of the Jewish Brigade began to travel across Europe in small groups on weekend passes. Carmi described their meetings with the survivors of the concentration camps: "We fling our arms around each other. They look upon us as saviors. Messengers from the Holy Land—the land they dreamed of. The dream that sustained them, helped them stay alive in the death camps. We look upon them as flesh of our flesh, blood of our blood."

Raquela put Carmi's letter in her apron pocket and descended to the large terrace on the second floor of the nursing school. She sat in a lounging chair, fanning herself. The June day was fiercely hot.

She shut her eyes. When would Carmi come home? Her body turned soft when she thought about him. She could feel his arms holding her close; her mind replayed their all-too-brief evenings together, that first night at the soldiers' club, their walks on Mount Scopus. She could taste his kisses on her lips. Then she remembered his strange jealousy when Shmuel, the young intern, approached them in the university garden. Maybe the war had changed Carmi, matured him.

In February, scarcely seven months away, she would be graduating. What would they do? In his letters he talked of going back to school, of studying agronomy at the Hebrew University School of Agriculture, in Rehovoth. He kept writing, saying he wished they were engaged. What would her life be like if she were married to a farmer? Nursing was her life; delivering babies. Would Carmi—

Her reveries were interrupted; she heard the terrace door opening behind her.

"*Shalom*, Raquela." It was Judith.

Raquela sat up. "Come join me and cool off." She motioned to a lounging chair beside her.

Judith walked out on the terrace. "I have only a few minutes. I'm on duty."

Judith was now a teacher in the nursing school. She had graduated in 1944 and received the coveted Henrietta Szold Award as outstanding student. Mrs. Cantor had recognized her unusual character, her empathy for other students, and prevailed upon her to give up her dream of becoming a midwife and to join the school staff. She was not only teaching now; she was also the assistant housemother.

Each week, when Mrs. Simonson went off duty, Judith was in charge. It was she who checked the beds at midnight with her flashlight. But unlike Mrs. Simonson, she closed her eyes when she saw an empty bed. And when the girls returned from their dates, their eyes often red from tearful good-byes, she comforted them. She herself had fallen in love with an oboe player, Elie Freud. They planned to marry now that the war was over.

A cool wind blew over the terrace.

"How welcome this breeze is," Judith said. "I think I will join you for a few minutes."

She leaned back in the chair and shut her eyes.

After a while Raquela spoke softly. "I had a letter from Carmi today. I feel so restless—even irritable. I keep worrying about the future. If only I knew when he was coming home."

"It's good you get letters. At least you know he's alive."

Raquela saw Judith lower her head.

Slowly, as if she were dredging the words out of a well

of pain, Judith said, "If I could only get one letter—one
little note from my mother telling me she's alive."

Raquela wanted to comfort her. But she could find no
phrases. How trivial her problems seemed compared to
Judith's.

Judith folded her hands on her white uniform. "I still
see her, that last day, filling up my suitcase with all those
hats and dresses. I see her face every time I sit on the bus.
I see it when they bring new patients to the hospital. I see
it in my dreams. I wake up screaming, 'Mama.'"

July 26, 1945

Again, elation in Jerusalem. The Labour Party in Britain was swept into office in the July 1945 elections.

For years, as loyal opposition, the Labour Party had
denounced the White Paper, deploring the pro-Arab stance
of the Conservatives. Even Churchill, who called himself a
proud Zionist, had continued the old policy all during the
war. Now Churchill and the Conservatives were out. The
British people, exhausted from the deprivations and
tragedies of the war, weary of the long separations from
their families, wanted a change, a clean sweep, new faces,
more-democratic goals.

In Palestine, the news seemed to herald the long awaited
end of the White Paper. But within days, Ernest Bevin, the
Labour Party's new foreign minister, reneged: election
promises were only promises; the White Paper was still the
law of the land.

"Why?" Raquela asked Arik. He was her mentor in politics, as in medicine.

It was early evening. They were sitting on the wide window ledge in the hospital overlooking the Arab village of
Issawiya, which lay just below.

"Why?" he repeated. "Because oil talks louder than
promises."

"Where do we go from here, Arik? Whom do we turn
to?" She followed his glance down the mountain.

"The United States," he said. "It's the new world power.
They will decide our fate. Listen to this." He drew a clip-
ping from the pocket of his white coat. "It's a story about
President Truman. He sent his representative, a man
called Earl G. Harrison, the dean of the faculty of law of

the University of Pennsylvania, to look into the conditions of the DPs in the camps. Truman was so shocked by his report that he has asked Bevin to let one hundred thousand survivors of the Holocaust be allowed to come here."

Raquela put her hand on Arik's arm. "Will Bevin do it?"

Arik shrugged. "Who knows?"

October 1945

Raquela looked up in the dining room. "Carmi!" she shouted.

"Who's he?" Arik asked, looking at the tall young officer standing in the doorway.

"My friend. He's back from Italy."

She pushed the chair from the table and ran toward Carmi. She felt Arik's eyes following her.

Carmi enveloped her in his arms. He shut his eyes. "I can't believe it," he whispered. "You're real. I'm not dreaming this."

Her body trembled. "Carmi! You didn't write me you were coming home."

"There was no time. A ship was leaving Italy and they let some of us from the Brigade go aboard."

She took his hand. "I want you to meet one of the gynecologists I'm working with. You remember I wrote you about Dr. Aron Brzezinski?"

She led him around the dining-room tables. Arik stood up.

"Dr. Brzezinski, may I present Lieutenant Eisenberg?"

The two men shook hands. "Pleased to meet you, Lieutenant. Will you join us?"

"Am I interrupting something—a medical meeting, or a—?" Carmi's eyes moved from Arik to Raquela.

"Not at all." Arik was expansive. "We're just having lunch together. It's an honor to have you with us."

"Carmi, you sit right down here next to Arik." Raquela moved a chair away from the table. "You two get to know each other while I go get you a tray of food."

She walked to the crowded cafeteria line, the words *Carmi is back* singing in her ears. The two men who meant most to her in the world were now sitting together. Carmi and Arik. Boyfriend and teacher.

The line moved slowly. She hardly noticed. She was fantasizing the next weeks. They were a threesome, walking along Mount Scopus, prowling the Old City. Carmi, twenty-one, dazzling in uniform, the war hero. Arik, thirty-five, in his white medical coat, wise, philosophical, her *rebbe*. And she, in her blue gown and crisscrossed white apron, walking between them, holding their arms.

She filled Carmi's tray with boiled chicken, chopped eggplant, rye bread, and tea, and smiled secretly as she carried it through the hospital dining room.

At the table, she stopped short. The two men were silent. What was going on? Carmi looked sullen and glum; Arik looked baffled.

She placed the dishes in front of Carmi and sat down.

She tried to start a conversation a few times, and failed.

Always ask people to talk about what they do, she had read somewhere. *It brings out the best in them.* She tried it.

"Carmi, I wish you would tell Arik some of those things you wrote me about, some of those things you did with the Jewish Brigade in Italy."

Carmi glared at her. "I'm not in the mood!"

Arik said, "It's all right. I understand."

Carmi shoveled the food angrily into his mouth. He was obviously trying to control himself. Finally he exploded, "Do you two eat lunch together like this every day? How long has this been going on?"

"Carmi!" Raquela snapped. "You have no reason, no right, to ask that."

Arik moved his chair away from the table.

"Please don't go, Arik," Raquela said. "You haven't finished your lunch."

"I'm sure you want to spend some time together. Raquela, I have to see Miss Landsmann anyway. Goodbye, Lieutenant."

Carmi nodded. Raquela thought she heard him grinding his teeth.

She tried to eat, but the food was gall in her mouth. She watched Carmi finish his lunch.

Her mind was churning. She had been so eager, so impatient, for him to come home. This was the moment she had dreamed of. Now it was ashes. *He really doesn't trust me,* she thought. *Maybe he's incapable of trusting any woman. He broke up with Debby because she was jealous of him. But maybe that wasn't it at all. Maybe he can't trust anyone. Maybe not even himself.*

How can I be a nurse and live with that kind of jealousy? A nurse has to associate with doctors, men and women. He'd go insane, and I would, too, if I had to come home every night and explain myself to him. What if I had night duty?

She shuddered. "Let's go," she said, "unless you want something else to eat."

"I've had enough."

Silently, almost without thinking, she led him along the ridge of Mount Scopus to the university garden. They walked through the pergola and descended to the circular bench, where they sat close together as they had done before, looking at the incredible panorama. But now Raquela was barely aware of the Old City.

They sat in stony silence, waiting.

Finally, Carmi broke the silence. "Who is this doctor friend of yours?" he asked truculently. "I can't even pronounce his name."

Raquela exploded. "He's one of the most respected doctors in the country. He's my teacher."

"The way he looks at you, I'd say he's a lot more than your teacher."

"Carmi, how dare you?"

"How dare I?" His blue eyes were iced with anger. "How dare I? You called him by his first name. What kind of teacher-student relationship is that?"

"You don't understand how informal most of us are in the hospital. I love nursing, and delivering babies, and Dr. Brzezinski is a great gynecologist and obstetrician."

Carmi sneered. "And I suppose he holds your hand every time you deliver a baby."

"Stop it, Carmi! I've been loyal to you. Dr. Brzezinski is just a good friend."

His face seemed drained of color. Raquela stared at him. He was a stranger to her and somehow frightening.

She bit her lip, feeling guilt. *He's been away so long—fighting Nazis, liberating the survivors of the death camps. A soldier's life is so lonely. . . . I must give him time.*

She gave him time. After work they walked the quiet streets of Bet Hakarem; they sat in cafés in downtown Jerusalem, drinking coffee; they went to the movies. She was determined not to give him a single reason for jealousy. Yet whenever she worked closely with Arik, she felt restless, vulnerable, confused.

It was a custom among the student nurses to arrange their schedules so that any nurse whose boyfriend came back from the war could spend three full days with him.

Raquela and Carmi planned their three days carefully. The first day they would go to Tel Adashim, so Carmi could see where she had done her "national service." Then they would visit Carmi's aunt Malka, in Petah Tikva, the oldest Jewish agricultural settlement in the land just outside of Tel Aviv, and the last day of their holiday they would spend in Tel Aviv proper and at the beach.

The October day was flawless, the air clean and cool, as they sat in the intercity bus, holding hands. In Tel Adashim, Carmi, his hair golden in the sunlight, moved through the rustic farm village like a native son, picking up the soil, smelling it, admiring the even rows of barnyard crops, stroking the bark of slender trees that opened to the sky, chatting easily with the farm families with whom Raquela had lived.

"This is what I want, Raquela." He spoke with quiet conviction. "This is my dream. All the time—all those years in Egypt, in Italy, in Europe—I saw the two of us spending our lives in a farm village like this one."

He put his arm around her waist. Raquela walked in silence. *Spending our lives . . .* could she spend her life on a farm? What about her work? There was always a need for nurses and midwives, especially in the rural areas. The thought of nursing brought Arik to mind. Guilt rose again. Why should she think of Arik during these three precious days with Carmi?

"We ought to get started for Petah Tikva," she said, "before it gets too late."

In the bus she put her head on Carmi's shoulder, relaxed in his contentment.

The two-hour bus trip brought them to Petah Tivka before dark. They walked from the bus stop through the streets of the little town, where each family owned its own home and cultivated its own land. It was a *moshav*, a cooperative village, and it looked like a European *shtetl* transplanted to Israel. Pioneers from Jerusalem had come here to farm in 1878, convinced they could redeem the malaria-ridden swampland. The determined farmers had turned the marshes into vast groves of citrus fruits and vineyards. Now Raquela breathed the air of Petah Tikva, of orange blossoms and pungent barnyard odors.

Aunt Malka's house was a typical Petah Tikva white stucco cottage with a door in the middle and a window on each side. The back of the house had a garden filled with flowers and shaded with lush green orange and lemon trees.

Carmi's aunt greeted Raquela effusively. Aunt Malka and Mama had been classmates at the Teachers' Seminar and had remained good friends. "And now," the older woman bubbled, "to think Tova's daughter is the girl friend of my favorite nephew!"

Raquela followed her into the scrupulously clean, simply furnished living-dining room, called the "salon." Through the doorway she could see the one bedroom and the large sunny kitchen.

"Sit down. Sit down." Aunt Malka took Raquela's arm and led her to the narrow sofa bed. Carmi followed them, smiling broadly.

"How about some coffee?" Aunt Malka said.

Raquela nodded. Aunt Malka was a slim pretty woman with long brown hair worn pioneer style over her ears and rolled into a bun. Her fair skin was made ruddy by the sun and wind, and like most Petah Tikvaites, her shapeless woolen skirt and bulky cardigan sweater were at least five years behind those of the more fashionable Tel Avivians who lived just a few miles away.

Aunt Malka's eyes swept over Raquela as she handed her a cup. "Everybody in Petah Tikva wants to meet you. And"—she turned to Carmi—"they can't wait to welcome you home."

"I've known some of them," Carmi explained to Raquela, "since I was a child. I was always coming over here to stay with Aunt Malka and help out on the farm."

All evening Aunt Malka's neighbors came in a steady stream to welcome the returning hero, resplendent in his uniform, and to meet his girl friend. They were warm, friendly, some rambunctious, all unabashedly curious, openly taking her measure. Was she good enough for their war hero, their young and handsome Carmi?

Across the little salon, Raquela saw Carmi slap his thighs with laughter, joking with some of the villagers. She felt alien and alone.

The next day, Carmi and Raquela headed straight for the seashore. They walked along the beach, watching the foreign ships anchored in the Mediterranean; small tenders and motorboats plied between the ships and the shore.

"Aunt Malka approves of my choice, Raquela." Carmi took her arm.

Raquela kicked a pebble on the promenade. The sense of alienation she had felt last night clung to her. Carmi was talking of the neighbors and she could hardly follow his voice. She saw him again in Petah Tikva, far more at home there than in her Jerusalem, reveling in the little farming town with its warmth, its liveliness, its sharp provincial curiosity, the neighbors pumping his hand, kissing him on the cheek, asking him about the war. She looked at his bronzed profile as they walked. There was so much to admire in Carmi—his good looks, his sensitivity, his readiness to lay down his life for the land and the people he loved.

Then what were the flaws that troubled her? She remembered his jealous outburst against Arik. So childish, she thought. Was that it; was it his immaturity as well as his jealousy that filled her with a growing apprehension?

"Let's walk in the sand," she said.

They descended the few steps to the beach, took off their shoes and sat down. The Mediterranean was greenblue and inviting. Impulsively, Raquela jumped up and ran to the water's edge. Carmi leaned back in the sand, watching her. She rolled her skirt around her thighs, waded into the water, letting the sea lap about her legs. She felt a sense of release; Carmi had not followed her. She was alone in the water—and free.

Two soldiers approached her. *"Shalom, motek"*—Hi, Sweetheart.

Raquela smiled, and the next moments were a blur of water splashing, of Carmi shouting at the soldiers, grabbing her arm, pulling her out of the sea. His mouth twitched angrily.

"Why were you flirting with those soldiers?" he demanded.

"Carmi, I was not flirting," Raquela insisted.

She was confused, torn by desire, need, anxiety. Was she really innocent? Had the soldiers detected something even she was not fully aware of?

The energy drained from her, she said, "I think we'd better go back to Jerusalem, Carmi."

She wiped the sand from her feet, slipped into her shoes, and silently climbed the promenade steps. The sea lay behind them. Soon they were on the intercity bus, climbing the hills to Jerusalem. They hardly spoke; Raquela stared out the bus window, but she saw nothing. Carmi sat beside her, his handsome face sullen, anguished.

They caught the bus to Mount Scopus. "Don't go in yet," Carmi pleaded. "Let's walk to the university garden."

They sat on the stone bench, the turrets and towers and embattlement walls below them washed in the afternoon haze.

She heard herself saying, "Carmi. Let's end it now, before we hurt each other too deeply. I can't live with your jealousy, with someone who doesn't trust me."

"Forgive me, Raquela." He tried to embrace her.

She drew away.

"It's only because I love you so much." His lips trembled. "I know this weakness in my character. But I'll change. I promise you."

Raquela searched his face. Her eyes moved toward the Jewish Brigade insignia on his sleeve. It woud be so easy to accept his promise; to wait, always hoping he might change.

"Carmi"—she shook her head sadly—"I've watched the surgeons operate. I've watched them take a knife and cut clean. That's what we have to do. Cut it clean now, Carmi."

"Raquela, give me another chance. I can't live without you. Please, Raquela."

She trembled, frightened by her own strength. She realized she was destroying her own dream.

She would throw herself harder than ever into nursing. She would absorb, as never before, everything Arik and the hospital taught her. She shivered.

"Carmi, for both our sakes, let's say good-bye now."

He looked at her, his lips parched and white.

He drew himself up to his full height, turned, and walked away.

Raquela watched him disappear. She ran blindly back to the nursing school and up to her room. She flung herself on her bed and wept.

⸜❈ Chapter Nine ❈⸝

October 1945

Judith searched the published lists of survivors for news of her family. She haunted the halls of the Jewish Agency for people who might have information. She put ads in the newspapers in Palestine and in the camps for displaced persons in Germany, Austria, and Italy, where hundreds of thousands of homeless and stateless refugees were now being sheltered.

> WILL ANYONE WITH ANY INFORMATION CONCERNING THE STEINER FAMILY OF BRNO, CZECHOSLOVAKIA, PLEASE WRITE JUDITH STEINER, HADASSAH—HENRI-ETTA SZOLD SCHOOL OF NURSING, JERUSALEM, PALES-TINE.

One day she received a letter from Eva Grunberg, a school friend.

> DEAR JUDITH,
> It is good to know that you are alive in our be-loved *Eretz Israel.* I saw your ad on the wall newspa-per in Zeilsheim, a DP camp near Frankfurt where I and thousands of other Jews are waiting. After the liberation, when the American Army freed me—I was working in a Nazi slave-labor camp—I went back to our home in Brno. I looked for my family. But they were all dead. Then I looked for the families of my friends. Judith, dear, it grieves me to tell you that your family, too, were all exterminated.

Judith's tears blotted the handwritten note. She shut her eyes in anguish. Six years of nightmares had become reality. Silently she screamed, *It can't be true. Someone must be alive.*

She forced herself to go on reading.

> The only one for whom I could find no witnesses and no records is your little brother Joseph.

Joseph! He had just had his Bar Mitzvah when she left, in 1939.

Was it possible that the miracle had happened? Could Joseph be alive, wandering somewhere across Europe?

Judith was numb, torn between grief and a glimmer of hope.

Raquela watched her go about her work, serious, never missing a day teaching or comforting other students and nurses who were now learning of their families' fates. Raquela, longing to comfort her, invited her home on weekends, hoping Mama and Papa might give her the warmth, the sense of family, that she had lost.

Late one Friday afternoon they were on bus 9, descending Mount Scopus into the Arab quarter of Sheikh Jarrah, when British police stopped the bus.

"Everyone out!" the policemen commanded.

They lined the men up separately from the women, searched the men for arms, and checked everyone's ID card against a list they carried.

The Arabs of Sheikh Jarrah poured out of their houses and shops to watch the drama on the street.

The policemen pulled Judith aside. Her name seemed to match a name on their list. They searched her purse and questioned her at length. Raquela could not hear the questions. But anger choked in her throat. Had Judith not suffered enough?

The war was nearly six months over in Europe, but in Palestine the White Paper War was escalating. The Mandatory Government passed severe emergency regulations. Anyone could be arrested for being a member of a group, if even a single person of that group had been arrested; it was collective guilt as well as guilt by association. Anyone could be detained and deported to one of the British prisons in Africa, without charges or a trial. Newspapers were censored. Radio broadcasts were censored. Civil liberties were dead.

What were the police planning to do to Judith? Raquela stared at them in anger.

Finally, Judith was released. "Case of mistaken identity," she told Raquela.

In the bus they spoke in whispers, knowing some of the passengers might be agents of the CID, British Counter-intelligence.

"They kept you so long I was sure they were going to arrest you," Raquela said. "I was already planning how I would ask Jacob to get the Palmach to spring you out of jail."

The image of Palmach commandos breaking into jail to rescue her brought a smile to Judith's face.

They both had many friends in the Palmach, the spectacular striking force of the Haganah, established in the dark days of 1941 when Rommel was at the gates of Palestine.

The British, grateful for their help, had trained hundreds of young men and women as guerrilla fighters. Arab-speaking Jews, like Moshe Dayan, had been sent, disguised as Arabs, on dangerous missions to help liberate Vichy-held Syria and Lebanon, and to Iraq to help quell the pro-Nazi uprising.

In Europe during the war, it was these young Palmach boys and girls who had parachuted behind the Nazi lines to make contact with the anti-Nazi resistance, to bring word to the trapped Jews that they were not abandoned, that help was on the way.

As soon as the war in Europe was over, the war against the White Paper escalated, and the Haganah was forced to go underground.

The Friday-afternoon Sabbath peace descended on the tree-lined streets of Bet Hakerem as Raquela and Judith walked from the bus stop down the street. They entered the garden fragrant with autumn flowers.

Raquela flung the door open, overjoyed to find that Jacob and Meira had come with their baby for the Shabbat meal.

Everyone talked gently to Judith. They knew the tragedy had ebbed her strength. At the table they surrounded her, trying to assuage her agony and pain. Jacob, who knew the most about the tragedy in Europe because of his position in Shai, understood best how to comfort Judith.

"The word is hope," he said. "Never give it up. Keep searching; keep on putting those ads in the papers. And maybe your brother Joseph will turn up on our shores."

Judith's eyes, wept out, filled again. But now she was smiling through her tears.

"Let me tell you what's happening in Europe," he said. "A mass migration—such as the world has never seen. Spontaneous. The people who went to their old homes and couldn't live there anymore are now migrating by the thousands back to Germany."

"Germany!" Raquela blurted. "How can they go back to Germany? The deathland."

Jacob nodded. "Yes, the deathland. Why Germany? Because the Americans are there, and the Americans are helping. The Displaced Persons camps are filling up every day with more survivors. And now, from the DP camps, the people are making their way almost instinctively, like lemmings; but they're not going to their deaths; they're coming here, to life, to Palestine."

"Someone has to help them," Papa said. "Who's helping?"

"We are, Papa. The Haganah. We have two arms helping—on land and sea. The Bricha and the Mosad."

He explained that the Bricha—the word means "flight"—was a clandestine body of emissaries from Palestine with a large contingent of Jewish Brigade men still in Europe, who were guiding the mass movement across the frontiers.

The Mosad le-Aliyah Bet—the Committee for Illegal Immigration—headed by top Haganah leaders, was in charge of buying boats, outfitting them, and getting the DPs onto the ships.

Jacob turned to Judith, who hung on to his words as though they were a lifeline. "Nearly every able-bodied man and woman, boy and girl, in the DP camps wants to get on one of our boats. Maybe one of those boys will be Joseph."

Judith whispered, "Dear God, make it happen."

Now the ships were coming, slipping through the Mediterranean, landing on the coast in the dead of night. Haganah men and women waded into the water, helped the refugees jump off the ships, then rushed them into kibbutzim and towns along the coast. They hid them out until they could get them ID cards, give them a history and a past, and teach them the answers to give soldiers and police if they were stopped on the street or pulled off a bus at a sudden checkpoint. When the British caught wind of the operation, they sent naval vessels into the Mediterranean to halt the mass movement; they patrolled the coast of Palestine with planes, ships and radar stations.

Some of the little boats escaped the dragnet, but many were caught. The British pulled the people down, put them on trucks, and transported them to Athlit.

An ancient and beautiful port, Athlit lay just below Haifa, on the Mediterranean. In the Middle Ages the Crusaders had built a strategic castle overlooking the natural harbor for the Knights of the Cross. The castle ruins were still standing. Here during the Arab riots of 1936–39 the British erected one of their chain of police stations, "Tegart Fortresses," named for Sir James Tegart, the architect who had planned them. Now the British were adding a new chapter in Athlit's history: a detention camp for the survivors of the fire in Europe.

By the fall of 1945 the camp was already overflowing with more than two hundred refugees, captured, dragged off the little "illegal" boats, herded into tents and barracks, and caged behind barbed wire: one more concentration camp in the wake of the tragedy and the passion. To the terrible rollcall of Auschwitz, Dachau, Treblinka, Maidanek, a new name was inscribed: Athlit. But this camp was on the soil of the Holy Land itself.

In October 1945, again in the warm glow of the Sabbath candles, Jacob announced, "I've brought a stock of reports and papers. I'm going to tell you the newest story of Athlit."

And for the next hour, Raquela, Meira, Mama, and Papa sat spellbound, as Jacob told the story.

Nahum Sarig, commander of the Palmach First Battalion in the north, waited in his underground command post in Bet Hashittah, his kibbutz in the valley of Jezreel.

Two twenty-three-year-old Palmach commanders, in khaki shorts and shirts, entered.

Sarig looked up from his desk. "*Shalom*, Yitzhak. *Shalom*, Nehemia." He motioned them to sit down. One was a handsome fair, blue-eyed commander, Yitzhak Rabin; his dark-haired companion was Nehemia Schein.

Sharig's leathery face was tense; his eyes were hard.
"We've just received secret information. The two hundred
eight refugees in Athlit are to be deported to Eritrea."

A swift glance passed between Rabin and Schein. Eritrea, on the east coast of Africa, near Ethiopia, had been
used by the British during the war to imprison members of
the Irgun. They had called it Devil's Island.

Sarig went on: "Haganah headquarters in Jerusalem has
ordered us to prevent the deportation."

He rose and began to pace the floor.

"We have no intention of shedding blood—British,
Arab, or Jewish. But we are prepared to pay the price, if
need be, to overcome any opposition. Our objective must
be measured by how many of the two hundred and eight
refugees we set free. Alive."

The young commanders nodded silently.

"We will assemble one hundred fifty Palmach men and
women for the operation," Sarig said.

He spread a diagram of the Athlit detention camp on
his desk, its entrances and exits carefully drawn. Code letters marked the refugees' tents and barracks in the
northern half of the camp and the buildings in the southern half where the soldiers and police were billeted. Surrounding Athlit were three British military camps and the
Athlit police station filled with hundreds of soldiers and
police. Next to the detailed sketch, he spread a map of the
Athlit-Haifa area and the Carmel mountain range.

Sarig began his briefing: "This action is against the
British, but it has wider political and moral meaning. It is
the first action *by force* undertaken by instructions from
the Jewish Agency." He had emphasized the words "by
force." All previous actions of the Haganah had been
without arms.

"There are three things we must calculate: how to release the people, how to transport them, and how to bring
them to safety."

October 10, 1945

Just after dusk one hundred fifty Palmach men and
women moved out from Kibbutz Bet Oren, at the top of
Mount Carmel. The kibbutz was only four miles from
Athlit, but the road wound around the mountain through

deep crevices and rough terrain. In trucks the Palmachniks drove west, toward the Haifa–Tel Aviv highway.

All forces were deployed. One group—under Amos Horev, who later became president of the Haifa Technion—hid at the side of the road, to secure the operation and block the highway in case of trouble.

Another group huddled opposite the Tegart fortress–police station, to prevent the police from moving to the support of the guards inside the camp that lay a mile off the main road.

Others, led by Rabin and Schein, waited for H-hour in the fields some forty yards outside the camp.

One A.M.

Inside the detention camp, young men and women "teachers" stirred in their bunks. They had been living in the camps as representatives of the Jewish Agency, holding classes for the imprisoned refugees; actually, they were the best athletes in the Palmach.

Inside the double rows of barbed-wire fences that surrounded Athlit, six Arab guards stood watch around the perimeter. An Arab policeman, hearing noises, began to shout. A Palmach soldier clamped his hand over his mouth.

A second Arab raised his gun and fired. Nothing happened. He tried again. Still no fire. He examined his gun and flung it on the ground in anger. The pin in his rifle had been broken. That afternoon the "teachers" had broken the firing pins in all the police rifles.

The "teachers" now gagged and tied up the six guards. Thirty more Arab and British police slept in the barracks, unaware.

A flashlight signaled to Rabin outside the camp. Armed with wire clippers and guns, Rabin's Palmachniks cut the barbed wire and slipped into the camp. Behind Rabin's group came Nehemia Schein's.

Rabin's people were deployed all over the camp, prepared to use force if necessary, while Schein's group headed straight for the tents and barracks.

The refugees lay in their beds fully dressed. They had learned of the breakthrough one hour earlier. At the signal, they jumped out of bed and followed Schein's young commandos out of the camp.

Schein led them, not along the one-mile asphalt road to

the highway but across the fields, out of sight of the police station and possible patrols.

Meanwhile, hidden in darkness, Nahum Sarig's group waited with trucks, east of the main road, to transport the refugees across Mount Carmel to Kibbutz Yagur, seven miles southeast of Haifa.

The scheduled time for getting the people out of the camp, across the field, and into the trucks was thirty minutes.

Rabin looked at his watch.

H-hour plus fifteen minutes. All was well, Rabin could hear light footsteps as the people stole out of the barracks and tents.

He saw a guard moving. Should he shoot him? Under the camp light he caught sight of the guard's face. The guard seemed terrified. Shooting would wake the sleeping policemen. He did not shoot. The guard moved away.

H-hour plus twenty minutes.

Rabin waited. Would the guards wake?

H-hour plus thirty minutes. Silence.

Rabin ordered a swift last-minute search. Every refugee was out of the camp. Not one shot had been fired.

Rabin and his Palmachniks, the last to leave the camp, moved stealthily through the gaps they had cut in the barbed wire and began running toward the trucks waiting east of the main highway.

Halfway across the field, Rabin saw disaster.

The men, women, and children were moving slowly, dragging sacks and pillowcases. They had refused to leave their pitiful possessions in the camp. The packs contained all that remained of their families, their homes, their history, their past.

The timetable was broken. By now every refugee should have been safely across the highway and climbing into the trucks. If the British caught them, there would be bloodshed everywhere. The people, aware of the danger, began dropping their sacks and pillowcases; the fields were littered with all they had salvaged of their lives.

Rabin raced to the main road where Sarig was standing. "Things are not working according to plan."

Sarig had more bad news. "Nehemia Schein is seriously ill. He's burning up with fever. Let's get the first hundred or so refugees, the stronger ones who've already reached us, into the trucks. We'll make a dash to Kibbutz Yagur and get Schein to the doctor. We don't dare wait for the slower ones, or we'll foul up the whole operation. You'll have sixty Palmachniks to help you protect about one hundred of the weaker refugees. You'll have to take them on foot to Bet Oren; they'll never make it to Yagur."

Kibbutz Yagur, one of the largest kibbutzim in the country, lay in the eastern foothills of the Carmel Mountains, in the Zebulun Valley. It was the Haganah's central arms cache. Most of the rifles for the raid on Athlit had come from Kibbutz Yagur.

"What about the trucks we can't use?" Rabin asked. "There'll be a fleet of empty trucks."

"We'll send them out in convoys on the road. Empty. To throw the British off our tracks. Good luck, Yitzhak."

Rabin organized his new formation of sixty young Palmach men and women. First they searched the fields to make sure not one straggler was left behind. Then, with Palmachniks protecting the people on all sides, they moved across the highway.

"We have to move fast," Rabin said, encouraging the slow, fragile men and women, still damaged from the war. "Crossing the highway is easy; it's flat. We just have to slip past the British police station. But then we have to climb seventeen hundred feet up the side of Mount Carmel."

There were children, babies, sick people. Rabin ordered the Palmachniks to carry the children on their backs. The older people followed.

Rabin put a little boy on his shoulders. Soon the child's trembling legs squeezed his neck. Rabin felt a warm trickle down his back. His shirt was already soaked with sweat. This was just one more hot stream. He grinned, patting the child's legs reassuringly.

Slowly, grasping rocks and tree branches, holding on to one another, they began the climb up the western slope of the mountain.

Meanwhile Sarig's trucks lumbered to the top of Carmel range, then down the eastern slope, until they saw the lights of Kibbutz Yagur.

The gates of the guarded perimeter were flung open.

The entire kibbutz was awake. The kibbutzniks ran to the trucks, helped the refugees jump down, embraced them, and hurried them into their cottages, where they gave them kibbutz pajamas, cold sandwiches, and hot tea.

Long before dawn, news of the breakthrough reached the British.

They rushed jeeps, armored cars, and patrols on the Haifa–Tel Aviv highway. They stopped the two convoys of empty trucks moving in opposite directions on the road. They searched each truck. But they found neither refugees from Athlit nor arms.

They waved the convoys on their way, and continued searching.

On the western slope of the mountain, Rabin, still carrying the child on his back, shepherded the weary and terrified people.

No one spoke. Not a child whimpered. The only sounds were the clicking of displaced rocks, the crunch of leaves, the labored breathing of the climbers.

The young Palmach men and women moved up and down, helping, encouraging, taking the hands of those who moved the slowest. But there was no way to hurry the march. Auschwitz had sapped their strength.

Rabin surveyed the uneven march and realized it would be impossible to reach the safety of Kibbutz Bet Oren before dawn. The path zigzagged around the mountain, with huge boulders and deep treacherous ravines below the hairpin curves.

Just before dawn, Rabin halted the march a mile from Bet Oren. He heard British reconnaissance planes scouting for them, and he sent one of his men to reconnoiter. He was told the British had surrounded the kibbutz with armored cars, tanks, and troop reinforcements. Kibbutz Bet Oren was under siege.

Rabin mulled over the whole new set of problems: how to secure the people from British fire in case of fighting; how to deploy his force of Palmachniks; how to enter the kibbutz.

In a hidden wadi, a dry riverbed, he gathered the exhausted men, women, and children. Here they would be safe from shell fire. Then he organized his sixty Palmachniks in a cave, prepared for battle.

Five A.M.

Had the British detected them? The air was silent.

Six A.M. He singled out two young commandos, Amos Horev and Dvora Flum, a Palmach fighter from Kibbutz

Hulatah, in the Huleh Valley. Most of the members of Dvora's kibbutz had come from Germany, parentless, with Youth Aliyah.

"Find out what's going on in Bet Oren," he told the two young people. "See if there's some secret way to get the people into the kibbutz without the British seeing us."

In half an hour Dvora and Amos returned. "The British," they reported, "have surrounded three sides of the kibbutz, including the main entrance. But on the fourth side there's no road, and no British. Just mountain and bushes and barbed wire. It's possible to enter that way."

Rabin mobilized the tired refugees for the last mile to Bet Oren. His men cut the barbed wire, and one by one the people pushed into the unguarded side of the kibbutz.

Rabin was convinced the British could see the operation, but they did not open fire.

Inside Bet Oren, the kibbutzniks were waiting. They hurried the marchers into their homes, fed them, handed them kibbutz clothing, and put the children to bed. Kibbutzniks, Palmachniks, and refugees were all told to hide their ID cards. If the British conducted a search, no one could be identified.

Meanwhile, the Haganah members in the kibbutz opened the slicks. Rabin and his troops carefully lowered their weapons into the underground shelter, and the slicks were resealed.

Twice the British attempted to enter the kibbutz with armored cars but did not open fire. Each time they were forced back.

A short while later, the British stared, confounded.

Hundreds of trucks, buses, cars, motorcycles, and bicycles moved like armies of ants up the mountain roads toward the kibbutz. Thousands of people had come from Haifa, emptying out of nearly every office, factory, school, restaurant—even from the ships in the harbor. They found their way through the concealed passage into Bet Oren.

By evening the British knew they had lost the battle. It was impossible to differentiate the "illegal" refugees from the "legal" kibbutzniks and the citizens of Haifa.

The refugees from Athlit were home in Palestine. And safe.

⊰ Chapter Ten ⊱

November 1945

Outraged by the Athlit breakthrough, the British brought in more soldiers. They searched houses and kibbutzim for arms. They made wholesale arrests. They placed ransoms—thousands of pounds sterling—on the heads of the underground leaders.

The tougher the British became, the stronger the resistance grew.

The Haganah joined forces with the two other national-liberation movements; the Irgun, under the leadership of Menachem Begin, and the Lehi, or the Stern group. Together they formed the Jewish Resistance Movement.

In a united front the resistance fighters began sabotaging bridges, railways, military installations, and the British patrol boats scouring the coast for the illegal ships.

Meanwhile, in Europe, more and more Jews were streaming into the DP camps and more and more boats were being outfitted, to carry the DPs through the British blockade to Palestine.

President Truman, shocked by the conditions in the DP camps and the continued suffering, asked England's foreign minister, Ernest Bevin, to allow one hundred thousand DPs to enter Palestine.

Bevin dared not refuse. The Labour Party was sorely in need of American aid to bolster the crumbling Empire. On November 15, 1945, Bevin announced the creation of the Anglo-American Committee of Inquiry on Palestine.

It was the eighteenth commission on Palestine since the Mandate. Meanwhile, the White Paper would remain the law of the land.

Early in the morning of February 7, 1946, Raquela hung her student uniform away. She pushed the clumsy black oxfords and gray stockings to the back of her closet and drew on white silk stockings that caressed her long legs. Then she bent over and carefully laced her white oxfords.

She trembled a little as she slipped the new white uniform over her head. Walking to her desk, she studied herself in the small mirror, turning slowly, as if she were on a pedestal. The starched uniform with its white-bibbed apron seemed to reveal her best features—her firm rounded bosom, her trim, sinewy hips, her shapely legs. She stood tall and erect.

Señora Vavá would have approved, she thought. *If only she were alive for this day. . . .*

She combed and recombed her hair, long and brown, like Mama's, with glints of gold. She finally worked it into a high pompadour. Then she lifted the new cap that marked her as a graduate nurse and pinned it into the pompadour. It was a simple starched white cap with a red star of David in the center.

She touched her lips with lipstick, fluffed some powder on her nose and chin, took one more swift survey in the mirror, and hurried through the pergola into the hospital.

The vast entrance hall was transformed. Hundreds of people had crowded into the white-marbled lobby, talking in low excited voices. It reminded Raquela of a theater, of the mystery and anticipation before the curtain goes up.

On the broad marble steps, ninety undergraduates in blue and white student uniforms and white starched cowls arranged themselves, looking like blue and white cornflowers.

At the foot of the stairs, seated behind a long table, were Dr. Yassky, Mrs. Cantor, Miss Landsmann, and Mrs. Simonson.

In front of the speaker's table, Raquela took her place with her class. Behind them, in rows of wooden chairs on the marble floor, sat their relatives and friends.

A woman violinist opened the ceremonies with selections from Mendelssohn's Violin Concerto. Raquela turned her head and saw Mama and Papa sitting proudly. She scanned the rows of spectators. Dr. Brzezinski sat near the back. Their eyes met and held. She was full of happiness.

The speeches began. Dr. Yassky spoke of this special wartime class that he knew would distinguish itself in nursing. Even their graduation day was special, held in

February rather than in September, to mark the end of their three years of study.

Mrs. Cantor made a brief speech. "These are critical days. Our country needs you as never before. I hope as you make your rounds as nurses, you will go on learning, studying. We have requests for you from all over Palestine. I hope you will accept the challenge."

She called each girl forward to present her with the mark of the Hadassah nurse—the large round silver pin. Raquela heard her name. She walked to the table, shook Mrs. Cantor's hand, accepted her pin, then moved down the length of the table, shaking all the hands, and returned to her chair.

She examined the pin carefully. The word "Hadassah" was superimposed over the star of David. Circling the edge of the pin, in tiny Hebrew letters, were the words "The Healing of the Daughter of My People" and the name "Hadassah–Henrietta Szold School of Nursing, Jerusalem."

She turned the pin over. Engraved on the back, under her name, were the year 1946 and the numbers 26 and 417. She understood. Hers was the twenty-sixth graduating class, and she, Raquela Levy, was the four hundred seventeenth graduate. She fastened the pin on the left lapel of her uniform. Pictures—fragments of the three years she had spent on this mountaintop—flashed through her mind. The dark tragic war years. Now what lay ahead?

"Raquela Levy." She heard Mrs. Cantor call her name again. "Will you please come forward?"

Her knees shook as she walked to the speaker's table. Mrs. Cantor was beaming. "You have been selected as the outstanding student in your class. I am proud to present you with the Elsa Sterling Award. It's an award from America given in memory of a young woman who was president of Junior Hadassah and died an untimely death."

Raquela tried to control the excitement in her voice. "I—I—thank you very much for this honor."

Mrs. Cantor handed her two volumes. Her eyes scanned the titles. One was *Medical Dictionary,* and the other, *The Principles and Practices of Nursing.* Mrs. Cantor went on. "I hope, Miss Levy, that you will find these books useful for the rest of your life, and we hope you'll always remember your years at our school."

"I know I will."

"There's also a gift of money, but I'm sure you would like to donate it to Miss Szold's favorite project—Youth Aliyah."

A ripple of laughter ran through the student section. Raquela looked up at them and suppressed a smile.

"I'm pleased to give it in memory of that wonderful woman."

Behind her she heard the hall burst into applause. Returning to her seat, she caught a glimpse of Papa's scholarly face wreathed in smiles. She felt a surge of love toward him and Mama. Dr. Brzezinski's hands, high in the air, were applauding her. She sat down in her chair, her heart beating wildly.

The ceremony was over. The people spilled out into the hospital garden set with tables of food and soft drinks under the Jerusalem pines. Raquela was surrounded by well-wishers. Mama reached up to kiss her. Papa embraced her. "You were right to fight us, Raquela. I think it was *beshert*—destined—that you become a nurse."

Arik stood at a distance, watching. Finally, as the crowd around her began to thin, he approached.

"*Mazal tov*, Raquela. I was sure you'd be chosen best student."

She blushed, trying to hide her pleasure. The prize had seemed somehow unreal; Arik's approval gave it reality. The hospital garden was filled with graduates in white holding little bouquets of fresh sweet-smelling violets, talking excitedly, kissing their boyfriends.

"I'd like to help you celebrate," Arik said. "Are you free for dinner?"

Her heart ticked like a speeding clock. "I am free, but first I want you to meet my parents."

She led him to the table where Papa and Mama waited discreetly. Arik bent low to kiss Mama's hand. Then, shaking Papa's hand, he said, "I know your School for Boys, Mr. Levy, and your reputation as one of the great teachers of the Bible."

Papa smiled modestly. "I am afraid Raquela exaggerates."

"I have heard it from others as well."

Raquela slipped her arm through Papa's. She could feel his hard muscles rippling. She remembered marveling as a child, watching him lift huge boulders from their garden with his bare hands. And how carefully he tended his delicate calla lilies. Papa was all strength and tenderness. And now, looking at Arik, she realized she had never felt so close to Papa. Was there some link between the two men? The same strength and tenderness, though they worked in different fields, lived their lives in different worlds? Was Arik another father figure?

"Excuse me," she said to Mama and Papa. "I've got to go up and change. Dr. Brzezinski has asked me to dinner."

Mama nodded. "We're going home now. Good-bye, Dr. Brzezinski."

He bowed slightly again and kissed her hand.

Hesse's Restaurant was up a flight of stairs in downtown Jerusalem, near Zion Square. It was elegant, with white tablecloths and flower vases. At least half the graduates had come to celebrate with their families or their boyfriends.

Each one looked up, smiling, as Raquela and Arik greeted her. A waiter in a black jacket and black bow tie led them to a table in the far corner against the wall.

They ordered shish kebab and a bottle of red wine.

Arik raised his glass. "To you, my dear. To a brilliant future as a midwife."

Raquela's eyes shone. She clinked her glass against his. "And to you, Arik. To my teacher."

They sipped the wine slowly, watching each other's faces.

It seemed to her he was looking at her differently, now that she was a graduate. Was graduation a kind of climax? An end, and a beginning? Arik had taken a volume of Sholom Aleichem from his coat pocket and was thumbing through the pages. "This is the story I was looking for," she heard him say. "Listen to this: 'You've got to stay alive even if it kills you.' That's Sholon Aleichem's philosophy," he said. "And it works for me, too. It tickles my patients."

She laughed, watching his face radiate love for the Yiddish writer.

" 'You may as well laugh,' Sholom Aleichem says. 'Even if you don't see the joke, laugh on credit. You may see the joke later, and if not, you're that much to the good.' "

She chuckled.

She wanted to tell him how she felt.

He would always be her teacher, in everything: in medicine, literature, politics, life. She wanted to be open with him. But now he was entering her life in a new way. And she could not talk.

Was it possible to fall in love with a man fourteen—nearly fifteen—years older than she?

She looked again at his face. It seemed to her it was the kindest face in the world. She had a yearning to know him better.

The next weeks gave her ample time. For whenever shootings and explosions made it too dangerous to get back to town, the doctors and nurses stayed for days on Mount Scopus. The hospital became a haven. A small city within the city, with its own special quality of life and healing.

The Holy Land became a police state. The British brought in more troops, until there were one hundred thousand soldiers. Some of the Black and Tan policemen, who had once suppressed the Irish, were sent to Palestine to keep order.

Jerusalem was hacked into ugly forbidden barriers, with streets and roads blocked off by great rusted coils of barbed wire. Hotels and office buildings were guarded by concrete pillboxes dubbed "dragon's teeth." Tanks and armored cars patrolled the streets.

Curfew was imposed from seven at night to five in the morning. Anyone caught on the streets without permission could be arrested or shot on the spot.

Raquela had special permission to be out during curfew, as did all the doctors and nurses. After graduation, she had moved back home with Mama and Papa in Bet Hakerem. Whenever she had night duty, Hadassah's eight-passenger station wagon called for her at home at 11 P.M. and then picked up fifteen more nurses. When the station wagon was halted at surprise checkpoints, the British soldiers stood baffled, as they watched white-aproned nurses jump out, one after the other, like performers in the circus.

During the curfew, the streets were deserted, quiet as a graveyard. The nights were punctuated with explosions and gunshots. Guerrilla fighters planted bombs. Soldiers and police, frightened, fired at anything that moved, even shadows.

But on Mount Scopus there was no curfew.

Raquela and Arik spent all their free time together. Often, while he worked at his desk, she sat reading on his divan against the wall. Then, his work finished, he joined her. They read together. They walked around the garden, smelling the roses and oleanders, holding hands as they strolled among the Jerusalem pine and the spreading eucalyptus trees that shaded the garden.

She felt happy and safe.

Yet she had doubts about him. He was attentive, affectionate. He brought her gifts he made himself. He picked mosaic, in empty candy boxes. When a flu epidemic felled pansies in the hospital garden and arranged them, like a her for a week in the infirmary in the nursing school, he brought her a fresh rose every morning.

Her roommate in the infirmary, Lea Gur-Aryeh, a short, bubbly student nurse, watched enviously.

"You're so lucky, Raquela. None of my boyfriends would even dream of bringing me a rose. He's like somebody out of the old world."

Raquela nodded. But she was silent. Not once had he said he loved her. Until he said it, she would never be sure. . . .

March 1946

Evening in Arik's room. His desk, the coffee table, the floor, were strewn with newspapers, even the Paris edition of the New York *Herald Tribune.*

Arik, at the desk, and Raquela, on the divan, sat tense. The radio in the bookcase was turned up. They sat glued to the words.

Dr. Chaim Weizmann was testifying in Jerusalem's handsome, towered YMCA.

The Anglo-American Committee of Inquiry on Palestine had arrived in the Holy Land on March 7, 1946. Dr. Weizmann, president of both the Jewish Agency for Palestine and the World Zionist Organization, was the first witness.

For the last two months Arik had clipped newspaper and magazine articles for Raquela as the committee listened to Jewish and Arab leaders in Washington, London, Vienna, and Cairo. With red pencil he had marked the stories of the subcommittees' interviewing survivors in Europe and the DP camps. The reporters described the hor-

ror-filled faces of the committee as the survivors showed
them pictures of their families. All burned. All dead.

In every DP camp, the survivors told them, "Palestine
was promised as our homeland. We want to go home."

Now the evening radio was broadcasting highlights of
the morning testimony. Dr. Weizmann was talking.
Raquela had seen the photos of this old, weary, nearly
blind man. It was hard to believe those photos now as she
listened to his voice. Strong. Passionate.

"We warned you, gentlemen," he said. *"We warned you.
We told you that the first flames that licked at the
synagogues of Berlin would set fire, in time, to all the
world."*

Raquela heard him pause. He talked about the promises
the Labour government had made. The room seemed to
echo with the plea of the old man who had spent his life
trusting the British government.

His voice broke. *"I ask you to follow the course of least
injustice in determining the fate of Palestine."*

Arik whispered, "The least injustice."

Raquela nodded, absorbed in the words that followed.

*"European Jewry cannot be expected to resettle on soil
drenched with Jewish blood. Their only hope for survival
lies in the creation of a Jewish state in Palestine. The
leaky boats in which our refugees come to Palestine are
their Mayflowers, the Mayflowers of a whole generation."*

The next witness was David Ben-Gurion, chairman of
the executive of the Jewish Agency, the short stocky leader
with a halo of white hair around his strong face.

Ben-Gurion was discussing the Jewish state. It was not a
new idea. Back in June 1937 the Royal Commission of
Enquiry, meeting around the same huge semicircular table
in the YMCA, had recommended partitioning Palestine
into an Arab and a Jewish state. Ben-Gurion, with
Weizmann and Moshe Sharett, had accepted the recom-
mendation, believing even a small Jewish state would give
the Jews a homeland. But the British government rejected
the findings of its own commission and instead issued the
White Paper in 1939.

In May 1942 Ben-Gurion, visiting the United States,
once again called for the creation of a Jewish commonwealth "integrated in the structure of the new democratic
world." It became known as the "Biltmore Program,"

from the Biltmore Hotel in New York, where the extraordinary Zionist Conference took place.

Now the committee was asking Ben-Gurion to define a "Jewish state."

His powerful voice blared through the radio. *"By 'Jewish state' we mean Jewish independence. We mean Jewish safety and security. Complete independence, as for any other free people."*

Ben-Gurion's words were carried live throughout the country. There was new hope. This committee was different from all the others. It had six Americans—sitting with the six Englishmen. The Americans understood the meaning of a "free people." The Americans would make a difference.

After the hearings the committee flew to Lausanne, Switzerland, to write their report in the neutral repose of the Hôtel Beau Rivage. The twelve men strove for unanimity. They sincerely believed Bevin's promise that if their report was unanimous, he would carry it out.

It took a month of debates and compromises and soul searching. Some of the committee members had gone through a genuine conversion in the DP camps and in the Holy Land. They voted unanimously to accede to President Truman's request: one hundred thousand DPs would be allowed to enter Palestine.

Truman enthusiastically approved the report.

Joy spread through the DP camps and Palestine. The suffering of the DPs would soon be ended.

Almost overnight, the joy turned to bitterness.

Prime Minister Clement Attlee, speaking in the House of Commons, announced that the Haganah and all private armies must be disarmed before any large-scale immigration could begin.

The report of the eighteenth commission was scuttled.

Palestine was burning.

The Jewish Resistance Movement attacked the Tegart police fortresses. They organized mass demonstrations fighting the British army and police. On June 17 they blew up all the bridges on the borders of Palestine.

Two weeks later the British decided to break the back of the Jewish Resistance Movement and, they hoped, to crush the Jewish will to establish a state.

At four-fifteen A.M. on "Black Saturday," June 29, Raquela, sleeping in her bedroom at Bet Hakerem, was awakened. Tanks and armored cars rumbled through the streets. In a country-wide military action soldiers burst into homes, searched attics and cellars, ripped up mattresses looking for ammunition, used dogs in kibbutzim to ferret out slicks, and arrested 2,600 men and women.

The leaders of the country, men like Moshe Sharett and David HaCohen, the Haifa labor leader, were imprisoned in the police fortress at Latrun on the Jerusalem-Tel Aviv Highway. Others were kept behind barbed wire in a camp in Rafa, on the Mediterranean Sea. Still others were imprisoned in Athlit.

David Ben-Gurion was in Paris, and he escaped.

Golda Meir, who had already distinguished herself in the Palestine labor movement, was chosen as acting head of the political department of the Jewish Agency, to replace the imprisoned Sharett.

Menachem Begin, leader of the Irgun, eluded the search.

Dr. Weizmann, who was not arrested, held a press conference.

In her room that night Raquela turned on the radio to hear Dr. Weizmann's voice. *"First the situation is allowed to deteriorate almost beyond hope,"* she heard him say. *"Then it is the victims of that deterioration that are punished."*

She sat at the edge of her bed, helpless with anger.

Dr. Weizmann, who had always talked of moderation—trust the British; cooperate with them; they are still our friends—now spoke bitterly.

"Is it not a most grotesque state of affairs," he asked, *"that the mufti should be sitting in a palace in Egypt, enjoying freedom, while Moshe Sharett, who raised an army for Britain of more than twenty-five thousand men, is behind barbed wire at Latrun?"*

Too agitated to sleep, Raquela switched off the radio and put on a robe. She found Mama and Papa sitting in the living room, still listening to the broadcast.

"We can't sleep either," Papa said. "Let's have some tea."

"I'll get it," Raquela said.

She busied herself in the little kitchen, fixing a tray with teacups and home-baked cookies.

She returned just as the voice on the radio announced, *"We interrupt this broadcast to bring you a news flash."*

She froze, clutching the tray.

"A pogrom today in Kielce, Poland, has taken the lives of many Jews. Exact details are not yet known."

The broadcast was over. Papa switched off the radio and began to pace restlessly.

"These are the Jews who went back to their homes in Poland. Not the DPs. These are the people who believed the propaganda. That the world had changed, that there is no more anti-Semitism."

Raquela poured the tea and handed the cup to Papa. "How can any Jew want to go back to such countries?"

Papa shook his head.

The Kielce pogrom started a new mass migration to the DP camps. More ships were outfitted to carry the DPs to the Holy Land. The struggle intensified.

Fear and terror spread throughout the land.

On July 22, 1946, the Irgun, with the approval of the Haganah, telephoned the offices of the British Government at the King David Hotel in Jerusalem, warning them to evacuate immediately. The building was to be bombed.

As the White Paper war continued, the southern wing of the hotel had become a fortress, housing military GHQ, the secretariat and the British civil government. Next to it were the British military police and headquarters for the Special Investigation Bureau, with soldiers and police on twenty-four-hour duty guarding the hotel, the offices, and the files kept by the British on the Jewish underground.

The commander of the Irgun, Menachem Begin, was the object of a large and intense manhunt by the British, his clean-shaved, bespectacled face on every "wanted" billboard. Begin was posing as Reb Israel Sassover, a bearded scholar living in a small detached house on Joshua Bin-Nun Street in Tel Aviv, not far from the Yarkon River. He spent much of his time in a synagogue studying the Talmud and biblical commentaries.

While his house and neighborhood were under constant surveillance by the British police, Begin and the Irgun planned the daring attack on the headquarters of the British rulers. At first, the Haganah command would not approve the plan. They feared an attack on the British headquarters would inflame the British to even more drastic repressive measures.

But after Black Saturday, June 29, when the British had

swooped down and arrested more of the leaders of the Haganah, the Palmach, and the Jewish Agency, the Haganah command approved Begin's plan.

Just before noon on July 22, Irgun men dressed as Arabs carried large metal milk cans into the "Regence Café" in the basement of the southern wing of the King David Hotel. Inside the milk cans were explosives manufactured by the Irgun operations chief "Giddy" (Amihai Paglin); they had a double mechanism—one to explode half an hour after they were delivered, the other to prevent the cans from being dismantled or removed.

The next steps were carefully planned to prevent casualties. To clear the streets, a small firecracker was exploded opposite the hotel. As soon as the bearers of the milk cans were safely out of the hotel, a young woman "telephonist" made three calls. First she phoned the King David Hotel, warning that explosives were to go off in a short time. "Evacuate the whole building!" she shouted.

Next she called the Palestine *Post*: "Bombs have been placed in the King David Hotel, and the people there have been told to evacuate the building."

Her third and final call was to the French consulate, right next to the hotel, telling them to open their windows to prevent shattering. They followed her instruction; the consulate was undamaged.

Twenty-five minutes passed. Reporters from the Palestine *Post* had already reached the King David Hotel to cover the expected explosion. Yet, to the horror of the underground fighters, there was no evacuation from the hotel.

Later the Haganah radio reported that Sir John Shaw, the chief secretary of the British administration, had refused to accept the telephone warning: "I give the orders here. I don't take orders from Jews."

Twelve-thirty-seven P.M. The whole city seemed to shake. The entire southern wing exploded in the air. Ninety-one people were killed and forty-five injured.

The British arrested 376 men and women, cordoned off the Old City, and sent twenty thousand troops on a house-to-house search to find Begin and the other leaders. Begin's cover held.

Palestine became an armed camp. The British were desperate. No more Jews must enter.

But the illegal ships continued to sail.

The patrols on the Mediterranean scoured the waters, found the ships, and imprisoned the people in Athlit. By August 1946 Athlit could hold no more.

The British opened new camps on the island of Cyprus as more ships with refugees were captured on the high seas.

Now there were two concentration camps after the war: Cyprus and Athlit.

March 1947

Raquela was in the delivery room, helping a young mother onto the delivery table, when a nurse opened the door.

"There was a telephone call for you. Dr. Yassky would like to see you as soon as you finish the delivery."

"Dr. Yassky!" Raquela turned. "Do you know what he wants?"

"No idea." The nurse shrugged her shoulders and closed the door.

Raquela helped the young woman push her feet into the stirrups. What could Dr. Yassky want?

She had been working as a registered nurse-midwife for a whole year—ever since graduation—and he had not once called her to his office. Mrs. Cantor or Miss Landsmann were always the intermediaries. He summoned the doctors; they summoned the nurses.

But she had no more time to worry. Her patient was ready to deliver.

Mazal tov. She placed the baby, washed and wide awake, in its mother's arms. Then she cleaned up, changed into a fresh uniform, and hurried down the steps to the row of administrative offices off a narrow corridor on the main floor.

Her mind was churning. What did Dr. Yassky want?

To most of his staff, he was a remote, almost mythical figure. He was the boss, the director general of the Hadassah Medical Organization.

Arik had told her stories of how Dr. Yassky and his dark-haired, dark-eyed wife, Fanny, had fled the Russian Revolution and come to Palestine in 1919. How appalled he had been by the sight of blind children in the Holy Land. Ninety-nine out of every hundred Arab children,

forty out of every hundred Jewish children, had eyes
scarred with the milky white film of trachoma which
would blind them.

He had become a school doctor in Haifa, treating
trachoma with a copper-sulphate stick, steeling himself
against the pupils screaming at him in pain, "You mur-
derer." He cured them. Henrietta Szold asked him to take
the fight against blindness to the whole country. He became *the* itinerant ophthalmologist, traveling with a little
cart and horse or on a donkey.

Raquela relaxed and smiled a little, trying to picture Dr.
Yassky, six feet tall, his legs dangling, sitting on the back
of a donkey.

But as she knocked on his door, her body grew tense
again. She was entering the private domain of the man
Miss Szold had selected in 1931 to become the head of the
Hadassah Medical Organization.

"Come in." She heard his voice.

He was sitting behind his desk, a silver and black cigarette holder in his mouth. Even in his long white medical
coat he looked austere. Formal. Aristocratic. His, the tight
hand of authority.

"Sit down, Miss Levy," he recommended.

She sat at the edge of the chair.

"I hope the delivery was routine."

"It was a normal birth," she said.

He ground his cigarette in an ashtray and filled a pipe
with tobacco.

"I am sure you know about Athlit, Miss Levy."

She nodded. "The British will probably be shutting it
down soon," she said, "now they have much bigger
camps—for tens of thousands—on Cyprus."

He focused his green eyes on her; she was struck by
their sadness.

"They're not closing it. It's full of refugees. Nearly three
thousand. Many have been there a long time. They've
asked us to send a midwife."

Raquela blurted, "A midwife in a concentration camp!"

The sad eyes closed for a moment. "Even in a concentration camp, men and women find ways to be together."
He wafted smoke in the air. "You're the youngest midwife
in our hospital." His austere face broke into a smile. "But
even in this office I hear when a nurse is gifted. When she
never complains. Willingly takes night shifts. When she is

completely dedicated to the mothers and the babies she de-
livers." He walked around the desk and put his hand on
her shoulder.

"Can you imagine, Miss Levy, what it would mean to
these survivors, still homeless nearly two years after the
Holocaust, to see an attractive young woman from
Jerusalem helping them bring a child into the world? It
won't be an easy job. We would like you to stay three or
four weeks." He looked at her face. "Will you accept it?"

"When would you like me to go?"

"The moment you're ready."

She knocked at Arik's door. The cries of infants filtered
down the staircase.

Arik was at his desk, reading, He looked up.

"You've accepted," he said.

She stopped short at the door. "Then you knew?"

"Dr. Yassky asked my opinion. He knew all about you;
his only hesitation was that you were so young."

She walked slowly to the divan. He followed her and
put his arms around her.

"It's good you're going," he said. "Not only for the refugees, but for us."

"Why?"

He took her face in his hands. "I've been monopolizing
you. It's not right. You must have a chance to meet other
men—younger men."

She was frightened. "Are you trying to get rid of me?"

"I'm trying to protect you."

"From what?"

"From me, Raquela. I'm too old for you."

"Fourteen years isn't such a big gap." *Why couldn't he
see that?* "Your beloved Sholom Aleichem would find an
etza," she said. "He would see that I'm twenty-two going
on thirty; and you're thirty-six going on—let's say—
thirty-three. So you're only three years older than I am."

He kissed her cheek.

"Let's not discuss it," he said. "You're leaving on an important mission. You're going to be the first Hadassah
nurse these refugees will have seen." He paused. "A
ninth-generation Jerusalemite—you're the fulfillment of all
their dreams."

They walked slowly, hand in hand, to the portico entrance to wait for the station wagon that would take her

down the mountain, past Sheikh Jarrah, through the silent curfewed streets, to Bet Hakerem.

"*Le'hitraot*, Raquela," he said.

"*Le'hitraot*," she repeated. It was not good-bye; it was a hope that they would see each other again.

In a country where so many had experienced tragedy and loss, *le'hitraot* was an amulet, a rabbit's foot to clutch against destiny.

-*₭ Chapter Eleven ₭*-

April 1947

At five-thirty in the morning, Bus 8 pulled up at the station in Bet Hakerem.

Mama and Papa kissed Raquela good-bye.

Papa blessed her. *"Behatzlaha.* May you succeed."

She climbed into the bus in her nurse's uniform and set her light suitcase near her seat. She waved good-bye to Mama and Papa, sensing their mixture of worry and pride.

The darkness was lifting. Jerusalem took on its special shimmering light as the sun rose swiftly, a delicate pink glow warming the hills. The bus window was open. She heard the birds chattering as they darted in and out of the tall pines and eucalyptus, chirping busily, like people in the marketplace.

Bus 8 sped around the empty road, passing an occasional Arab or Jewish farmer. In all of Jerusalem, there were only a few private cars, and at this hour, there were none on the road. But British tanks and armored cars were already patrolling.

She disembarked at the Central Bus Station, then boarded an Egged intercity express bus to Haifa.

"Wouldn't it be possible," she asked the driver, "to let me off near the camp at Athlit?"

He looked at her uniform. "For a young nurse going to that desecration—that dung heap—I'd even make a detour."

She settled herself at a window seat, watching the bus fill up with Jews in open shirts and dark trousers and Arabs in long black gowns and *keffiyehs*. Police and soldiers guarded the terminal, searching for explosives, scanning every face for men and women "wanted as terrorists." Raquela felt the tensions in the bus terminal like raw nerves under her skin.

For the cycle of violence and repression was spinning faster than ever. Repression begat violence. Violence and terror begat more repression.

The three underground groups had split apart, differing on how to fight the repression. The Haganah and Pal- mach, supported by most of the population, focused on immigration, on filling the "illegal" ships with "illegal" im- migrants. The paramilitary Irgun declared open guerrilla warfare; they mined roads, blew up British installations, attacked the Tegart police fortresses. The Stern Group, the smallest and most militant, set the oil tanks in Haifa ablaze, hoping to prevent the British prison ships from sail- ing to Cyprus with the people captured on the illegal boats.

The British reacted with more house-to-house searches and whosesale arrests. The prisons in Jerusalem, Tel Aviv, and especially in Acre, on the northern coast, filled up with underground fighters. The Irgun broke into Acre to free their comrades. Two hundred prisoners escaped.

Meanwhile, the mufti and his followers sat back, watching the war between Britain and the Jews with satis- faction. And the violence and repression intensified.

Bevin finally threw up his hands; on February 15, 1947, he announced to Parliament that he was turning the Pales- tine problem over to the United Nations. After the revolt of the American colonies and Ireland, Palestine was the greatest political failure in the history of the Empire.

The soldiers and police in the Central Bus Station waved the bus on. They had found no terrorists.

Raquela, leaning back, relieved, watched the bus pull away from the station. Jerusalem, with its coils of barbed wire and dragon's-teeth pillboxes, lay behind them.

Now they were in the Jerusalem corridor, swerving around the hairpin curves.

Raquela looked down at the biblical valleys that fell away abruptly from the winding highway. Across were the barren stubbled Hills of Judea, with huge boulders bleached white, baking in the sun since the days the prophets had walked among them.

They descended to Bab-el-wad, the gateway to Je- rusalem. A long graceful yellow building swept into view around a delicate slope. It was the Latrun Monastery, whose Trappist monks had taken a vow of silence and whose vineyards had made the monks famous. Raquela looked up above the monastery toward the Latrun Tegart police station and barbed-wire camp, staring in anger. Here the British had imprisoned the Haganah leaders that "Black Saturday," June 29, when she had heard the tanks rumbling through the streets of Bet Hakerem. They had held them for five long months.

Her mood followed the road. Ahead were the green and golden wheat fields of Ajalon, where Joshua had commanded, "Sun, stand thou still upon Gibeon, and thou, Moon, in the Valley of Ajalon."

She breathed in the peaceful air, the strong scent of orange blossoms.

What did Athlit look like? Would it be like this gently rolling land with fruit orchards, carob groves, and vines creating their own green roots as they stretched along the sticks planted in the soil?

Or would it look like that flat land and brick-red-clay earth of Hadera, the Jewish settlement they were now passing? Or Binyamina, whose rich orange groves and banana plantations lined the road, giving way to green vineyards?

The mountains of Carmel began to rise ahead, first bare-backed, like the wrinkled skin of dinosaurs, then covered with fir trees and boulders.

The driver called out, "Athlit," and stopped. Raquela picked up her bag and cape and hurried down the steps.

Two doctors stood in front of a white ambulance on whose side she saw the words MAGEN DAVID ADOM. The shield of David. Palestine's Jewish Red Cross.

The doctors introduced themselves—Dr. Mossberg, Jewish Agency doctor in charge of health services in the camp; Dr. Altman, eye, ear, nose, and throat man. Each day, they explained, a different specialist came to the prison camp from Haifa.

Raquela and the doctors climbed into the ambulance for the mile drive down the access road.

The prison camp loomed before her. Wooden watchtowers, manned by British soldiers, pierced the sky. Rows and rows of barbed wire stretched around an arid, dusty landscape of brown wooden barracks.

At a barbed-wire gate the doctors produced their identity cards. A British soldier studied Raquela's ID card.

"You're a bloody sight prettier than this picture, ma'am."

A second soldier made his personal examination. "And

a hell of a sight easier on the eye than those people inside."

Raquela ignored their compliments. "May I enter now?"

"No need to get huffy, ma'am. It's no fun sitting in this bloody heat guarding a bunch of illegal Jews."

He stopped short, aware that the tall, attractive young nurse was also a Jew.

The gates were unlatched. Raquela followed the doctors, then stopped abruptly.

Hundreds and hundreds of people were milling together on a hot dirt road. Some were half naked; others wore tattered rags, like shipwrecks on an uncharted island. Only this was no island with tropical trees and lush green foliage. It looked more like the pictures she had seen of concentration camps transplanted onto a scrubby hillside.

Dirty brown wooden barracks stood in martial rows as far as she could see, interspersed here and there with army tents. No grass, no green. Even the tall scrawny palm trees looked dusty gray and threatening. The fronds sat atop gigantic trunks, sad, wilted, defeated, like the people she saw waiting to be released. To be liberated in the Promised Land.

At the right, near the entrance, Raquela saw the delousing station, with stalls where British soldiers were now delousing some people, spraying them from their heads to their toes with white DDT powder.

"The men and women are separated," Dr. Mossberg told her. "The women are in the barracks at the left, down the main road; the men at the right. And over here, at the left, is the hospital compound."

Each compound was surrounded by barbed wire. Camps within camps, Raquela thought dismally. Prisons within prisons. The British in their camp outside the perimeter. The women in their prison camp; the men in theirs. Even the whitewashed hospital was sealed off behind a tall barbed-wire fence with a wire gate through which they entered.

She felt as if a giant lock were being turned, she was trapped.

"This first hut," Dr. Mossberg said as he led her into a white wooden barracks, "is the outpatient clinic. Here's where you'll find dozens, sometimes hundreds, of patients waiting for you at all hours of the day."

She nodded dully. Some thirty people sat on camp

chairs, their bare legs and thighs covered with open sores and impetigo. Flies and mosquitoes buzzed around them.

They led her through the four compartments of the hut: the patients waited in the first partition; they were treated in the second, gave birth in the third, and the fourth was the office of Dr. Herman Carr, the camp gynecologist.

She was in Dr. Carr's office, waiting to meet him, when a middle-aged woman in nurse's uniform burst in.

"I didn't believe you were ever coming. Every day they told me I was getting a replacement. They kept telling me 'tomorrow, tomorrow, tomorrow.' I began to doubt you existed."

"But it was only yesterday Dr. Yassky asked me to come."

"Maybe everybody else turned him down. They must have heard what our life is like."

"I don't understand—"

"Let's not waste any time. I'm due back at the British Government Hospital in Haifa. You'll be the only midwife here. Is there anything you want me to tell you?"

"I'd like to see the delivery room and the equipment."

"What kind of equipment?"

Raquela was flustered. "Well, I mean, I know you must have clamps and sputum tubes. What about sterilized sheets and towels?"

"Where do you think you are? Mount Scopus? Who has anything sterilized here? You'll be lucky if you can get some sheets and towels from the government hospital. Then you'll have to boil everything. At least there's water."

They entered the delivery room. Raquela saw a conventional white leather delivery table with stirrups. The midwife talked rapidly. "Here's a sheet. The only time a woman sees a sheet in Athlit is in this room or in the hospital. But you'll be able to sleep on a sheet—that's on condition you ever have time to sleep."

Raquela decided to ask no more questions. Nausea overcame her. The heat. The grueling bus trip. The filth. The dust. The dark throngs of people moving back and forth in the camp, like sheep in a pen. The look of hopelessness and despair.

She leaned against the delivery table to steady herself. The nurse-midwife looked worried. "You're pale. Don't you feel well?"

"I'll be all right in a minute. I know you're anxious to leave. Just show me where I'm to sleep."

They walked out the back door past a second barracks painted white. "This is the hospital," her guide explained. "You'll have plenty of time to see this later." They moved on to a third barracks, to the right of the hospital. This one was brown, like the barracks of the refugees, but it was partitioned into a chain of rooms—a dining room, kitchen, storage room for food, and three small bedrooms for the hospital staff.

"This is your room," the midwife said. "You're right next to the storage. Don't worry about the food smells. You won't have much time to enjoy them."

Raquela set down her bag.

"I'll just wash my hands," she said, "and get right to work."

"You're sure you're all right?" the midwife looked at her askance.

"Positively. Thank you."

"You're pretty young to be sent to this hell on earth. I hope you last. . . ."

She picked up her carpetbag and walked out.

Raquela washed her hands and face. Her hair felt like straw under her cap. Her once-starched uniform stuck to her body. She pulled off her white stockings and changed to ankle socks. At least her legs would be cool.

She hurried to the hospital and went from bed to bed, introducing herself, talking to the patients, learning what she could of their illnesses.

Lunch was at one o'clock. She entered the barracks dining room, already crowded. A compact young woman in a spotless white shirt and pleated black skirt put out her hand.

"*Shalom*," she said. Her voice was crisp. "I'm Ruth Berman. I'm the Jewish Agency liaison officer between the British and the refugees. Welcome to *Gan Eden*." (The Garden of Eden).

Raquela smiled. "*Gan Eden* with barbed wire."

"After a while you won't notice the barbed wire. It's the other things that will bother you. But why should I frighten you? You've got plenty of time to discover for yourself."

Raquela found herself attracted to the efficient-looking woman with black curly hair, sharp dark eyes, and good strong features. Ruth talked in clipped phrases, like a British officer. She had joined the Haganah in Haifa before her eighteenth birthday and was one of the first women to volunteer for the British army in 1942. She had risen swiftly to junior commander in the Auxiliary Territorial Service, serving in Egypt.

"I suppose you've toured our camp facilities here?" Ruth asked Raquela.

"Some of them."

"Consider yourself lucky. It's pretty clean where you are in the hospital compound. And you're apart from most of the sounds and smells."

"And you? Where do you sleep?"

"In the delousing station."

"You're pulling my leg."

"Not really. It's the partition next to the room where the British delouse all the newcomers with DDT powder."

"How do you breathe?"

"Who breathes?" She shrugged her shoulders. "When the DDT gets too much for me, I sleep outside, in a tent."

Raquela nibbled at the army rations the British served the staff—bully beef, pea soup, white bread, and coffee— and then left to make rounds in the barracks.

Down the length of the camp was a long dirt road called the Walkover. Here hundreds of people milled together, talking, shouting; some hurried, some stood apathetic; the hubbub seemed to have a chain reaction, as if the noise fed upon itself.

Raquela walked among them. Some stared at her curiously: a new face; someone from the outside world. Others brushed past her, turned in on themselves. They seemed to Raquela like people from another planet.

She felt hot anger. These people had come through so much—the blue numbers of the death camps were on their arms as they moved around her on the Walkover. They had survived. They had come to the Holy Land. They were on the holy soil. Yet it was denied them. No wonder some of them stared catatonically through the barbed wire. Where was reality? Here in the prison, or out there, just beyond the iron fence, in the Promised Land?

At seven, exhausted, Raquela returned to her room in the brown barracks.

From the top of her ankle socks to her skirt, her legs were blotched with mosquito bites. She was smearing them with calamine lotion when a woman wearing a tentlike sack made from an army blanket stood before her.

"My time has come," she said.

"Come with me," Raquela said. She led her through the compound to the first white wooden hut and into the delivery room.

She examined her on the delivery table.

"You still have time," she said. How could she send a woman in labor back to one of the women's overcrowded, broiling barracks?

"You can stay here," Raquela said softly. "I'll stay right here with you."

"I'm so worried. I've just arrived in Athlit."

Raquela frowned. "I thought no new prisoners were brought here. I thought they were all transported to Cyprus."

"Maybe so. I guess I'm special."

"How's that?" Raquela helped her descend from the high delivery table and tried to make her comfortable in a chair.

"We were on a small boat. The British captured us outside of Haifa. Soldiers and sailors came on board with guns and tear gas. We were empty-handed. Some of our people picked up cans of food to fight them off. Many were wounded by the soldiers; two of our best friends were killed. Then the British pulled us into Haifa."

Raquela shook her head in silence.

The woman moved her heavy body in the chair. "On the dock the British began to load the people onto big ships. We knew they were taking us to Cyprus. My husband went to one of the officers. My husband"—she chuckled—"the SS couldn't scare him; nothing scares him. He said to the officer, 'My wife is due any minute. Do you want her to give birth on your prison ship? Can't you be human? Send her to a decent hospital in Haifa!' That's why I'm special. They put us in a jeep and brought my husband and me to Athlit."

Raquela brought the woman a cold drink. Her name was Pnina Kaczmarek; her husband was Gershon. Growing more relaxed as she talked, she told Raquela she was born in Czechoslovakia. When she was fourteen, the Nazis had deported her with her whole family to the death camp in Auschwitz. Children of fourteen were almost always sent, by the infamous Dr. Mengele, directly to the gas chambers. Pnina pretended to be sixteen. She was sent to the barracks with the women strong enough to work.

Gershon, also fourteen, had made the journey to Auschwitz from the ghetto in Lodz, Poland. He, too, had lied that he was older.

They were both liberated in April 1945, nearly dead of hunger and typhus. They had made the pilgrimage back to their homes, found no one, and returned to Germany, where they met in a DP camp and fell in love. They married in the camp and vowed they would get to Palestine. The route had led to Athlit.

"How old are you now?" Raquela asked.

Pnina looked forty, but she had to be younger.

"Nineteen."

Raquela averted her face. Four years younger than she, yet she looked older than Mama.

Pnina's voice began to tremble. "What if the war years did something to me? What if I have an abnormal baby?"

Raquela heard the panic mounting. "Don't be afraid. You've come through everything—Auschwitz, the war. You'll come through this." She wiped Pnina's forehead with a damp cool cloth. "Just think. Your baby will be a Sabra."

"I dreamed of this. That's why I insisted we get on that little overcrowded boat. I wanted my baby born in *Eretz Israel*. But who dreamed it would be born in a prison camp?"

"They can't keep you here forever. You'll be free soon."

Pnina shut her eyes. "I hope I have a daughter. I'll name her Etya, for my mother. She died in Auschwitz. In the ovens."

The contractions came closer together.

Raquela helped Pnina back on the table and delivered the baby.

"You have a daughter," Raquela said.

Pnina's face, still wet with sweat, relaxed. She studied her baby, counted her fingers and toes, stroked her forehead and soft rounded cheeks.

Suddenly, Pnina was young and radiant.

"She's the image of my mother," she said.*

---

* Twenty-five years later, Pnina's baby, Etya, became secretary to Dr. Moshe Prywes, Raquela's second husband.

—◄ *Chapter Twelve* ►—

The next morning, Raquela crossed the hospital compound, passed a few people already out on the Walkover, and entered the bathhouse. It was Ladies' Day.

Inside the long tin building, she secluded herself in one of the shower stalls, grateful for the privacy, letting the warm water cascade over her body and hair as she covered herself with lather.

She changed into fresh clothes, a new uniform to begin the day. She had been one of the first in the bathhouse; now dozens of women were queuing up in front of the shower stalls. She saw a few women standing in front of a gray-white asbestos partition in the center of the bathhouse. Curious, she walked toward them. They were scrawling their names on the partition. She looked closer. Hundreds of names were on the asbestos wall, some with the dates of their arrival in Athlit, some with drawings of the ships on which they had made the journey.

Her eyes fastened on a single line: DAVID POLAK—BERLIN, BUDAPEST, BERGEN-BELSEN.

In six words the man called David Polak had recorded the story of his life: Born in Berlin, Escaped to Budapest. Was deported to Bergen-Belsen. Refused to die. Was liberated. Dreamed of Palestine. Sailed to *Eretz Israel*. Ends up—the irony of survival—in a prison camp called Athlit.

She no longer felt clean. She had washed the dirt of Athlit off her body; now she was returning to it. She walked slowly back to the hospital compound and immediately began making rounds.

With the shortage of doctors and nurses, she worked not only as the camp's midwife but as a regular nurse. It was the nurses who decided when a doctor was needed; then they called the doctor who was on duty for the day.

In the heat of mid-afternoon a scantily clad woman entered the clinic. "My friend has terrible cramps. She's in our barracks, vomiting. She's very hot; she must have a fever."

"I'll come with you," Raquela said.

Mobs of people were swarming back and forth on the Walkover as they crossed the dirt main street to the women's compound, surrounded by barbed wire, and entered one of the brown wooden barracks.

Raquela gasped. In opening the door they had pulled aside a hanging blanket. A couple lay naked on a cot, making love.

She hurried past them to the bedside of the sick woman, who was writhing in pain. Raquela felt her stomach, pressing her fingers, probing. She diagnosed the illness as gastroenteritis endemic to the Middle East. She would not need to call the doctor. She took a supply of sulfaguanidine tablets out of her bag, gave her seven to take at once with a glass of water, and assured her she would return every four hours with four more pills.

Several other women lay on the cots, watching in silence. Now they called out to Raquela, each with a different complaint—headaches, rashes, infected mosquito bites. She treated them and suggested they come to see her again in the clinic. She tried to forget the couple making love. She dared not look to see if they had covered themselves.

The smell of stale and rancid food filled the barracks. Half hidden under some of the pillows were pieces of bread, herring, and remnants of army rations. She had learned that although the soldiers, doctors, nurses, and Jewish Agency representatives were given bully beef, the refugees were given dairy foods, since the British army could not supply kosher food or utensils.

"Why do you put this bread and herring under your pillow?" she finally asked the woman who had complained of a headache. "Don't you get enough food in the dining room?"

The woman looked at her in surprise. "Of course there's enough to eat. But I never finish a meal. I always take some of it back with me. How do you know that if there's bread today, there will be bread tomorrow?"

The worst disease was boredom.

All day the people herded up and down the Walkover, endlessly waiting. Occasionally they glanced up at the hill outside the camp that separated them from the sea. They hated the hill. It was the hill that blocked the cool breezes from the Mediterranean. It was on the hill that most of the wooden search towers stood, looming over the landscape. Beyond the hill, a few yards away, lay freedom.

But there were no days of boredom for Raquela.

On call at any hour, she sometimes worked around the clock. The first few days she tore the pages from her small desk calendar and drew a red circle around May 1, 1947, the day her four weeks' stay was scheduled to be over.

But soon she forgot the calendar. In Athlit time was not marked by the chronology of day following day. Time, like boredom, was a disease marked by crises. Or by desperate attempts to escape.

A few prisoners succeeded by furrowing under the barbed wire. But most were caught and arrested by the ever-vigilant sentries in the watchtowers and in the huge soldiers' camp outside the barbed wire.

Each month a few hundred were allowed to leave legally. Under the White Paper, fifteen hundred certificates were allotted every month until the day, envisioned by the White Paper, when no more Jews would be allowed to enter Palestine. The war had sidetracked the original date— 1944—when all immigration was to have ceased, and with it the end of the homeland.

The fifteen hundred certificates were given to the Jewish Agency to administer: seven hundred fifty for the Jews in Europe and the DP camps, and seven hundred fifty for the refugees in Athlit and Cyprus. The rule in the camps was "first in, first out." Any missing refugees were deducted from the quota.

At four in the morning, a week after her arrival, Raquela walked out into the night air. The camp lay in darkness, the searchlights making eerie circles on the Walkover.

She saw a figure moving about with a flashlight. It was Ruth Berman.

"What are you doing out here at four in the morning?" Ruth asked. "Is someone sick?"

"I needed fresh air. My room is so stifling I can't sleep. But what are *you* doing up at this hour?"

"Making my nightly head count," Ruth said crisply. "I make two a day: the first one at ten P.M., and this one at four in the morning."

Raquela, dressed in a cotton robe, walked beside her. "I thought the men and women are all locked up inside their barracks after supper. Locked in for the whole night."

"That doesn't mean," Ruth said, "they won't hide someplace before the lockup and make a try to get out of here. It's bloody lucky the British trust *me* to make the head count. How would you like to have British soldiers unlock the womens' barracks every night to make the check? You might have more business than you can handle in your delivery room."

"I won't be here that long."

Ruth put a key in each barracks door, entered quietly, and made her check. When the head count was finished, they started back toward the hospital compound. A soldier in a watchtower beamed his light on them.

"They greet me this way every night," Ruth said. "They're victims, too. They're taking orders from Whitehall. You can't blame all the British people for Bevin's anti-Semitism. I got to know a lot of British soldiers when I was with the army in Egypt. Decent, humane, compassionate. The policy is monstrous, not the boys. Never forget, these British soldiers are not Nazis. They're interning our people; they're not killing them."

Raquela glanced up. It seemed to her the sentries were waving to them. "Looks as if your coming out here every night helps them get through their boredom."

The circle of light followed them like a spotlight on a darkened stage.

"Bismarck wrote you can do anything with bayonets except sit on them," Ruth said. "These boys up there in the search towers are sitting on their bayonets. And most of them hate it. But they've got to keep watch twenty-four hours a day."

"Who can blame the people for trying to escape," Raquela said.

"Sure, but the British can't afford another breakthrough like the one the Palmach pulled off less than two years ago. You remember when Nahum Sarig and Yitzhak Rabin freed more than two hundred refugees slated to be deported to Africa?"

"I remember very well." Raquela's voice was muffled.

She felt a pang of homesickness; she was home again. It was Friday night in Mama's living room; Jacob was telling of the breakthrough in Athlit.

Ruth seemed to sense her quietness. "If you're not ready to go to sleep, why don't we have a cold drink in my tent. That's where I go when I can't sleep."

The tent had a wooden table, a few chairs, a narrow cot. Ruth lit a kerosene lamp and placed it in the center of the table. A warm amber glow suffused the darkness.

She poured *gazoz* into two glasses. They sat for a while in silence.

Raquela realized she had a need to talk to someone, to clarify her own feelings. Ruth, ten years older than she, sensitive and philosophic despite her no-nonsense air, made her feel comfortable.

"The first time," Raquela said slowly, tentatively, "the first time I saw a man and woman making love, I was in shock. But now, after a week, I hardly notice it."

Ruth nodded. "Camps dehumanize people. That's what the Nazis tried to do: dehumanize our people. What you see is sex. Physical contact. Not love. They need to prove to themselves they're alive."

She refilled their glasses.

"When the war ended," Ruth said, "I was coldly hysterical. Every time I saw a Jewish survivor, I felt guilty that I was alive. We should have done more to save our people. We should have marched on Whitehall. We should have marched on the White House. We should have screamed, 'Save our people!' "

She stopped and stared into the light. "Now, when the Jewish Agency asked me to come here, I felt maybe at last I could do something for the survivors. Then I saw the things that you're seeing now. The results of the Nazi dehumanization. People with no belief in the future, apathetic, quarrelsome, no morals. I tried to bribe some of the women with chocolate bars if they would wash their hair. I change my clothes three times a day. They don't care what they look like."

Raquela looked out the tent flap. The camp was still dark; the people were still asleep. Soon they would begin milling again, hiding food, making love, waiting, waiting. Jerusalem, only eighty miles away, seemed light years distant from the bedlam in the hot, overcrowded camp.

Ruth went on. "One day I called some of the older people—those in their thirties—to my tent, and I said, 'why do you behave this way?'

" 'Madame Ruth,' they said—that's what they call me when they're trying to be polite—'Madame Ruth, what do you want from us? Who remained alive in the concentration camps? A few, by a miracle. And there were very few miracles. Maybe once we're out of here, we'll change, we'll do the things you'd like us to do. But for now, leave us alone, Madame Ruth. Leave us alone.' "

A few days later, a group of men burst into the hospital.

"What do you want?" Raquela asked.

"We suspect you've got a Nazi hiding in one of your beds."

"A Nazi? In Athlit? Have you lost your senses?"

One of the men drew her aside. "Some of the people think they recognized a Nazi. Why not? It would be a good cover for an SS man wanted for war crimes. He throws away his uniform, poses as a Jew, gets into a DP camp, and then boards a ship for Palestine. You must let us search. If you have a Nazi here, you must let us find him."

Silently Raquela led them to the men's ward. They approached the first patient. She watched as one of the refugees drew down his eyelids. Then he raised the patient's arms, leaning down, examining him closely.

"What are you looking for?" she asked.

"Two tiny letters: *SS*. They tattooed those two letters on their eyelids or inside their armpits."

They went from patient to patient. In the fifth bed they found a man squeezing his arms under the blanket. They forced his arms apart.

His tattoo was in his right armpit.

They stretched the skin to make certain. Then they called Raquela. There it was: ss. Tiny, but indelible. The hated Sturmstaffel. The Storm Troopers.

The men pulled him off the bed. He lay trembling on the floor, pleading, "Don't kill me. Don't kill me."

Raquela felt weak with nausea and fear. Would the men torture him, as they must have been tortured? Would they kill him?

"What will you do?" she whispered.

"We'll turn him over to the British. Too bad we can't do to him what he did to our people. But the Allies, we hope, will try him for war crimes. If they call us as witnesses, the people who recognize him can testify how many hundreds of Jews he killed with his own hands."

Two weeks passed. There were no telephones in Athlit. She wondered how Dr. Yassky would get word to her to come back. Perhaps he would send a replacement. Then she could go home. She could call Arik immediately.

She saw herself sitting on the divan in his room on Mount Scopus. His arm was around her. The dirty wooden barracks fell away. She felt warm and clean and loved.

A few nights later a woman in labor entered the hospital compound. Raquela placed her stethoscope on the woman's abdomen.

"You're carrying a big baby."

The woman was too weary to answer. Raquela listened to the baby's heartbeat. It sounded faint. She examined the woman. Her pelvis was far too small for the large baby she was carrying.

"Just lie here and try to relax," Raquela said soothingly. "I'll be with you in a moment."

She hurried through the partition to the office, praying silently that Dr. Carr, the gynecologist, would be there.

"He's gone home to Haifa," a nurse told her. "You know his wife just had a baby."

"Get any kind of transportation," Raquela ordered. "We've got to get this woman to the hospital in Haifa right away. Only a caesarean section can save her baby."

Raquela returned to the delivery room. She dabbed the woman's face with a damp cloth. Minutes passed. *Arik, I need you.*

Arik was the master of caesarean sections. Arik could perform a caesarean in three minutes.

The nurse burst into the delivery room. "We have a panel truck. I'll go with you to Haifa."

They wrapped a blanket around the woman and helped her lie down in the back of the truck. The driver raced to the government hospital in twenty minutes. They were in the delivery room. A resident doctor performed the caesarean.

The baby was dead.

Two nights later, another woman lay on the delivery table. The procedure seemed routine. Raquela held the woman's hands in her two strong hands. "Now push against me."

The woman cooperated. She pushed hard. Raquela turned white. The umbilical cord was preceding the head.

She knew—Arik had taught her well—that she had seven minutes to save the baby's life.

The umbilical cord contained the blood vessels that brought blood and oxygen from the mother to the fetus. If the umbilical cord prolapsed—if it came out first—then the head of the baby could press down on the remainder of the cord and stop the flow of blood and oxygen. There was enough oxygen and blood in the baby for just seven minutes. If the birth took longer, the baby might survive, but it would be brain-damaged.

What should she do? There was no time to call Dr. Carr from Haifa. Should she give the mother ether? Anesthesia would relieve some of the pressure. The baby's head would no longer press down on the umbilical cord. The flow of blood and oxygen could start again. If only she could use forceps. But midwives were not permitted ever to use forceps.

If only we were in a hospital, she thought frantically. In a hospital we might save this baby. Why don't the British let us deliver our babies like human beings, in the hospital in Haifa?

She began to give the mother light anesthesia. Then she helped her bear down. Three minutes passed. Four minutes. Five minutes. Ten minutes. The baby was born. A purple, lifeless child.

Raquela felt blood rush to her head. What kind of world do we live in that women have to give birth in a prison? What crimes have these woman committed? That they're Jews? And they want to go home?

The mother woke up from the anesthesia. "How is my baby?"

Raquela stood at her side. "Your baby was stillborn. But you're all right."

The mother screamed, "Even this they deny me! They take away my land. My freedom. Now my baby. Let me die. I want to die."

Raquela held the sobbing woman in her arms. Tears ran down her cheeks. "You're young," she told the mother, her own voice choking. "You're healthy. You'll have other babies in the Holy Land."

"Let me die."

The next morning, Raquela confronted Dr. Carr in his office. Her face was ashen.

"I will not do another delivery unless there is a doctor on the grounds all the time."

He looked at her in amazement. "I've never seen you so upset."

"I've lost two babies. Both of them might be alive, if you—if a doctor—were here."

"You know why I go home at night, Miss Levy. My wife needs me. My baby needs me."

"These women need you, too. Unless a gynecologist is on duty all the time for emergencies, I will not deliver another baby."

"My dear young woman, you're being unreasonable."

"I'm sorry, Dr. Carr. I'm going back to Hadassah today. You'll have to find another midwife."

"Not so hasty, young lady. I know I should have been here when you needed me. I'll get Haifa and ask them to send me some clothes. I'll move into a barracks in the hospital compound. Now, please, let's not have any more difficulties."

Raquela was not ready to agree. "What happens on your day off?"

"I'll send a doctor from Haifa to cover."

Raquela nodded. "I'll stay."

Four weeks passed.

The desk calendar lay untouched.

Six weeks. Seven weeks. She knew she could go to Haifa and telephone Dr. Yassky. *You said it would be for three or four weeks. It's nearly two months. Why don't you send a replacement?*

She never telephoned.

On a boiling-hot afternoon she lay on her cot for a quick nap. Little steps scampered overhead on the tin roof. She knew they were rats searching for food in the storage partition next to her room. Often they kept her awake at night. But this was afternoon.

Day or night, rats terrified her. With her head on the pillow, she shut her eyes.

Suddenly she screamed. A rat had found its way into her room and leaped, landing in her long hair. She shook her head free and raced in panic out of the barracks.

I've got to get out of here, she thought frantically. *Out. Out. I can't take anymore.*

She was running down the Walkover, toward the entrance gate. Men and women crowded around, some touching her arm.

"My baby is sick. . . ."

"Can you get me more milk? . . ."

"The sore you bandaged is healing. . . ."

"How can I thank you? . . ."

"I felt some pains this morning. Do you want me to come to the delivery room this afternoon? . . ."

"You look so pale. Soon you'll look the way we do. Please take care of yourself. We need you. . . ."

She stopped running. She felt currents of love eddying toward her from the ragged people. What was a rat, compared to their agony and need? She turned around and reentered the hospital.

Late in the afternoon, Raquela put on a bathing suit beneath her white uniform and took a shortcut across the hill to the sea. Before her eyes stretched an expanse of bleached white sand and beyond it the blue Mediterranean. Two worlds separated by the hated hill: back of her, dirt, filth, barracks, barbed wire, the foul smell of imprisonment; before her, cool breezes, the sea breaking on the dazzling sand, freedom.

She kicked off her white oxfords, stepped out of her uniform, and ran into the water.

❈ Chapter Thirteen ❉

June 1947

A car drove up to the barbed-wire gate. A tall man showed the sentries his credentials and made his way to the hospital.

"*Shalom*, Miss Levy," he extended his hand.

"*Shalom*, Dr. Yassky."

They looked at each other in silence. Finally, Dr. Yassky spoke.

"I'll send a replacement for you at once," he said.

"You've seen the camp."

He nodded. "Take a holiday, Miss Levy. Go home to Jerusalem and rest for a few weeks. Then come and see me. If you decide not to come back, I'll understand completely. Your job is always waiting for you at the hospital. Meanwhile I'll send a temporary replacement."

She nodded silently.

Two days later, her replacement arrived. She said goodbye to her patients, boarded the intercity bus to Jerusalem, and slept most of the way.

At home, she kissed Mama and Papa, then retired to her bedroom. She folded back the clean printed bedspread, lay down, and fell asleep. She slept around the clock. For three days she called no one. Not even Arik.

At last she phoned him. He hurried from Mount Scopus to Bet Hakerem, held her in his arms, then stood away to look at her.

"You look good," he said. "Do you feel the way you look?"

"I'm all right."

"How about going downtown? There's a Philharmonic concert tonight. Let's have dinner early and celebrate your homecoming."

She nodded.

Soon they were on the bus, riding past Bet Hakerem's peaceful gardens and myriad playgrounds. In Romema the bus picked up Arab passengers; the memory of the Arab attack on the bus before her Bat Mitzvah slipped dream-like in and out of her mind. On the street, the men in robes and *keffiyehs*, smoking their water pipes, looked shadowy, like sepia figures in a painting.

Now they were in the old Jewish quarter; Zayda and Bubba seemed to be dancing a Hassidic dance midair, Chagall-like. She saw them through half-opened eyes. She had long decided that a trip in a Jerusalem bus was like an instant voyage through the Middle East and the *shtetls* of Eastern Europe. But now, she thought, talking to her-self, the *shtetls* of Eastern Europe are exterminated, wiped out. Still, the people live on, here in Jerusalem. Survivors, too.

As the bus continued its route, she looked at the little stone houses and open kiosks, at the men in long black coats and curled earlocks, the women in long-sleeved dresses and cotton stockings, dressed in traditional Has-sidic garb despite the summer heat. But she saw them all through a haze, like a patient coming out of ether.

"You're so quiet, Raquela," Arik said. "Still tired?"

"A little. Though I should be slept out."

They were now in the bustling modern quarter of new Jerusalem. Women in attractive summer dresses, men in shorts or slacks and cool open shirts, walked briskly. The buildings looked new, the shops well stocked. "Look at those people." Raquela shook her head in disbelief. "Look at them sitting in cafés, as if nothing has happened. Eating, talking, laughing. Look at them in front of that greengrocer, filling up string bags with fresh fruit. And over there—queuing up for a movie!"

"What's wrong with that?" Arik interrupted.

"Don't they know about Athlit? Does life just go on?"

"This is reality, too, Raquela. I'm worried about you."

"I don't think I can sit through dinner and a concert," she said.

"What would you like to do?"

"Let's go up to Mount Scopus."

They changed for Bus 9, as Raquela had done for more than four years. She felt her spirits lift a little as the bus passed the hospital, the nursing school, and then dropped them in front of the university.

Together they strolled slowly on the mountain she loved. The sun, setting on the Old City, washed the domes and steeples in pastel and gold.

"I kept expecting you to go to Haifa, to call me on the telephone," Arik said. "When you didn't call, I figured you must be working night and day."

"The truth is, I didn't have time to miss you. I was so busy—and so angry."

"Anger is good, Raquela. Remember the words of the Jewish sage: *'b'kisso, b'kosso, b'kasso.'* 'A man is known by three things: by his pocket, his cup, and his anger.' Your anger, my darling, is righteous anger."

A cool wind blew up from the desert behind them. Arik put his arm around her as they walked through the university garden. The flower-scented air, the peace and serenity on the mountain above the turbulent city, Arik's nearness, were like balm. At last the words came, released in a torrent. She began to tell him about the babies she had lost, the rats, the lack of privacy, the boredom, the open lovemaking, her feelings of guilt when she sought refuge in the sea.

He took her hand and held it between both of his. "You had a right to push the camp away for a few hours whenever you could. People like us, doctors and nurses, live with tragedy and death every day. If we don't escape occasionally, we can't function. We can break under the pressure."

Tears formed behind her eyes. "But Arik, *I* could run away from the camp; they couldn't."

Raquela strolled through new Jerusalem looking at shop windows. She entered a dress shop on Ben Yehuda Street and rummaged through the racks. She'd been gone only two and one-half months, and already the styles had changed. The skirts were longer now, and the shoulders of suits were padded, like a football player's uniform.

The salesgirl approached her, holding up a voluminous brown taffeta dress. "It's 'the new look.' Christian Dior designed it. Why don't you try it on? With your height and figure, you'd look *eisen beton*—supercolossal."

Raquela smiled. *Eisen beton,* literally "iron concrete," meant "terrific," "supercolossal." It was part of the new "slanguage"—a mixture of colorful words from all over the world, with Hebrew syntax.

In the fitting room she tried on the dress. Imagine turning up in Athlit with the "Dior look." Athlit! She pushed
it swiftly out of her mind. She still had time to make the
decision. She looked at herself in the mirror. The dress
was brown, Señora Vavá's favorite color. That was good.
And it had another advantage: it made her look older
than did the cotton skirts and blouses she usually wore.
Would Arik notice?

"I love it," she told the salesgirl. "I'll take it."

She walked down Ben Yehuda Street as if she were a
stranger in Jerusalem, feasting her eyes on the window dis-
plays of leather pocketbooks, cosmetics, bathing suits, oriental rugs, shining brass coffeepots, and round hammered
trays. Ben Yehuda Street was a narrow hilly avenue that
descended like an arrow into new Jerusalem's main thoroughfare, Jaffa Road, which came all the way from Jaffa
up to Jerusalem, to the portal of the Jaffa Gate, entering
the Old City.

Now, at her left, she saw coils of barbed wire sealing off
the big government buildings in the vast "Russian compound" with its onion-domed church and its complex of
old buildings. Here were the headquarters of the British
police, the CID, and the Central Prison, a low ugly stone
building that was said to have been a monk's retreat when
it was built, in 1860. Now its tiny dark cells were filled
with "dissenters," the men of the underground, who could
look through their iron bars at the noose and the trap.

It seemed to Raquela that the rusted wire, the concrete
"dragon's teeth," the soldiers with submachine guns—the
whole complex—had become a war zone. With typical
Galgenhumor—gallows humor—the Jews nicknamed it
"Bevingrad." The British, she thought ruefully, have become prisoners of their own security measures.

She continued walking down Jaffa Road as it curved
around a small hill, became King David Street, and
emerged the most elegant boulevard in Jerusalem, with the
King David Hotel set back on its left and the YMCA rising majestically on its right.

This is the way America must look, she thought. The
Y—the Young Men's Christian Association—had been
built by Americans, and the two small streets that flanked
it were named for George Washington and Abraham Lin-
coln.

But now armored cars and personnel carriers were lined

up on King David Street, and soldiers with submachine guns stood on the steps of the Y, pushing back a crowd of people who seemed to be waiting for a big event.

"What's happening?" she asked a woman.

"The members of UNSCOP are opening their hearings. We want to see what they look like."

She nodded. She had read about UNSCOP—the United Nations Special Committee on Palestine, composed of delegates from eleven small, neutral countries.

Two months ago, on April 28, the United Nations had held a "special Palestine session." Bevin seemed to be giving up. He had thrown the Palestine problem into the lap of the UN. The fifty-five member nations, meeting in the special session, had voted to send another committee to investigate and make recommendations.

It was the nineteenth commission on Palestine. But this committee was different: for the first time Britain was not a member of the group investigating her own role in the Holy Land.

The people watched as a fleet of Studebaker limousines pulled up. The eleven members of the committee climbed the wide stone stairs to the tree-shaded veranda, and entered the conference chamber.

Raquela stood in the crowd, holding her package in her arms. Strangers talked to one another; everyone was involved.

"Do you really think this UNSCOP committee is any different from all the others?" a woman in a large straw hat asked her neighbor, a man, carrying a briefcase, who looked like a civil servant.

"And if it is different, and they do come up with a real solution"—he shrugged his shoulders—"do you think Bevin will accept it? Remember how he turned down the Anglo-American Committee report last year?"

Raquela questioned him. "Don't you think, this time, Bevin's had a stomachful? After all, *he* went to the UN and threw it in *their* lap."

"Bevin will never give up Palestine. He's pretending now that he is neutral. You heard his line, 'The Jews want to go to the head of the queue.' He's incapable of neutrality. He loves Arabs and hates Jews."

"Then why did he turn the problem over to the UN?" she asked.

"It's his newest trap. He didn't go to surrender the Man-

date. He wants a new mandate—this time from the UN.
He's probably sure he can convince the countries of the
world that Britain is the only one that can keep law and
order here."

A boy broke into the crowd, waving a newspaper. "The
three Irgunists have been sentenced to hang!"

The crowd gasped. The three Irgunists captured after
breaking into the prison at Acre on May 4, 1947, were
being tried in the British Military Court nearby.

The man with the briefcase turned to Raquela. "That
shows you who's running this country. Imagine choosing
today. The very first day the UN committee holds its
meetings. *Today* they have the *chutzpah* to fling this death
sentence in the committee's faces."

Raquela had seen the pictures of the three condemned
prisoners on wall newspapers pasted up at night by the Irgun. They looked barely eighteen or nineteen. They had
hardly lived; now they were sentenced to die at the end of
a rope.

From the back of the crowd, Raquela heard the voice
of a young woman: "The Irgun will fight back! The Irgun
will avenge this terrible deed!"

Raquela spent the next days at home, with Mama and
Papa. Jacob and Yair came with their wives, and Arik,
welcomed affectionately, especially by Mama, came in the
evenings.

All conversation stopped the moment Papa turned on
the radio in the living room for the nightly broadcast of
the UNSCOP hearings.

Raquela sat on the straight-backed sofa, beside Arik,
trying to concentrate. But her mind kept wandering back
to Athlit. Soon she would have to make the decision. Return to Athlit—or stay.

She looked around the room; all the people she loved
were here, in the small, simply furnished cottage. *It's so
good to be here,* she thought, *and Jerusalem is so beautiful, even with all the tension and the violence and the soldiers. Listen,* a voice beguiled her, *you can sleep in your
own clean bed. No tents, no dirt, no rats on your roof.
Privacy.*

But another voice spoke even more insistently: *Go back
to Athlit. They need you.*

Vaguely she heard the radio announcer describe the
eleven members of UNSCOP. *Eleven strangers,* she thought,

trying to decide the fate of Palestine. The fate of the Jews, the Arabs, and the British. Eleven Solomons pondering what to do with the "baby." Give it to one of the mothers? Give it to the foster mother—Britain? Or cut it in half?

"Listen to B-G," Jacob said, breaking into her thoughts. Ben-Gurion was Jacob's idol.

"What the Jews need," Gen-Burion told the committee, *"is immigration and statehood; what the Arabs need is economic development and social progress."*

Immigration and *statehood*, she thought. That's what my people in Athlit want. Her mind no longer wandered, as she heard Ben-Gurion say, *"We feel we are entitled to Palestine as a whole, but we will be ready to consider the question of the Jewish state in an adequate area of Palestine."*

Jacob blurted, "It's the first time B-G has come out for partition. Until now the Jewish Agency Executive has held to the original promise of a Jewish homeland in *all* of Palestine."

So they might cut the baby in half after all, Raquela thought.

A few nights later, Arik came to the house for dinner. After the meal, they were to go into town, to the Philharmonic. Raquela decided to wear the new brown dress.

Arik noticed it instantly. "Turn around, Raquela." he said, examining the strange long hemline and the padded shoulders. "Fine. Gorgeous."

Delighted, she asked, "And don't you think it makes me look older?"

He laughed. "Positively ancient." Then he frowned. "But it may bring you bad luck."

"What do you mean?"

"Don't you know I'm very superstitious? People will envy you, you look so beautiful. They'll give you the *ein hora*—the evil eye."

She chuckled. "Are you afraid of black cats, too?"

"And I won't walk under a ladder. Do you have some red thread?"

"What do you want with red thread?"

"Just give me some with a needle."

She went to her bedroom and returned with a needle, through which she had pulled red thread.

"Here." He lifted the back of her hemline and sewed a few stitches. "That will keep the evil eye away."

At the dinner table in the little foyer, Papa said, "Dr. Weizmann appeared today before the UNSCOP committee. It must be heartbreaking for him—the nineteenth time he's had to testify. Once he was so full of hope, and now—what must he be feeling?"

"Maybe we can hear some of his testimony," Arik said, "before we leave for the concert."

They took their coffee cups into the living room. Papa switched on the radio as the announcer described Dr. Chaim Weizmann's being led by an aide to the semicircular mahogany table in the YMCA. Raquela and Arik took their customary seats on the sofa. She fluffed the brown taffeta skirt over her lap; it brushed Arik's leg. The living room grew still. Raquela leaned forward, fascinated, as Dr. Weizmann's voice came over the radio. Age and near blindness had not dimmed his wisdom or his wit. _"What is a Jew?"_ he asked the committee, and then answered: _"He is a man who has to offer an explanation of his existence. As soon as you have to offer an explanation, you are under suspicion."_

Arik whispered to Raquela, "The old man may be nearly blind, but his mind is nimble and graceful. He moves around those men like a ballet dancer."

Raquela smiled. Dr. Weizmann went on. _"Why, of all places, have the Jews chosen Palestine, a small country which has been neglected and derelict for centuries?"_

She heard him talk of Moses and of the biblical promise. That's why they had come. At different times. All through the ages. Four thousand years ago. This was the Land of Promise.

"I am old enough to warn you," he was saying. _"For us, the question is of survival, and it brooks no delay. All that you have seen here constitutes national progress. All of it we did with our own hands. Here in Palestine there were marshes, and we drained them. There were no houses, and we have built them. All that has been done here, from the modest cottage of the settler to the university on Mount Scopus, is the work of Jewish planning, Jewish genius, and of Jewish hands and muscles—not only of money and initiative."_

Reluctantly Arik stood up. "I wish we could stay and hear all of his testimony, but it's getting late."

They hurried into town. Inside the concert hall, Arik whispered, "It's a lucky thing I sewed that red thread in your dress. Everybody's turning around to look at you."

Raquela beamed with secret pleasure as she settled herself into her seat.

The members of the orchestra took their places on the stage. The lights were dimmed. Arik placed his hand on her two hands, crossed in her lap, as they listened to Brahms and Beethoven. He took his hand away only long enough to let her applaud the performance.

After the concert they walked along Jaffa Road and entered a coffeeshop. Once again, women and men stared at Raquela's dress. She overheard a woman at the next table whisper, "I wonder how it would look on me."

But Raquela was no longer interested in the dress. She was agitated. She still had not resolved her conflict over Athlit.

"Arik," she said, "we have carefully avoided discussing something very much on my mind."

"I waited for you to bring it up," he said.

"I wasn't ready to talk about it."

"Then you've made your decision?"

"Not yet. I'm in conflict, my teacher, my *rebbe*. What do you think?"

"I think you've given so much of yourself that you shouldn't feel any guilt if you decide to stay in Jerusalem."

"It's not guilt that would make me go. It's all that's been happening since I came home. UNSCOP. Listening to Ben-Gurion the other day, and Dr. Weizmann tonight. Those Irgunist kids sentenced to be hanged. It makes me see Athlit in a different perspective."

He nodded and waited for her to go on.

"We're all part of the resistance. Even in the misery of Athlit, prisoners are asserting their right to a home for their babies. They need me to help bring those babies into the world. How can I let them down?"

"I'll miss you, Raquela," he said.

She put her hand to her throat to ease its choking.

The days seemed shorter now in Athlit; the weeks meshed. One morning, Dr. Carr entered the hospital. "I've just come from Haifa; they telephoned me from Jerusalem to give you a message. A friend of yours"—he opened a little notebook—"let me see, ah, here it is—her name is Judith Steiner—she'll be here this afternoon."

"Judith!" she exclaimed. "But I thought no visitors were allowed in Athlit."

"She's not coming as a visitor. She's discovered her brother is here."

So Judith's little brother, Joseph, had survived. She shut her eyes. *Thank God.*

"We're telling the guards," Dr. Carr explained, "that she's coming as a nurse to replace you for a little while. You looked rested when you came back; now you're beginning to look weary again. It won't hurt you to get a little rest."

Late in the afternoon Judith arrived, wearing her nurse's uniform. Raquela threw her arms around her. She noticed Judith was wearing dark sunglasses. Was it to hide her tears?

"Sit down for a few minutes, Judith. Let me get you a tranquilizer."

Judith steadied herself in the chair. "I don't know if I'll even recognize him. I haven't seen him for seven years. He was thirteen—" Her voice broke.

Raquela drew up a chair beside her.

Slowly Judith tried to regain her composure. "Everyone in Jerusalem sends you love. I phoned your parents; they're fine. Dr. Brzezinski sends you special greetings. He wants to know when you're coming back."

"I've no idea. So long as they need me. . . ."

Judith nodded; her body was trembling. Raquela realized she was still too overwrought to move.

"Tell me what's happening in Jerusalem," Raquela said. "Athlit's like a desert island. We're cut off from the whole country."

Judith answered slowly. "The tension is worse than ever. A few days ago—July thirteenth—the Irgun retaliated for the sentencing of the three boys. They picked up two British sergeants in Natanya and now have them hidden somewhere. They've threatened to hang the sergeants if the British hang the Irgun boys."

"My God! And what are the British doing about it?"

"They've put Natanya under martial law. There's no communication; no phones, no telegrams, no food can be brought in; nobody can enter or leave Natanya. They've got more than five thousand soldiers making a house-to-house search. And they haven't found the sergeants yet."

"Is UNSCOP doing anything about it? They're still in Jerusalem. Can't they do something?" Raquela demanded.

Judith had stopped trembling. "What can UNSCOP do? What can anyone do? The three Irgun boys are already in Acre—the prison they liberated. That's where the British are planning to hang them."

"They mustn't hang them," Raquela said, her teeth clenched. "If only UNSCOP can make the British see that they mustn't hang them."

Judith stood up. "I'm feeling better now, Raquela. Your tranquilizer is working."

"Do you want me to come with you?" Raquela asked. "We can look for your brother together."

Judith shook her head. "I must find him myself. Just tell me where to look."

They went outside the hospital to the Walkover. "The men's barracks are on this side." She pointed to the right. "They've been kept together pretty much according to their countries of origin—Poles, Rumanians, Hungarians, Czechs. Just ask the people where the Czechs are."

Judith started down the Walkover. Raquela watched her stop several men. "Can you tell me where Joseph Steiner is?" Judith asked. A bit farther along, she saw Judith stop a young man. "I'm looking for Joseph Steiner."

"I am Joseph Steiner."

The sister and brother embraced and wept.

Raquela slipped quietly back into the hospital.

Friday, July 18, 1947

Raquela was in the outpatient clinic when she heard a commotion. She stepped outside to see the whole camp on the Walkover, talking agitatedly.

"What's happening?" she asked a man who seemed a little calmer than most of the others.

"Somebody just brought us news from the Haganah radio," he said. "The biggest refugee ship in history is on its way to Haifa. They say forty-five hundred people are aboard."

"Forty-five hundred! That's more than the three thousand we have here in Athlit." She looked at the man in disbelief.

"That's right. Picture a whole Athlit and fifteen hundred more on a little ship on the high seas."

Raquela moved along the Walkover. She heard people talking: "Maybe my cousin is aboard. . . ." "Maybe my brother. . . ." "My sister. . . ."

The man she had first talked to sought her out. "You should know—the name of this ship is *Exodus. Exodus 1947.*"

She nodded. They were all people of the Exodus, all the survivors.

She had to know more; her patients in the outclinic would wait. She ran to the tent where Ruth Berman had once held office. But Ruth was no longer in Athlit; her tour of duty had ended. New Jewish Agency liaison people now sat in the tent, listening to a shortwave radio.

"You're just in time," a young man in a cool white shirt told her. "*Kol Israel* is picking up a broadcast that's coming from the desk of the *Exodus.*"

The radio came alive. A voice with an American accent spoke urgently:

"This is the refugee ship *Exodus 1947.* Before dawn today we were attacked by five British destroyers and one cruiser at a distance of seventeen miles from the shores of Palestine, in international waters. The assailants immediately opened fire, threw gas bombs, and rammed our ship from three directions. On our deck there are one dead, five dying, and one hundred twenty wounded. The resistance continued for more than three hours. Owing to the severe losses and the condition of the ship, which is in danger of sinking, we were compelled to sail in the direction of Haifa, in order to save the forty-five hundred refugees on board from drowning."

In the afternoon word came that the forty-five hundred were being dragged off the ship in Haifa. They were transferred to three prisons ships. The British announced they were sending them to Cyprus. Two members of UNSCOP who were in Haifa had watched the refugees being pulled off the *Exodus* and herded onto the prison ships.

Days passed. The ships did not arrive in Cyprus.

The air in Athlit was charged with desperation. Raquela felt the new strain among the people: the *Exodus* people were missing. Where were the British taking them?

Finally, caged in the prison ships, the refugees were taken back to Port-de-Bouc, in the south of France, the port from which they had sailed for Palestine. But the people refused to come down from the prison ships. "We will come down only in Palestine," they said, defying the British.

In Acre, in the middle of the night, the British woke the three young Irgunists to tell them they were to die at dawn. The boys asked to speak once to their parents. The request was denied them. Their parents were told, "You must be outside the prison walls at eight A.M. with a truck, and we shall deliver the bodies to you."

The Irgun carried out its threat. They hanged the two sergeants from a tree in a woods near Natanya.

Listening to *Kol Israel* in the Jewish Agency tent, Raquela lowered her head. What did the world gain by having five young lives—Jewish and British—snuffed out?

When would the hatred and agony end?

For three weeks Raquela waited restlessly with the prisoners of Athlit for news of the *Exodus*; the forty-five hundred people on the three prison ships still refused to leave their iron cages, even in the blistering heat of the south of France. Bevin tried to pressure the French into forcing the people off the ships. The French refused; Marseille, they said, was not Haifa; there would be no use of force in France's waters; there would be no broken skulls.

Dr. Carr brought a newspaper from Haifa; Raquela read of an American journalist the French had smuggled aboard one of the prison ships, disguised as a nurse. She described the ships as "floating Auschwitzes."

"There are a thousand orphans who came on the *Exodus*," the journalist wrote. "Now on these prison ships, it is the children who keep morale high. There are schools in the iron cages; the children are learning the Hebrew language and literature and the Bible story of the 'Exodus.'

"On one of the prison ships, the *Empire Rival*," Raquela read, "the officer commanding the soldier-guards has ordered all books in Hebrew and Yiddish burned. Among the books is the Bible. These are the people of the Bible. They are the People of the Book and the Land, and on these prison ships both have been taken from them."

People of the Book and the Land.

Would she have the strength, Raquela wondered, to go

on as they did? What lay ahead for the people of the *Exodus*?

On August 22 she rushed out to the Walkover. The refugees were shaking the barbed wire, waving their fists, screaming curses at the guards.

"Haven't you heard?" a man shouted to her. "The British are taking the people of the *Exodus* to Hamburg. To Germany." His voice and face changed "They will fight back. They will get out of Germany. They will get on more ships. They will come home. Now you will see the birth of a Jewish state."

In Geneva the members of UNSCOP continued their search for a solution. Their deadline was September 1. At five minutes before midnight on August 31, they signed their names, in alphabetical order, to their report. They recommended to the General Assembly of the United Nations that the British mandate be terminated and Palestine divided into a Jewish state and an Arab state.

All that fall, the debate raged at the UN, which met at Lake Success. Arab leaders denounced the recommendations; Jewish leaders declared that partition meant "a very heavy sacrifice"; they had been promised all of Palestine, yet reluctantly they would accept partition.

In Athlit, Raquela and the refugees waited.

Would the nations of the world accept UNSCOP's recommendations?

Would there be a Jewish state and an Arab state where Jews and Arabs could live side by side, helping one another, in peace?

While the debate continued, Britain still held the Mandate, sending "illegals" to the prison camps of Athlit and even worse, to Cyprus. Athlit, at least, was on the soil of the Holy Land; Cyprus was more than two hundred miles away.

Early in November, Raquela's replacement arrived. Raquela examined the new midwife with a critical eye. Young. Pink cheeked. Fresh. Naive. She too had come young, rosy faced, innocent. She would not frighten the young woman as she had been frightened.

She took her into the hospital and through the barracks, introducing her to the people. Soon word spread that Raquela was leaving. Men and women streamed into the hospital compound bearing gifts. A woman brought a small hand mirror she had saved; a man came with a wooden bird he had carved from an old crate. Raquela blinked back tears; the people were giving her their most precious possessions.

Back in Jerusalem, Papa held her against his tall body. Mama kissed her. Raquela picked up the telephone. "Arik!" she shouted. "Arik, I'm home!"

--⊰ *Chapter Fourteen* ⊱--

November 1947

On Mount Scopus, Raquela returned to the routine she loved—delivering babies in the clean white delivery room.

Two weeks later Dr. Yassky sent her a message through Miss Landsmann: "Come see me as soon as you can."

This time Raquela entered his office without trepidation. Miss Landsmann was sitting in the chair opposite his desk. Dr. Yassky stood up to greet Raquela.

"You must know how proud we at Hadassah are with the job you did in Athlit."

He offered her a chair and returned to his desk. Raquela watched him fit a cigarette into his black and silver cigarette holder. Had the busy chief called her to his office just to thank her?

He took a long puff and blew smoke into the air. "Now we have an even tougher assignment for you, Miss Levy."

"What kind of assignment?"

"Cyprus."

The word ripped through her like a blade. Her stomach hardened.

"There aren't many young women I would ask to serve, Miss Levy, but Miss Landsmann has recommended you highly." He paused. "I want you to know the truth. There are better facilities in Cyprus, I'm told, than you had in Athlit for delivering babies. But the place itself might be a lot tougher. This time I promise you—it will be for only six weeks."

"Do I have to give you my answer immediately?"

"Perhaps you will want to discuss it with your parents and"—he hesitated—"with Dr. Brzezinski."

She stood up. Arik was very much on her mind. They had spent a few evenings together; on Saturday they had walked, hand in hand, through the Old City. It felt good being with him, comfortable, yet something was missing. Was she to be forever his pupil? His favorite disciple? And nothing more? Words flowed easily between them. He seemed to want to talk of everything—of his admiration for his parents, of politics, of the fear and tension in Jerusalem, of the impending vote on Palestine at the UN—everything except how he felt about her. *Still,* she had told herself, *I'm home now; there will be time to find out how he really feels.*

Now there would be no time, if she went. . . .

"I will let you know, Dr. Yassky," she said.

She left his office and walked pensively down the stairs to the ground floor of the maternity wing. She knocked at Arik's door. There was no answer. She entered, looked around at the familiar desk, the bookcase, the sofa bed, the long narrow windows Erich Mendelsohn had designed to keep out the hot summer sun and the cold winds of winter. It was winter; the room was heated, but she was shivering.

She stretched out on Arik's sofa bed.

He came in after dark. "Raquela! What a pleasure. What can I offer you?" He opened the door of his closet. "Coffee? Wine? Chocolates? Here's a whole box—un-opened—a gift from a grateful new father."

"Arik, sit down. I need your advice."

He walked to the sofa and waited for her to speak.

"Dr. Yassky has asked me to go to Cyprus."

"Cyprus." He said the word slowly. "So they've selected *you.*"

"They didn't ask you, then? It was not your sugges-tion?"

"No."

She was sure he spoke the truth.

"What do you think, Arik?"

"It's just two weeks since you left Athlit. Are you ready for another descent into hell?"

"Arik, for God's sake, what about us? We've been sep-arated for so many months."

Arik moved restlessly around the room.

"I love you, Arik," she said.

"I love you, too, Raquela."

She leaned back on the sofa and shut her eyes. He joined her and put his arms around her. "I love you as I have never loved any woman." He pressed his lips against hers. She clung to him, her body flushed with joy. He stroked her hair; his skillful fingers traced her cheeks, her chin. Long minutes passed.

At last she spoke. "Arik," she paused. "I can't bear the thought of being separated from you again."

"Did Dr. Yassky say how long you're to stay in Cyprus?"

"Six weeks."

He relaxed. "For heaven's sake, what's six weeks? Before you turn around you'll be back again."

She moved away from him. "Arik, you're telling me to go. Why?"

"Dearest, you're just twenty-three and I'm in my late thirties, nearly forty. I'm afraid. . . ."

"Afraid? Of what?"

He walked to the window and looked out at the lights twinkling over Jerusalem. His back was to her as he spoke.

"I'm afraid that I love you so much that if I married you, after a while you . . . you might grow tired of me. Because I'm too old. And that would destroy me."

Raquela went to the window and stood beside him, looking down at her beloved city. "Arik, why would I grow tired of you? You're the kindest, warmest, dearest man I've ever known."

He smiled indulgently. "How many men have you really known? I've heard about Carmi. Dearest, that was puppy love. I want you to meet more men. Young men. Younger than I. I want you to be sure that it is really me you love."

"Arik, you're sending me away."

"No, Raquela. The decision was yours. You knew deep down, the moment Dr. Yassky asked you, you would say yes."

She was silent.

On the morning of November 21, 1947, Arik called for Raquela in a cab. In town, they climbed into a *sherut*—a seven-passenger intercity taxi—bound for Haifa.

Raquela took the rear middle seat; Arik was at her right, a taciturn man at her left. The moment the seventh passenger entered the car, the driver took off. He handled the steering wheel as if he knew this road blindfold. He was short, barrel chested, and bald headed, with a red handlebar mustache. He wore an open blue shirt and khaki shorts whose pockets were stuffed with papers. Jovially he said, "Call me Yitzhak."

Outside Jerusalem, he braced himself, racing his car past the Arab village of Kastel. Its white stone houses sat ominously atop the highway. Raquela knew that Arab snipers chose Kastel to lie in ambush, hidden by the trees and houses, sniping at the cars. This road was Jerusalem's lifeline. Virtually everything the people needed—food, drugs, clothing—was trucked up this winding highway to the Holy City in the hills.

No one spoke in the cab. Arik clutched Raquela's hand.

There were no shots from the trees above them. No Arab ambush. Kastel was behind them. The tension lessened. But the danger was not yet over.

A roadblock of military cars loomed ahead. Yitzhak spoke swiftly. "If any of you have guns or grenades, hand them over to the women."

The taciturn man at Raquela's left slipped two hand grenades into her lap. She placed them carefully inside the cups of her brassiere and draped her nurse's cape over her shoulders.

At the roadblock soldiers surrounded the car.

"Everyone out!" they commanded.

Two soldiers searched the men, but they did not touch the women passengers. Other soldiers poked their heads under the hood of the car. They tore apart the seat-cushions and ripped up the floor mats. Then they unlocked the trunk of the car. Raquela watched as they opened her suitcase, rummaged through her uniforms and her party dress. She blushed as they held her underwear to the light.

"What do they think," she whispered to Arik, "that I'm smuggling a Haganah message in my panties?"

The soldiers found nothing. "You can shut everything now," they said abruptly.

Raquela spoke under her breath. "Arik, you close the suitcase. I'm afraid to bend down."

The passengers helped Yitzhak push the lacerated cushions and the floor mat back into place. They stood aside to let Raquela enter first. When they were all in, Yitzhak put his foot to the throttle. With a roar and a cloud of black smoke, the cab pulled away.

Everyone began to talk at once, brought close by the narrow escape. Discovery of the grenades could have led to their imprisonment.

"Someday, maybe they'll search Arabs instead of Jews," one of the men said.

Yitzhak concentrated on the road. The sky had turned slate gray. "We're running into rain."

Arik put his hand out the window to feel the first drops. "Welcome, *yoreh*, the first rain." He turned to Raquela. "It's good we have a name for every first, as if every day were Genesis."

Raquela rested her head on his shoulder and napped. She woke as they neared Haifa. She gazed up at the white city of stone, terraced on biblical Mount Carmel.

They entered the city. Yitzhak drove through the port area. Kingsway, the broad crowded avenue, was alive with buses, trucks, people hurrying in and out of freight offices, ships' handlers, and navy supply stores. The air smelled of the sea.

The taxi pulled up at a curb. Surreptitiously, Raquela drew the grenades from her brassiere and returned them to the silent man. He slipped them into a briefcase. *Where was he taking them,* she wondered? *What was he planning to blow up?* She could not ask him.

On the street, Arik said, "We'd better get you some sandwiches for the flight. I know that plane you're going on. They don't even serve you water." He turned back to Yitzhak. "Would you have time to become a 'special' and drive us to a place where we can get some food and then take us on to the airport?"

"Get back in the car," Yitzhak commanded. "After what your lady friend did, I'll drive you for nothing. Haifa's my town."

He stopped at a small sandwich shop. "You stay right here." He jumped out, smoothed the ends of his mustache, and entered. Soon he emerged with two cheese sandwiches wrapped in a paper napkin and handed them to Raquela. "Consider this a war medal."

Raquela laughed. "You're right, Arik. It's a day of firsts. My first war medal. My first airplane trip. My first journey abroad."

"I'll show you another first," Yitzhak said. "When is your plane leaving?"

"At four." She looked at her watch. "We've still got a couple of hours."

Yitzhak turned the cab down the narrow side street to the waterfront. They drove past British tanks, trucks, and jeeps lined up near the harbor. In the turrets of the tanks helmeted soldiers looked around warily, primed for action.

He parked the car unobtrusively. "Come with me."

The rain had petered out. They followed him to an isolated area of the wharf, strewn with rocks and debris. Yitzhak motioned them to crouch behind the rocks. Raquela looked at Yitzhak, wondering if he might be a Haganah commander on whose head the British had a price.

A shabby wooden vessel, its prow smashed, pulled by a British tug, hove into sight. Weary and shattered people stood on the deck, their eyes riveted on Mount Carmel.

"A first for them, too." Yitzhak said in a bitter voice. "Their first view of the Promised Land."

The crushed vessel was tied to the dock. The voices of people floated down to them; they were singing *Hatikvah*, the "Song of Hope."

Somewhere a loudspeaker boomed. "The commanding officer wishes you to disembark quietly. Women and children first."

Red-bereted British soldiers affixed a gangway and ran up to get the people. First came the stretchers with the wounded from the battle at sea. Then women and children followed by their men came down, their faces dark with fright and hunger.

Surrounded by troops to prevent escape into the city, they made their first step on the so-long-promised land. They breathed the air deeply and tiredly.

Raquela heard screams. The British were separating the men from the women. Separation in the concentration camps always meant death! They disappeared into search pens made of sackcloth, and then reappeared, some buttoning their blouses or adjusting their pants. British soldiers now sprayed them with DDT, shooting the white flourlike powder at their hair, into their clothes, and over their legs.

Raquela tasted blood. She realized her teeth had been clenched over her lower lip.

The soldiers herded the people single file down the wharf, onto a ship with the name, printed in bold white letters, RUNNYMEDE PARK.

"Only the British would name a prison ship," Yitzhak said, "for the spot where the Magna Carta was signed."

Raquela stared at him, now certain he was not just a taxi driver.

The soldiers sped the people up the gangway; they looked unreal, covered in white powder, their faces bleak. The rain had resumed and was pelting them.

"They're going to the same place you are," Yitzhak said shortly. "Come on, let's go."

A tiny four-passenger plane was poised on the runway in the makeshift airport on the right curve of the bay.

Arik pointed to the plane.

"Your '*primus*,'" he said. The *primus* was the one-burner kerosene stove Mama and most people cooked on: small, unsteady on three spindly legs, but serviceable; the plane looked just as fragile.

He kissed Raquela. "I'll see you in six weeks."

She ran through the rain, climbed the shaky ladder, fastened her seat belt, and waved to Arik through the rain-streaked window. The pilot opened the throttle. The little plane shook like a machine gone mad. She felt it taxi down the runway, grow light, swerve sharply, and then ascend over the Haifa harbor, above the British naval ships and the graveyard of broken hulls on which the Jews had desperately sought to enter Palestine.

Now they were in a blanket of ominous clouds. The little "primus" was lashed by heavy rain. Raquela tried to control her fear as the plane bounced in the black sky. She heaved and put her hand to her mouth. She was grateful she had no food in her stomach; the cheese sandwiches lay uneaten in her bag. She took out her knitting needles to begin a new sweater for Arik. The passenger beside her opened his prayer book; in a singsong voice he intoned the Prayer for Travelers. She hoped he was praying for her, too.

Flying blind in the storm, the "primus" took three hours to make the two-hundred-mile trip. It was dusk; the rain had stopped when they crossed over the island. In the vague light Cyprus looked like a green and brown fish with a long tail rising unevenly out of the sea.

The plane landed in a small airport outside Nicosia. Passport Control, Immigration, and Customs took a few minutes. A young man approached her. "Miss Levy?"

She nodded, relieved that someone had come for her. He was tall, painfully thin, somewhere in his mid-twenties.

"I'm Yakov, from the Joint," he said. The Joint—also

called the JDC—was the familiar name for the Joint Distribution Committee. Part of the United Jewish Appeal, it
was the largest and most famous Jewish overseas welfare
organization in the world; its function was to help all Jews
in need. The British had allowed the JDC to come into the
camps to run the health and welfare services, set up
schools, and bring in relief supplies. Raquela, on temporary loan from Hadassah, was to be part of the JDC
team.

Yakov picked up her bag. "It's too late to take you to
camp. You're spending tonight in a hotel."

A taxi drove them across the island, to the Palace Hotel
in Famagusta. Yakov promised to return in the morning.

Alone in the hotel room, Raquela felt small and
frightened. The strange wide bed, the nondescript chest of
drawers, the heavy damask drapes, the sense of total
aloneness, unnerved her.

"Arik, it's another first," she whispered, trying to cheer
herself up. "The first time in my life in a hotel."

Remembering she had not eaten, she washed her face
and descended to the dining room. She stopped in the
doorway. It was a huge salon with formal tables covered
with white linen and sparkling goblets. British army officers and haughty-looking women in formal evening
gowns sat at the festive tables, eating and drinking. She
felt like a country girl from the provinces.

The smells from the kitchen pervaded the air, food fried
in rancid oil.

The maître d' approached. "Would you like a table,
madam?"

She fled up to her room. Slowly she munched one of
her cheese sandwiches. She would save the second one for
breakfast.

Yakov returned the next morning, took her bag, and
helped her into a taxi. They drove through the sleepy
white streets of Famagusta down toward the harbor. The
stone seawall rising above the Mediterranean reminded her
of the Old City walls of Jerusalem. She fought off a wave
of homesickness.

"The Greeks call Cyprus 'Love's Island,' Yakov told
her, "because Aphrodite rose, not as a child, but full
grown, out of the waves."

She looked out the window at a stone turret, the remains of an old castle. "That's Othello's tower," he said, "where Othello killed Desdemona in jealousy. It's a romantic island all right; Richard the Lion-Hearted was married on it."

"Romantic? With a concentration camp?"

"That's only a small part of the island. Remember, this is a British crown colony; the English love to come here for their holidays."

Raquela listened as she wiped the sweat under her eyes, grateful she had changed into a cotton dress. The rain had ended, and the day turned fiercely hot.

"You can boil in Cyprus, even in November," Yakov said, "and you can also freeze."

"Sounds just like Jerusalem."

Was everything to remind her of home? Time to put Jerusalem out of her mind.

"We're getting close to the Caraolas camp," Yakov said.

From the dusty road near the bay she saw barbed wire. Endless miles of barbed wire. Ten-foot walls of barbed wire.

Nineteen forty-seven, she thought bitterly, *and Jewish history is still written in barbed wire and prison camps.*

The taxi pulled up before the barbed-wire entrance gate, where a contingent of British soldiers sat at a table outside the camp.

"This is Miss Levy," Yakov said. "The new nurse-midwife from Jerusalem."

The officer hardly looked up as he scribbled a pass. "This is for today only. She'll have to get fingerprinted, give us two photos, and then we'll give her her ID card."

Raquela looked through the gate into the camp compound. Thousands of people in rags and tattered blue shorts moved in and around a giant maze of green tents clustered together in uneven rows; some of the tents were arranged in circles, punctuated here and there with iron Nissen huts. A tent city on sand.

Still outside the barbed wire, she followed Yakov to a Nissen hut on whose side the letters JDC were painted in white. He set down her bag, introduced her to the director, and hurried out. his assignment completed.

"I'm Morris Laub," the director said in an American accent. He looked like a Jewish scholar; of medium height, in his late thirties, dark-haired, with dark glasses, with a strong, sensitive face. He reminded her of Arik.

"I can't tell you what your coming means to us, Miss Levy. We've got lots of pregnant women ready to deliver; and more come with every batch the British intercept and bring here on their prison ships."

Raquela nodded. "I've already seen a few pregnant women inside the gates. Where will I be working?"

"We have a prison wing in the British Military Hospital in Nicosia. That's where we want you to set up the maternity ward."

A small, wiry man in a white shirt and khaki shorts entered the office. "This is Josh Leibner, my associate, also an American. Now you've met the only two 'outsiders' on the staff. All the rest are recruited Palestinians like you, or IJIs, as the British call them."

"IJIs." She tried to figure what the letters stood for.

Laub helped her. "Illegal Jewish Immigrants—that's the British name. To me, the first initial stands for 'Intercepted.' You'll find we have among them famous doctors, writers, musicians, great teachers. But in the hospital, even in the prison wing, the British won't let us use our IJIs except as aides."

"If you're ready, Miss Levy," Josh Leibner said, "I'll take you to the hospital in Nicosia."

"Can I see a little of the camp before we go?"

"Of course."

They entered the gates and walked through the streets of sand. Under the scorching sun women in shorts stood in front of their tents, washing laundry in little pans. Men and women were cooking over open stoves, sweat pouring into their makeshift pots.

She looked down the streets of tents and iron huts; Caraolas seemed to stretch to the horizon. Athlit, in comparison, seemed very small.

Near the barbed-wire boundary, she saw half-naked children holding on to the wire, looking longingly at the Mediterranean, which creamed their shore. She watched them intently. *Even the cool sea is denied them,* she thought bitterly.

Suddenly there was a commotion. A squat British water truck materialized out of the dust. Several boys carrying tin cups flew down the camp streets shouting "Water! Water!" A man emerged from a tent with a five-gallon tin. A woman followed him with a small evaporated-milk can.

"There's no water in the camps," Josh explained. "The

British have to bring it in. It comes to about a cupful for each person per day. That's for everything—drinking, cooking, washing."

People pushed and shoved to get to the spigots. A youth shinnied up onto the tank and pounded it madly, as if he expected a spring to spurt forth under his hand. The tank emptied quickly and the supplicants moved carefully away with their treasure.

Josh's face was tormented. "No water is only part of the degradation. No privacy is worse. A girl came to me yesterday and asked if she could use our kitchen shack in the camp. 'I'm getting married this afternoon,' she said, 'and I'd like to use it for our honeymoon. It's the only place in the camp where we can be alone.' "

They walked back toward the JDC hut. "That debate in the UN," Raquela said tentatively. "They should be voting soon on partitioning Palestine. Maybe there won't be any more IJIs."

"I wish I could share your optimism," Josh said.

He picked up her suitcase at the hut. A taxi with a Cypriot driver waited nearby. "He's a friend," Josh told her as they climbed into the cab and drove off. "A lot of the Cypriots are our friends. They want the British off their necks as much as we do."

"We?" she asked. "I thought you were American." She looked at Josh more closely. He seemed young—in his late twenties, perhaps; he had a poetic face with a cleft chin, full, sensuous lips, and wavy brown hair. But it was his eyes that held her—deep, mournful eyes that for the moment lost their sadness and seemed to twinkle.

"I'm a City College boy from Brooklyn," he said. "My wife's a New Yorker, too. But now we're *kibbutzniks,* with a couple of Sabra kids. We live in Ein Hashofet."

Raquela knew the kibbutz, in the hills overlooking the Jezreel Valley. Young American pioneers had founded it and named it Ein Hashofet—"Spring of the Judge"—for their hero and benefactor, Justice Louis Brandeis of the U.S. Supreme Court.

"We were neighbors for a while," she said. "I did my national service at Tel Adashim."

He seemed to regard her with new respect. "Here's our telephone number." He gave her a slip of paper. "Phone me any time of the day or night. At the office or at home."

The British Military Hospital lay on a hill on the outskirts of Nicosia. A typical army hospital, it was a vast complex of iron huts guarded by soldiers.

Two soldiers looked at their passes and waved them in.

Josh led Raquela to a Nissen hut, introduced her to Matron White, and took leave.

Big bosomed and large bottomed, Matron White studied Raquela's name on the JDC-personnel-appointment form Josh had left with her.

"Nurse Leev-eye." She spoke in a braying voice. "These are our tours of duty. We work on twelve-hour shifts. One month on day shift. Following month on night shift."

Raquela was silent. The matron seemed to be looking through her.

"Since this is the twenty-second of November, Miss Leev-eye, and almost the end of the month, I will permit you to start on the day shift. Beginning December one, you will work the night shift. You work the entire month, no days off until the end of the month. Then you get four and one-half days."

I'll need them, Raquela thought silently. *I'll probably do nothing but catch up on sleep.*

The matron was still braying. "You work for the JDC, Miss Leev-eye; you're on their payroll. But at the hospital, you're under British military command. You take orders from me."

She must be a one-woman outpost of the British Empire, Raquela thought.

"Finally, Nurse Leev-eye, when I enter the dining room, you will stand up. No one touches a knife or fork before I do."

Then the matron called out, "Nurse Welles, show Nurse Leev-eye to the nurses' quarters."

A kindly gray-haired English nurse led her to a long arched metal hut. Inside, it was partitioned into small rooms, each with two army cots, a cupboard, a small table, and two chairs.

Nurse Welles spoke softly. "Don't let Old Battleship scare you. She's hard on all of us, but you learn to live with it."

Old Battleship, Raquela thought, *looks as if she'd like to ram me through like some of those broken "illegal" ships lying in the Haifa harbor. She'll discover I don't break easily.*

Nurse Welles was talking. "How long will you need to get into your uniform? Matron White wants you to begin working the minute you're ready."

"Fifteen minutes."

"I'll be back."

Raquela changed swiftly, pinned her silver Hadassah pin on her uniform, and fixed her cap in her hair.

She waited for Nurse Welles outside the iron barrack. The sun and heat had evaporated. Dark clouds hid the sky; the winter rain fell again, turning the dirt paths into mud.

Nurse Welles ran through the rain. "I'll take you directly to the Jewish wing," she said.

Again the dismal pattern Raquela knew all too well: the barbed-wire fence surrounding the prison wing, soldiers outside the barbed-wire gate, and, inside the enclosure, rows of iron huts, black and desolate.

Plodding through muddy, nameless streets, Nurse Welles began pointing out the huts in the compound. *Are you ready for another descent into hell?* Raquela heard Arik's voice.

"This hut's for surgery," Nurse Welles was saying. "This one's for medicine, this for pediatrics, this for isolation, and now"—she stopped in front of a strange array of barracks different from all the others—"here's Maternity."

"It looks like a prehistoric bird or monster." Raquela stared. Composed of three barracks, its sides were two elongated black wings and its front was a short round protrusion painted white. A door in the protrusion was the opening, with three windows and a chimney stack.

They entered the door. A round, friendly-looking coal stove dominated the arched hall; this was the kitchen. They walked down the right wing; this barracks held the nurses' station, the admitting room, the labor room, and two small delivery rooms. Raquela recoiled at the delivery rooms; they were filthy.

They walked back to the protrusion, then down the left wing, a long barracks with twenty-four cell-like arches and a recessed window between each arch. Below each window a woman lay on an army cot, covered with a khaki blanket. The women looked like the patients in the black and white woodcuts of cluttered, unclean medieval hospitals she'd seen in her textbooks.

A few of the women sat up in bed as the two nurses entered. A woman near Raquela burst into tears. "We have a Jewish nurse," she shouted. "Look, everybody. Look at her cap. The star of David."

Now all the women pushed themselves up to look; some climbed out of their cots to come closer.

"Where are you from?" one of them asked Raquela.

"Jerusalem." She said it simply, slowly.

"Jerusalem! *Yerushalayim!*" The women's voices picked up the word and repeated it up and down the barracks until the prehistoric-looking monster seemed to change, to turn modern, light, hopeful, as if the hut itself were singing the word *Ye-roo-sha-lie-im*.

Nurse Welles was startled. "What are they so excited about? They seem to be saying one word. What is it?"

"Jerusalem."

The kindly English nurse shook her head. "I never imagined people could get so passionate about a city."

"It's more than a city," Raquela started to say, and then stopped. How could she explain that these women had risked everything to reach Jerusalem?

In the hospital administration building, Raquela telephoned Josh Leibner.

"We've got to clean up the filth. It's inhuman to treat women in labor like so much—" her voice faltered. "It's like an insane asylum."

"What do you need?"

"Some good, strong girls."

"Okay. What else?"

"More sheets."

"I'll try my best to get you some, but there are only a few here. The people in the camps sleep on the tent floors. I *can* get you more army blankets."

"They stink. We'll wash the blankets we have. I can still smell the soldiers who slept under them."

Within the hour Leibner headed a contingent of six young refugee women. One of the soldiers summoned Raquela to the entrance gate. She explained that the young women were her aides.

"How do I know they're not smuggling guns?"

Raquela looked at their ragged clothing. "I'll be responsible."

He waved them in. Each of them had a blue number tattooed on her left forearm—all death-camp graduates.

Raquela organized her small battalion with quiet precision. They scrounged for basins, soap, a mop, rags, and first-aid supplies. The hospital had ample water. Then they set to work. One mopped the floor; another dusted the iron walls; a third scrubbed the windows; a fourth cleaned the beds.

Raquela studied her aides; then she selected two to help her sponge-bathe the patients. Gerda was a young Polish woman with dark piercing eyes and black ringlets framing her heart-shaped face. She was short, compact; she looked like a fighter. Lili, a Hungarian, was tall and fragile and so gaunt her skin seemed wrapped around her face. But her blond hair and green-blue eyes bore witness to the beauty she must once have been, and, Raquela thought, when all this is over, might become again.

Gerda and Lili learned fast. Gently they bathed the patients whose bodies were blotched with rashes. "They're the signs of deprivation," Raquela explained to her two aides. "It's the lack of hygiene, proper food, decent medical care."

She went to the hospital pharmacy and found salves to alleviate their discomfort.

The maternity ward was cleaned just in time. A woman entered. Raquela greeted her, smiling. "You're going to have your baby under the best conditions we can create for you."

The woman spoke wearily. "I've been through so much already. I just want to give birth."

Raquela helped her secure her feet in the metal foot grips.

"Just try to relax." She spoke gently.

"Relax! I'll relax when I get home."

"It'll be soon. And you'll bring a new citizen with you."

The delivery was easy and fast. Gerda wept as she saw the baby's head emerging.

"It's a boy," Raquela announced. She handed the baby to Lili to wash while she massaged the mother's uterus, through the abdomen, coaxed the placenta down, and examined it to make sure no pieces had broken off.

"*Mazal tov!*" she called out jubilantly.

"Is he normal?" The mother asked the first question all her mothers asked.

"Normal? The most beautiful boy in the world."

She placed the baby in the mother's arms.

Later, scrubbed and clean, with the mother and baby sleeping, Raquela turned to Lili and Gerda. "I couldn't have chosen better assistants."

"Are you as excited as we are?" Lili asked.

"If you stop being excited, you'd better stop being a midwife. Let's have tea and celebrate."

They sat in the kitchen, around the coal stove, the experience of the birth drawing them together.

"I've never seen how a baby is born," Gerda said. "I gave birth to my son in a cave."

Raquela put down her teacup and glanced at Lili. They nodded and waited for Gerda to talk, or to remember in silence.

She talked. Her eyes stared unseeingly out of the hut's window, as if she were looking back to another landscape, another time.

"It was winter. The Carpathian Mountains were covered with snow. My husband stood guard outside the cave. He had to watch not only for the Germans but also for the Ukrainians. They either raped the women and then killed to steal whatever we had or they turned us over to the Germans for ransom."

Raquela lowered her eyes from Gerda's face. To deliver your baby in a cave. The terror outside. All alone. No one to help. They never taught you that in the school for midwives.

"I was in labor—I don't know for how many hours. I didn't dare scream. Any sound would have given away our hiding place. I was weak from lack of food. All we ate were grass and berries. But we had water; we made it from snow. My son was born. I bit the cord and tied it with a piece of cloth I tore from my skirt."

Raquela and Lili stared through the windows; the Nissen hut closed around them; they were with Gerda in the cave in the Carpathian Mountains.

"He lived a few days. I had no milk in my breast. We tried to give him water from our hands."

She paused. "It was better he died so soon. He could never have survived. We lived in the woods for three years before we were liberated."

"Three years!" Raquela blurted out. "Surely you couldn't have survived in a cave that long!"

She was back in reality. Back in Cyprus. She regretted

her remark, but surely Gerda didn't expect her to believe she could stay alive in a cave for three years.

Maybe something happened to the people of the Holocaust. Maybe the hunger, the terror, the dying all around them, did things to their sense of time.

"It was three years," Gerda repeated dully. "We went into the cave in June 1941, and we came out in July 1944, when the Russians drove the Nazis back. But my husband was very weak; he weighed only sixty pounds. He died after we were liberated."

That night Raquela wrote her first letter to Arik.

> Athlit was just a beginning. I think that's where I began growing up.
> But Cyprus! Tens of thousands crowded into tents and iron huts. There is so much to do, so much to learn, Cyprus is going to age me so fast in these next six weeks, I think I'll bridge the fourteen-year-gap between us.

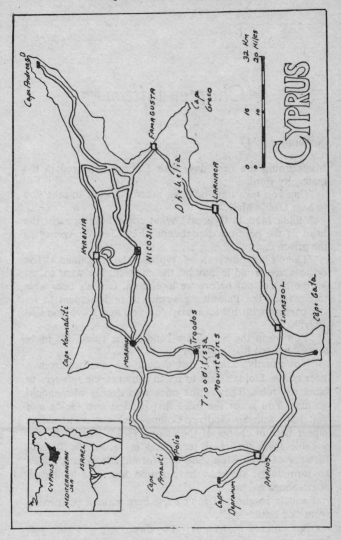

-◆ Chapter Fifteen ◆-

November 1947

Midmorning the next day, Josh Leibner appeared in the maternity ward.

"Can you take time off?" he asked. "I want to take you to hear Golda Meir."

"Golda Meir in Cyprus!" What could have brought the head of the political department of the Jewish Agency to the prison camps?

"There's an outbreak of typhus," he explained. "The doctors are afraid it may hit the children. We want to get all the babies out before we lose them. Golda's been able to convince the Palestine government in Jerusalem to let the parents with babies under one year old leave immediately."

"You mean the British are bending the rules? No more seven-hundred-fifty-a-month quota?"

"Not exactly. They'll just deduct the number from a later quota. Golda's here to try to convince the *refugees* to bend the rules. They're the ones who decide who should go first. You know the rule: first in, first out. Golda met yesterday with Sir Godfrey Collins—he's the commanding officer here in charge of the camps. Golda learned he got a cable from the chief secretariat in Jerusalem. It said, 'Beware of Mrs. Meir. She is a formidable person.' She's so formidable, she may have scared him into letting all our orphans go, too."

Raquela laughed. "I can't leave here without permission from Old Battleship."

They entered Matron White's office. "Are you sure you have enough aides to cover you?" the British nurse demanded.

"Two excellent young women," Raquela said.

The matron waved her hand impatiently. "You can go, but don't make a practice of this."

Raquela hurried to her room to pick up her cape. The day was somber; rain threatened.

The Cypriot taxi driver opened the door of the cab. Soon they were driving to the second complex of camps, at Dhekelia, near the Mediterranean shore. It was called the "winter camp" and was eighteen miles from the camp at Caraolas.

They pulled up in front of a dilapidated wooden gate crisscrossed with the ever-present barbed wire. Soldiers inspected their ID cards and opened the gates.

Raquela saw a straggly line of people, in ragged European winter coats and shawls, waiting in front of a dark iron hut. Obviously newcomers, straight off a British prison ship, they milled around, bewildered, resentful. Behind them were the round black iron huts that looked like sewer pipes: their future homes.

"We've got more than thirty thousand in the camps," Josh said bitterly as they walked across an open area and came upon a crowd of people circling an improvised grandstand made of vegetable crates. Men, women, even small children, were talking, arguing, gesticulating.

Josh introduced Raquela to a small, attractive young woman with curly black hair and a smiling, freckled face. "This is my wife, Pnina, and this is Ehud, and Ruti."

Raquela shook hands with the two children—a boy of eight whose serious face was a carbon copy of Josh's, and a two-year-old freckled miniature of her mother.

"Josh has told us about you." Pnina's voice had a breathless quality. "We'd like you to visit us whenever you're free. We live in the first house near the port in Famagusta. You can't miss it; it's a two-story white stone house with a porch. We just have to be careful when we talk." She lowered her voice. "An important judge lives right over us."

"I'll be delighted to come on my days off." It was good to know there was an American family from Palestine with children; maybe she could relax with them away from the barbed wire.

The air grew still. A heavyset woman in a dark tailored suit and white shirtwaist, clutching a bulging black pocketbook, strode toward the makeshift platform. Golda climbed to the top of the crates and began speaking. The words, strong and simple, sounded to Raquela like the footsteps of a soldier marching.

"There is typhus in the camps. We cannot allow Jewish babies to die. We owe them life. I am asking you to make a sacrifice."

An angry voice interrupted. "Sacrifice! What kind of sacrifice do you want from us now? Haven't we sacrificed enough?"

Golda's voice grew a little softer. "We know what you have suffered. But we're asking one more sacrifice. Those of you whose turn it is to go to Palestine in December—we're asking you to give your certificates to families with babies."

A man in a tattered raincoat shook his fist in the air. "Hitler did enough to me in Europe. Now I've been in this hell for six months. I want to get *out!*"

"Listen to me!" The voice pealed forth across the crowd of angry people.

They grew silent.

"Friends, hear me out. They're talking about us right now at the United Nations. I am sure you will not have to remain on Cyprus much longer; eventually all of you will be released and you will all be free to come home to us."

Derisive laughter filled the cold winter air.

Golda looked down from the crates. "You must believe me. Whoever gives up a certificate now will be on the quota in January. If we delay getting the children right out, they may be dead of typhus. We want them to live. We want you to live. We want all of you to come home."

"She's right!" a woman called out. "I've waited so long, so many years. I can wait another month. Golda, take my certificate. I have no babies anymore to be saved. My babies are dead."

A few days later a "baby transport" sailed from Famagusta to Haifa.

November 29, 1947

Raquela sat with the Jewish doctors and nurses in an iron hut, listening to the shortwave radio.

At Lake Success, New York, the nations of the world were about to vote on the UNSCOP recommendations—

whether or not to partition Palestine into a Jewish state and an Arab state.

In Jerusalem, David Ben-Gurion sat at his desk surrounded by the leaders of the Jewish community.

In the camps in Cyprus the refugees waited to learn their fate. A Jewish state, they were sure, would set them free.

The vote on partition was beginning. Raquela put her head close to the radio. Her temples throbbed. The roll call began:

"Afghanistan votes no."

"Argentina abstains."

"Australia votes in favor of partition."

Raquela held her breath. Would Golda's prophecy be fulfilled? She remembered Golda's voice, speaking in Dhekelia. . . . *You will all be free to come home to us.*

The votes continued. The Soviet bloc and most of Latin America were voting in favor of partition. Even the Commonwealth countries were breaking away from the motherland. The United States and France voted yes. The eleven Arab states voted no. Great Britain abstained.

Raquela looked up at a calendar on the wall. *It's the twenty-ninth,* she thought. She had long ago decided that twenty-nine was her lucky number.

From Lake Success she heard a voice tallying the results.

"Thirty-three in favor. Thirteen opposed. Eleven abstentions."

Tears rolled down the cheeks of the doctors and nurses.

A new voice came over the radio, speaking from Jerusalem:

"Tens of thousands of people are in the streets, singing and dancing. Mobs are crowding into the courtyard of the Jewish Agency. Mrs. Golda Meir has just appeared on the balcony."

Golda's voice entered the iron hut. Raquela shut her eyes. She saw her again, her dark hair pulled back, her words simple, forceful. She was describing the Jewish State that would be born of this vote:

"The Jewish State will offer equal rights and opportunities to all its citizens. The Arabs have nothing to fear; we reach out to our Arab brothers the hand of friendship."

The doctors and nurses sprang up, hugging and kissing one another, then linking arms and dancing the hora.

Raquela ran through the hospital compound into the prison wing. "Wake up! Wake up!"

"What's the matter? What's happened? What now?"

"The UN has just voted. We have a state!"

Cries of joy swept through the iron wings of the maternity ward.

A woman reached up to touch Raquela. "My baby was born in Cyprus, but he will grow up free. In a Jewish state."

A young woman turned her head to the wall, sobbing. "If only my mother and father could have lived to see this day."

Lili began the *Shehekhiyanu*, the prayer of thanksgiving. A hush fell on the crowded maternity room. Even the infants were still. Raquela, Gerda, the mothers and nurses and aides, all joined Lili in the prayer.

"Blessed art Thou, O Lord our God, Who has sustained us and brought us to this day."

December 1947

The air of the maternity ward had changed. The prehistoric monster had been transformed. On sunny days rows of white diapers flapped outside the huts like flags in the wind. On rainy days the wet diapers were strung on lines inside the arched walls. The nursery at the far end of the ward, heated by a small kerosene stove, became a white island of bassinets lined with sail cloth and protected with white netting. The babies nestled in pieces of army blankets that had been softened by countless scrubbings and purified by the sun.

A new midwife arrived—Hava Rosenbusch, a dark-haired, blue-eyed woman. Originally from Germany, where her father had been a doctor, Hava had been a classmate of Raquela's in nursing school. Hava's coming made Raquela's life easier. They shared their days and nights and the burden of responsibilities for the maternity ward.

Even Old Battleship's tyranny in the dining room was circumvented; the doctors and nurses convinced a British officer that they needed a separate kitchen for their kosher diet. They found an empty hut and moved in; now they had rooms of their own and their own dining area where

they no longer had to jump when Old Battleship entered.
There they could relax together.

"May I help you, Sister?"

Raquela, holding a warmly wrapped premature baby in
her arms, looked up.

A young British soldier stood in the doorway.

"You know about premies?" she asked.

"My sister had one. I used to feed him all the time."

He tiptoed toward her and looked down at the tiny
bundle. "Why don't you let me feed the baby?"

Raquela wasted no time accepting. She gave him a
white apron, a diaper for his shoulder, and a surgical
mask, which he put over his nose and mouth. He settled
himself comfortably in a chair. Raquela handed him the
baby girl and a bottle of milk. Tenderly, he fed the premature baby. Raquela smiled at the paradox—a premature
refugee snuggling in the arms of a British guard.

The young soldier looked longingly at the white island
of babies. "It's a bit of home here," he said. "Not like the
rest of this bloody camp."

He lifted the baby over his shoulder, carefully rubbing
her back until he heard a tiny burp. "Guess she's had her
dinner. I'll come back and feed her again if you'll let me."

"You're welcome anytime."

"I'll bring my buddies, too, if I may. By the way, Sister,
my name is Richard."

The next night, Richard appeared with another soldier.
"We guard different gates," he explained. "But we each
left a buddy on duty. They'll come to feed more premies
for you when we get back."

They fed the babies; then Richard and his friend tucked
them in their cribs, wrapped them in extra blankets, and
warmed them with hot-water bottles. Raquela invited the
young men to stay for a spot of tea. She fixed a tray with
American biscuits and the canned peaches she received
from the JDC, and soon, joined by more young nurses,
they sat around the coal-burning stove, chatting as if they
were in an English drawing room.

Raquela kept their nocturnal visits a secret lest Old Battleship have them punished for invading her domain.

Soon Raquela's six weeks would be over. Meanwhile,
she was determined to use every day to win more conces-
sions for her mothers and babies. She had to sign for ev-

ery diaper and shirt she requisitioned from the neat stacks on the shelves of the Red Cross hut. Colonel John Richardson, a pleasant, sandy-haired Englishman in charge of the hut and its sorely needed supplies, told her one day, "I'm being shipped back to England soon. From now on, when each baby leaves the hospital to go back to the camps, I want you to give it an extra shirt and diaper."

"You're very kind, Colonel Richardson."

A few days later he entered Maternity. "Nurse Levy," he said, "please come with me."

She followed him to the Red Cross hut. "I want to give you *all* these diapers and shirts. But you'll have to find a place to hide them."

Raquela stared at him, "I . . . I can't find the words to thank you, Colonel. What a gift for these new mothers."

The colonel explained. "My replacement has just arrived. I'm afraid he's so hostile to your people he won't even give you the things you're entitled to."

Raquela yearned to say yes immediately. The kindly Englishman was offering her a bonanza. But it was too big a haul to accept on her own. She ought to get permission from Dr. Mary Gordon, the JDC's medical director.

"Can I let you know in a few minutes?" she asked Colonel Richardson.

"You're not turning me down, are you?"

"Oh, no. But I'll be right back."

She hurried to Dr. Gordon's office in the administration building. Dr. Gordon was a South African in her fifties who had served for years as a Jewish officer in the South African army. In the turbulence of the camps she was calm, tough, unflappable.

Dr. Gordon listened to the offer.

"Don't accept it. You're an attractive young woman, and he's been here a long time without his wife. He's going to demand something from you."

"I don't believe that for one moment." Raquela turned on her heels.

She sped back to Maternity, looked at her aides, and chose Henya, a small gray-haired woman. She had long been struck by Henya's urbanity and air of quiet strength. Raquela asked her to come along to the Red Cross hut. On the way, they picked up some laundry duffel bags.

"We're back for your offer, Colonel," Raquela said.

His face broke into a smile. "I'll help you."

The three of them, the tall sandy-haired Englishman, Raquela, and Henya swiftly emptied the shelves and stuffed the baby's layettes into the duffel bags. The two women thanked him, dragged the bags to Raquela's room, and hid them in her closet.

Henya looked at Raquela's clothes hanging there.

Her face changed. "Let me sew something for you," she said. "In fact, you're looking at the best seamstress in the whole Caraolas camp. I'll make you a dress—like from Paris—if you can get me some real silk."

Raquela was intrigued. "Maybe we can buy silk in Nicosia."

Henya shook her head. "You know the British won't let me out of the compound."

Raquela closed the closet door on the babies' bounty. "Meet me here tomorrow morning, right after I come off night duty."

Raquela could hardly wait until Henya arrived. She had borrowed a dress, a cape, and an ID card from one of the Jewish nurses. The postage-stamp-size picture on the identity card was sufficiently vague to bear a slight resemblance to Henya.

Henya arrived, breathless with excitement. She tried on the dress. It was a little big. No matter; the cape would hide it.

"You'll pass," Raquela said. "But don't say a word at the gate. If you open your mouth, they may begin to question you and get suspicious."

At the gate, they showed their cards to the soldiers and continued walking nonchalantly until they were on the road.

Henya took deep drafts of the cool, clean morning air. "So this is what free air smells like."

Raquela held her arm. "For today, forget the camps. Forget everything. We're going to town."

She hailed a cab. "Downtown Nicosia, please," she told the driver.

Soon they were driving past the circle of fortifications and ramparts that girded the capital city. Within the double walls of brown-earth embankment and green trees, they drove past Gothic churches, domed mosques, and Turkish baths, past palm trees and orange groves. The minarets of St. Sophia, once a great cathedral and now the principal mosque of Nicosia, rose above the narrow streets.

Henya whispered, "I don't know where to look, where to throw my eyes first." She stared at the crowded shops and the white stone houses with overhanging balconies covered with tile. "So today there really exists in the world," she said slowly, "a place without barbed wire."

They left the cab in the bazaar and walked through a network of streets and lanes crowded with villagers and townspeople shopping for fruits and vegetables. They wandered in and out of open shops with huge, cavernous interiors.

"It's like the Old City," Raquela said. "You'll see—when you get to Jerusalem."

"When I get to Jerusalem," Henya sighed. "It's more than two weeks since they voted in the UN. What's holding the state up?"

"The British still have to get out of Palestine," Raquela explained as they walked down streets where coppersmiths hammered metal trays and carpenters turned wood into furniture.

"So when will the British get out?" Henya asked.

"I heard on the air just the other day—it was about the eleventh or twelfth of December—that Bevin told the House of Commons the Mandate will end on the fifteenth of May, 1948."

Henya counted on her fingers. "Five more months! Five more months of imprisonment."

Raquela felt a twinge of guilt. Her tour of duty would be ending in three weeks.

They stopped in front of a shop that displayed pure silk and damask brocade in its windows. They entered the shop; the shelves were stacked with bolts of fabric. Henya was like a hungry child at a banquet. "That's the one." She pointed to a bolt of periwinkle-blue silk with a fleur-de-lis pattern woven into it.

They bought three yards of the silk, a rainbow assortment of threads, a tape measure, pins, and needles.

"Let's have some ice cream," Raquela said. They sat in an ice-cream shop, talking about the dress soon to be created. Henya, savoring every spoonful, shut her eyes. "Don't wake me. I'm dreaming this whole day."

It was midafternoon when they returned to Raquela's room. Henya changed into her own clothes. "I feel like

Cinderella after the ball," she smiled ruefully. "But let's not waste any time. Do you have a pencil and a piece of paper? I'll need to take your measurements."

Measuring the length she wanted, from the shoulder to the hem, Henya stopped the tape measure just above Raquela's knee. Raquela looked down. "That's too short!!"

"Why do you want to hide your legs?"

"Skirts are much longer now," Raquela explained. "It's the new style by Christian Dior."

"Who's that?"

"He's the latest rage in Paris."

Henya drew back. "There was no Dior when I worked for a couturier in Paris. I was there a few months." She paused. "I went home to Warsaw to my husband and my two little girls just before Hitler came, on September first, 1939. See my gray hair. I know I look like an old woman. I'm thirty-eight. My hair turned gray overnight."

She leaned against Raquela's small table, unconsciously stroking the blue silk. "One day Nazi trucks came down the street, rounding up all the children. I saw them grab my two little girls and throw them into a truck. I ran after them, screaming, 'Give me back my children.' The Nazi officer stopped the truck.

" 'Which are your children?' he asked me. I pointed to them."

Henya stopped talking. Tears streamed down her cheeks. Raquela's eyes filled up. Henya went on.

"The Nazi officer took my two precious children to the back of the truck, where I was standing.

" 'Choose one,' " he said.

"I stood there screaming. How could I choose? 'Give me back my children.' I kept pleading.

"He laughed and drove away."

-*◄ *Chapter Sixteen* ►*-

January 1, 1948

Levi, Morris Laub's ten-year-old son, woke early on the first day of the new year. He wheeled his bicycle out of the garden of their house on Franklin Roosevelt Road.

Near the Famagusta harbor, he saw the port filled with British naval vessels escorting two huge ships.

Levi pedaled home as fast as his legs could spin the wheels.

"Daddy, Daddy!" He woke his father. "The two biggest ships in the whole world are in the harbor."

Laub put on his trousers and shirt, jumped into his car, and rushed to the port.

Raquela had stayed the night with the Leibners after a New Year's Eve party. Now they hurried to the harbor.

They saw British soldiers lining the dock, armed to the teeth, as if they were preparing for an invasion. Out in the water, thousands of men, women, and children were crowding the decks of two huge ships.

Josh spoke in an undertone to Raquela and Pnina to prevent the soldiers from hearing. "We had word, there are more than fifteen thousand refugees on the two ships."

Raquela was appalled. "Fifteen thousand more! Where in the name of humanity are we going to squeeze in fifteen thousand more human beings? The camps are already overflowing. No water. No plumbing. No electricity. My God, there was no privacy before. What will there be now?"

"The British will have to open new compounds for them," Josh said. "There'll be no sleeping for any of us for at least a week until we make life a little bearable."

"I'd better get right back to the hospital," Raquela said, "and see if I can scrounge some more supplies. It's lucky I've go all those extra diapers and shirts."

194

She taxied to Nicosia, entered the hospital on the hill overlooking the city, and hurried to Maternity.

"Gerda, Lili, Henya," she called. "We've got to get to work right away. Fifteen thousand new refugees are being unloaded in Famagusta."

In the early afternoon there was a knock at the white door of the protruding entrance. Gerda opened the door and reported to Raquela.

"There are two funny-looking *shmendricks* outside. They say they want to see the midwife in charge. I told them you were busy, but they refuse to go away."

Raquela walked to the entrance. Two men who looked barely out of their teens, wearing khaki shorts, waited impatiently. One, slight but muscular, had curly hair, thin lips, and light eyes; the other, taller than she, was also spare and muscular with bright Mediterranean-blue eyes.

"What can I do for you?" Raquela asked.

The taller man spoke. "We have fifteen babies who were born during the voyage. And I don't know how many pregnant women. They need medical attention. We want to be sure they're taken care of properly."

"We take care of all our women," Raquela said. "Who are you, anyway?"

"We're the captains of the *Pan Crescent* and the *Pan York*."

"You're the captains! Then I'm Napoleon!"

The shorter one spoke first. "I'm Ike. I was the captain of the *Exodus*."

The nurses and aides who had followed Raquela to the door burst into laughter. "The *Exodus*!" Gerda scoffed. "Who's he kidding?"

Belligerently Ike whipped his seaman's identification card and an envelope of newspaper clippings and photos out of his shirt pocket. He handed them to Raquela for examination. He had indeed been the captain of the *Exodus 1947*.

Raquela was embarrassed. "I've never seen a sea captain before; we don't have any in Jerusalem."

The taller man seemed to enjoy her confusion. "I'm Gad, captain of the *Pan York*. We'd like to bring our patients and the newborn babies right here in ambulances."

"We can arrange that," Raquela said.

*   *   *

The next hours were spent in feverish preparations. Dr. Mary Gordon appeared in the maternity ward. "We're setting up another Nissen hut, fully equipped with cots, cribs, blankets. I'm getting it from the British commandant. We'll annex a hut right next to Maternity."

It was already dark when a convoy of ambulances moved into the prison compound. Every nurse, midwife, and doctor was on duty. British soldiers lifted the stretchers out of the ambulances and carried the women into the new maternity annex. It was lit by a few unshaded light bulbs. There was no flooring. Only dirt. The hollow hut looked eery and haunted. Some of the women seemed terrified. The babies sensed their mothers' fright and began to howl. Even the sleeping babies awoke and joined the infant chorus.

Raquela tried to comfort a tiny, frail baby, lifting it out of the crib. The mother, a somber-looking woman, ran toward Raquela, pulled the baby out of her arms, and screamed, "You can't have my child. Where's my husband? They separated us when they put me on the ambulance. God only knows where they've taken him. It's like Auschwitz."

Raquela spoke softly. "This is not Auschwitz. You'll see your husband soon. This is a Jewish maternity ward, and we're going to take care of you and your baby."

Women lying on cots nearby stared at Raquela. One woman shouted joyfully, "Look at her cap! The star of David! She *is* Jewish. Now our babies will be safe."

Willingly now, the women surrendered their babies to the nurses and aides who washed their tiny bodies and fed those whose mothers had no milk to nurse them. The doctors and nurses examined them; aides weighed them, put name tapes on their wrists, and tucked them, clean and warm, into the cribs heated with hot-water bottles.

Before dawn, Raquela and another midwife delivered two babies.

One of the new mothers took Raquela's hand gratefully. "I didn't want my baby born on the ship. It was like a dungeon. All around you everyone seasick, vomiting."

Raquela looked at the woman resting on a cot against the iron walls. *Sure, it's better than a ship*, she thought. *But damn it, you're still giving birth in a prison.*

All the next day doctors and nurses worked, forgetting hours, forgetting shifts, taking time out only for coffee or tea. Raquela's eyes were burning with weariness; she was suddenly consumed with longing for Mount Scopus. In a few days she would be back; her six weeks' tour of duty would be finished; and Arik would be there.

At five in the evening Mary Gordon entered the new ward. Raquela was at the bedside of the somber woman who had snatched the baby out of her arms.

"Some of you"—Dr. Gordon's eyes searched the hut, "are scheduled to leave here next week. We are asking you to prolong your stay. With these fifteen thousand—and who knows how many thousands more will be coming— we need every nurse and midwife."

The staff stood in the arched hut, listening.

"This is no military order. It must be your decision. But you must make it immediately."

"How long do you think we'll have to stay?" Raquela asked.

"It depends on how many more people break their necks to get to Palestine and wind up here. It could be weeks. Who knows?"

The nurses answered, "We'll stay."

Dr. Gordon's tough, unflappable face grew soft.

The lights were low in the Chanticleer nightclub in Nicosia.

Raquela and her friend Esther Nathan, who was now head nurse in Surgery, were beginning their four-and-a-half-day leave.

The nightclub atmosphere—people relaxing, laughing, sipping drinks—excited them. They needed the change; January had been the roughest month in Cyprus. It had taken four days to unload the human cargo; the British had interrogated every single passenger, and filled out more than fifteen thousand forms. The soldiers had forced the people to leave their belongings on the ships, then for two more days had made a fine-combed search through the pitiful baggage. The Foreign Office announced to the press in London that they were looking for evidence of "fifth-column communists." They found none.

Josh had told Raquela that one of the passengers was a world-famous brain surgeon, Dr. Harden Ashkenazy, who had refused to leave the ship without his bag of precious instruments. Josh slipped aboard, rescued the bag, and gave it to the brain surgeon, who, with his wife, was now a prisoner in the camps, waiting restlessly, his skills wasted. And all month in the hospital, the maternity annex had been on emergency footing. The medical staff worked as if they were in combat, on the front lines of war.

It *was* war. Though the British had begun closing some of their offices in Palestine, relaxing their control over everything—except immigration—planes and ships patrolled all the waters around Palestine; agents combed the seaports of Europe. The UN had ended the Mandate, but Bevin was adamant. Not one Jew must enter Palestine.

In the nightclub, Raquela and Esther celebrated like two schoolgirls. Both Jerusalemites, they had met for the first time at the British Military Hospital and had become instant friends. They were the same age, just twenty-four, with the same love for nursing, the same affirmation of life, which Cyprus made more poignant and urgent each day.

Yet their childhoods were totally different. Esther was born in Germany; she and her family had fled in the mid-1930s. Her father was a dentist, and Esther had finished the Government Nursing School in 1945.

Esther was shorter than Raquela, her hair darker, her eyes lighter and softer. Only their smooth complexions and the fact that both were strikingly good-looking could have explained why Old Battleship was forever confusing them.

They played on her confusion to the hilt. Whenever one was tired, the other took her place for the morning report. Now, in the gaiety of the nightclub, they were regaling their escort, Dr. Renzo Toaff, with stories of Old Battleship's confusion.

Dr. Toaff had just arrived in Cyprus, the first qualified gynecologist in the military hospital. Until now the only doctor in gynecology had been a British woman who had just graduated from medical school in England. Raquela had little confidence in the young woman and had called upon her for assistance only when there were problems that required an obstetrician.

Dr. Toaff's arrival was a blessing. There were now three Jewish doctors and eight Jewish nurses in the military hospital: several from Hadassah, some from the *Kupat Holim*—the Sick Fund of the Histadrut—and some from the government hospital in Haifa.

Dr. Toaff, who came from Hadassah, was a tall distinguished-looking man in his early thirties who had been born in Italy and still spoke with a musical Italian accent. Since the nurses would not go out alone at night, he had become their favorite escort. Now, at the club, they sat surrounded by Englishmen in army and navy dress uniforms and Englishwomen in colorful evening gowns. Esther wore a short dress, and Raquels, the periwinkle-blue outfit Henya had turned into a flattering Paris creation.

In the muted light Raquela saw two familiar figures come through the door—the captains of the *Pan Crescent* and the *Pan York*. Dapper in dress whites, they walked jauntily through the nightclub, peering at all the tables, searching for a familiar face. They saw Raquela and Esther and came over.

"What a stroke of luck," Gad said. "Do you mind if we join you?"

Raquela introduced Dr. Toaff. "By all means, join us," he said. He called the waiter to bring two more chairs.

"Have you ordered yet?" Gad asked.

"Not yet," Dr. Toaff said.

"Then you'll be our guests." Gad spoke to the waiter. "Bring us two bottles of Retzini. We'll start with that."

Soon the waiter returned with the golden-colored wine. Gad poured a small amount, tasted it, nodded, then filled the glasses.

"*L'Hayim.*"

During the meal Ike raised his glass again. "To the two best-looking nurses in the whole military hospital."

Raquela looked at the two captains. Ike had an impish grin and a restless manner; Gad was calm and composed.

Gad leaned toward her. "Can I see you at the hospital tomorrow?"

"I'm off duty tomorrow," she said. "In fact, Esther and I are off for four and a half days."

"Four and a half days' leave!" He sounded as if it were a lifetime. "Why don't the two of you come visit us on our ships?"

Raquela looked at Esther; both of them smiled. "We'd love it," Esther said.

"And will you have lunch with us?" Ike asked.

"Anything to get away from that hospital food." Raquela tried to hide her excitement.

At ten the next morning, a taxi pulled up in front of the hospital. Raquela and Esther were already waiting. The day was warm; the air smelled of early spring; crocuses dotted the hillside. Nicosia spread below, low white houses, a city of white with graceful turrets and minarets in its perfect circle of trees and earthen embankment.

Ike and Gad jumped out of the taxi and helped the two young women inside. They drove to the Famagusta harbor, and then walked along the dock. Commercial ships flying flags of many countries were anchored in the harbor. An English captain in stiff whites and gold braid, and with a tobacco-stained mustache, strutted along the waterfront.

"That's the way I thought a captain should look," Raquela said, "not like the two of you."

"The British don't know we're professional seamen," Gad said. He wore a sport shirt and chinos. "They must not know our real identities, or they'll throw us in the jug. They think we're refugees with a little knowledge of seamanship. All the foreigners we had helping as crew members have been allowed to go home. Only our Palestine Jews are left. Since we're in charge, we're known around here as Captain Gee and Captain Ike."

Gad sought out a young Greek Cypriot, chunky, with tough arms and legs and a sun-leathered face. A fringe of black lashes curled around his sleepy brown eyes.

The young man saluted smartly. "Morning, Captain Gee. Morning, Captain Ike. Ready whenever you are."

Gad acknowledged the greeting. "We're ready right now, Mikos."

Lithe as a dancer, Mikos leaped into a small motorboat. Ike jumped in after him, holding up his hands to catch Raquela and Esther. Gad followed.

"Mikos," Gad said, smiling, "meet two girls from my country. They take care of our babies in the British Military Hospital."

Mikos' eyes woke up. "They hate British—like us?"

"We don't hate all the British," Raquela said. "There are good and bad."

Mikos looked belligerent. "*You* want freedom from the British. *We* want freedom from the British, too! We want our own homeland—like the Jews. Who needs the British to rule us?"

Soon Mikos' motor began to sputter, but finally, like a singer finding his voice, the motor hummed a welcome tune. The *Pan York* loomed above them.

"You'll have to climb the Jacob's Ladder," Gad said. "It's a good thing the sea is calm today."

Raquela looked at the swaying rope ladder hanging down the side of the ship. On the deck the whole crew of Palestinian Jews and the British soldier-guards seemed to be watching her as she made her precarious ascent. A sailor took her hand as she reached the top of the ladder and helped her over the railing.

Still breathless, she leaned over to watch Esther climb the ropes. Excited and relieved, Esther jumped over the railing. "I hope the ladder in Jacob's dream looked steadier than this one."

Gad led Raquela around the deck while Esther and Ike moved off in a different direction. Raquela looked out at the blue sea, dappled with sunlight. "I've never been on a ship in my life," she confessed, as her eyes scanned the water all around her. "The only water we see in Jerusalem is water to drink."

Gad laughed. "You're like a breath of home to me. It's a long time since I've seen Jerusalem; we've been at sea for months. And now, even if we're free to move around Cyprus, we're still detainees. See those soldiers." He pointed to two British guards patrolling the vessel. "They make sure we don't try to sneak our ships out of the harbor. And they keep constant tabs on us; we had to give the British our word that Ike and I and the crew won't try to get out of Cyprus."

He looked at her. "You and Esther—you're the ones who are free. You can just pick up and go home to Jerusalem. What keeps you here?"

She leaned against the rail, looking down into the water. Finally she waved her hand as if she were encompassing his ship. "You brought seventy-five hundred people on this ship, and Ike another seventy-five hundred. It's like those waves out there. I see waves of Jews coming into Palestine. After what happened in the Holocaust, it's something to see the strength of our people. The courage, the will, the guts, to fight the British, even if they end up here, like you, in Cyprus. I don't know any other place in the world where this is happening."

Gad nodded. "That's why I can't wait to get out, to get back to Europe, so I can bring more people, and more, and more; get them out of those DP slum camps in Germany. Bring them home."

He looked at her; her face was illuminated by the sun and the sea. "But you haven't answered my question. What keeps a girl from Jerusalem on this island?"

"There's something about that maternity hut—the fear in those women's eyes when they first come in. Those women you brought straight from this ship. They had that look. I don't want just to deliver their babies; I want to wipe that look of pain out of their eyes."

A crew member approached him. "Excuse me, Gad, I have a problem."

Raquela stepped aside to let the two men talk. She was surprised by the soft manner and gentle tone with which Gad spoke to his crew, who were busy all over the ship, scraping the hull, painting, polishing, repairing, preparing for the day the ships would be released.

She recognized the sailors as typical Sabras—Palestinian Jews who had made their own place in the world, confident, friendly, informal, totally unimpressed by titles. Yet they seemed to recognize Gad's authority. He strode the ship secure in his identity. He was the unquestioned master of this world.

Trim and graceful, he looked younger than his twenty-seven years. He was both amusing and serious, handsome yet rugged, with blue eyes that dominated his suntanned face. Surrounded by the turquoise Mediterranean water and his respectful crew, he seemed romantic, adventurous, bigger than life.

Arik, she thought. Arik, you may yet regret . . .

Ike and Esther joined them; Ike was pointing to his ship, the *Pan Crescent,* riding at anchor about a hundred yards away.

"How in the world did you squeeze fifteen hundred people into these two ships?" Esther asked.

"I'll show you," Gad said, "Just follow me."

He led them down the companionway to the hold. At the entrance Raquela sucked in her breath. She felt she was entering a dungeon with endless shelves. Thousands of wooden planks were arranged in columns of twelve that covered the entire hold and reached from the floor to the ceiling. She could still smell the bodies of the people who had spent six days and nights on these shelves.

"People actually slept here!" she gasped.

Esther shook her head. "There's not enough space for a person even to sit up."

Ike put his hand on Esther's shoulder. "This wasn't exactly billed as a luxury cruise. We love these two boats, but where they used to carry cargo, we carried people."

"How did you feed them all?" Raquela asked.

Ike grinned. "Just the way they prepare the menu for the *Queen Elizabeth*. We had all our menus prepared before they boarded."

"With American canned rations," Gad added. "From the JDC."

Raquela's eyes swept the dungeonlike hold again. "What did you do about toilets?"

"Toilets!" Gad shook his head. "That was one of our worst problems. We built lavatories all over the ship. Even on the decks. And there were always lines waiting to use them."

Raquela shook her head. "I hear there were terrible storms."

"That there were," Gad said. "It's strange what happens to people. We had twenty-four doctors and forty nurses among the refugees and a fully equipped operating theater. When the ship began to roll, the doctors and nurses took to their bunks—as seasick as the rest. The minute they were needed to operate, take care of an emergency, or deliver a baby, they stopped being seasick. As soon as they finished, they got seasick all over again."

Totally absorbed, Raquela stood in the empty plank-filled hold and shut her eyes for a moment. She heard Dr. Weizmann's voice talking to the Anglo-American Committee: *The boats in which our refugees come to Palestine are their* Mayflowers, *the* Mayflowers *of a whole generation.* Were not these refugees pilgrims, too? Modern-day pilgrims leaving Europe in search of political freedom? To give birth to a new nation.

Gad and Ike ushered the two young women up the companionway to the captain's ward room. The cook set the captain's table with a gay red-and-white-checked cloth and soon placed before them heaping platters of fried chicken, coffee, and for dessert, a bowl of figs and grapes.

"I'm so stuffed," Esther said. "I can hardly move."

Raquela patted her stomach. "I haven't tasted food this good in years. Especially not in Cyprus. Most of our food at the hospital comes in cans."

Gad beamed. "There's plenty more aboard. And you're always welcome."

The muted light in the wardroom cast a soft glow on his face. Raquela felt his presence, his outward gentleness and quiet inner strength. There was something electric about him. Magnetic. Mysterious.

Eager to know more about the young sea captain, she said, "It's hard to think you and Ike—you're both so young—could have captained this whole incredible mission."

Gad spoke softly. "It's a fascinating adventure. Would you like to hear about it?"

Raquela nodded. Esther said emphatically, "You bet we do."

While they sat around the table, as the ship rolled gently at anchor, Gad began the tale of the unsung voyage of the two ships.

In the summer of 1947 in New York City, three people, intimately involved in buying ships for the "illegal" immigration, found the United Fruit Company's *Pan York* and *Pan Crescent,* called the two *Pans* because they had sailed under the flag of Panama.

The three people were Rebecca Shulman, a Hadassah president; Morris Ginsberg, president of the American Foreign Steamship Corporation; and Dani Shind, one of the three top men of the "Mosad." The Mosad le-Aliyah Bet, the Committee for Illegal Immigration, ran the whole operation; by this time they had already moved three hundred thousand Jews across Europe and had purchased one hundred thirteen ships. The two *Pans* were the first "big ships," old, built in 1901, but cheap and fast.

In the States the ships were repaired, and to help pay some of the Mosad's skyrocketing costs, they were loaded with trucks and cars and regular cargo for ports in Europe.

They discharged their cargo and prepared for their new assignment. The *Pan Crescent* sailed to Venice, where some two hundred Italian workmen undertook to make repairs. The *Pan York* waited in Marseille.

The crews of the two *Pans* were made up of Italians. Spaniards, Palestinian Jews from the Palmach, and a half a dozen Americans who had sailed the *Exodus.*

At last the work on the *Pan Crescent* was completed.
The day she was scheduled to sail, a mine exploded in the
engine room. An underwater plate blew out. Water rushed
into the hold. The ship listed and began to settle in the
sandy bottom. Ike and the handful of American and Palestinian Jews on board got the pumps working and emptied
the water. Italians nailed up the huge crater with wooden
boards, and the *Pan Crescent* rose from the dead.

Investigation convinced the Mosad the British had sab-
otaged the vessel. The British Foreign Office had set up a
special espionage office called "Illegal Jewish Immigration"
and flung a network of agents around the globe to halt the
march to Palestine—by any means, even sabotage.

Gad was ordered to take on huge supplies of food and
oil, and to stand by in Marseille until he could rendezvous
with Ike.

But Ike was having more trouble.

The Italians, pressured by the British agents, refused to
sell him fuel. For three weeks he waited, and still no fuel.
He decided to make the run with the scant oil left in his
tanks. He ordered the engines fired. Under cover of
darkness, the *Pan Crescent* slipped out of Venice.

The two *Pans* now sailed for Constanza, in Rumania,
where they were to pick up their human cargo. British
destroyers were instantly on their tail, as they moved down
the Adriatic into the Mediterranean, then through the
Aegean toward the Straits of Bosporus.

Nearing Constanza, they were caught in a storm; the
Black Sea lived up to the fearsome name the mariners had
given it. Torrential rains tossed the ships like matchboxes
in the sea.

With his last drops of fuel, Ike navigated his ship
through the wartime mines still floating outside the harbor.
He joined Gad and the *Pan York* crew in Constanza.

Here the two *Pans* were transformed for their historic
mission. The planks Raquela and Esther had seen in the
hold were nailed into place. Each of the fifteen thousand
refugees was to be allowed the same area—the size of a
coffin, six feet long, two feet wide, with forty inches between the bunks.

"If they were to load the *Queen Mary* with this den-
sity," Gad calculated, they'd be able to take aboard one
hundred sixty thousand people."

The afternoon light filtered through the *Pan York*'s port-hole. Soon it was twilight, but Esther and Raquela did not move. Both Gad and Ike took turns telling them the odyssey.

Still in Constanza, workmen outfitted the ships with sinks and toilets, with bunks even on the decks, an infirmary, and the operating room. They took aboard more than fifty tons of bully beef, flour, powdered milk, powdered eggs, cans of fish and fruit juices, and forty tons of biscuits—almost all of it from the JDC.

Bevin was enraged. He sent the British minister in Bucharest to Ana Pauker, Rumania's foreign minister and leader of its Communist party to try to halt the exodus.

He was late. The Mosad had already seen Madame Pauker, and she had agreed to grant the fifteen thousand exit visas.

The British minister brought more pressure. Madame Pauker compromised. She would not withdraw the visas. She would allow the fifteen thousand Jews to leave Rumania, but she would not allow them to board the two *Pans* in Constanza.

Swiftly, the Mosad dispatched a man to neighboring Bulgaria. The Bulgarians were friendly; they agreed to let the refugees enter Bulgaria by train from Rumania and to sail from the port of Burgas.

It was now December 1947, and bitter cold. In Rumania the fifteen thousand people had sold all their belongings, packed their suitcases, used wood from some of their house to keep warm, and waited for word. Months had passed, the timetable thrown out of kilter by the sabotage in Venice, by the fruitless wait for oil, and now by British pressure.

Bevin, determined that these two ships—the largest refugee ships in history—must never sail, bore down on Washington. On Bucharest. On Jerusalem.

Cables crossed the ocean. The leaders in Jerusalem were warned to stop the ships, with threats that they might lose sorely needed American aid in the next critical weeks and months.

Ben-Gurion called into his office the man known only as "the Chief." Shaul Avigour, the head of the Mosad, was a short stocky man with deep-set eyes, a high forehead, and the cool, quiet air of integrity. A farmer in Kibbutz Kinneret on the Sea of Galilee, the Chief had helped found the Haganah, built its intelligence service, bought arms, and had been saving refugees since the beginning of World War II.

Ben-Gurion showed the Chief the cables.

But even as they talked, nine special trains at nine railway stations began picking up people from the villages in the Carpathian Mountains, in northern Rumania, from Cluj, from the Transylvanian Alps, and from towns and cities like Ploesti and Bucharest.

A transport officer was in charge of each train; the people traveled in "platoons" of fifty, with a platoon leader, who was to remain their commander until they reached their destination. There were doctors, nurses, and orderlies to care for the sick, the pregnant women, and the newborn babies. The coaches were unheated. The people huddled together, with only their body heat for warmth.

On one of the trains a baby was born, and in the freezing cold he died.

The platoon commanders held a discussion: should the baby be buried as soon as the train arrived in Bulgaria, or buried at sea? It was decided to bury the baby in Bulgaria. But the burial was delayed. The trains were halted at the Rumanian border on orders from Jerusalem.

The pressures on the Executive of the Jewish Agency from Washington and London were intense. The vote on partition had been taken at the UN; the Arabs had stalked out of the General Assembly and declared war on the Jews. With the shortage of arms and planes and men to fight back, the Agency needed every friend it could find abroad. The majority of the Jewish Agency voted to halt the ships.

Ben-Gurion was still in a dilemma. He told the Chief, "Fly to New York. See Sharett (head of the Jewish Agency Delegation to the UN). Get the pulse. And then, decide what to do. When you and Sharett reach an agreement, I'll abide by your decision."

The Chief flew to Paris and learned how critical their position was in Rumania. He decided human needs outweighed political pressures. He did not fly to New York. Instead he telephoned his man in Bucharest. "I will let you sail—white or black." It was their code for legal or illegal.

The trains crossed the Rumanian border.

Ike and Gad were waiting in Burgas aboard their ships as the trains pulled in. The platoon commanders transferred their people onto the ships, and kept them together in the holds. Loading the fifteen thousand people took two and a half days.

The Palmach commander in charge of the two ships was a young man in his late twenties, Yossi Har-el. Trained in warfare and sabotage, he had been Dr. Weizmann's bodyguard.

It was Christmas Day. Yossi, sailing aboard the flagship, the *Pan York,* with Gad as his captain, ordered the anchors raised. Fifteen thousand voices filled the port of Burgas singing "Hatikvah."

It was dusk when the ships began to move, with Gad and Yossi at the wheel of the *Pan York* and the local pilot at their side. The pilot insisted only desperate men would dare steer through the eighty-mile-long channel infested with mines, in the dark of night.

Nothing would stop them.

The sun rose warm and welcome; they were safe, but not out of danger.

They set their compasses for the Bosporus. Here they would have to face the Turks. Would Bevin succeed? Would the Turks turn them back?

Turkish officials boarded the ships in the straits. Ike and Yossi filled the Turks' pockets with money and gold watches.

The pleased officials overlooked the overcrowding in the holds, approved the health and sanitation conditions, and stamped the papers.

The ships sailed through the straits, and were immediately met by three British destroyers and three cruisers.

Again, the cables, angrier than ever, passed between London, Washington, and Jerusalem. Bevin had failed to force the ships back to Turkey or to Burgas. Under no circumstance, even if there were violence and bloodshed, would he allow fifteen thousand Jews to enter Haifa.

Washington pressured Sharett to find a compromise that would save lives and save face.

A compromise was reached. The ships would sail directly to Cyprus. There would be no violence, no pulling people off in Haifa. And the refugees would go straight into the camps.

Aboard the ships, using their public-address systems, the Palmach commanders explained to the refugees, *"We are*

not going to Haifa. Our orders have been changed, to pre-
vent bloodshed. We are sailing directly to Cyprus."

Cries of anger and frustration swept the decks and the
holds.

Men and women waved their fists in the air. The platoon commanders moved swiftly among their platoons,
calming the people.

"These orders are only to save our lives. To spare us
being beaten and maybe killed in Haifa. We would be
shipped to Cyprus anyway, in prison cages. This way, we
shall go there in our own ships."

"Don't you see?" one of the platoon leaders explained,
"we've made our point. Fifteen thousand of us on two
ships of Jews have won our battle against the British."

The people grew silent.

New Year's Eve. Nineteen forty-seven was drawing to a
close. The two ships turned in the wind toward the prison
island.

And the next morning, New Year's Day, 1948, they
sailed into Famagusta.

It was dark now in the wardroom. Raquela and Esther
leaned back on the leather cushions, too exhilarated to
talk, looking anew at the two young captains whose fire
and guts and courage had brought the fifteen thousand
people to Cyprus.

Raquela glanced at her watch. "Heavens. It's nearly
eight o'clock. We have to get back to Nicosia."

"Why don't you spend the night on the ship?" Gad said.
"You two can have my cabin. I can sleep out here in the
wardroom. And Ike can go back to the *Pan Crescent.*"

"Why not?" Raquela said. "We still have two and a half
days' leave." Esther agreed.

The cook served a light supper; the two young women
walked around the deck for a while with Gad and Ike,
breathing in the fresh salt air.

Ike said good-bye, then descended the ladder into a
small boat, to return to the *Pan Crescent.* Gad led them to
his cabin, wished them a good night's sleep, and left.

Esther and Raquela took off their dresses and, in their
slips, stretched out on the captain's bunks.

Raquela lay on the bunk, reliving the day. *Another first,*
she thought, and smiled, and fell asleep.

-◄ Chapter Seventeen ►-

February 4, 1948

Lili burst into the maternity hut.

"Raquela, a sailor handed me this newspaper. He said Captain Gee got it from someone who just flew in from Palestine and Captain Gee knew you'd want to see it."

It was a single sheet of newsprint.

"What does it say?" Lili said, pressing Raquela. "Please read it to us."

The nurses and refugee aides clustered around her. Raquela's eyes swept the headline. She read it aloud, trying to control her mounting panic: " 'Palestine *Post* press and offices destroyed; bomb and fire gut three buildings.' "

She steadied herself and went on:

"Just before eleven P.M. on Sunday, February first, a British-army truck loaded with dynamite pulled up in front of the Palestine *Post* building. The driver, an Arab, disappeared. Minutes later his truck exploded. Buildings and homes for blocks around have been shattered; even cafés on Zion Square have been blown wide open. Hundreds have been wounded in the blast.' "

The date on the newspaper was February 2, 1948. In the middle of the night, on a private press—its own presses destroyed—the *Post* had printed the story of its own injuries.

Lili begged, "Go on, please—read us the whole paper, Raquela. Every word."

Raquela was devouring the sheet. "I'll read you column one. It's written by an Englishman under the name of David Courtney."

The aides and nurses moved closer; the women in the beds raised themselves to listen better.

" 'The bomb in Hasolel Street for a moment closed the

mouths of the messengers of the world, and shut off, as a telephone is shut off, the news from a score of capitals.' "

Raquela looked up at the women. "Those capitals he's talking about," she said, "they're the capitals of all the Arab countries that surround us—Egypt, Lebanon, Syria, Transjordan, Iraq. Everybody who reads English in those countries reads the Palestine *Post*."

Then she continued: " 'It did but throw into still sharper relief, and sound with still farther-reaching voice, the truth of this land and the sureness of its triumph.' "

Slowly she reread the words in the silence of the iron hut: " '. . . *the truth of this land and the sureness of its triumph.*' "

The words seared her.

Thoughts of the explosion made her frantic with fear. What was happening in Jerusalem? Were Mama and Papa safe? Jacob and Yair, and their families? And Arik—was he safe on Mount Scopus?

She hoarded every piece of news, hungering for details. The radio was instant, swift. Letters and newspapers took weeks; they were more informative than the radio, yet more terrifying.

Papa had written soon after the November 29 vote on partition, telling her what the reaction was in Jerusalem. The joy and ecstasy had given way, almost overnight, to terror. The commercial center, a series of little shops and workrooms near the Jaffa Gate, had been blown up. Papa described how hundreds of Arabs had marched out of the Old City with guns and sticks and stones.

Raquela trembled, reading his letter. Was it an Arab replay? 1921. 1929. 1936. Now 1948. Memories of the little girl in the unfinished Yellin fortress-school made her hands sweat as she held the lined notepaper, reading how Papa had taken refuge in a hallway.

> When it seemed quiet, I peeked out. The whole area looked like a bombed-out city. Dead bodies and glass and broken timbers were strewn all over the streets. The Arabs did this—but how many British help them, we can only suspect. We know that British deserters are happily joining the mufti's gangs in acts of terror.

The British were writing their final epitaph in Palestine in violence and chaos.

Each day the British machinery of government disintegrated further. The railways stopped running, except sporadically. Postal services became disorganized. Palestine was burning—its arsonists both Arabs and Englishmen. It was a tragedy, for the British had done much that was admirable in this land.

They had changed it from a neglected Turkish outpost into a Westernized land with British courts of law, British police, the graceful amenities of British culture. They had made many friends among the Jewish and Arab populations. They had shepherded Palestine into the twentieth century.

Statesmen like Balfour and Lloyd George, believers in the Bible and the prophecy, had laid the cornerstones for the Jewish national home.

But the other face of British rule now showed itself naked and clear: political expediency in its most treacherous form; betrayal of the promise and the hope; surrender to the Arabs for their petroleum favors.

Bevin dropped all pretenses. In these last days of Empire there would be no cooperation with the Jews. There would be no help in setting up the Jewish state.

Immigration must be stopped at all costs, lest men of military age from the DP camps and Cyprus enter Palestine and join the Haganah forces to fight the Arabs. Even in the quota system of first in, first out, the British barred all ablebodied men from leaving the camps.

One day Josh Leibner appeared in the maternity ward with Dr. and Mrs. Harden Ashkenazy. It was Dr. Ashkenazy who had refused to leave the *Pan York* until Josh had rescued his bag of surgical instruments before the British could confiscate it.

Josh introduced Raquela. "Will you show Dr. Ashkenazy and his wife, Nina, around. I've got a few things to take care of in Nicosia."

He turned to Dr. Ashkenazy. "I'll be back in a little while to take you to Caraolas."

Dr. Ashkenazy's fame had spread throughout the hospital. Raquela had learned that the forty-year-old Bucharest brain surgeon had spent two years in Boston, working with the renowned neurosurgeon Dr. Harvey Cushing.

"It must be terrible for you to be a refugee," Raquela said, "to be idle here when you're so needed in Palestine."

"It is," he said. "It is terrible."

Handsome and dignified even in their prison garb, the surgeon and his wife walked down the rows of beds in the arched huts, stopping to talk to each woman. Some of the women recognized him from Bucharest and the *Pam York*. *What a waste*, Raquela thought ruefully. *In all of the Middle East there is not one brain surgeon. How many head wounds, how many damaged brains, how many lives, could he be saving? Instead, here he is, waiting.*

Raquela offered her guests coffee. They sat around her potbelly stove, chatting. Dr. Ashkenazy leaned back in his chair. He was well built, with a face both strong and poetic, and eyes that seemed to penetrate the very walls and windows of the hut.

Through the window he watched the white diapers flapping against the barbed wire, like free-floating flags defying the prison.

"This must surely be the warmest, friendliest, most unusual maternity ward in any prison in the world," he said.

His wife, Nina, laughed. It was obvious she adored him. In her twenties, she was slender and graceful, her features finely structured, her hair soft and blond.

"How long have you been here?" she asked Raquela.

"A few months—and a lifetime."

Nina took her hand. "We don't have a salon in Caraolas—not exactly an interior decorator's dream—but we'd love to have you visit us in our tent."

"Come soon," Dr. Ashkenazy added. "Be our guest."

More mail arrived: letters from Arik and her brother Jacob. She tore open Arik's letter first.

> We go up to Mount Scopus in convoys. Our patients come only when a convoy assembles in the morning. We wait downtown in a long line of trucks and ambulances until the British give us the all-clear sign telling us the road is safe. Then we race through the Arab quarter at Sheikh Jarrah. . . . I miss you, Raquela. When are you coming back?

When? Maternity was overflowing. The two *Pans* had brought the equivalent of a whole town—judges and lawyers, doctors, nurses, rabbis, engineers, merchants and tradespeople, artists and writers, musicians, farmers, peasants—and countless pregnant women. How could she leave them?

Jacob's letter, written hurriedly in a few lines, assured her the family was well. "We're managing," he wrote. "You have too much to do to be worrying about us."

But were they managing? Did they have enough food?

From newspapers that Gad brought her she knew, as if she could feel it herself, that the Arabs had their hands around the throat of Jerusalem, trying to starve it to death.

The grocers' shelves were nearly empty. Women and children foraged in the hills and parks for grass to feed their families.

Water ran low. The cisterns were drying up. Men with horse-drawn water wagons brought meager rations to the Jerusalemites, who filled their pails and jugs and cans.

The battle was for the highway that climbed nearly three thousand feet from Tel Aviv to Jerusalem. The Arabs held nine danger spots—a few on the coastal plain; the rest, the most treacherous, in the mountains. Hiding behind bushes, high over the winding snakelike road, the Arabs had an easy shooting gallery. The road was dubbed "the Murder Road."

Jerusalem had to be saved. Food had to get through.

The Jews created "sandwiches"—thinly armored trucks and cars covered with two sheets of steel plate with a wall of wood between. The "sandwiches" traveled in convoys, with young Haganah men and women armed with Sten guns shooting back at the snipers.

Convoys broke through, but many were ambushed. The ditches along the highway were a graveyard of burned "sandwiches."

Anxiety and worry crept under Raquela's skin. If only she could hear Mama's voice. And Arik's. . . . *I miss you, Raquela.*

After a long day's shift, Raquela decided to spend the evening with the Ashkenazys in the Caraolas camp. She threw her cape over a fresh uniform and taxied from the medical compound to Famagusta. The British soldiers guarding the gate glanced at her ID card and waved her in.

At night Caraolas looked like a gypsy camp. Bonfires

made circles of light almost to the horizon. Around the
fires sat the refugees. Having lost their families in Europe,
they formed themselves into new "families"—most of the
members twenty or thirty or forty years old.

The women, recognizing Raquela, invited her into their
tents and huts where the infants she had delivered lay on
blankets on the sand floor. She bent down to lift the babies, their faces amber and pink in the glow of candles
burning in little cans.

She continued weaving her way through the camp
toward a group of tents close to the seashore. Through the
double walls of barbed wire she could see and smell the
whitecaps of the Mediterranean lapping the dark beach.

She found the Ashkenazys' tent, close to the sea.

Nina jumped up from a rude wooden crate as Raquela
entered. Dr. Ashkenazy offered her another crate. Nina lit
a candle in an American tin can that had once held fruit
and was now weighted down with sand.

In the candle glow Raquela saw two cots with neatly
folded army blankets. Wooden crates served as chairs, and
in the center of the sandy floor stood another crate set
with two tin plates, two tin cups, and two crude tin
spoons: regulation issue for prisoners.

Dr. Ashkenazy questioned Raquela closely about
Jerusalem and the bombing of the Palestine *Post*. "I'm
afraid the whole world will explode," he said, "before we
get to Palestine."

A young Haganah man entered the tent. "Dr. Ashkenazy," he said, "there's a meeting going on. It concerns
you. Will you come with me?"

"Of course."

He walked to the open flap. "Please stay with Nina until
I come back," he said to Raquela.

Nina looked worried. "The fate of a doctor's wife: he's
always being called away."

She lit a cigarette. "We almost didn't make it—coming
here."

Raquela leaned forward. She realized Nina needed to
talk to calm her own fears.

"We had permission to go, but, you know, we couldn't
take anything with us. We walked out of our apartment
with ten kilos—about twenty-two pounds—of belongings.
But there were my husband's instruments. He was chief of
neurology at the Caritas Hospital, in Bucharest. We were

sure there would be no instruments for brain surgery in this whole region. Fortunately, he had brought back two sets of everything from America. Finally we managed to get one set into a bag."

"Then what was the problem getting out?" Raquela asked.

Nina puffed at her cigarette. "We were all assembled in a Jewish school in Bucharest. It was just before Christmas. They began calling the names; people went outside and got into buses to get on the special trains."

Raquela nodded. Gad had told her about the trains.

Nina went on. "Our names were not called. We kept waiting. Then someone came and said, 'The government has just decided not to allow Dr. Ashkenazy to leave. He is too important.'

"Everyone left. The two of us were all alone in the school. We took our bags and went to the Athenée Palast Hotel. My husband left me there and went to see Ana Pauker. He was allowed right into her office. She was sorry; she agreed it was not fair. We had exit visas. But it was a government decision, she said. 'Don't worry'—she tried to make him feel better—'we'll get you a new apartment, new furniture, everything.'

"He left her office and came back to the hotel. We didn't sleep all night. Who else could help us, when Ana Pauker herself—the boss of the Communist party running the government under young King Michael—seemed helpless?

"In the morning—it was Christmas morning—he said, 'I'll go to see Theohari Georgescu.' He was an important government minister.

" 'You can't see him on Christmas morning,' I said.

" 'I'll try.' He went to the minister's office. He was told Georgescu was at Christmas Mass with King Michael.

"He decided to wait. He walked up and down on the snow-covered streets. The clock was ticking. Had the people all boarded the ships? Had the ships left? He paced the streets; I paced the hotel. They were the longest hours of our lives.

"Finally the minister drove up to the building, got out of his car, and saw my husband. At the age of six they had been schoolmates. Georgescu was the son of a poor worker. He recognized Harden; he had followed my husband's career all these years.

" 'What are you doing out here on Christmas morning?' he asked my husband.

"Quickly Harden told him what had happened.

" 'Come inside. Come up to my office.'

"At his desk, he said, 'Tell me, Harden, why do *you* want to go to Palestine?' "

Why indeed, Raquela wondered? *Giving up everything—job, apartment, security, his great skill recognized by his own government? Going to a land he had never seen, a land in turmoil.*

She thought of Gerda, Lili, Henya—the women with Auschwitz numbers on their left arms. They had lost everything—husbands, children, homes. They had no options. Dr. Ashkenazy had a choice. Why had he chosen this route of sacrifice and suffering?

"What did your husband tell the minister?" Raquela asked.

Nina's tapered fingers struck a match in the tent's semi-darkness. She lit another cigarette. "He said, 'I want to be in my own country.' "

The words hung in the tent like Nina's puffs of smoke. *I want to be in my own country.*

"My husband was shocked by Georgescu's answer: 'Listen to me, Harden, it isn't worth your while going there. There will never be peace in the Middle East. We—and the Russians—will see to it. *There will never be peace.*' "

Raquela put her hands to her forehead. *Never be peace! Must we always have enemies? The Romans. The Crusaders. The Spaniards. The Germans. The British. The Arabs. Now the Communists.*

Only the sound of the waves outside the barbed wire broke the stillness. The two women sat in the tent, silent. Nina went on.

"My husband was desperate. He has a passion for freedom. When Georgescu saw that he could not lessen Harden's determination, he called his secretary to come in. 'Give Dr. Ashkenazy and his wife a slip of paper with permission to leave. I will sign it.' We caught the very last train. When we pulled into Burgas, we saw these two ships; every porthole was lit up; the decks, the gangplanks, strung with lights. Snow on the docks. It was a fairy tale.

"Almost everybody on the ships had heard that we were barred—the only ones of the fifteen thousand who were held up. The story must have gone from mouth to mouth.

Because now there was a collective shout. Fifteen thousand people seemed to be shouting in one voice, welcoming us aboard."

Raquela pulled her cape around her.

"You can't imagine how happy we were on that ship," Nina said.

"On those terrible planks—in that hold?" Raquela gasped.

"Sure, they were terrible. Horrible. But I tell you, I've taken elegant cruises in my life, and never, on any cruise, was the spirit so high. We were ecstatic. Happy beyond belief. We didn't care what the ship was like, that we had almost no clothes and had left behind everything we owned. It was like Paradise. We were free."

A shadow fell across the tent flap. Dr. Ashkenazy entered.

"Nina." He spoke rapidly. "The meeting *was* about us. The refugee committee voted to let us leave immediately. Two kind people—the Schwartzes—gave up their certificates so we can go right to Palestine."

Nina threw her arms around her husband. "When do we go, Harden?"

"Tomorrow."

Raquela stood up, tears in her eyes. The great surgeon would soon be in her homeland. Healing the wounded. Performing the most delicate of all procedures: brain surgery.

She shook Dr. Ashkenazy's hand and embraced Nina. "Can I be of any help?" she asked. "I can change shifts with a friend at the hospital and come back tomorrow if you need me."

"I would like that," Nina said. "Come back."

Dr. Ashkenazy put his hand on her shoulder. "The British must not know we're leaving."

"I understand," Raquela said. To let the famous brain surgeon into Palestine would mean helping the Jews. The British would sooner throw him in jail.

The next morning Raquela returned to Caraolas. She accompanied Nina and Dr. Ashkenazy as they returned their two blankets, tin plates, tin cups, and tin spoons to the camp depot. The refugee in charge gave them a receipt.

All over the camp, people stood up as the trio approached, to say farewell.

An elderly man took Dr. Ashkenazy's hand. "I am a rabbi," he said. "God give you strength to save our people."

"What about your instruments?" Raquela asked.

"Josh Leibner has already got them past the British. They'll be waiting for us aboard the ship."

Raquela helped them carry their bags to the barbed-wire entrance gate. "Your reception committee." She nodded in the direction of the British officers sitting at a table just outside the gate.

Nina whispered hoarsely, "Harden, look. The same officers who interrogated us when we came off the *Pan York* six weeks ago. What if they recognize us?"

"Don't worry. They see hundreds of people."

They walked through the gate; Raquela, showing her ID card, waited at the side. Seven hundred fifty people stood in line. Finally it was the Ashkenazys' turn.

At the officers' table a second lieutenant with an antler-like red mustache looked up at Dr. Ashkenazy.

"Your name?"

"Yakov Schwartz."

"Your receipt for returning the camp equipment?"

Dr. Ashkenazy handed him the paper he had just received. The lieutenant stamped and signed it.

"Move along. Next, please."

Dr. Ashkenazy waited. "She's my wife. I'd like to wait for her."

"Keep moving. . . . Your name?" The second lieutenant looked up at Nina.

"Rivka Schwartz."

He stared. "What did you say your name was?"

"Rivka Schwartz."

"You sure you didn't pass through here a few weeks ago?"

Raquela and Dr. Ashkenazy looked at each other. Nina was calm. Pretending not to hear, she repeated, "Rivka Schwartz."

The second lieutenant stroked his mustache slowly. Raquela saw him wink.

"Good luck, Mrs. . . ."—he paused significantly— "Mrs. Schwartz."

He stamped and signed her paper. Nina hurried to her husband's side.

Raquela accompanied them and the 748 other refugees traveling in lorries to the dock.

A graceful white yacht waited at anchor. It was the *Kedma*, the Mosad's ship for "legal" immigration. Raquela looked at it longingly.

She kissed Nina good-bye and shook Dr. Ashkenazy's hand. "I know how busy you'll be the minute you land," she said, "but if you get to Mount Scopus, if you meet a doctor—his name is Brzezinski—give him my . . . my regards."

"Be glad to," Dr. Ashkenazy said. "We'll look for you in the Promised Land."

With the rest of the day free, Raquela rode back to camp in a lorry. The sound of an accordion and people singing filled the air. A group of refugees sat a few yards from the watchtower.

"Raquela, come join us." The accordionist, Adi Baum, beckoned to her. He was a constant visitor in Maternity, where he came to play his accordion for the mothers and their babies. Young, skinny, with a shock of curly brown hair and dark eyes, Adi had been a chef on the *Pan York*. Now, inside the camps, his culinary accomplishments no longer needed, he became a musical director. He set up an orchestra of talented musicians, composed music, and arranged concerts for the refugees.

"Sit down, Raquela," he said. "We need you."

She tried to read his face. Why would an accordionist need her?

She sat next to him in the sand.

In a low voice he said, "Four young men are making a break for it through the tunnels. We want to divert the soldiers up there in the watchtower. We want to keep them looking down here at us, not outside the barbed wire when the boys surface."

The tunnels were the biggest secret in Cyprus.

There were two reasons for the tunnels: to smuggle *out* young men of military age; and to smuggle *in* Haganah teachers, from Palestine, with guns, for drilling the refugees.

In all the camps young men and women were training to be soldiers, to join the Haganah the moment they arrived in Palestine. When British officers came upon groups openly drilling in a compound, the British were told, "It's physical culture, the only way to keep up morale."

Seven tunnels were built; Haganah and refugee engineers worked out the techniques. In the floors of carefully selected tents and huts they sank shafts seven or eight feet into the ground. Since sand runs and earth collapses, they shored up some of their shafts with pieces of wood from broken-up crates.

Now they began mining horizontally. A human conveyor belt of men and women passed the dirt back in baskets. Then a pulley lifted the basket up the shaft.

Other refugees quickly "broadcast" the dirt, spreading it in front of the huts and tents, planting it with vegetables and flowers.

The English soldiers in their watchtowers were oblivious of the refugees digging their escape routes. The prisoners used old-fashioned bellows to pump fresh air down the shafts to keep from suffocating. The tunnels varied in length, depending on the distance to the barbed wire and the spot chosen for the exit. They were just wide enough for a man to crawl through: about three feet wide and three or four feet high. Finally, they built the exit shaft, digging from the bottom up and surfacing in areas concealed by trees or bushes or hidden in a farmer's field. Here the refugees climbed up, then lay on the ground, hiding until Haganah men slipped them into cabs, drove them to the dock, and put them on little fishing boats or rowed them out to the *Kedma*.

The tunnels came alive each time the *Kedma* sailed into port for legal immigrants. Hundreds more escaped through the underground and boarded the white yacht for Palestine.

Now, sitting in the circle, Raquela was part of the diversionary action, singing with the little group, clapping her hands and taking her cues from Adi. His repertoire seemed endless; he knew songs in every language, including the Scandinavian. He ran his fingers up and down the ivory keyboard; he folded and pleated the bellow, glancing up at the watchtower to see if the soldiers were watching.

They were indeed; they even applauded when he struck up a medley of English tunes. Raquela hummed and sang, but her mind was on the *Kedma*. Dr. and Mrs. Ashkenazy were safely aboard; by now most of the seven hundred fifty people with certificates had undoubtedly been processed.

But would the four young men in the tunnel reach the *Kedma* in time?

The singing went on, unabated. Adi seemed tireless. The circle of refugees did not move, even for food.

It was late afternoon when a teenager joined them. "Keep playing," he said in a muffled voice. "They haven't come out of the tunnel yet."

Adi's accordion grew louder, faster, full of passion.

Raquela looked at the watchtower. Did the soldiers recognize the change? The new urgency? Were they growing suspicious? What did they think—a group of crazy people singing and clapping and humming for hours on end?

Adi seemed to sense something. He struck up another medley of English tunes. Then he stood, his tall spare body erect, holding his accordion like a soldier going into battle, and he played "God Save the King."

In the watchtower the soldiers, too, stood at attention, their faces turned solemnly to the music, their backs to the field where the tunnel surfaced.

It was twilight when a Haganah man dropped on the sand, joining the circle.

"They're aboard the ship," he said. "They sail at midnight."

-⊰ *Chapter Eighteen* ⊱-

February 22, 1948

Gad was waiting for Raquela at the Famagusta dock. Soon they were in the motorboat with Mikos, the young Greek Cypriot, maneuvering through the sun-dappled waters to the *Pan York*. Raquela climbed the Jacob's ladder confidently.

She and Esther had come aboard several times for lunch or dinner, their friendship with the two young sea captains a welcome reprieve from the prison-hospital routine and the fears for their families in Jerusalem.

Raquela walked the deck in the warm sea breeze, beside Gad, relaxed and happy. She told him how Nina and Dr. Ashkenazy had escaped from the heavily guarded camp. "He's probably already operating on soldiers with head wounds," she said.

"Maybe now," Gad said, "there won't be so many death notices on the walls."

He took her below to show her a newspaper photo of walls and billboards in Jerusalem covered with small square obituary notices framed in black. The names of the dead young men and women were printed below the photos, with the words WE STAND TO ATTENTION BEFORE THE MEMORY OF OUR COMRADE———.

She studied the faces. Two of them had been her classmates in high school.

The day seemed to grow dark; fear and worry gnawed at her.

"What's going to happen, Gad? This is only the beginning." She continued to look at the faces. "I've read that the mufti's gangs are being reinforced with Polish and Yugoslav volunteers, and with British deserters and German Nazis specially released from prisoner-of-war camps in

223

Egypt. I wonder how the British officers in Palestine are reacting."

"From the reports on our shortwave radio, it looks as if each British commanding officer makes his own decisions. Some are on our side, holding off the Arabs with even a few men; others are openly siding with the Arabs. They've even withdrawn their troops from some of the borders, so Arabs from outside can join the battle. There's a so-called 'Palestine Liberation Army' made up of irregulars and troops that have come all the way from Iraq. They're battling our boys in the north; their leader is Fawzi el-Kaukji, an Iraqi Nazi; like the mufti, he spent World War II with Hitler in Berlin."

Gad studied her face. "For heaven's sake, Raquela, don't look so glum. We're not helpless. We're fighting back. The Haganah has just blown up six bridges leading from Palestine to the neighboring countries; Kaukji's men won't have easy access. Now, let's have lunch. The cook's always so tickled when you come aboard he dreams up concoctions he never makes for the crew."

He took her arm and led her into the wardroom, where the cook greeted her with obvious pleasure. The food was delicious; Raquela downed it with a glass of cool wine, relaxing into the air of salt and brine that enveloped her each time she boarded the ship. Maternity was a woman's world; this ship, devoid now of women passengers, was an all-man's world. She welcomed the change.

After lunch the cook cleared the table and left them alone. Gad put his arm around her. "Raquela, do you realize this is the first time we've been together without Esther and Ike?"

She grinned. "Of course."

"Are you comfortable?"

Her eyes sparkled. "Do you need to ask?"

"I want to be sure. I'm growing very"—he paused—"very fond of you, Raquela."

She put her hand on his. "I'm . . . I'm fond of you, too, Gad."

"You've made these last weeks tolerable," he said. "You and Esther, both. Ike and I would be going out of our minds, tied up here, if not for the two of you. We should be out, sailing our ships back and forth to Europe to get every DP who can fight into Palestine. God knows how we need every single soldier."

He paused. "But I don't want to talk about that. I want to talk about you. In fact, if you want to know the truth, I don't want to talk at all."

He moved closer to her at the table, cupped her face in his hands, and kissed her.

She rested her head against the ship's wall, her hair falling softly around her face.

Gad kissed her again, on her lips and eyes; then he leaned back a bit to look at her. "The first time I saw you, Raquela, in that black maternity hut in your white uniform, something opened inside of me."

She shut her eyes. Something was opening in her, too; her body was growing soft against his. He was kissing her again; her lips returned his kisses; her mouth parted.

The *Pan York* was rocking gently at anchor; there were no sounds from the decks. Perhaps the men were taking their siesta. Gad was stroking her cheeks.

"Talk to me, Gad," she said. "I've never known anyone like you."

"No talking." He covered her mouth with his lips. The blood shot through her veins.

Suddenly she drew back. Arik, am I disloyal? But it was you who told me . . . *I want you to meet more men . . . young men . . . younger than I.*

An urgent knocking on the wardroom door startled them. They moved apart.

"Come in," Gad said.

His radio operator stood in the doorway, his face white.

"There's been another explosion in Jerusalem. It just came over the air."

Raquela's stomach turned over. "Do you know where?"

"Ben Yehuda Street"

Raquela's hand flew to cover her mouth.

"Ben Yehuda Street. The Fifth Avenue of Jerusalem. The hilly slope of narrow streets lined with shops, cafés, hotels, and modern apartment buildings with little balconies. The street where she had bought her "new look" dress.

She turned to Gad, her voice hoarse with fear. "Esther's family lives in Ben Yehuda Street."

"Esther's family!" Gad stood up, in command again. "Come on, Raquela, let's go to the radio shack. Maybe we can get more details."

They hurried down to the room that housed the wireless

and made contact with the radio ham in Jerusalem. Raquela sat motionless, praying silently that no one was hurt. Praying for a miracle.

The radio operator in Jerusalem was talking: *"No word yet how many were killed."*

Pan York: "How did it happen?"

"Arabs and British deserters—joint operation."

Arabs and deserters. Like a dirge, a song of death. *Arabs and deserters.* She felt faint. She heard the voice say, *"The Vilenchik Building . . ."* She saw it, six stories high, one of the tallest buildings in Jerusalem. She had many friends living in it.

"The stone wall buckled outward and collapsed into the street."

She pressed herself down in the ship's chair, steadying her body.

"It was early this morning. Two apartment buildings are rubble. The Amdursky Hotel fell inside itself. The streets are rubble. Hundreds of people are in the streets now, running out of burning buildings; they're in their nightclothes. Pieces of bodies are mixed in with glass and bricks."

"Oh, my God," Raquela moaned.

The shortwave conversation ended. Gad came toward Raquela and placed his arm around her protectively.

She looked up at him, her eyes blurred with tears. "Esther will go out of her mind."

"Don't tell her anything yet. Not until we learn whether or not her parents are safe."

"But somebody might tell her at the hospital."

Gad took his handkerchief and wiped her cheek. "When is your next four-and-a-half-day leave?"

"The end of this month. Another week."

"Why don't the four of us go somewhere—get her away? Meanwhile, you alert the doctors and nurses not to mention the explosion in front of her."

Raquela dried her eyes. "Where do you want to go?"

"I'll check into some places with Ike. You two have seen only the seamy side of this island. It has some beautiful spots, too."

Esther was delighted with the plans.

But Raquela, eager to get Esther away until the casualty list reached them, found herself in a quandary. She spent most of the night before they were to leave tossing on her bed, repeating Arik's words over and over: *"Younger man ... younger man ... younger man."*

Was she being disloyal to Arik? Was she in love with Gad?

What if the British suddenly allowed the two ships to sail? What if Gad, sailing the DPs to Palestine, was attacked and his ship bombed? *Arabs and deserters.* What if these were the last four and a half days she would ever see him? She twisted in her bed, a mass of longing and yearning tinged with a sense of impending loss.

I'm human, too, she thought. *Sure, I could throw in the sponge and leave this island. Tell the JDC to get itself another Hadassah midwife. I've served enough.*

No, I can't. I can't leave my women now; I've got deliveries every single day.

Then why should I feel so torn about going off with Gad? I've been living like a prisoner myself. I deserve some escape. Maybe it's all going to blow up. One big Ben Yehuda Street explosion! We'll all be killed. Mama. Papa. Jacob. Yair. Arik. Gad.

Arabs and deserters. Arabs and deserters.

The words finally lulled her to sleep.

The next morning, two cabs pulled up on the hill outside the hospital compound. Raquela and Esther waited, their small suitcases beside them. Gad and Ike jumped out; Ike helped Esther into the first cab; Gad and Raquela followed in the second.

Inside the taxi, Gad kissed her. "You should always wear that blue cape. It makes you look like a princess in a fairy tale."

Her eyes shone. "This whole adventure seems unreal. I keep wanting to pinch myself."

"It's real, all right. We're going to have four wonderful days."

"Where are we going?"

"The Troodos Mountains. There's a lot of snow up there this time of the year."

The two cabs drove down the hill into Nicosia. Raquela, looking out the window, thought again of Jerusalem. Like new Jerusalem, Nicosia had spilled out from the old embattlement walls, a panorama of old stone houses and modern apartments, of churches and mosques, a blend of Europe and the Middle East, of the Middle Ages and the twentieth century.

Even the jewel-like St. Sophia Cathedral seemed to symbolize the clashes between people and cultures in this Mediterranean enclave. The conflict here was not, as in Palestine, between Jews and Arabs, but between Greeks and Turks, between two religions and two diverse cultures. The cathedral became a mosque—the grand mosque in a city of more than one hundred thousand Cypriots. The conflict between Christians and Moslems remained unresolved.

Raquela watched the landscape change as the cab left Nicosia and drove across the wide treeless plain—the Mesaoria—that stretched from east to west across the island. They traveled southwest until, fifty miles from Nicosia, they reached the foothills of the southern mountain range. They began the ascent to Mount Troodos.

A fresh snow carpeted the mountain. Tiny villages seemed painted into the landscape, guarded by tall poplar trees standing like silver sentries. The two cabs navigated the winding hilly road past apple orchards, cherry orchards, and vineyards, their branches and foliage heavy with snow. The warm morning sun cast strong shadows; the world was a study in black and white.

Raquela's eyes swept with pleasure across the white-carpeted fields. "It snowed the first day I entered nursing school," she told Gad. She laughed. "We were even called the Class of Snow Whites."

Gad kissed her cheek. "You're still Snow White—beautiful Snow White with a bunch of adoring men."

She looked at him, startled. What did he mean? Did he know about Arik? Or Carmi? On Mount Troodos both Carmi and Arik seemed part of another world, another life.

The two cabs pulled up in front of a rustic lodge. A few guests milled around the cheerful lobby. They registered, then followed a porter up the stairs. Esther and Raquela entered a large inviting bedroom, smelling of pine needles. A white hand-crafted bedspread covered the bed in the center of the room.

Gad and Ike checked into a room on the next floor.

The four unpacked swiftly, changed into ski pants and sweaters, and hurried out to walk in the snow. They raced through the fields, tossed snowballs at one another, built a funny snowman, and then, famished, returned to the inn for lunch.

The four and a half days melted into one. They ate, drank, romped in the snow, danced in the evening, sang, laughed, took midnight walks, and were inseparable.

On the last evening, after dinner, they walked along a snow-covered path framed on both sides with snow-clad oaks and pines.

Gad drew Raquela aside. "Let them walk ahead," he said.

His hands reached inside her cape. He caressed her body; then he drew her close and kissed her. She put her arms around him, returning his kisses, her body flaming in the snow.

"I'm in love, Raquela."

Gently she put her hand on his lips. "I'm in love, too, Gad," she whispered.

"Snow White," he kissed her. "My darling, I dream I hold you in my arms every night." He brushed his lips across her eyes, her cheeks.

"I love you, Gad. I love you." She held him tightly.

Slowly, they walked back to the inn.

Esther's parents were safe. The whole family had rushed into the street wearing only their nightclothes. Their apartment, with everything they owned, was ruined.

March descended on the camps with sudden brutal heat.

Raquela counted the days. Seventy-five days until May 15, 1948—Bevin's announced target date. On May 15, all the troops would be withdrawn. The last Englishman would be out of Palestine.

The gates of Cyprus would surely fling open. She—and all the prisoners—would go home to the so-long-promised land. They would have their own state.

In the March heat the two and a half months seemed millennia away. The air burned. The iron Nissen huts were furnaces.

Raquela, touching the door of her maternity hut, felt her hand scorch.

The Haganah stepped up the drilling and marching and kept morale fairly high among the adults. But in the children's village, a mound in Dhekelia housing the orphaned children whose parents had been killed in Hitler's gas chambers, the teachers fought a desperate war against the children's rage and frustration.

Hanoch Rinott, Henrietta Szold's disciple in Youth Aliyah, had come from Jerusalem to set up schools and activities for the children. He pleaded with the British, "Let the children go swimming. The heat in the camps is making them physically and emotionally ill."

Finally, the commander yielded. "No adults may go swimming. Only children."

Raquela was visiting a young mother in Dhekelia when the children were lined up for their first swim. Hanoch Rinott invited her to go along as an escort and to be available for medical help.

Flanked on both sides by armed soldiers, the children were marched through the camp grounds like prisoners in a chain gang. Raquela marched beside them, her own rage boiling.

Outside the camp a British tank with a soldier standing up in the turret led the parade; for a mile and a half in the relentless sun the children marched behind the tank, guarded by soldiers lest they escape. *And where would they escape to?* Raquela looked around bitterly as they trudged past Cypriot fields and the gaze of curious and astonished farmers. *Where would they hide?*

The next two hours were magic, as they swam, bathed, dug castles and tunnels in the sand, and seemed to forget the camps.

Then, reluctantly, they dressed for the long march back.

Raquela's body sagged as she watched the children reenter the hated gates, march to the children's village on the mound, and fall wearily to the ground.

What could they make of their lives? Could they pick up skills and professions? Could they be reclaimed? Could a child who had never been inside a house, who had never seen a bathtub, or a flush toilet, who had long forgotten what his parents looked like before they were shot or burned, ever be normal?

A few weeks later, Major Maitland, a kindly British officer who spent his Sundays driving through Cyprus, trying to buy shoes for the children, made an announcement: "All orphaned children who arrived on the *Pan York* and the *Pan Crescent* will be allowed to leave on the next transport to Palestine."

The adults helped the children prepare for their voyage; they brought them presents and helped them pack their little knapsacks. The camps for once were filled with smiling people. The children would go directly to Youth Aliyah children's villages and kibbutzim in Palestine, the whole country ready to put its arms around them, adopt them, welcome them home.

And still the conceiving and the birthing never stopped. More than two thousand girls and boys were born in the prison maternity ward—each newborn an answer to Hitler.

A few days after the orphaned children had left, the thousandth boy was born. The records of circumcisions were carefully kept.

Meir Noy, a Rumanian musician, composed a song, and Moshe Sakagio, a well-known poet, also from Rumania, wrote the words for "A Hymn of Joy to the Thousandth Boy."

Soon nearly everyone in the camps and the hospital was singing the song.

> The thousandth boy is born today
> Rejoice! In all the camps
> A *mazal tov*; a holiday
> The thousandth boy is born
>
> Men and women of Zion at war
> Soldiers of *Eretz Israel*
> Greet
> A thousand boys and one more.
>
> Asleep in his cradle and warm
> The thousandth boy dreams,
> A builder in peace, a fighter in war,
> The thousandth boy is born.
>
> Men and women of Zion at war
> Soldiers of *Eretz Israel*
> Greet
> A thousand boys and one more.
>
> In the swiftly setting sun
> Iron barracks strike gold;

A regiment of children marches,
Marches to Jerusalem.

Men and women of Zion at war
Soldiers of *Eretz Israel*
Greet
A thousand boys and one more.

Each day Raquela joined the women in Maternity, singing the new theme song of Cyprus. Nursing and midwifing
had never seemed more needed, more meaningful: delivering the babies of survivors, babies who would themselves
soon be allowed to grow up in their own state in their own
land. But would there be a state? Would fifty million Arabs, surrounding little Palestine, destroy what generations
of Jews, like Papa's family and Mama's, had created?

Meanwhile she was delivering babies. Delivering babies
was itself an act of faith.

On Friday, March 12, 1948, the third Arab attack
rocked Jerusalem. This time the target was the Jewish
Agency Building itself, the heart of the Jewish government.

Papa wrote Raquela how most of the top Agency officials—Ben-Gurion, Golda Meir, the leaders of the
Haganah—were in the building when the trusted Arab
driver of the U.S. consul general drove his American car
flying the stars and stripes into the barricaded and heavily
guarded Agency compound. The driver told the security
guard he was going to a café to get a pack of cigarettes.
Another guard was suspicious of the empty car; he was
Haim Gur-Aryeh. "You know him," Papa wrote. "He's
the brother of your nursing-school friend Lea. Haim
jumped into the car, drove it a few feet away from the
buildings, still inside the courtyard. The car exploded. A
whole case of TNT was found in the trunk. Haim was
blown to pieces."

Thirteen others were killed, among them Papa's gentle
seventy-one-year-old friend Leib Jaffe—one of the pioneers who had helped turn the swamps into farmlands.
Leib Jaffe, who loved all living things, was dead.

Raquela was still mourning Haim's and Leib Jaffe's
deaths when a letter from Rena Geffen arrived. She
opened it curiously. Why was Rena writing her now?

The letter began simply.

> I've just come back to Tel Aviv from visiting my
> mother in Jerusalem. I walked down the street to say
> hello to your family; they're all well. In fact, your
> brother Jacob was visiting, and he gave me your
> address in Cyprus.

Raquela smiled inwardly. What a friendly thing for
Rena to do—and in these days when she must be up to
her ears in work, to take time out to write. Even Arik
hardly wrote at all, occasionally dashing off a few lines to
tell her how bone weary he was and how he missed her.

She went on reading.

> Maybe you've heard this from somebody else. If
> not, I hate to be the first to write you about this
> tragedy. It's about Carmi.

Raquela had been standing inside the door of the maternity hut, reading. She reached out to the potbelly stove to
support herself. What had happened to Carmi? What
tragedy?

> Carmi had joined the Palmach. He was com-
> mander of a convoy that was trying to evacuate the
> people in Atarot and Neve Yaakov.

Raquela knew the places well; two Jewish communities
in the hills of East Jerusalem, side by side with Arabs.

> The Arabs had turned hostile and threatening.
> Carmi was in an armored truck leading the operation.
> He succeeded in evacuating all the Jews. Then he
> headed his convoy through Sheikh Jarrah to reach
> our old love—Mount Scopus.

She shut her eyes. Sheikh Jarrah. Bus 9. How many
times had her heart stopped beating as the bus stopped in
front of the mufti's villa and the Nashashibi houses on her
way to Scopus.

She forced herself to read on.

In the Sheikh Jarrah quarter, Arabs ambushed the convoy. Carmi jumped out of his lead truck and shouted, "Everyone jump into ditches. Save your lives."

The people jumped into the ditches by the side of the road and miraculously saved themselves.

But Carmi was killed. A hero's death. I am so sad, dear Raquela, to write you this news.

Raquela ran blindly from the maternity hut to her room. She wept for Carmi. She wept for all the young men and women dying every day. For all who would still die before they could have their own state.

But now! What about Arik and Gad?

She sat up in bed. Carmi's death made it urgent to see things clearly. Was it possible to love two men? Did each one fill a different need within her?

Arik—the teacher, the father figure, the compassionate doctor, the respected gynecologist intimately involved with her own career as a midwife.

Gad—romantic, exciting, young. Gad meant fun and adventure. Gad meant release from the tensions of Cyprus and her terrors about the danger in Jerusalem.

Gad was immediacy, reality. Arik was two hundred miles away.

A phrase that Papa loved to quote from Goethe's *Faust* went through her mind: *"Zwei Seelen wohnen, ach! in meiner Brust . . ."* Two souls dwell, alas! in my breast.

"Raquela, are you there?" It was Gad's voice.

She wiped her face hurriedly. "Come in, Gad," she said.

She had never seen him look this way, his face distorted in agony.

"There's terrible news about Mount Scopus."

"What's happened? Tell me, quickly."

"There's been a massacre. Seventy-seven people killed."

Raquela flung herself on Gad. "No! It can't be. It mustn't be. Do you know any names?"

"Only one so far: Dr. Yassky."

"No!" The word ripped up through her stomach to her throat. "Not Dr. Yassky." Founder. Creator of Scopus.

Gad held her in his arms, trying to calm her.

"Can you get off?" he asked. "We can go back to the ship and try to get more news on the short wave."

"I'm free this shift."

"Let's go, then. I have a cab waiting."

They hardly spoke in the taxi. She lay in his arms, her eyes shut; she was in a dark room watching pictures of Dr. Yassky, Arik, Judith Steiner, Mrs. Cantor, all her friends, in still frames, frozen frames on a screen. Maybe, she thought, if she could keep conjuring them up, she could keep them alive.

Aboard the *Pan York,* the wireless was tuned to Tel Aviv.

Raquela settled into a deck chair next to the radio. The wireless operator began turning the dials.

"Come in. Come in, Tel Aviv. This is the *Pan York* in Cyprus. Do you read me? Over."

"Roger. This is Tel Aviv. I read you fine. Over."

"Can you give us details on the massacre at Scopus? Over."

"I've got some newspapers in front of me. I'll read you one of the reports. Over."

"Roger."

Raquela strained to hear every word.

"Here goes." The radio operator in Tel Aviv began reading: *" 'Dateline Jerusalem, Tuesday, April thirteen, 1948.' "*

He described how the convoy had set off from downtown Jerusalem for Scopus: one hundred thirty doctors, nurses, patients, university professors.

The Haganah escort was in a "sandwich," a Dodge truck with armored plates; then came the white ambulance also armored, with Dr. Yassky, Mrs. Yassky, six other doctors, the assistant matron, and a patient on a stretcher. Behind them came more "sandwiches"—buses, trucks, another ambulance. All moved down Jaffa Road to East Jerusalem, then turned at the hilly bend in the road to Sheikh Jarrah.

A mine in the middle of the road exploded. The convoy was trapped. Arabs lying in the ditches tossed hand grenades and fired guns at the stalled vehicles.

A few managed to turn and dash back to the city. But most were sealed in, paralyzed in the narrow road.

Raquela held the arms of the deck chair so tightly her knuckles turned white.

"Do you still read me okay, Pan York?" the Tel Aviv operator asked.

"Roger. I read you okay. Over."

The operator in Tel Aviv continued the account.

" *'A few tried to jump from the buses. They were instantly gunned down and killed. The rest sat for hours in the armored buses and ambulances with no air, no food, no light. As time passed, hundreds of Arabs streamed out from neighboring areas and the Old City with more guns, hand grenades, and Molotov cocktails. British soldiers watched from their post less than a hundred yards away and did nothing.*

" *'From the rooftops of Mount Scopus, doctors could see the whole action. They telephoned downtown. The British army controlled the road. The Haganah demanded it be allowed to send men and arms to the rescue. The British refused. They told the Haganah the sight of armed Jews would only inflame the Arabs.'* "

Static pierced the room and penetrated Raquela's body.

" *'Mobs of Arabs encircled the buses, poured gasoline on the thin metal plates, put torches to the gasoline, and the people inside were all burned alive.'* "

Raquela cried out in horror. *Dear Lord,* she prayed silently, *don't let Arik be in one of those buses.*

Gad leaned over and stroked her shoulder tenderly.

The words kept coming from the set. " *'For seven hours, from nine-thirty in the morning, the convoy was under fire. It was about three in the afternoon when Dr. Yassky turned in his seat in the ambulance, next to the driver. He put his hand on Mrs. Yassky's arm. "Shalom, my dear. This is the end," he said.*

" *'A bullet penetrated the floor of the ambulance and hit him. He fell back in her arms, dead.'* "

Raquela slumped in her chair. "Dr. Yassky," she moaned. "Dr. Yassky."

" *'Half an hour later, the British appeared on the road in tanks and armored cars with mortars and machine guns.*

" *'The Arabs fled.'* "

Tears rolling down her cheeks, Raquela walked to Gad. "Can we ask him—does he have the names of any others who were killed?"

"Tel Aviv. Do you have the casualty list? Over."

"Roger. Seventy-seven names. Do you want them all? Over."

Raquela nodded. "Please." Her voice was strangled.

She listened to the list. She could see them. Doctors she had worked with in the white hospital. Midwives. Nurses.

University professors. Some she knew intimately. She kept brushing the tears from her cheeks.

"*That's it.*" The wireless operator in Tel Aviv finished the list.

Arik's name was not among them.

⊸⊷ Chapter Nineteen ⊶⊷

May 14, 1948

Late Friday afternoon.

Raquela sat with the doctors and nurses in their hut in the hospital compound. No one spoke. They leaned their heads close to the radio.

For days they had been waiting, arguing and debating three questions: Would Britain pull out of Palestine on Bevin's target date—May 15, 1948? Would the Jewish state be proclaimed? Would the Arabs invade?

David Ben-Gurion's military advisers told him two things were certain: The British would pull out. And the Arabs would invade.

Fifty million Arabs in seven neighboring Arab states, five regular Arab armies, a million Arabs in Palestine—against 650,000 Jews.

Yigael Yadin, the Haganah's chief of operations, summed up the army's position: "We have a fifty-fifty chance. We are as likely to win as we are to be defeated."

Ben-Gurion made his decision: the state would be born. And it would come into existence on Friday, the fourteenth of May, because the Sabbath fell on the fifteenth.

Now, in the hut in Cyprus, the radio came alive. Ben-Gurion, standing up in the little museum in Tel Aviv, was speaking in a high quiet voice.

"I shall read the Scroll of Independence."

Independence!

After two thousand years of exile. Independence. Tears streamed down Raquela's cheeks. She did not notice. Her whole body listened.

"The land of Israel is the birthplace of the Jewish people."

She nodded. Papa's family had been there for generations. Abraham had been there, and Isaac and Jacob.

238

David and Solomon. The birthplace of the Jewish people. The land promised by God.

"Here they wrote and gave the Bible to the world."

They were the people of the Bible, reclaiming their right to the Land of the Bible, the Book they had given to the world.

She could almost see Ben-Gurion as he talked, the leonine head, the strong face framed in the cowl of white hair, like a prophet himself. Now his voice was filled with promise:

"The State of Israel will be open to Jewish immigration and for the ingathering of the exiles."

The exiles! The fifty-two thousand men and women who had been imprisoned in Cyprus; the two thousand babies she had helped deliver in the prison maternity ward. The tens of thousands in the DP camps. The thousands more fleeing persecution in Europe and pogroms in the Arab lands. Now they could all be ingathered.

The dark night of the Holocaust was over.

The quotas and the certificates and the illegal ships were over.

The State of Israel was open to Jewish immigration.

The words washed over her, but she had stopped listening. She was thinking of Dr. Yassky and Carmi, and the hundreds of young men and women who had been massacred bringing food to save Jerusalem.

The road to statehood had been strewn with blood.

But was not every birth shrouded in blood? Who knew better than she? And how much more blood would be spilled in this birth?

"We extend our hand to all neighboring states and their peoples in an offer of peace, and appeal to them to establish bonds of cooperation for the advancement of the entire Middle East."

Peace . . . cooperation . . . the advancement of the entire Middle East. Was it possible? Was it a dream? Why not?

Ben-Gurion's voice rang out:

"We hereby proclaim the State of Israel."

Raquela stood up with Dr. Toaff and Esther and all the doctors and nurses.

They sang "Hatikvah," the "Song of Hope." It had never seemed so meaningful.

Raquela and Esther hugged each other. Dr. Toaff kissed them both, laughing and wiping his eyes. "Do you realize"—his musical Italian accent was thick with excitement—"now we're a nation like all other nations? For the first time in two thousand years, we won't be standing before kings and rulers with our hats in our hands. We're in charge of our own destiny. Children, we should celebrate."

"I must tell my women first," Raquela said.

Raquela bounded across the compound to the maternity ward.

"Women!" she shouted. "Listen. Ben-Gurion has proclaimed the State of Israel."

The women jumped out of bed. Some had just delivered; some were heavy with babies ready to be born. They encircled Raquela, kissed her, hugged her until she was out of breath.

"Wait a minute," she finally gasped. "I only delivered the news. I didn't deliver the state."

"Raquela, Raquela," one of the women sang out, "we're going home. Our babies will grow up in Israel."

When the excitement died down and the women returned to their beds, Gerda asked Raquela, "Do you know when they'll let us out of here?"

"I'll go to Caraolas in the morning and bring back whatever news they have."

At seven the next morning she taxied to the camp. Inside the gates she stopped in her tracks. A mass of people swept across the campground, marching, stamping, parading. Banners waved in the air: LONG LIVE ISRAEL . . . LONG LIVE THE NATION OF THE JEWS.

The paraders, dressed in their Shabbat clothing, wove in long lines about the tents and huts. Fiddlers played. Adi Baum pumped his accordion. Drummers beat rhythms on makeshift drums.

Thousands of people were marching in different lines. Raquela joined one of the lines, marching happily until her group spontaneously formed a circle and danced a hora, faster and faster. Adi Baum joined them, playing his accordion; then, the folk dance over, he led them in a parade again, toward the watchtowers.

Joyously waving their banners, the people called out to the soldiers, "Long live Israel! Now you too can go home."

The soldiers leaned out of the watchtowers, smiling broadly, waving back.

Raquela caught sight of Josh and Pnina Leibner and their children marching in another line. She stepped out and hurried toward them; they too stepped out of line.

Raquela and Pnina hugged each other. *"Israel."* Pnina said it was if she were trying out a holy word.

Only yesterday they had called their land "Palestine."

But Palestine was derived from the name "Philistine," the people who were constantly at war with the ancient Israelites. No, the name "Israel" was right. For thousands of years they had called it *Eretz Israel*—"the Land of Israel."

"Josh," Raquela said, "my women are clamoring to know when we can all leave. Have you got any word?"

"Nothing yet on Cyprus closing down. But we've heard Egyptian planes have dropped bombs on Tel Aviv. The Arab armies are massing at all the borders."

She looked sadly at the people parading and waving their banners in ecstasy. In a few days, perhaps, they would be descending the gangways of Ike's and Gad's ships; immediately the men would plunge into the fighting, and the women and children into the war.

"I'm going back to the hospital," Raquela said. "One of the nurses is holding the fort until I get back for the day shift. Will you let me know the minute you hear anything about closing the camps?"

She taxied back to the hospital. She found Gad waiting in the entrance to Maternity.

"Raquela," he said, "we've got to celebrate the birth of Israel. Can you and Esther get off tonight and come out to the *Pan York*? Bring your bathing suits. Ike wants us to have dinner on the *Pan Crescent*. I thought it would be fun if we swam from my ship to his."

"A night swim? It sounds fantastic, but is it safe?"

"Ike and I do it all the time."

After dusk Raquela and Esther, dressed in summer cottons and carrying bathing suits, taxied to the Famagusta harbor.

A full moon threw stabs of light into the sea.

Looming up, the *Pan York* and the *Pan Crescent* seemed like two giants chained and fettered in the black water.

Aboard the *Pan York* Raquela saw two British soldiers

patrolling the ship. Gad kissed Raquela and greeted Esther.

"We have to be careful," he whispered. "The soldiers mustn't know what we're planning."

"Why?" Esther asked. "Is it illegal to go swimming?"

"Off these ships it is. Remember, technically, we're still their detainees."

An explosion detonated under the water. The two women flinched.

"What was that?" Raquela asked.

"A little game the British play with us every night. They drop one or two small bombs around us in the water to make sure we don't have any frogmen trying to free our ships. Don't worry. They've dropped their quota for tonight."

Raquela looked across the water at the *Pan Crescent* a hundred yards away, its decks festooned with lights.

"Why don't you two go into my cabin," Gad suggested, "and put your bathing suits on under your dresses. The crew and I already have our bathing trunks under our pants. The British mustn't see us in bathing suits."

Soon Raquela and Esther were back on the deck, their dresses concealing their swimsuits, waiting with Gad until the patrol moved out of sight.

"Okay, everybody," Gad commanded in a low voice.

Swiftly, they stepped out of their clothes, hid their dresses and shoes in a box on the deck, and climbed down the Jacob's ladder. A dozen or more crew members surrounded the two women as they swam through the dark cool water toward the *Pan Crescent*.

Gad reached Raquela with long smooth strokes. He drew her to him in the water and kissed her. Her face glistened with pleasure. She raised her head high in the salty water, tried to tread water, put her hands around his neck, and returned his kiss. The moon made a path to Ike's ship; she could see him standing with his crew on the deck.

"We'd better get out of this moonlight," Gad said, "or the soldiers on one of our ships may see us."

Raquela turned over and floated luxuriously, letting the water lap over her. Gad swam at her side, guiding her.

Arik, she thought, *in a million years you couldn't guess what I'm doing right now*.

After a while she turned over, moving her arms rhythmically in a breast stroke.

"Have you seen Esther?" she asked Gad.

"She's probably swimming with the crew, but I'll go check. You keep on heading toward the ship."

"Hi, Raquela." Esther splashed beside her. "I haven't had this much fun since I got to Cyprus."

A bullhorn shattered the night.

"Attention! All personnel! Have sighted frogmen! Alert all naval craft!"

Raquela and Esther sped toward the *Pan Crescent,* their hearts racing faster than their strokes.

A motorboat pulled up beside them. Strong arms reached down and dragged them into the boat; soon half a dozen of the crew were hauled up.

Raquela sat on a wooden ledge, searching anxiously for Gad. The British kept scouring the water for more swimmers. Apparently convinced they had captured them all, the seamen pulled into shore. The swimmers clambered onto the dock. Raquela's teeth chattered with cold and with fear.

"What are you going to do with us?" she asked a British officer who seemed in charge of the soldiers waiting for them.

"Take you to jail."

"Jail!"

A paddy wagon pulled up. The captured swimmers were loaded into the wagon. Raquela shivered, her bathing suit dripping on the seat as they drove in the night air. She sat close to Esther. They did not speak.

In the Nicosia jail, a guard led them through a corridor. He unlocked the door of a large cell and pushed the crew members inside; farther down the corridor he locked the two women into a smaller, narrower cell. "You sure look like drowned rats," he said.

Soon he returned and handed them two army blankets. The familiar-smelling blankets had never seemed so welcome. They wrapped them togalike around their bodies and slipped out of their wet suits.

Now warm and dry, they looked around the cell. Two iron cots flanked the walls.

Esther shuddered. "They're probably full of bedbugs and cockroaches."

"Still, we can't stand up all night," Raquela said. "It must be about ten o'clock."

The two nurses gingerly brushed the dirt off the cots, then sat down at the edge of the beds.

"I wonder if Gad was caught," Raquela said worriedly. "I pray he got away."

They heard heavy footsteps outside their cell. A British military officer rapped his stick on the bars.

"Now would you two like to explain what you were doing? Frogmen, aren't you?" He glared at them.

"Frogmen!" Raquela gasped. "We're nurses from the British Military Hospital."

"You don't expect me to swallow that cock-and-bull story. No nurses from the BMH would carry on like this. You're a couple of terrorists from Palestine."

Raquela pulled the blanket closer around her body. "Please, sir, call the BMH. Ask for Dr. Mary Gordon. She'll vouch that we're not terrorists."

He turned on his heels.

A few hours later, still unable to bring themselves to lie on the cots, Raquela and Esther saw the jailer approach. "You've got a couple of visitors. We've let them in because they brought you dry clothes."

He handed them the summer dresses they had concealed on the deck, their shoes, and their purses, which held their wristwatches and ID cards. "I'll let you see your visitors for a few minutes."

He returned with Ike and Gad.

"Thank God, you're safe," Raquela whispered to Gad through the bars. "I was so terrified not knowing what happened to you."

He looked contrite. "I saw them catch you. It was too late to help you get away. I swam underwater and managed to escape their net."

Ike put his hand through the bars and touched Esther's face.

"Some jailbird!"

"They think we're terrorists, Ike," Esther said. "We told some officer to get in touch with Mary Gordon. I don't think he believed us."

"We'll call her ourselves." Ike tried to reassure her.

"Time up," the guard shouted.

Alone in the cell, Raquela and Esther changed into their clothes. Sleep was out of the question.

Sunlight began to filter through the prison corridor. Somewhere in Cyprus the sun was rising. Raquela could visualize the people stirring in the tents and iron huts. "One night behind bars and I feel as helpless as the refugees—like a trapped animal."

"What a way to celebrate the birth of Israel," Esther said. "In jail!"

The jailer appeared, unlocked the cell door and handed them each a cup of tea and a slice of rye bread. Famished, they ate the bread slowly to make it last longer.

The hours dragged. When would they be released?

They looked at their watches. Eight o'clock. Nine o'clock. Ten o'clock.

No one came.

Twelve o'clock. The jailer brought two bowls of soup.

"How much longer before we can go?" Raquela asked.

"Who knows? Maybe thirty days." He shrugged his shoulders.

"But we haven't done anything wrong!" Esther protested.

"Never met a prisoner yet that didn't say that. Why did two good-looking girls like you want to blow up those bloody refugee ships?"

"It was only a swimming party," Raquela said.

"Hm." He slammed the cell door.

Raquela and Esther sipped the soup. More hours passed. Shadows were growing long in the prison corridor. Raquela looked at her watch. "It's five o'clock."

"I'm getting exhausted," Esther said, "but I can't see myself sleeping on this bed. Still, I guess if we're tired enough, we'll have to."

Six o'clock. The jailer reappeared, his keys dangling. He opened the cell door.

"You two sure fooled me. It's the first time I ever locked up nurses."

Sighing with relief, they followed him outside the jail. In the street, Gad and Ike embraced them.

"How did you get us out?" Raquela asked.

"Hop into the cab," Gad said, "and we'll tell you everything. But you've got to report immediately to the matron."

He ordered the cab to drive fast to the hospital.

"It was Dr. Mary Gordon," Gad told them. "We got in touch with her and she went right to the top, screaming that no one had a right to lock up her nurses."

"What about the crew?" Raquela asked. "Will you be able to get them out right away?"

"It's harder with them. But we've hired the best lawyer in Cyprus to work on it."

The cab sped up the hilltop to the hospital. Raquela and Esther leaped out, said good-bye, raced through the complex of iron huts, and knocked on the door of Matron White's office.

The matron was imperious in her rage.

"You—you prostitutes."

Her huge bosom rose and fell inside her starched white uniform.

"It was a perfectly innocent swimming party," Raquela said through her teeth.

"I can imagine how innocent."

"What's wrong with swimming with our friends? You know how hard we're working. We're entitled to some relaxation."

The matron's cheeks were purple, apoplectic.

"You don't even look remorseful. Your own Jewish women are in labor—and you go whoring with sailors in the middle of the night."

Esther drew herself up tall. "We'd never have been arrested if it weren't for your Englishmen. They'd arrest mermaids, if they could, and call them frogmen."

"I don't know how they bring you up in Palestine. No English nurse would ever behave like you."

Raquela and Esther stared at her, their faces impassive.

"I ought to have you fired. And I would, if I didn't need nurses so badly. The two of you—*ugh*—you're a disgrace to the profession."

She dismissed them with a wave of her hand.

Outside the matron's hut, Raquela and Esther looked at each other. "I thought it would be worse," Raquela said.

Esther was worried. "We still have to see Dr. Gordon."

They hurried to Mary Gordon's quarters.

Her face was sad. "Maybe someday I'll understand this crazy young generation."

Events began tumbling over one another.

In Washington, President Truman recognized Israel eleven minutes after Ben-Gurion's Proclamation of Independence. The United States thus became the first nation in the world to recognize the new state.

The Soviet Union followed. And the third was little Guatemala, whose ambassador to the United Nations, Dr. Jorge García-Granados, had been a pivotal member of the historic Unscop committee whose recognition of the rights of the Jews had started these wheels turning.

Unscop had hoped the state could be born in peace. The Jews had accepted partition. The Arabs declared war.

Egypt, Transjordan, Syria, Lebanon, and Iraq, with troops from Saudi Arabia and Yemen—seven Arab states—crossed the borders, invaded Israel, and attacked. The armies of fifty million Arabs hurled themselves against Israel's 650,000 Jews. The War of Liberation began.

And even as she fought for her life, Israel began to take in new immigrants, sometimes a thousand a day. For was not this the reason she had been created?

When would the men imprisoned in Cyprus be allowed to join her Army? Every man who could hold a gun was desperately needed.

Each day, the refugees in the camps, Ike and Gad on their ships, Raquela and Esther and the staff in the hospital, waited for word from London.

Why the delay? The state had been declared. On the Hill of Evil Counsel, in Jerusalem, Sir Alan Cunningham, the British high commissioner, had closed the door of Government House behind him. The British soldiers and police sailed back to England. British power was ended.

But Bevin had one last card: Cyprus.

He gave new orders.

"The Jews in the camps and aboard the impounded Pan York and Pan Crescent are guilty of having attempted illegal entry into Palestine. As such, they are still internees under our jurisdiction on the British Crown Colony of Cyprus."

In the tents and iron huts the people reacted first with disbelief, then with outrage.

No one could leave: no men, women, or children. Nor Gad and Ike. Nor would Raquela and Esther and the hospital staff leave so long as they were needed for the thousands who were now beating their fists against the barbed wire. How dare the British hold them prisoners when they had their own state.

Two weeks had passed since Israel's birth; battles were raging on every front; the Arabs were attacking isolated kibbutzim; Jerusalem was under heavy fire; and the gates of Cyprus were still sealed.

The island temperature rose to one hundred degrees Fahrenheit, and the rage of the people mounted.

For Raquela, surcease came on her evenings off with Gad. But he, too, was restless and angry.

On a boiling afternoon she saw him hurrying toward her across the hospital compound. She ran toward him, trying to read his face.

"You've had word," she said. "You're free to leave."

He shook his head. She had read him wrong.

"I came because I couldn't stand another day without seeing you."

She nodded. "I need you, too. Even my maternity ward has lost its calm. The women are ready to scream every minute. These last days have made them wild, as if they're unhinged. I don't know how much more they can take. Or how much more I can take."

"Come on the ship," he said. "Let's be together tonight."

At seven, Raquela fled the hospital grounds.

Gad met her on the dock in Famagusta. Soon they were pacing the deck of the *Pan York* under the watchful eyes of the British patrol.

Gad put his arm through hers. "If we don't get out of here soon, Raquela, I swear Ike and I will explode."

Raquela held her hand to her hair, feeling the wind and salt run through it.

"Sometimes I wake up in a sweat," she said. "I dream you and Ike have somehow managed to sneak out past the British. And I'm not sure whether or not I want you to be gone."

"You would miss me, Raquela?"

"I would miss you very much, Captain Gee. I love coming out here. I love being with you on your ship. Out here on the water, everything seems timeless. I wish all the clocks in the world would stop ticking. In camp, in the hospital, I have such a sense of urgency; I'm as restless as all the prisoners. I must get back to Jerusalem. I must help there. I must help in the war. Time is like something breathless. But here . . ."

She put her face to his and kissed him.

He held her tightly. The dark night and the dark sea bowled around them.

She looked out at the water. Across the sea lay Jerusalem . . . and Arik. *Two souls dwell, alas! in my breast.*

They returned to Nicosia and the hospital compound.

A letter from Arik lay on her bed.

> DEAREST RAQUELA,
>
> Not a day passes that I don't think of you. We've had to give up the hospital on Scopus. We've moved down to the old English Mission Hospital on the Street of the Prophets. We call it Hadassah A. You'll be working here with me when you come back.

When you come back. She looked around the iron hut. When? When would Bevin allow the twenty-five thousand remaining refugees to leave? Could she go before then? She went on reading:

> I know you worry about us, but with all my superstitions . . .

She smiled, remembering the red thread he had sewn into her "new look" dress to guard against the Evil Eye.

> . . . with all my superstititions, I am a fatalist. I think we're all inscribed in God's Book—who shall live and who shall die.

May 28, 1948, the Old City of Jerusalem fell. Starved out of food and ammunition, seventeen hundred people in the Jewish quarter huddled into cellars and ancient synagogues, to save themselves from the bullets and shells of Transjordan's Arab Legion. Most of the historic synagogues were already rubble. Only the great Hurva Synagogue, its cupola a landmark in the Old City, held out until it, too, was captured. Two rabbis, defying the pleas of the handful of Haganah defenders, walked with a white flag toward the Arab Legion's headquarters in a school in the Arab quarter, and surrendered.

The Old City. Raquela mourned, where she had walked those quiet Shabbat mornings with Arik. The Old City, where Papa's family and untold generations of Jews had lived and borne babies and worshiped and died.

The Legion allowed some thirteen hundred women and children to pass through the gates of the crenellated wall into new Jerusalem. But the Arabs took the men, young and old, to a prison in Transjordan. Three were Hadassah doctors.

Anger and sorrow at the loss of the Old City tore through the Cyprus camps.

"If we were there!" Some of the men beat their fists in the air. "We're eleven thousand young men who could be fighting! We might have saved the Old City!"

The refugees, moving in mobs, brandished sticks at the British soldiers in the watchtowers. Raquela saw their anger turn to violence; their frustration, to hostility and rage.

Each night a handful of men escaped through the tunnels where trusted Cypriots drove them to little fishing boats waiting in Famagusta and Larnaca. They sailed to Haifa and from the dock went instantly into battle. But most of the men were trapped in the furnacelike huts and tents of the May inferno.

On every front the newborn state was battling for its life. In the south and west the Egyptians crossed the Suez Canal, cutting the Negev off from northern Israel and driving on to Tel Aviv.

In the north the Syrians and Lebanese, and the Iraqi Arab Liberation Army, led by the pro-Nazi Fawzi el-Kaukji, marched across the Galilee, attacking the kibbutzim.

From the east King Abdullah's Arab League crossed the Jordan, and now, along with the Iraqis, they battled for the cities on the West Bank and, most of all, for Jerusalem.

Word came on Gad's radio. New Jerusalem was on starvation rations of food, water, fuel, and ammunition. Yet, one hundred thousand Jerusalemites and units of the Israel Army were still holding off the soldiers of the Arab Legion.

The road to Jerusalem, the single lifeline from Tel Aviv, was immobilized; the Arab Legion, steamrolling from the towns they captured on the West Bank, surrounded Latrun, in the foothills of the Jerusalem corridor.

To save Jerusalem, a secret road was built through a steep wadi. Mickey Marcus, an American Jew and a West

Point graduate, who had flown over to help the fledgling state, planned the road. Hundreds of elderly men built it in the darkness, carrying sacks of dirt on their backs. The old "Murder Road" harassed by Arabs was bypassed; on the new road of dirt and gravel, dubbed the "Burma Road," trucks from Tel Aviv, raising clouds of dust, reached Jerusalem just as it was down to its last two days of bread and flour.

The siege of Jerusalem was over.

In New York the UN Security Council was meeting in endless sessions. Some of the members sought earnestly to arrange a cease-fire, but so long as the Arabs were winning, the Security Council failed to reach agreement.

Now the Arab offensive began slowing down; kibbutzniks were hurling Molotov cocktails at Arab tanks trying to conquer the kibbutzim. The tanks blew up; the men inside, if they were lucky, jumped out and ran away. Most were burned to death.

Information that the Jews were going on the offensive reached New York. The security Council agreed to a four-week cease-fire. It would last from June 11 to July 9.

It gave both sides a breathing spell. Instructed by the UN to do nothing during the truce to improve their positions, both sides paid no attention. They regrouped their forces and brought in more arms.

Mickey Marcus, tragically killed by one of his own sentries who mistook him for an enemy when he walked out of his tent one night, was flown to the United States and buried with full military honors at West Point. Colonel Moshe Dayan accompanied the body, and then rushed home.

Golda Meir barnstormed America describing the war; she raised fifty million dollars.

Golda's dollars bought arms and planes from the only country willing to supply the new state: Czechoslovakia. Local pilots, like Ezer Weizman, who had fought with the RAF in World War II and volunteers from abroad ferried the planes and armaments to Israel.

The Arabs bolstered their numbers and planned their strategy of attack to be used as soon as the cease-fire ended.

And Bevin relented a little.

He made a new announcement; all refugees—*except men of military age*—could leave the camps.

The joy at being freed was poisoned. But Britain, he explained, must remain evenhanded. They could not allow Jewish soldiers to create an imbalance.

Imbalance! Raquela shook her head in disbelief. Fifty million Arabs against fewer than a million Jews was no imbalance. But eleven thousand young men of military age might tip the scales.

The *Pan York* and the *Pan Crescent* were freed. They would begin ferrying the refugees, *all except men of military age.*

Gad sent Raquela a message. "Can you come at once? We're sailing today."

She switched shifts and rushed to the ship.

Lines of women and children and old people—erstwhile prisoners of the Empire—overflowed the dock. Many were sobbing or staring blankly ahead.

A woman carrying a baby stood forlornly. Raquela approached her.

"They're separating us." The young mother's eyes were flecked with fear. "God knows when I'll see my husband again."

Raquela put her arm around the frightened woman's shoulder. "They can't keep the men here forever. You'll see; he'll join you soon in Israel."

Raquela looked up at the two ships. Some of the happiest hours of her life had been spent aboard the *Pan York*.

But it was no longer the *Pan York*. Fresh white paint spelled out its new name: KOMEMIYUT, a Hebrew word for "independence." The *Pan Crescent* had become the *Atzmaut,* another word for "independence."

On each ship Palmach sailors unfurled the blue and white flag of Israel and hoisted it to the top of the masthead. On the dock the people lifted their faces to the flags and sang "Hatikvah." The minute they set foot on the ships, they would be on the soil of Israel.

Raquela climbed the gangway of the *Komemiyut* and hurried to the bridge. Gad, dressed in summer whites, every inch the commander, was bending over charts, talking to his first mate, giving orders to his bosun. Raquela waited.

At last he looked up. "Raquela!"

He pressed her into his arms. "I thought they'd give us

a little notice. That we'd have at least one last evening together. But the moment word came to sail, all hell broke
loose."

"Will you be coming back?" she whispered.

"We'll keep making the run to Haifa until we get everyone out of here."

"Even the young men?"

His handsome face grew sober. "As soon as they're released. Would you believe this?"

He showed her a document. "It's the bill of health the
British gave us to clear out. Read it."

She read: "The flag flown by this vessel is not recognized by the British Government."

She laughed. "Will Bevin never give up? His government still hasn't recognized the state of Israel."

The first mate waited anxiously for Gad. The people
were already lining the decks.

"Good-bye, Gad."

"Good-bye, my darling."

She hurried down the gangway.

In the hospital Raquela worked feverishly, delivering the
babies of women too close to term to risk sailing. By now
twenty-five hundred babies had been born on Cyprus.

Gad returned every few days. But they had only
minutes together. The moment the ships hove into sight,
the lines of women, children, and old men queued up to
board.

A few young men managed to hoodwink the British officers at the checkout table. Some dressed as women with
wigs borrowed from Orthodox women; some lined their
faces with black-crayon wrinkles; some had fake casts on
their legs; some wore dental overlays to look like toothless
old men.

A few hundred escaped and made their way to Israel to
join the army. But most of the eleven thousand young men
watched the long processions file out of the camps; they
were lonely, bitter, enraged. The camps took on the air of
an all-male prison, like the male sections of Hitler's
concentration camps. The women and children had made
internment tolerable. Now, in Bevin's final anti-Semitic
stroke, he inflicted the last indignity, the one act that com-
jured up death: separation. Separating them from the
wives who had survived the Holocaust, or the new wives

they had found and married in the camps, separating them from the babies who had given them back their manhood.

The four-week truce continued; so long as there was no war, Gad and Ike could ferry the people safely to Haifa.

The day came—a day, in early July, so hot it blistered the huts—when Raquela got word. "Come quickly. This is my last trip."

On the bridge Gad looked drained.

"Others will finish cleaning out Cyprus. They're sending Ike and me to Europe to reoutfit our ships. From now on we'll be sailing back and forth from Naples with refugees from the DP camps and thousands of other Jews pouring into Naples from all over Europe."

Already she felt a sense of loss.

He seemed to understand. "This is not good-bye, Raquela. I'll come to Jerusalem. I'll find you wherever you are."

She clung to him. Would Arab planes bomb him? Would Arab submarines slide through the waters and rip his ship apart?

"I'll come back, Raquela." They kissed passionately.

He walked her to the gangway and stood watching her descend.

On the dock she turned around. She waved. "Good-bye, Gad." She looked at the handsome captain.

Would she ever see him again?

A few days later, her replacement arrived. She boarded the plane for Haifa.

❧ Chapter Twenty ❧

July 1948

The engines revved, and within minutes the plane rolled down the Nicosia airstrip.

Cyprus fell away; below lay the Mediterranean, turquoise in the morning sun. In an hour Raquela would be landing in Haifa.

The plane flew smoothly through the blue cloudless sky, but Raquela's mind was in turmoil. Who was she? What did she want of life?

Love. Fulfillment. Fulfillment as a woman. Fulfillment in the field she had chosen.

Marriage? Yes. She wanted a man to hold her in his arms. She wanted marriage and her own children. But marriage to whom? Gad, or Arik? *Does every young woman,* she wondered, *discover herself through the eyes of the men who love her?* For she was beginning to see herself as the two men saw her.

Gad made her aware of her sexuality, of herself as a passionate and warm-blooded woman. Arik made her proud of her career—life-loving, life-giving, life-nurturing. Under his tutelage she would move to the top of her profession. Arik, too, made her aware that she was a desirable woman.

Married to Gad, she would probably have to move to Haifa, waiting and watching for his ship to come in. Her life with him would be like the sea that was his life—uncertain, stormy, with days of great beauty and calm, and weeks, maybe months, of loneliness. A life forever fraught with danger.

As the wife of a sea captain in Haifa, she would be the outsider. Her roots, her background, everyone she loved, was in Jerusalem. The city was almost human, like a beloved person in her life.

255

Were her feelings for Gad strong enough to overcome her apprehensions?

Married to Arik—she would live in Jerusalem. She would work at his side. She would never be alone; he would be her constant companion.

Arik's life was the life she knew and had loved before Cyprus. It would be more serene, more even-keeled, than Gad's. Did she love Arik enough to compensate for the excitement that Gad stirred within her?

The plane landed in Haifa. A sign greeted her:

WELCOME TO ISRAEL

Israeli soldiers guarded the airport. Israeli officials sped her through Immigration. Israeli customs men inspected her suitcase. She wanted to fling out her arms and embrace them. She was home. In Israel. And the British were gone.

On the streetcorners of the broad main avenue the old name, Kingsway, had been changed. The street signs, in Hebrew and English, bore the words REHOV ATZMAUT— "Street of Independence." Even the air seemed to breathe the word "independence."

On the dock she asked the cab driver to wait. She walked past shipping offices and small warehouses until she found the office of the Jewish Agency.

A young man glanced up from a cluttered desk. "What can I do for you, miss?"

"Can you tell me—is Captain Gad of the *Komemiyut* in Haifa?"

He looked at her. "He sailed an hour ago for Naples."

Raquela taxied back to the Street of Independence and pulled up at a curb where an intercity *sherut* waited with a sign on its windshield: TO TEL AVIV. She climbed into the front seat of the seven-passenger cab. It filled up almost immediately; the driver turned the ignition key, stepped on the gas, and maneuvered his way through the port city.

Circling the harbor, Raquela saw the graveyard of "illegal" ships and the famous American riverboat, the *Exodus 1947. "The Mayflowers of our State,"* Dr. Weizmann had called them.

Soon the white stone houses of Haifa and the biblical

Carmel Mountains lay behind them; they were driving along the Mediterranean coast.

Raquela looked out the window as army trucks and jeeps filled with Israeli soldiers rolled by. In some of them the men were singing Palmach songs; they waved to the people in the *sherut*. She waved back, her joy tinged with apprehension. The truce was holding, but the soldiers made her realize the war was far from over.

"*Shelanu!*" The driver pointed proudly to the soldiers.

"*Ours.*" *That's the word, she thought. Our soldiers. Our cities. Our country. No longer owned by the Turks. No longer ruled by the British. Ours.*

The road suddenly looked familiar; it was the crossroad to Athlit.

She turned to the driver. "Do you know if all the refugees are out—if Athlit has been closed?"

"But of course. As soon as the state was born. They're citizens already. The first act of our Provisional Council of State was to end all restrictions on immigration."

She stared straight ahead. Athlit was closed, but not Cyprus. Judith Steiner's brother, Joseph, and all the able-bodied men who had been imprisoned in Athlit were probably in the army. In a few days, on July 9, the truce would end. Unless the Security Council could prolong the cease-fire, the war would erupt again on every front.

Arriving in Tel Aviv, Raquela was stunned. She discovered there was no passenger traffic to Jerusalem: only convoys of jeeps led by the UN or the International Red Cross were allowed to make the journey. She sat on a café veranda on Allenby Road, sipping iced coffee, trying to figure out how to get home.

All around her Tel Aviv shrieked, honked its horns, ground its brakes. On terraces women beat their carpets with a *rat-tat-tat* like machine gun fire. It was nearly noon. The sun beat fiercely on the concrete street. Yet the Tel Avivians moved along urgently, purposefully, carrying briefcases or newspapers under their arms.

How different our three big cities are, she thought, still worrying how to get transport to Jerusalem. *Haifa is a morning city—workers hurrying to their jobs in the harbor, the factories, the oil refineries. Tel Aviv is high noon, the city of frenzied commerce and even more frenzied traffic. Jerusalem is the sunset city. Jerusalem is the eternal "going home." Every trip to Jerusalem is a pilgrimage, a going up, a return. Jerusalem is my city. But how am I to get there?*

She was beginning to panic. An army jeep drove slowly down Allenby Road. From the café veranda she caught sight of the driver, an officer in uniform. "Ze'ev," she called out. He was a good friend of her brother Jacob's.

He stopped the jeep.

She ran down the stairs to greet him. "Can you help me?" she said. "I've got to get up to Jerusalem."

"Hop in," he said. "I'm just on my way."

"God, Ze'ev. Somebody up there sent you to me."

She ran back for her suitcase. Ze'ev tossed it in the back of his jeep and helped her climb up into the high front seat.

Soon they had joined a convoy of jeeps at the outskirts of Tel Aviv. Ze'ev, preoccupied, hardly spoke as they drove along the coastal plain through Jewish settlements, vineyards, and fruit orchards. A few miles before the approach to Latrun—the police-station roadblock from which Israel had failed to dislodge the Arabs—the convoy swerved onto a dirt road.

It was the "Burma Road"—the road that had been built at night, the secret lifeline that had broken the siege and saved Jerusalem. *Our road,* she thought.

It was steep and unpaved, winding through a wadi along the foot of the hills.

The line of jeeps churned up a cloud of dirt and dust. Her hair, her face, her clothes, were covered with dust. She smiled, even as the dust entered her nostrils. *Our dust. Our dirt.*

Near Bab-el-wad—the Gate of the Valley—they drove past coils of barbed wire. The "Burma Road" ended. They turned sharply left back to the old highway she knew. They were beginning the ascent, climbing the ancient Hills of Judea, the steep hills the Arabs had controlled during the winter war that had begun in November 1947.

Now the road was safe; the Arabs, defeated, had run away. But the sides of the road were a monument to war, a cemetery of burned-out trucks and cars that had failed to reach Jerusalem.

They drove past the village of Abu Ghosh, whose Arabs had chosen to stay with the Jews, past fertile kibbutzim in the hills, winding through the hills to the crest. Jerusalem lay ahead. Raquela could see its skyline. Her breath was short.

Separated from the convoy, they were driving now down Jaffa Road. She knew every shop, every kiosk, every house. The signs of war were everywhere; glass and rubble littered the streets. She saw gaping holes in stone buildings, and pockmarks where bullets had entered. Some of the buildings were stained ugly black from fires. But the city of stone had withstood the shelling.

A few women walked quickly, carrying string bags through which she could see a loaf of bread or a tomato and a cucumber.

The jeep drove up Ben Yehuda Street. She saw the bombed-out Vilenchik Building, the collapsed Amdursky Hotel, the apartment building where Esther's family had lived. The buildings looked like London in the blitz.

"I have to drop something in an office," Ze'ev told her. "If you can wait a few minutes, I'll take you home. You'd have a hard time trying to find a cab. Gasoline is harder to get than . . . than blood."

"Of course I'll wait."

He returned in a few minutes and drove toward Bet Hakerem. The early-afternoon traffic was light; it was siesta time. Did people still take siestas these hectic days?

The jeep stopped in front of her tree-shaded stone cottage. She thanked Ze'ev, picked up her suitcase, unlatched the garden gate, and ran across the little patio, shouting, "Mama! Papa!"

"Raquela!" They flung open the door. Her mother reached her first and lifted her arms to embrace Raquela. Papa folded her in his strong arms.

"My child," he whispered.

"Are you all right?" Mama asked. "Let me look at you. You're covered with dust. Are you feeling all right? Even your face is all gray, like a mask. I can't see what you look like."

Raquela laughed. "I'm fine, Mama. Especially now that I'm home. All I need is a good shower."

"Come on inside," Mama said, businesslike. "Now I know why I saved all my water today. I must have felt you were coming home."

As they entered the house, Papa explained. Jerusalem had no running water. The Arabs controlled two of the pumping stations that brought water to Jerusalem—at Latrun and at Ras el Ein. They had cut off the water supply, hoping that thirst might make Jerusalem surrender. But Israel held two other stations—at Bab-el-wad and, not far from it, at Saris, and was already beginning to lay pipelines. Meanwhile, the little water they had was brought in by trucks and horse-driven carts and was carefully rationed.

"We use the water five ways," Mama said. "Drinking, cooking, bathing, sponging the floor, and finally the toilet. Today is so special we'll celebrate. You'll have the water."

"I can't let you do that," Raquela protested. "You can't be without water."

"No, no, you'll see."

In the bathroom Mama gave instructions. "Now undress and step over here."

She placed a large basin inside the bathtub. Raquela stood in the basin and dipped a bar of soap in the pail of water Mama held. She was a little girl again as she scrubbed and soaped her hair, her face, her body, until she was coated with lather. Then Mama, now standing on a chair near the tub, spilled the pail of water on Raquela's head and watched it flow into the basin.

Raquela stepped out of the basin, clean and refreshed. The soapy water was saved; Mama assured her it would serve two more purposes—the floor and the toilet. Raquela, dressed in fresh clothes, joined her parents in the living room, full of energy, eager for news.

"How are Jacob and Yair?"

"Thank God, well," Papa said. "They've been on different fronts in the war."

Mama smiled mysteriously. "You have a new brother."

"What? Have you adopted a baby?"

"We adopted him, but he's no baby. He's just two months younger than you."

"Where is he?" Raquela glanced swiftly around the living room.

"Sh-sh, he's sleeping. We've given him our bedroom."

"I can't stand this suspense. If I have a new brother, I'd like to know about him."

"All right, sit down," Mama said. "I'll tell you."

Raquela settled herself on the sofa. Mama sat beside her, watching her face. "You know, there are so many soldiers in the hospitals, nearly every family in Jerusalem has taken in a wounded boy or girl. We try to help them get better and at the same time we free the beds in the hospitals."

Raquela nodded.

Mama went on. "They sent us this nice young man—handsome, good character. His name is Itzhak Elkhanim. He's from Hungary. His family were all killed in the concentration camps. He himself survived Auschwitz."

"But what's this about adopting him?" Raquela asked.

"Not so fast." Mama put up her hand. "Don't be in such a hurry. I'll tell you. He fought in the Old City; an Arab put six bullets in his stomach. He and his best friend, who was also badly wounded, crawled to one of the first-aid stations that we had set up in the Old City. His friend bled to death. But our boys were able to get Itzhak to the Bikur Holim Hospital."

Raquela waited for her to go on. Bikur Holim was the large red hospital on Straus Street, right off Jaffa Road.

Mama had jumped off the sofa. "You must be hungry. I'll get you some food; I bet you haven't had lunch yet."

"Mama, lunch can wait. I want to hear about my adopted brother."

"All right, then." Mama perched next to Raquela again. "In the hospital they performed a temporary colostomy. Then he was brought to us. Papa and I took turns taking care of him. After two weeks he needed another operation. We took him back to the hospital. And we nearly lost him. He was critically ill. Now he's with us again, slowly convalescing." She paused. "I'll let Papa finish the rest. I'm going to fix you some food."

"There's really not much more to tell," Papa said. "When he wakes up, you'll meet him yourself. You'll see why he walked right into our hearts, and, since he had no parents, we adopted him."

After a scrambled-egg-and-salad lunch, Mama tiptoed to the bedroom.

"Come here, Raquela," she called out. "Itzhak is up."

Raquela entered the bedroom. A young man looked up at her, smiling; his face was pale and drained; he had dimples in his chin and his cheeks. His eyes were dark; a neat black mustache lined his lip.

"How do you feel?" she asked.

"Are you asking as a nurse—or as a sister?"

Raquela chuckled. "Both."

"In that case, I'm already feeling better."

They chatted for a little while. "You rest now, Itzhak. We'll have plenty of time to talk. I'm home now for good."

She plumped up his pillow and straightened his covers. "Good-bye . . . my brother," she said.

She went to her childhood bedroom. Mama had already fixed it with freshly washed sheets that smelled of the Jerusalem sun and wind. She lay down and was asleep instantly.

The next morning Raquela walked to the bus stop and caught the bus to Zion Square. She walked up Rabbi Kook Street to the corner of the Street of the Prophets where the old English Mission Hospital now housed Hadassah A.

It was a massive Romanesque structure that curved around the street with balconies, tall arched windows, and annexes with sloping red-tiled roofs. It was topped by a steeple, and surrounded on all sides by a stone wall and thick trees.

She entered through a courtyard and walked up the stairs to the department of obstetrics and gynecology. In the hall she saw the back of a familiar figure. "Arik!" She started to run.

He wheeled around. "Raquela!"

He gathered her in his arms. "I can't believe it's you."

"Arik. It's so good to see you. Are you well? Are you working too hard?"

"I'm strong as an ox. But let me look at you."

Then he stood back. "My God, you're more beautiful than I remembered."

All around them, nurses, doctors, patients, were scurrying through the narrow stone corridor. The hospital, in the July heat, was bedlam.

"I've got to talk to you, but it's so hectic here," he said. "It's been so long. I'll be free in a couple of hours and we can go off somewhere for coffee."

"Fine. Why don't I go right to the maternity ward and pitch in. I've brought my uniform."

He kissed her. "I'll pick you up the minute I can take a break."

Raquela, in a fresh uniform, entered the nursery. The infants lay in cribs against the rough stone walls, yet the warmth, the cacophonic sound, unlike any in the world, of a dozen babies' announcing their presence enveloped her.

One nurse was on duty. The rims of her eyes were swollen and red. Her body sagged with fatigue.

"Are you a new nurse here?" she asked Raquela.

"Not really," she said. "Just an old one come home. Why don't you lie down for a while?"

For the next three hours Raquela changed diapers, fixed formulas, bottle-fed babies, and brought hungry infants to nursing mothers.

The Jerusalem sun was setting over the Old City; the mountain winds were cooling the nursery. Raquela tucked blankets around the infants—not coarse army blankets but soft white ones. It was twilight when she felt someone looking at her. Arik stood in the doorway.

He was smiling. "Even the babies are happy you're home. It's as if you never left us."

He planted a kiss on her cheek. "I'm free now. As soon as you're ready we can leave."

Raquela called the nurse on duty, and soon, still in their hospital uniforms, they walked out into the courtyard.

Zion Square was crowded with soldiers and their girls. Boys who seemed barely old enough to shave and men who looked like grandfathers strode the streets in motley uniforms and an incredible assortment of stocking helmets, GI overseas caps, French berets, Italian fedoras, Australian profile hats—mirroring all the countries they had come from. Unabashed, the soldiers stood in the middle of the square, clinging to their girls, kissing them, their bodies speaking the fear they might never hold each other again.

"Let's go to the Patt Bakery," Raquela said, "for old times' sake."

In the bakery Mrs. Patt, catching sight of Raquela, came from behind the counter.

"Welcome home, Raquela." She embraced her, her blue eyes wide with pleasure. "And good evening, Dr. Brzezinski."

Raquela returned the warm greeting.

"Is Shula around?" she asked.

Mrs. Patt shook her head. "Shula's in Tel Aviv—in Army Intelligence. Come along." She took them to the garden. "You're both my guests. How about some of my apple strudel? With this rationing we can only make a little, and I save it for my special friends."

"I dreamed about your apple strudel in Cyprus," Raquela said.

Mrs. Patt ushered them to a table in the garden.

All around them doctors and nurses in uniform nodded and exchanged greetings with Arik. Several, catching sight of Raquela, came to their table. "So good to see you back with us, Raquela."

A wave of nostalgia swept over her. This garden, the Patt bakery, the people—they were all part of her past.

Arik was studying her face, beaming. "Now my friends will know why I haven't stopped smiling all afternoon. I haven't felt this good since you left." He reached for her hand. She felt a glow of warmth.

"You can't imagine how I felt," she said, "when I learned that you weren't with Dr. Yassky on the convoy. That you were safe."

"It was the worst experience of my life. I stood on the roof of the hospital, watching through binoculars. I was in charge of the hospital, and my friends were in the buses, being burned alive. It was horrible—the worst nightmare. We couldn't rush down to save any of them. We had no guns. We had nothing to fight them with."

Raquela shuddered. "What it must have done to you— seeing it all happen before your eyes."

"Awful. It aged us all a hundred years. We were desperate. We had more than seven hundred people in our institutions up there—doctors, nurses, students, professors, workmen—and, most serious of all, more than a hundred fifty patients. We couldn't get down for three weeks, surrounded all the time by Arabs. We were able to hold out because of one man: Benjamin Adin, the driver."

"I remember. He used to pick me up during the curfew. We called him the *meshugana*—the crazy guy."

"Crazy like a fox. He refused to let us starve. He would take his truck and drive through Sheikh Jarrah like a shot to bring us supplies. He even brought us matzoh and sacramental wine so we could celebrate Pesach. We had Seders all over the place—in the hospital, in the nursing school, everywhere. I went from one to the other—"

"Like the prophet Elijah," she said, laughing.

"If you can picture Elijah dropping in at every Seder to sip wine and tell some Sholom Aleichem stories."

"Only you would think of Sholom Aleichem to make the people forget for a little while."

The waiter brought their coffee and a small square of strudel.

"Mrs. Patt must really love you, Raquela. Do you know what our rations are this week? I can tell you exactly. Each of us gets one tomato, half a carrot, one cucumber, two onions, one green pepper, and a few string beans."

"My God, that's a starvation diet."

"You're right. It's so ironic. We've got this UN Truce Commission and Count Folke Bernadotte, the UN mediator. They say that there mustn't be any improvement of any kind during the truce. If we had no food at the beginning of the truce, we should have none now. It's madness when you think that UN officials, supposedly idealistic and humanitarian, spend all their time figuring out how to keep Jerusalem starving."

She put her hands to her face. "I feel so guilty. Mama made me a scrambled egg for lunch. I may have used up the family's ration."

"Things are a little better now. We've got a tough Jerusalem boss—Dr. Dov Joseph, a former Canadian. He's head of the Jerusalem Emergency Committee. He's finally made the UN agree to let more food come up to Jerusalem in convoys. Now we're getting an egg a day and some milk and cheese, and once in a while some frozen fish. But I can tell you, Jerusalem is still hungry."

The waiter refilled their cups.

Arik sipped slowly. "It's only since the truce that we can even have coffee in a café. During the fighting everything was shut down." He looked at her. "Now I want to hear about you, Raquela."

For the next half hour she entertained him with stories of Old Battleship, of the kindly British officer who gave her his supply of diapers for her babies, and of the homesick Tommies who fed her premature infants. Then she told him of the frustration and despair of the young men of military age whose wives and babies were evacuated. "They're still there, Arik. I don't know what's going to happen to them if the British don't free them soon."

"Did you meet anyone special?"

She took a long swallow of coffee. "Some wonderful people. Real heroes. The people who ran the JDC. Dr. Harden Ashkenazy."

He nodded. "The army is sending him every tough head injury. He's already training other surgeons in neurology."

Raquela hardly heard him. "And I met the captains of the two biggest illegal ships." She paused.

"I want to hear more." He looked at his wristwatch. "Good grief. I had no idea we'd been gone so long. It's so good being with you again, sweetheart. Now that you're in Jerusalem, we'll have a lot more time to be together. Right now, we'd better get back to the hospital."

But there was little time in the next days to be together.

At six A.M. on July 9, the cease-fire ended.

Raquela was already at work in Hadassah A when shells began to fall on Jerusalem.

The Arabs had used the last days of the truce to erect strong fortified positions on the walls and parapets of the Old City near the Tower of David and the Jaffa Gate.

From the nursery window Raquela could see the new gun positions. She hurried to Arik. "I'm uneasy. I'd like to move the babies to a safer room. I found a good-sized room downstairs that's like a shelter. It needs to be emptied and cleaned up. Is that okay?"

He smiled. "I put you in charge."

Raquela helped a porter empty the room; the floors were scrubbed, the stone walls washed.

Back in the nursery she handed each baby to a nurse who carried it down the narrow stone stairs; she brought the last infant down herself.

Minutes later, a blast pierced the air.

The massive hospital trembled. The babies screamed. Raquela's knees buckled.

She heard a commotion in the corridors and on the stairs. People were rushing up and down; voices called out, "Is anyone hurt?"

Arik came in, shaken. His kindly face was chalk.

He took her in his arms and held her close.

Finally he spoke. "A shell just exploded in the nursery upstairs. It would have killed every baby." He stopped. "I can't bear to think—it would have killed you, too."

The Old City was gone. New Jerusalem was encircled by the mufti's gangs, Kaukji's pro-Nazi Arab Liberation Army, Arab irregulars and mercenaries, and by Transjordan's Arab Legion.

The Arab Legion was the most formidable—twelve thousand soldiers trained by the British, armed by the British, and leb by the English general Sir John Glubb.

King Abdullah* of Transjordan hungered for Jerusalem and the West Bank.

His desert kingdom of thirty-four thousand square miles on the East Bank of the Jordan had been an integral part of the original territory of Palestine promised by the Mandate for the Jewish homeland. Then, in 1921, the British had given it to Abdullah as a reward for the assistance of his father, Hussein ibn Ali, in defeating the Turks in World War I. The British had promised Syria to Hussein's son Feisal. But the French, taking Syria for themselves, kicked Feisal out. So the British consoled Feisal with Iraq and gave his brother Abdullah the largely unpopulated sands on the East Bank of the Jordan River.

Winston Churchill, then colonial secretary, boasted that on a Sunday afternoon with a stroke of his pen, he lopped the East Bank off the Palestine map, took it from the Jews, and handed it on a platter to Abdullah. Even the name was significant: Transjordan—the other side of the Jordan.

Now Abdullah had crossed the Jordan with Sir John Glubb commanding his Arab Legion. His purpose: to annex the West Bank and Jerusalem. He had, of course, no legal right to the territory. Had the British intended to give him Jerusalem and the West Bank—biblical Judea and Samaria—Churchill would have done it that Sunday afternoon in 1921 when he gave him the East Bank of the Jordan.

The battlefront was the streets of Jerusalem. Arik, Raquela, every doctor and nurse, and every volunteer worked to exhaustion. Raquela served wherever she was needed—the delivery room, the nursery, tending the wounded, civilians as well as soldiers.

To get to Hadassah A from the bus, she crept along the sides of buildings, for the Arabs were shooting almost incessantly from the nearby wall of the Old City. The sidewalks were stained with blood.

The wounded from the streets and the burning battlefields were rushed to the nearest hospitals. Hadassah, after moving down from Scopus, had set up five emergency hospitals in town with three hundred beds. Hadassah A, in the old English Mission Hospital, had been the first; Hadassah

* King Abdullah was the grandfather of King Hussein of Jordan.

B was in St. Joseph's Convent, a former nun's school for six hundred Arab girls—a sympathetic French Government official had turned it over to Shulamit Cantor to house her nursing school. The nearby Straus Health Center and the Hasolel Street Clinic were also converted. But the most exotic facility was the men's ward of Hadassah D: it had originally been a Turkish harem. Even the wounded enjoyed knowing their upstairs rooms encircled the white-tiled indoor courtyard where once the women of the harem had danced and entertained their pasha.

Basements and cellars were converted to operating rooms, and when the sporadic electricity gave out or the high-tension lines were damaged, Arik and the other surgeons operated and Raquela and the midwives delivered babies by flashlight.

Each day gruesome casualties were rushed to the operating rooms, young men whose arms and legs and pieces of their faces were blown off. Many of the soldiers were new immigrants; some went directly into the army from the ships ferried by Gad and Ike and other captains. Straight out of the DP camps, these men had little or no training; everything was strange to them—the language, the customs, the climate, the terrain. Some could barely understand their commanders' orders. The fighting was brutal; thousands of young men lost their lives.

Yet, the tide of battle was turning.

The Israelis had a secret weapon—*Ein Brera*, "no alternative." Against all the predictions that the armies of fifty million Arabs would slaughter the Jews within a few days, the Jews were routing the Arabs.

In the center of the country, Colonel Moshe Dayan, who had lost an eye on a reconnaissance mission for the British in Syria during World War II, led a special commando unit of jeeps and half-tracks and a captured Jordanian tank his men had nicknamed "the Tiger." Dayan, who believed in speed, mobility, and the element of surprise, astonished the enemy by racing his crack commandos through the Arab lines and capturing the vital Lydda Airport, then speeding through the towns of Lydda and Ramle. The well-trained troops of the Arab Legion fled back toward the West Bank; the local populace surrendered.

In the north, Kaukji's Iraqis and mercenaries were headquartered in Nazareth. Using diversionary tactics, the

Israel Army confounded the enemy. Kaukji and his mercenaries took flight, and at six-fifteen on July 16, the notables of Nazareth surrendered. Not a single church or religious shrine had been harmed. As dusk fell on Nazareth, monks and priests and parishioners prayed near the Grotto site where the angel Gabriel had announced to Mary, "And behold, thou shalt conceive in thy womb, and bring forth a son, and shalt call his name Jesus."

In the south, King Farouk, of Egypt, insanely jealous of Abdullah, sent his army across the Sinai Desert into the Negev to get his piece of the Israel pie.

The strategic center of the Negev was Kibbutz Negba, a square green oasis of three hundred fifty people in the midst of the rolling yellow desert. It lay near the crossroads of the vital Majdal-Faluja road from Gaza to Jerusalem and the Julis-Kaukaba road from Tel Aviv to the Negev. Whoever controlled those roads controlled the gateways to Tel Aviv and Jerusalem.

The British, who had realized the strategic importance of Negba as far back as 1941, had built a Tegart fortress-police station called "Iraq Suweidan" nearby. Nothing had been more welcome then; building it had given Negba's people protection against Arab thieves and brigands and a fortress against a possible Nazi invasion of Palestine through Egypt.

But on May 14, 1948, the day of Israel's birth, the Iraq Suweidan Police Station was taken over by the Moslem Brotherhood, the irregular Egyptian forces, who handed it over to the Egyptian army.

The Egyptians immediately took control of the friendly neighboring Arab villages and captured two Jewish colonies near Negba, Nirim and Yad Mordekhai, leaving Negba surrounded by hostile Arabs and cut off from the vital crossroads. To the beleaguered Jews, it seemed obvious that the Arabs were planning a blitzkrieg drive on Tel Aviv. If Negba fell, the whole southern front would crumble, and the heart of the new state would be punctured.

The Israel High Command sent orders: "Hold Negba until your last bullet and your last man."

The Egyptians shelled Negba with cannons and mortars all through May, waiting for the kibbutz to surrender. A new style of life began in the settlement. The people moved out of their houses, into the underground warrens.

With no heavy weapons to start an offensive, they fought back with homemade Molotov cocktails—soda bottles filled with gasoline and a fuse—keeping the enemy at bay. Finally, toward the end of May, reinforcements arrived— three-inch mortars and one antitank Piat with ten shells— to hold off the Egyptian army.

On June 2 Arab tanks, fanning out from the Iraq Suweidan Police Station, opened fire against Negba. The kibbutz was ruptured with explosions—every house was demolished. Four Arab planes roared overhead, crackling the air with machine-gun fire.

A key machine-gun crew in the trenches covering the barbed-wire entrance to Negba was short of ammunition. Negba's commander, Kuba Wayland, turned to eighteen-year-old Tzigane Hartman, his prettiest runner, who had been one of the parentless children in Cyprus. Her parents had been burned by the Nazis. Could Kuba send Tzigane into the foray to carry ammunition?

But Tzigane was the only one he could spare. She carried the ammunition through the trenches, crouching, listening for Arab fire, discerning its direction, and making her way through in the opposite direction. Kuba sighed with relief when Tzigane returned to headquarters alive.

In the middle of the morning, twenty-four Arab tanks moved toward the settlement. The first row pushed through the outer barbed-wire fence. One tank broke through the two inner fences and was almost on top of one of the trenches when Tamara Weinfeld, one of the original settlers, tossed her Molotov cocktail. Flames encircled the tank. The Arabs were killed.

From their posts in other corners of the kibbutz, the men and women opened flank fire on the Arabs. The Egyptian infantry were caught in the middle, unable to advance on the village, unable to retreat to the police station.

At two in the afternoon, the Arabs withdrew, ending the first tank battle for Negba. The handful of settlers had held out against more than a thousand Arabs equipped with tanks and planes and cannons.

The first truce began. Negba was in ruins, every house shattered; the children's home, which housed more than a hundred children, had been blasted open. Yet, there was no time to rebuild; every moment had to be used to dig more underground hospital space and more trenches, to store water, food, and ammunition in preparation for the second round.

On July 9 the month-long truce ended. The Egyptians rushed to the offensive and captured Hill 113, which lay a mile west of Negba and overlooked the entire colony.

On July 12 the Egyptians coordinated a massive attack: a barrage of artillery followed by a row of tanks, then artillery with a cover of Spitfires, and a final row of tanks and troops.

The Egyptians' fire cut the telephone wires. A chain of runners rushed through the trenches, relaying messages and commands. Tzigane's red sandals flew through the ditches.

From the watchman on the water tower, she relayed the disastrous news that the Egyptians had captured another strategic area, Hill 110. Negba's last road to Tel Aviv was cut off. The kibbutz was caught in an iron ring.

Thirty-two Egyptian tanks maneuvered about, searching for a weak point in the village's defenses. But Negba had set up antitank minefields. Seven Egyptian tanks were blown up. All the men inside were killed.

Egyptian infantry surged down the road; Israel's machine-gun fire mowed down the soldiers. The sounds of the wounded and dying on both sides carried above the noise of the bullets.

The posts around the village were filled with wounded men and women and others fainting from exhaustion. The human telephone system was disrupted; Tzigane and all the runners were sent to man the guns.

Three more waves of infantry poured down upon the village and were repulsed. At three-thirty in the afternoon, the watchman on the water tower saw fresh troops of a fourth wave rushing down from Hill 113. He heard them shouting, "*Alai-hum, alai-hum,*" "Seize them, seize them."

Commander Kuba Wayland ran to the hospital shelter and spoke to the wounded, who were lying on slabs built against walls of earth.

"The enemy are pushing through. If they conquer us, they will slaughter us all. Whoever can move, pick up a gun and go to posts three and five."

The sick and wounded, with bandages around their heads and limbs, pulled themselves off the underground ledges and crawled through the trenches to feed the machine guns.

At four o'clock the tide ebbed. But all the next day, the Arabs shelled Negba from every angle of the encirclement. That night, the Israelis attacked Hill 110. The Arabs surrendered. Their ammunition—four Bren carriers and two pieces of heavy artillery—lay in Israeli hands. The ring was broken.

On the night of July 13, Negba, still under immobilizing artillery fire, emerged from its trenches. The offensive began.

In a radial pattern, three units from Negba attacked the semicircle of Arabs surrounding them. The Israelis were thrown back.

Colonel Moshe Dayan, with his commando unit of jeeps, half tracks, and "the Tiger," was rushed south. The commandos cut the vital Majdal-Faluja road and overwhelmed the Arabs surrounding the kibbutz.

Negba was saved. "The lesson we learned," Kuba Wayland told his exhausted but exhilarated comrades, "is that if you love your soil, if you never leave it, they cannot conquer you."

Dayan drove to an army hospital to visit his wounded commandos. He found two with severe eye wounds, their eyes bandaged, their faces drawn with pain.

Remembering his own feelings when he had lost his eye on a mission for the British, Dayan stopped at their bedside to cheer them up.

"Boys," he said, "for all that's worth seeing in this wretched world, one eye is enough."

In Jerusalem the Israeli army sought desperately to recapture the Old City.

They had already breached the New Gate; a few more hours, they felt, and they could drive out the Arab Legion. They were forced by the UN to halt. The second truce, ordered by the Security Council, went into effect July 18 at seven P.M.

Reluctantly the Israelis agreed.

Nine tenths of Jerusalem was now in Israeli hands, though the Old City and East Jerusalem flew the flag of the Arab Legion. Mount Scopus held, but the Arabs controlled Sheikh Jarrah and the road to Scopus.

Bone weary, Raquela had little time to be with Arik or to think of Gad. For the second truce brought as little respite as the first. The shelling and sniping and bombing continued, and the hospitals overflowed. Raquela nursed wounded in the hospital and took care of her new brother, Itzhak, when she could get home.

July. August. September. Hardly a day or night went by without shells and mortars splitting the air of Jerusalem. Tracer bullets streaked across the sky. Civilians were caught in the deadly range of machine-gun bullets.

The UN mediator, Count Bernadotte, recommended to the UN that Israel, winning on nearly every front, hand over Jerusalem and the Negev to the Arabs in exchange for peace. Outraged, three men, wearing soldiers' uniforms and Afrika Korps caps, assassinated Bernadotte on September 17.

He was rushed to Hadassah A and died within minutes, before the surgeons could remove the bullets. The Jewish community recoiled with shock and horror.

The provisional government of Israel issued an ultimatum: the dissident groups must disband. Four days later, the Irgun accepted the ultimatum, the leaders of the Stern Group were arrested. In the aftermath of the tragedy the new state was united.

October 10, the second truce ended. The battlefields were blazing again. On October 15, the Arab Legion launched a dawn attack on Mount Zion, just outside the Old City wall, the biblical mountain with King David's tomb and the room of the Last Supper.

The battle was mercifully short; the Israel Army was determined to hold every inch of Jerusalem. They drove the Legion back to its old lines.

In Hadassah A, Raquela prepared a brutally wounded young soldier for surgery.

"Nurse," he pleaded, "lift me up. Let me take one last look at my Jerusalem."

Ben-Gurion faced a dilemma: whether to drive the Arab Legion out of the Old City and off the West Bank or the Egyptians out of the Negev.

Steeped in the Bible, Ben-Gurion, always a dreamer and prophet, saw the Negev as Israel's future. Here in the empty desert were Solomon's copper mines, gold and minerals, and, maybe, oil. He opted for the Negev.

The Egyptians controlled the road that cut the country in half. Under Yigal Allon, the Palmach commander, the

Israel Army went on the offensive and with the air force and navy attacked King Farouk's legions.

They cleared the roads, took command of the sky, and on the Mediterranean, near Gaza, sank the *Emir Farouk,* the flagship of the Egyptian navy.

Four A.M., October 21, they entered Beersheba.

Eight A.M., the Egyptians raised a white flag on the roof of the police station.

Nine-fifteen A.M., ancient Beersheba, where Abraham had dug his wells, was captured. It would become the capital of the Negev, Ben-Gurion's dream.

October 31, the UN Security Council proclaimed the third cease-fire. Just before the deadline, Kaukji's Arab Liberation Army and his mercenaries were routed. The entire Galilee was open.

There was no stopping now; both sides breached the truce.

On November 9 the Israelis encircled the Egyptian stronghold in the Negev, called "the Faluja Pocket." Among the Egyptian soldiers was a young major named Gamal Abdel Nasser.

On November 30, 1948, Colonel Moshe Dayan, now commander of the army in Jerusalem, and Colonel Abdullah el-Tel, the representative of all the Arab forces, met in Government House, on the Hill of Evil Counsel. Under the supervision of the UN Truce Commission, they signed an agreement for a "complete and sincere" cease-fire in the Jerusalem area.

On the first quiet Shabbat of the "sincere truce," Arik asked Raquela to go walking. They could walk freely at last; no more huddling against walls, no more dodging in and out of doorways to escape bullets and mortars.

The day was warm and balmy; thousands of people thronged the streets in Shabbat clothes. Young fathers, still in uniform, wheeled their babies in carriages. Young mothers walked proudly, clutching their husbands' arms, as if they were telling themselves, He's mine; he's alive; he's whole.

But the joy in Jerusalem was tempered. Six thousand young men and women had died to give birth to Israel. And the Old City where Raquela and Arik had spent so many Shabbat mornings was denied them.

Instead they walked through the quiet streets of Bet Hakerem. Finally, in a tree-shaded playground where they could watch children playing, they rested on a wooden bench.

"I've neglected you all these months, Raquela," Arik said.

"Nonsense, Arik. Many times in that operating room, when I saw your eyes red from no sleep, I was afraid you might collapse. God knows where you found the strength to go on operating."

"And where did you find your strength? Don't think I was blind, Raquela."

He took her hand and caressed it.

His warm hand sent currents of electricity through her body.

"We can be together again," he was saying. "Take up where we were before you went to Cyprus."

Where we were. But Cyprus had changed her. And Gad had entered her life. *Do you ever go back to where you were?*

Gad had promised to find her when the war was over. All these months of the fighting, she'd had no word. Was he still ferrying refugees from Europe—coming in now at the rate of ten thousand a month? Where was he now?

She looked at Arik. Impulsively she stroked his cheek. She loved this man; she loved his strength, his gift for saving lives. The Jerusalem sunlight seemed to come from behind his eyes, deepening their compassion.

And Gad? Memories of the *Pan York,* of the moonlit sea, of the snow in Troodos, and of the nocturnal swim kaleidoscoped in her mind.

In her bedroom at home that night, she stared at herself in the mirror. *Look at yourself, Raquela. Look at your own strengths and weaknesses. What is it you want? What is it you need? What's best for Arik? What's best for Gad? What's best for you?*

She tossed on her bed, unable to find answers, unable to sleep.

-ᵈ Chapter Twenty-one ᵇ-

February 1949

At long last the gates of Cyprus opened.

Late in December 1948 with Israel now seven months old, Britain had ended its private war against the Jews and recognized the Jewish state.

A month later the restless, angry men on Cyprus, deprived of the right to fight for their nation, were allowed to leave. The first shipload left Famagusta on January 24, 1949, aboard an Israeli passenger ship, the *Galila*.

Raquela devoured the newspaper photos of the throngs of people meeting the men in Haifa. Flags and banners. Young wives, middle-aged mothers, weeping with joy as they embraced their men.

Early in February Raquela was in the nursery in Hadassah A when a cable was brought to her.

> BRINGING HOME LAST REFUGEES FROM CYPRUS. CAN YOU MEET ME TONIGHT AT JEWISH AGENCY OFFICE ON HAIFA DOCK? GAD.

She folded the cable carefully and tucked it into her pocket. She asked a nurse to cover for her, wrapped her cape around her shoulders, and walked out of the hospital toward the post office.

The streets were crowded with people holding umbrellas, lashed by the rain and a fierce wind. She walked blindly, trying to think.

This was the moment of reckoning.

She could go to her superior and say, "I've worked without rest. I need a few days off—to go out of town."

She would see Gad again; she saw him now, tanned, blue-eyed, in his white captain's uniform, standing at the wheel. She could feel his kisses on her lips.

276

She sat down on a park bench near City Hall, hardly aware that the rain was drenching her hair and her cape.

Gad was romance and youth and escape. Escape from the grim reality of Cyprus.

But is it Gad I really love?

Then why am I sitting here?

Why am I not in a sherut already, on my way to Haifa? Remember—she heard Señora Vavá's voice—*you are a ninth-generation Jerusalemite.*

She looked around her in the winter rain. She was only a few blocks from the Old City, the turreted walls and Jaffa Gate a stone's throw from where she sat.

She shook her head; the frontiers between Israel and Abdullah's Legion were bizarre: sometimes the frontier was a street or an ugly aluminum fence; the most famous was the "Mandelbaum Gate," the war-wrecked house of Abraham Mandelbaum with its ugly corrugated-iron shed that separated East and West Jerusalem.

The city was obscenely truncated, and she felt the separation physically, as though part of her had been amputated.

Closing her eyes, she saw Mount Scopus . . . the hospital . . . the nursing school . . . her first delivery . . . the birth fluid drenching her like a geyser . . . Arik at her side . . . Arik, teaching, guiding, making her feel her own strength.

The rain had turned to hail; stones pelted her face. She hardly noticed. Did she love him as teacher? Or man? Or both?

The answer was suddenly clear. Raquela ran across the street to the post office. She sent a cable:

HAVE DECIDED TO STAY IN JERUSALEM. GOOD-BYE DEAR GAD. RAQUELA.

She walked swiftly back toward Hadassah A. Thunder rumbled through the streets; streaks of light tore open the sky over the great Romanesque hospital.

Arik . . . she began to run, tears mingling with rain on her cheeks . . . Arik, it's you I want . . . you I need . . . you and Jerusalem.

On the island of Rhodes a gifted black American, Dr. Ralph Bunche, the UN mediator, began meeting with Arabs and Jews in armistice negotiations on January 13, 1949.

Wise and shrewd, Dr. Bunche brought the erstwhile warring factions together in a technique of diplomacy so simple, so obvious, it was conceded that only a genius could have developed and implemented it.

First he met alone in a room with each country's delegate. Then, when he sensed some movement toward agreement, he brought a delegate from one of the Arab states and the delegate from Israel face to face. When they reached agreement on armistice terms, he handed them the papers to sign.

His secret of success was twofold: face to face, and one Arab country at a time.

The Egyptians signed first, on February 24. Jordan signed next, on March 4; Lebanon, on March 23; Syria was the last to sign, on July 20.

Thus, on the twentieth of July, the War of Independence ended. Twenty months—nearly two years—since that day in November 1947 when the UN had voted to partition Palestine and the Arabs had marched out of the UN and declared war.

Twenty months. Six thousand dead. One out of every ten Jews dead on the battlefield.

The nation born—like all births—in blood.

On a warm October day in 1949, Raquela and Arik rode out of Jerusalem. They were bound, some seventy miles south and inland, for Beersheba.

Ben-Gurion had already begun implementing his dream of opening the Negev. He turned to Hadassah. The frontier needed a hospital. Would Hadassah establish a first-rate hospital in Beersheba?

Arik had spent most of September converting a group of houses the army had turned over to him for his department of obstetrics and gynecology. Now he was returning with Raquela; she was to set up the maternity ward and the delivery room.

They sat in the back of the *sherut,* talking to some of the passengers. The middle-aged couple in the jump seats were scientists: he, a government ecologist; she, a government botanist. Beersheba was to be their headquarters, but they were headed for a mountainous region forty miles farther south. With twelve others, including a cowboy from Texas, two meteorologists, and a zoologist-soldier in case they were attacked by Arabs, the couple were searching for water and grass to feed the pioneers who would someday live here.

The slim brown-bearded young man in the front seat was an archaeologist on his way to dig for the wells of the ancient Nabataeans, who had farmed and cultivated this land two thousand years ago.

Raquela looked out the car window at the empty rolling steppeland.

Not a tree, not a plant. Only sand dunes and bareback hills, broiling sun and thin translucent light.

The archaeologist was talking. "The Old Man," he said, speaking of Ben-Gurion, "sees this whole desert filling up with pioneers and cities. 'Go south, young men and women,' he says, the way the Americans used to say 'Go west.'"

In the shimmering light the colors of the sand were changing from yellow to reddish brown. Was this lunar landscape with its own strange beauty Ben-Gurion's dream?

Who lived here? Who would come to this hospital? She knew there was a chain of kibbutzim in the Negev. The first three had been started in 1943; then, defying the White Paper, a small army of young men and women, in one dramatic nighttime operation, had established eleven new kibbutzim in the Negev on Yom Kippur, October 6, 1946, as the Day of Atonement ended.

The kibbutzim were little islands in the desert, but what would life in Beersheba be like these next months?

Happy, but a little apprehensive, she looked at Arik. He was smiling. "There's a sense of peace here," he said, "a kind of eternal serenity, despite the constant tug of war between man and the desert. It was only after I began to work here that I really understood what Ben-Gurion meant when he asked us to open up a hospital for the whole Negev."

"What did he say?" Raquela asked.

Arik spoke slowly. "He said, 'If the state doesn't put an end to the desert, the desert will put an end to the state.'"

An end to the state?

The yellow arid desert enveloped them, another challenge to survival, another enemy.

The only sign of civilization they saw for miles was the

narrow road they were traveling, the artery that was to pump life-giving blood into the desert.

Suddenly against the horizon they saw the silhouettes of camels moving in a straight line in the yellow shimmering sunlight. A Bedouin nomad in a flowing black robe and white *keffiyeh,* stark and one-dimensional, followed the camels on a donkey. Behind him walked three women, black-gowned and veiled, with baskets on their heads. Across the sea of sand two barefoot boys shepherded goats. A little girl with enormous kohl-rimmed eyes stopped to stare curiously.

The car sped past them.

Again the desert, unpeopled, limitless, empty to the horizon.

They were approaching Beersheba.

Raquela had expected to find a small town; instead she saw a sleepy desert outpost with dirt streets, Arab houses in shambles with broken shutters, a single mosque, and a police station.

"There's Abraham's Well," the bearded archaeologist said as they drove on the main street.

"Can we stop for a minute?" Raquela asked. "I've heard about this well all my life from my father."

The driver pulled up on the side of the street. The passengers formed a circle around the well that had been dug four thousand years ago. The young archaeologist pulled a well-worn Bible from his pocket and read from Genesis: "And Abraham took sheep and oxen, and gave them unto Abimelech; and they two made a covenant."

Raquela stared down into the deep dark hole, listening as the archaeologist read of the seven ewe lambs that Abraham presented to Abimelech, the Philistine king of Gerar, in exchange for the grazing rights to the land.

"That's how Beersheba got its name." The archaeologist closed his Bible. " 'Be'er,' of course, means 'well,' and 'sheba' means both 'seven' and 'covenant.' Take your choice; I like to think of Beersheba as 'the Well of the Covenant.' We're renewing Abraham's covenant in the desert."

They reentered the taxi and drove a few hundred yards to the main street—a few little shops and one café with CASSIT printed over the doorway.

Raquela and Arik said good-bye to the two scientists and the archaeologist and wished them success.

"And good luck to you, too." The passengers shook Raquela's and Arik's hands.

Arik asked the driver if he would take them up the road about a quarter of a mile.

"What's up there?" the driver asked.

"We're setting up a hospital," Arik explained.

They drove along the dirt road, churning hot dust into the flat landscape. "We get out here," Arik said. They opened a gate and found themselves in a quadrangle of four short intersecting dirt streets.

"We closed this area off," he said, "as a compound for the hospital and the staff."

He pointed to a warehouselike building. "That's the combination staff kitchen, dining room, and laundry. And that"—Raquela looked at a jumble of scrub—"was once a garden and I hope will be again. See that little house behind the garden?" Raquela nodded. "Our pediatrician has already moved in, a young Englishwoman, Dr. Pearl Ketcher. I'm sure you'll like each other."

"I know her. I met her at Hadassah A after she came to Jerusalem; she had been working with the DPs in Germany."

He lifted Raquela's suitcase. "Come on, I'll show you the hospital and where you'll be living."

They entered a large courtyard surrounded by a jumble of one-story stone houses with flat roofs.

Arik was talking. "My friend Dov Volotsky was the first one down here—he came in June 1949. He's already begun repairs and construction to convert each of these buildings into different departments. Dov lives in a little house in back of the hospital. Now I'll show you your quarters."

They turned left through the courtyard to a small stone patio. A lemon tree shaded a white stone cottage.

"It looks different from the rest of the buildings, Arik. I like its feeling of privacy."

They walked up a few stairs and entered the small cottage. "There are two bedrooms," Arik said. "Four nurses. You'll be sharing your room with another nurse."

They left Raquela's suitcase in a bedroom just large enough for two beds and a small table. She hung her cape on a nail on the wall.

"If you're looking for indoor plumbing," Arik said, "there is none. The WC is across the courtyard. But you'll be able to shower in the hospital. We're putting in showers and toilets and our own generator. There's one generator in Beersheba already, but they shut it down at ten-thirty every night."

Raquela was impatient.

"Let's go, Arik. I can't wait to see what my maternity building looks like."

"We haven't done a thing there. We've left it completely for you."

They returned to the huge open courtyard. "Here it is." Arik led her into a small yellow building. Excitedly Raquela walked through the building's four small rooms. Surveying. Studying. Noting that each room had two windows. Admiring the tile on the floor, but concerned: the floor had been laid unevenly. She would have to cope with that problem later.

"I see the way to do it," she said, as much to herself as to Arik.

"We'll put the delivery room in this room, left of the corridor, with a little admission office near the door, and a shower and toilet next to it."

They continued to explore the empty building. "These two rooms at the right, off the corridor," she said, "will be for the mothers. We can get three beds in each room. Not bad for a new hospital in the desert." She paused. "You know, Arik, in Cyprus I began to realize it's not bricks and mortar that make a hospital. You can be in a tent or a hut. It's the way the doctors and nurses care for the patients. It's making a hospital homelike. It's what you taught me, Arik."

"My disciple has improved on her teacher."

"Never. You'll always be my master builder."

She went on. "Now, listen, on the two windows in each room I'll put green and white curtains. I don't want a separate nursery, Arik. I'd like to let the babies sleep with the mothers in these nice little cozy rooms."

"Why not? It could be a fascinating experiment. Babies lying in with their mothers."

"Beersheba is the place to try it out. Each mother taking care of her own baby—as soon as she's rested—after I put the baby in her arms."

He put his hand on her hair. "When do you want to get started?"

"I'll make a list of the things still missing. We need everything—from diaper pins to the delivery table."

"Okay, Sergeant. And now would you like to see where I live?"

They walked out of the courtyard, down the road, to an elegant stone villa. Several doctors had already moved into the six-room house. They entered and walked to Arik's room, at the left, a large corner bedroom flooded with sunlight.

The light fell across her face.

Arik embraced her. "It's a new beginning," he whispered. "And you have never looked so beautiful."

She shut her eyes with pleasure.

Now, at last, maybe we will have time to be together.

Her own future and Beersheba's future seemed to be interlocked. In all these months in Jerusalem they had worked closely together, but it was always work. Maybe now, in the desert isolation, away from the pressures of Jerusalem . . .

Arik interrupted her thoughts. He drew away, talking rapidly.

"We'd better get back to the hospital. We've got a great deal of work if we're to get this place ready before the opening in December."

The pleasure drained from her face. Was work his excuse? Why did he embrace her and then draw away?

Was he still frightened of her youth, afraid of their age difference?

Maybe in Beersheba, she could make him see how she'd changed. Matured by Athlit and Cyprus. Forged by the tragedies of the war.

The hospital was rapidly taking shape.

Dov Volotzky and his crew raced against time, repairing, painting, cleaning, installing plumbing, setting up the equipment they ordered from Jerusalem and Tel Aviv and the industrial kibbutzim.

Raquela was standing on a ladder, hanging green and white curtains in the maternity ward, when Dov and Arik entered carrying huge boxes.

She looked down at them. "What have you got there?" she asked.

"A present for you. From Hadassah in America," Arik said.

"For me? Who knows me in America?"

"It's really for your patients."

Raquela hurried down the stepladder. "Let me see." She helped Dov and Arik tear open one of the boxes and lifted out a package of carefully folded white sheets.

"They're beautiful. So soft and pure white. It's the best present I ever got."

"Well, don't wait," Arik said. "Put them on the beds. I want to see what they look like."

"Not so fast. I'm going to get this place finished and spotless before I put on these sheets. That's the last thing we'll do."

"Listen, you two," Dov interrupted. "It's Friday. How about coming for Friday-night supper?"

"I'd love it," Raquela said.

It was dusk when Arik knocked on Raquela's cottage door.

"Ready?" he asked.

"Come in," she called out through the empty house. The three nurses who would share the two bedrooms had not yet arrived.

Arik stood in the doorway looking at her as if he were seeing her for the first time.

The few days in Beersheba had already turned her skin golden tan.

He kissed her. "The desert becomes you."

He moved away for a moment. "And in this white dress, you look like an advertisement for wintering in the Negev."

She stroked his cheek—tanned, too, and smoothly shaved. "Maybe coming down here is what the doctor ordered for both of us."

He took her arm and led her in back of the hospital to Dov's cottage. Dov was Arik's height, with coal-black hair and sharp dark eyes, which squinted when he laughed. His eyes sparkled as he greeted them, holding his eighteen-month son, Chanan, in his arms.

Sarah came to the door; she was about five foot two, with light hair, a creamy pink and white complexion, and sparkling teeth. She seemed warm and ebullient.

Raquela felt a sharp stab of recognition. The cottage smelled of Friday night; the table was set with a white cloth and Sabbath candles; delicious odors of gefilte fish, chicken-noodle soup, broiled chicken, and carrots came from the kitchen.

"Can I help you?" she asked Sarah, forcing herself back to the present.

"Everything's ready. As soon as Arik is."

But Arik was carrying little Chanan on his shoulders, oblivious of everyone but the little blond blue-eyed boy. He got down on the floor and Chanan rode him like a donkey. He tossed Chanan in the air, cuddled him, tickled him, laughed with him, until Raquela found it hard to decide who was enjoying it more, Arik or Chanan.

"Arik, you're a born father," Sarah said, laughing. "What are you waiting for? Now give me Chanan and let's eat, or everything I've cooked will be ruined."

They sat around the Shabbat table, talking, laughing, reminiscing. Then Sarah put Chanan into a carriage in the living room. In minutes he was asleep and the talk continued. Raquela learned that Dov and Sarah had been married in 1940. When the Nazis overran Poland, they were interned in the ghetto of Kovno. In the hovels of the ghetto Sarah gave birth to a little girl, Elana.

To feed their baby and themselves, they worked in chain gangs outside the ghetto. Elana was two and a half when, on March 27, 1944, the Nazis held one of their infamous "children's actions." Dov and Sarah returned to the ghetto at night to find that Elana had been snatched away.

Raquela glanced at little Chanan, who was sleeping peacefully. No wonder he looked so loved.

When the ghetto was liquidated, Dov and Sarah were sent to concentration camps, separated, each not knowing if the other was alive. They discovered each other after the war in a refugee camp outside Graz, in Austria, boarded a fishing boat to Palestine with a thousand others. . . . Cyprus . . . then Palestine. . . . The life juices returned. Chanan was born.

"And now,"—Sarah's white teeth flashed—"here we are, with our few *shmattes*, our rags, and our most precious possession, living in this desert."

"Are you happy?" Raquela asked.

"Sometimes I still have nightmares. But I wake up. Dov is here. Chanan is here. I'm in Beersheba, building the new state. And you ask—am I happy. Look at me. Can't you see it? I only wish you should have the same happiness."

Raquela walked toward Sarah and took her hand. "Thank you, for this night."

Sarah smiled. "Come back tomorrow for lunch. Arik likes my chicken. He's a wonderful doctor, Raquela. We have to take good care of him," she said slyly. "But I'm sure you know."

Arm in arm, Raquela and Arik strolled out of the hospital courtyard and through the gate. "Where would you like to walk?" he asked. "To Cassit and have coffee? Or to the desert?"

"Is the desert safe?"

"I think so."

"Then let's walk there."

A full moon rode across the sky, lighting the sand as if it were a calm sea.

"I saw you in a whole different light, Arik," she said, kicking the sand with her sandals. "I never saw you before—the way you were with Chanan."

"I love that baby—as if he were my own."

"Arik—what about us?"

He stopped walking. He bent to pick a cactus flower. "For you, my love."

Raquela slipped the flower into a buttonhole in her dress.

"You haven't answered me. What about us, Arik?"

He put his arms around her, held her tightly, pressing his lips against hers. "I want you, dearest," he whispered. "There's nothing in the world I want more."

"I want you too, Arik," she whispered.

She felt his strength against her body. Silently, their arms around each other's waists, they walked back to the hospital courtyard and into the cottage.

In her room the cactus flower fell to the ground as he unbuttoned her dress.

~«Chapter Twenty-two»~

November 1949

The next morning was Shabbat.

They woke in Raquela's bedroom, dressed, walked slowly out of the empty cottage, breakfasted across the road, strolled back to the now-friendly desert, watched a bird wheeling in the sky, lunched with Dov and Sarah, played with little Chanan, and returned to the cottage, to seek and find each other.

Early Sunday morning, Arik went off to supervise the reconstruction while Raquela entered the maternity building; the supplies she had ordered were arriving almost daily.

A few minutes later he looked in on her and, with no one around, caught her in his arms and kissed her.

"Arik," she said, laughing, "do you realize you're slowing the march of progress."

"Any objections? Are you getting tired of me already?"

"Arik! Never!"

They held each other tightly; Raquela felt a circle of joy weld them together.

"I'd better leave now," Arik said finally, "but I'll be back soon. I love you."

She walked around the little building, singing to herself as she worked.

He loves me. He loves me. He loves me.

She unwrapped the heavy brown paper on the brand-new delivery table and ran her hand over the smooth white leather.

And I love him. Oh, God, I love him.

She unpacked a carton of medicine bottles, brown glass bottles whose labels fell off as soon as she lifted them out of the box. She borrowed a thin brush and white paint from one of Dov's workmen, and in fine English letters

she painted on the bottles ASPIRIN . . . PENICILLIN . . .
IODINE . . . SILVER NITRATE . . . SECONAL . . .

*He's the wisest, kindest, gentlest human being. And the
tenderest.*

He returned, and kissed her. Her body yearned for him.

"Tonight we'll be in my room," he said.

Swiftly the hospital was taking shape. Target date for
the opening was December 9, 1949.

The courtyard was cleaned up, with a little area of cactus and desert flowers and palm trees landscaped to give
shade. The scattered buildings began to merge into a hospital complex, as Dov Volotzky's men fixed broken windows, installed plumbing, and set up the medical
equipment.

Most of the laborers were newcomers, Jewish refugees
from Arab lands. For the war had created two great
streams of refugees—Arabs fleeing Israel, and Jews fleeing
Arab lands.

Refugees.

The terrible aftermath of every war. After World War
II more than forty million people had become refugees:
Hungarians, Germans, Indians, Pakistanis—the list went
on.

The Arab-refugee flight began with the winter war, in
November 1947, after the partition vote. The world,
watching the voting at the United Nations, saw the Jews
accept partition and the Arabs reject it.

There was no question in anyone's mind, as they
watched the Arabs march out of the UN, declaring war,
that if the Arabs were to win that war—as everyone expected—the refugees would be Jews.

The secretary general of the Arab League described the
Arab plan: "This will be a war of extermination and a
momentous massacre which will be spoken of like the
Mongolian massacre and the Crusades."

In Haifa the Jewish mayor pleaded with the Arabs to
remain in Haifa, to live peacefully with the Jews. The
Jewish leaders went down to the boats on which Arabs
were fleeing to Lebanon and Syria, begging their Arab
friends not to uproot themselves.

Some of the Arabs hesitated. They sent word to the
mufti and to the neighboring Arab states: what should we
do?

The answer came back: leave immediately, soon you will return, we will return, we will drive every Jew into the sea, we will lead you back with our victorious Arab armies.

The British superintendent of police, A. J. Bidmead, wrote to his government, in a confidential document, "Every effort is being made by the Jews to persuade the Arab populace to stay . . . [but] Arab leaders reiterated their determination to evacuate the entire Arab population."

So the Arabs fled, believing their leaders' promises.

Some fled in panic; some ran, as innocent people always run, from shelling and war. Some villages were demolished, among them, Deir Yassin, the hostile Arab village whose men had invaded Bet Hakerem in 1929, when Raquela and all of Bet Hakerem had taken refuge in the Yellin Seminar, and which had been attacked by the Irgun during the 1948 war.

In the wake of the defeat of the Arab armies, the trickle of Arab refugees turned into a flood tide. By the time Ralph Bunche began holding his face-to-face armistice negotiations, six hundred thousand Arabs had fled to the neighboring states, to the West Bank, and to the Gaza Strip.

At the same time, six hundred thousands Jews who had been living in Arab states began their refugee trek.

It was a mirror image: Arab refugees fleeing war-torn Israel, into Arab lands; Jewish refugees fleeing Arab lands, into Israel.

At the same time, more refugees fled from Europe to Israel, from countries in Eastern and Central Europe where anti-Semitism was a way of life.

The mirror image continued. The Arab refugees were housed in dismal camps, in tent cities in Arab lands.

The Jewish refugees were housed in dismal camps, in tent cities in Israel.

But there the mirror image ended.

The Arab refugees became the responsibility of the world. The UN, largely with dollars from the United States, fed and housed and educated the Arab refugees.

The Jewish refugees became the responsibility only of Israel—with help from Jews abroad.

The Arab refugees were kept inside the camps in misery and squalor.

Israel closed down its camps and moved the people out.

They built transit neighborhoods—*mabaroth*. These transit neighborhoods then gave way to new development towns.

And of all the development towns, Beersheba was the most important.

Mrs. Fanny Yassky led the delegation to the opening of the Haim Yassky Hadassah Hospital for the Negev.

Political dignitaries, doctors, and nurses journeyed from Jerusalem; Hadassah leaders who had raised funds in America flew across the Atlantic and the Mediterranean to attend.

They listened to brief speeches; they sipped soft drinks under the desert trees; they toured the buildings, admiring the equipment that had come from Irsael and from the United States.

Raquela led them through Maternity, where the beds were covered with the soft white sheets they'd sent.

Soon the operating theater was as busy as a big-city hospital's. Truck drivers were now hauling concrete and food down the Negev road to Eilat. That ancient harbor on the Red Sea, where King Solomon had welcomed the queen of Sheba to his kingdom, was to be opened, to become the window to Asia and Africa. The one road through the desert and the canyons of the Negev was 143 miles of dirt and gravel from Jerusalem, 212 miles from Tel Aviv.

Struggling to open the desert, the truck drivers often drove twelve hours or more each way over this monotonous terrain. Exhausted, they sometimes fell asleep at the wheel, caromed off the road, and overturned. Other drivers, finding them, would rush them to the new Beersheba hospital and carry them up a ramp into the surgery building.

Even in December, the days were hot. Sweat poured down the faces of the doctors and nurses when they worked during the day. Nights were freezing, and a small kerosene stove heated the operating room where the surgons tried to mend the limbs and save the lives of the weary drivers.

Ben-Gurion had expressly asked Hadassah to open this hospital for the Bedouin Arabs of the Negev as well as for the Jews. But the Bedouins of this region had never seen a hospital before. For weeks, no Bedouins came.

Finally, the first Bedouin sheikh arrived. Behind him came four wives, twelve children, two camels, and a flock of goats. He carried an almost lifeless young boy.

At the entrance gate he told the guard, "My son Abdullah is sick in the stomach. He cannot eat. No food stays in him. Can your medicine make him better?"

The guard escorted the sheikh and his entourage to the courtyard. The family and the animals bedded themselves under a palm tree while the sheikh and his young son entered the pediatrics building, where Dr. Pearl Ketcher was waiting.

For several days, the little boy hovered between life and death. The sheikh's family never moved; they ate and slept in the courtyard.

Abdullah was saved.

Word about the Jewish miracle doctors spread among the Bedouins. Soon more Bedouin sheikhs arrived with their families and their livestock.

The sheikhs sought help for themselves and their sons, but never for their wives or their daughters. No doctor, male or female, could examine their womenfolk.

Arik's OB Clinic and Raquela's delivery room held Jewish women patients, but no Arabs.

Raquela was frustrated. She left her ward and walked through the courtyard, past a family of Bedouins, to see Arik. He was bending over newly arrived gynecological instruments like a jeweler examining precious stones.

"Arik," she said, "the courtyard is filled with pregnant Bedouin women. They must have the highest birth rate in the country."

"And the highest infant mortality," he added.

"If Beersheba is to be Ben-Gurion's model for Bedouin Arabs and Jews' living together, we ought to be saving those babies."

He jumped up. "Maybe we *can* do something to save them."

The next morning they set off in a car with a young Moroccan Jew whose family had come from the *mellah*—the ghetto—of Casablanca. Ami, a tall thin young man with black hair and tawny skin, had worked in the GI camps, shining the boots of the soldiers stationed in Casablanca. Bright and quick-witted, he had learned English well enough for Arik to hire him as an interpreter for the Arab patients.

They drove deep into the desert until they reached a small compound of black goatskin tents. A gray-bearded sheikh in a long black gown and checkered *keffiyeh* received them. He was the sheikh whose young son Dr. Ketcher had saved.

"Welcome to our humble tent," the sheikh greeted them.

Arik introduced Raquela and Ami. The sheikh bowed.

Raquela saw several women and young girls peeping out of one of the tents, hiding behind the flap lest the men see them.

The sheikh led the way into the largest tent filled with pillows propped on the ground against the tent walls. Raquela, Arik, and Ami sat on pillows on one side; the sheikh sat alone, majestic, on the other.

"Your family is well, I hope," Arik said.

"Allah be praised. We are well."

An older son who closely resembled his father entered the dark tent carrying a tray of demitasse cups with Turkish coffee.

Raquela sipped slowly, listening to the polite words in the first part of the ritual.

Now the second stage began. The son collected the coffee cups and returned a few minutes later with glasses of hot tea.

"And your little son, Abdullah?" Arik asked. "How is he?"

Ami translated.

The sheikh stroked his beard and looked searchingly at Arik. "Ah, that lady doctor. She made the devil go out of Abdullah."

Raquela watched the sheikh's face closely as Ami translated his words.

"At first I was afraid to trust my little son to a woman. Every Friday I took him to the dervish. He used his powers. He put his hand on Abdullah's back and pushed and pushed and said, 'The devil is going out. The devil is leaving you.' But nothing happened. He pushed again. 'The devil is going out of your fingernails. The devil is going out of your toes.' But the devil went out in your hospital."

Arik nodded solemnly.

The third stage of the ritual was to begin. The tea glasses were gathered up, and the son returned with a fresh round of Turkish coffee in demitasse cups.

This was the moment Arik had chosen to launch his plan.

"Sitting here beside me in your tent, sir," Arik said, waiting for Ami to translate phrase by phrase, "sitting here is the best midwife I know. She has brought hundreds of babies into the world. I am hoping you will allow her to deliver your next child."

The sheikh focused his dark eyes upon Arik.

"You are asking me to send one of my wives to her. Why is your midwife better than ours?"

Raquela leaned forward from her pillow and spoke for the first time.

"I am sure I am no better than your midwives."

The sheikh sat impassively as Ami translated. Then he looked at her. "Why should I let my wife go to have a child in your hospital? Why is it better than my tent?"

"There's no reason why most women can't have their babies at home, provided there are no complications." Raquela was talking urgently. "If there are complications, a few minutes can mean the difference between life or death. In the hospital, if a baby or the mother is in trouble, they can be saved. There's a doctor. There's equipment. At least we have a fighting chance. At home, the baby can die and the mother can die."

She stopped. She had not meant to talk so long.

The sheikh lit his *narghila*. The desert silence filtered into the black goatskin tent.

Arik played his trump card.

"The government of Israel is deeply concerned that too many babies and too many mothers die in childbirth."

The sheikh puffed his water pipe, listening. Arik went on. "So they've voted to present every mother who gives birth in a hospital with a gift of money."

The sheikh pulled the pipe out of his lips. "Arabs, too?"

"Of course."

"Hm."

"It's a way of showing how strongly our government feels about saving Arab and Jewish lives."

The sheikh again blew smoke into the air. "I must give this some thought."

Overnight, it seemed to Raquela, concrete apartment houses rose from the sand. The town encroached upon the desert. New streets, new roads, new neighborhoods, new factories. A twentieth-century symphony of bulldozers and tractors and steam shovels pierced the desert air.

Each day new immigrants arrived—tailors from Tunisia, shoemakers from Algeria, shopkeepers from Morocco, cave dwellers from Libya, tradesmen from Egypt.

Great rivers of Jews began to pour home into the sea that was Israel.

From Yemen alone, fifty thousand came on the "eagles' wings" that Isaiah had prophesied; they were American planes.

Early in 1950 the entire Jewish community of Iraq—120,000 men, women, and children—fled from the hostile Arab land, still officially at war. Iraq had refused to sign an armistice agreement; now she ordered the Jews to get out within a year or be trapped forever. Among the refugees were financiers, doctors, railroad and telegraph workers. They were forced to leave everything they owned—property, jewelry, heirlooms—and permitted to take out only one suitcase of clothes. Even the rings on their fingers were torn off by Arab guards in the Bagdad airport.

From Rumania, legal ships brought legal refugees on legal routes from the Black Sea to Haifa—the same route the *Pan York* and the *Pan Crescent* had followed on their historic "illegal" voyage.

Eighty thousand came from Rumania. Others came from Hungary. From Czechoslovakia. From Bulgaria and Yugoslavia.

Each exodus was the biblical Exodus—out of Egypt, into the Promised Land—retold.

The Bible had said, "Gather yourselves together." Now, at last, they were being ingathered.

After the extermination of six million Jews, every life was valuable.

Israel became a pressure cooker, absorbing them all—Jews from Arab lands; Jews from the Western world; Sabras, like Raquela; and the two hundred thousand Arabs who had remained in Israel.

On a hot May morning the Bedouin family Raquela and Arik had visited in the desert made their way into the hospital courtyard. The sheikh settled three wives, a bevy of

children, and an assortment of livestock in a circle beneath
a palm tree and led his youngest wife, heavily veiled, into
the maternity building.

Raquela greeted the sheikh and his young wife, motioned them to chairs, and called out, "Monique, can you
come here."

A young woman in her late teens—her pink cheeks,
brown hair and white starched apron all freshly
scrubbed—entered the little admission office. Monique was
part of the Algerian exodus of Jews. Arabic had been her
mother tongue, and at the Alliance Israelite school in Al-
giers she had learned French and Hebrew; now she was
studying to be a nurse's aide.

"Monique," Raquela said, "please tell the sheikh that no
men, only women, will take care of his wife and deliver
his baby."

The sheikh nodded as Monique translated. "I leave her
in your hands," he said to Raquela. "May Allah watch
over her."

He left to rejoin his family in the courtyard.

Monique helped the young woman slip shyly out of her
long black gown and kept up a stream of soothing Arabic
as she turned on the shower in the little bathroom off the
tiny office.

Her face frozen with fear, the young woman followed
Monique into the delivery room. She stared at the white
leather delivery table and clutched her body tightly.
"What's that?" she cried out hysterically.

Raquela longed to put her arms around her, but she
feared even the touch of her hand might be misunder-
stood. She had never seen such panic in a delivery room.

"It's only a bed, a kind of hospital bed to make it easier
for me to help you have your baby."

"I'm not getting up on that thing." Her eyes darted
around the room. "Where's the pole?"

"She's asking about a pole," Monique said. "I don't
know what she's talking about."

The young woman had backed into a corner of the delivery room and crouched on her heels. Her childlike face
looked stricken.

She can't be more than fourteen, Raquela thought.

Monique sat on the floor beside her, talking quietly. The
terrified girl spoke between sobs.

Monique explained to Raquela. "She says when Bedouin

women have their babies, they hold on to the pole that goes through the center of the tent. She says they stay on their knees, and when the pains come, they push and push, but they keep holding on to the pole. She says she saw her mother deliver many times. She says that's the only way she's going to have her baby."

Raquela listened thoughtfully. Pictures she had seen in old textbooks of women in ancient China and of Eskimo women in igloos, kneeling to give birth, flashed through her mind.

"Tell her we know that kneeling is a natural way to give birth. Tell her she can kneel as long as she feels she wants to. But as soon as she wants me to help, then we will go to the table. I can't do much for her if she kneels; but on the delivery table I *can* help, and maybe the baby will come sooner."

The young woman barely heard.

"I want the pole." She tightened her arms around her swollen belly as if she were protecting her unborn child against the enemy.

A spasm of pain racked her body. She cried out, "Help me! Help me!"

"We will help you," Raquela said.

They lifted the young woman onto the delivery table. Raquela placed the stethoscope on her abdomen and listened to the baby's heartbeat. Then she checked the mother's heartbeat, pulse, and blood pressure and examined her internally.

"Tell her," she said to Monique, "she's almost ready. Tell her to push against me. Push. Push."

Raquela worked swiftly, skillfully. Suddenly the head, covered with straight black hair, emerged. She turned the shoulders and eased the baby down.

"The most beautiful baby girl in the world," she said, and then, as always, gently placed the baby on the mother's stomach.

The young woman opened terror-stricken eyes. "My husband wanted a son."

Raquela stopped working and looked at her for a moment. "I'm sure he'll love his new daughter."

The young woman turned her head away, sobbing.

Raquela finished the delivery and then went to find the sheikh in the courtyard. She beckoned him to come into her little office. Monique joined her as interpreter.

"You have a beautiful baby," she said.

"Allah be praised. A son?"

"You have been blessed with a healthy daughter."

He frowned. "I have too many daughters. What is wrong with my wives?"

Raquela swallowed hard. How could she help the young wife? She thought swiftly—a white lie would hurt no one. She spoke with authority. "So far as science knows, it's the seed of the husband that determines the sex of his child. If you have only daughters, then it must be something in *your* seed. But have no fear, I will not reveal your secret to anyone."

She paused. "Now I will take you in to see your wife and baby."

The sheikh gathered up his voluminous black gown and strode into the delivery room.

His young wife lay resting on the table with the baby in her arms. She saw him and instantly turned her frightened face to the wall.

He took the baby from her. "Allah be praised!" He kissed his infant daughter on the forehead.

Then he bent down and spoke to his wife. His voice was tender.

Her lips parted in a smile.

Raquela and Monique slipped quietly out of the room.

The Israel Philharmonic was performing in Beersheba.

Half the hospital staff arranged to attend. The orchestra was to play in the outdoor movie theater on the main street, opposite the Cassit Café.

Raquela and Arik left the hospital early in the afternoon to have dinner before the performance. Dressing for the desert night, Raquela wore a terra-cotta wool suit and the necklace of blue Hebron-glass beads Arik had bought her on their first walk through the Old City.

They walked arm in arm through the bustling streets toward Cassit. Little shops now lined the main street—dress shops, greengrocers, stationery stores, bookstores.

The restaurant had been enlarged and was nearly filled as the owner led them to a table in the rear.

"Let's celebrate and have some wine," Arik said.

"What are we celebrating?"

"Just being in love."

The waiter brought the wine. Arik lifted his glass. "To the lucky day on Scopus when we first met."

Raquela sipped her wine, looking across the table at Arik. Four years had passed since they'd first met. He had been the thread weaving through those years. He had been on Scopus, a shadowy backdrop in all the turmoil of her love affair with Carmi. In Cyprus, walking the ship with Gad, or kissing him in the snow-covered Troodos Mountains, she had never been able to drive Arik completely from her mind.

Now in these four months of intimacy in Beersheba, of nights of closeness and beauty in his bedroom in the villa, Arik had not once talked of a total commitment—of marriage. Why? She no longer believed his argument that he was too old for her. His lovemaking disproved it; he was as passionate as any young lover.

What was holding him back?

The waiter stood over them, reciting the menu. "*Humus . . . t'heena . . . felafel*"—Middle Eastern dishes—chick peas and sesame seeds ground with oil. They ordered *humus* with *pitta*. There was no meat; Israel was too poor to import beef and too young to produce it.

In minutes the waiter set the food before them.

"You're so quiet tonight, Raquela," Arik said.

She dipped her *pitta* into the *humus*.

"You're my *etze*-giver, Arik. I'm troubled. I need advice."

He straightened himself on the hard chair. "And what advice does my beautiful petitioner seek?"

"I had a dream last night. There I was, walking alone out into the desert. Walking—it seemed for hours and hours—on the sand. I was parched; my mouth felt stuffed with cotton wadding. Finally, far off, I saw the hot sun shining on a patch of water—the oasis. I began to run. I ran faster. I was ready to faint. But the oasis kept moving farther and farther back into the emptiness. I wanted to scream, but the scream choked soundlessly in my throat. I woke up in a sweat."

His eyes filled with sadness behind his glasses.

"One can never deny a dream, Raquela. Only the fears that cause it. I'm not drawing back from you."

"I've known you for four years, but I wonder if I really know you. You're a very complex man, Arik."

He fished a cigarette out of a pack. His hands trembled as he lit it.

Raquela kept searching his face. "There's some barrier between us, and I can't put my finger on it."

"Our ages—"

"It's deeper than that," she interrupted. "Even when I'm in your arms, I feel something dark—something unspoken—between us, and it scares me."

"But I've never been so completely in love." Anguish spread across his face.

"Are you sure? Completely?" She tried to stifle her doubts.

"With every cell in my body."

She shook her head.

Slowly he ground out his cigarette in an ashtray.

"You called me complex. All right, I am. Yes, I do have fears. The very things I love in you are the things I fear: your strength, your independence, your desirability."

"For God's sake, Arik, how can a man with *your* strength, *your* understanding of human nature, be scared off by"—she ticked them off her fingers—"by strength, independence, desirability?"

"I wish things could go on just the way they are now."

"You know they never can."

She leaned across the table and put her hand on his. "Do you still have doubts about me? After these last months in Beersheba? I'm over twenty-five. Don't you think I know what I want from a man?"

Around them people began to stand up.

"We'd better get to the concert," Arik said.

They crossed the street to the outdoor theater where Dov and Sarah waited for them. They took their seats together; the Hadassah staff filled the first three rows.

It was early evening. The raw frontier town was blanketed in a glow of orange and gold. Raquela tried to push the conflict out of her mind. The sun was setting; she watched the ball of flame drop abruptly out of the cobalt-blue sky. Night enveloped them as the musicians assembled on the improvised outdoor stage.

-*&Chapter Twenty-three &-

June 1950

"One-eight-one-nine-two-five!"

Raquela studied the rectangular disk hanging around her neck. She read her name, the number 181925, and her blood type engraved on two halves of the metal disk.

"Here," she called out. Her voice reverberated through the army warehouse stacked with clothing.

A young woman soldier shouted, "Over here, one-eight-one-nine-two-five. Sign the receipt."

Raquela leaned down on the warehouse table and signed for her gear—khaki shirt and jacket, khaki blouse, khaki beret, brown belt, brown sandals, pajamas, underwear, a duffel bag, and an aluminum mess kit.

She moved to the side of the warehouse to wait. Twenty-five Hadassah nurses smiled around the warehouse in Camp Tel Nof, an army training camp twenty miles south of Tel Aviv. Was it only a week since the notice had come from Hadassah in Jerusalem? "The army has requested every civilian hospital in the country to supply nurses. They've asked for twenty-five volunteers from our staff. Ages 21 to 25. URGENT!"

Raquela had read the notice carefully. In the war's aftermath, hundreds of young soldiers, blinded and burned and crippled, still filled the iron huts of Tel Hashomer, the military hospital outside Tel Aviv.

She leaned against Tel Nof's warehouse wall and shut her eyes. Her mind flashed back. She was in Arik's office in Beersheba. He was at his desk.

"Arik, the army has issued a call: they want nurses to volunteer to care for the soldiers."

He had stood up and come toward her. "You're not thinking of—?"

She nodded. "The soldiers need us, Arik. And since the

only way I can take care of them is by joining the army, I'm going to join."

His voice was strangled. "I know the army needs nurses, but . . ."

She didn't wait. She wanted to tell him her decision firmly, before she could change her mind. "Besides, if war breaks out again, it won't hurt me to have my training behind me. I can't get it staying in Hadassah and delivering babies."

He repeated slowly, "I know the army needs nurses, but so do we, Raquela. And so do I."

He came toward her and put his arms on her shoulders.

"It's a fine, patriotic thing you're doing, but that's not the only reason. You're leaving me. That's part of it; isn't it?"

Her eyes filled. "Yes, Arik."

"But these six months have been so beautiful."

She tried to keep her voice calm. "They have, Arik. But I can't go on—not on your terms."

Around her in the army warehouse the nurses were gathering up their gear. But she heard nothing. Her mind was still replaying the scene in Arik's office.

He'd returned to his desk and put his head in his hands.

"I have *etzes* for everybody except myself," he said. "I can't throw off my fears."

He lifted his head to her. His face was distraught.

"Oh, God, I love you so, but I feel it so clearly: some morning you'll wake up and see, next to you on the pillow, the face of an old man. And—I don't blame you— you might run into another man's arms. And I would die."

"It's no use, Arik. I can't deal with your fears."

She moved toward the door. "The longer we go on, the more we'll hurt each other."

In the warehouse, she felt again her desire for him and her frustration. Had she made the right decision? She felt an emptiness already.

She heard a voice snap: "Come on. Get moving. You nurses sure take your time." A young noncom with two diagonal stripes on her right sleeve tried to speed the line along. She was small, with a round baby face and huge black eyes. Her dark hair was cut short and straight.

"Call me Miriam," she said, bristling. "I'm the corporal in charge of your unit, and I can see I'm going to have a lot of trouble with you."

The tough voice coming from the baby face brought giggles from the nurses.

"What's funny?" she demanded. "Come on. Stuff your gear into your duffel bags and follow me to your barracks. Get moving. On the double."

The twenty-five nurses dragged their heavy khaki bags down one of the dirt paths that separated the rows of Nissen huts in the army compound

Inside their barracks, Raquela and Naomi Samueloff, a friend from Bet Hakerem who had enlisted with her, selected two empty cots. They tossed their kits on the foot of the bed and sprawled out.

"I'm bushed," Naomi said, and put her hands behind her head. She was strikingly handsome, with porcelain-blue eyes, ash-blond hair, and a finely carved face. Three years younger than Raquela, she had fled Hitler's Germany with her parents in 1939, studied nursing at Hadassah, and spent six months on Mount Scopus, after the convoy massacre, nursing patients too sick to be moved.

The barracks hummed with the voices of the nurses. They knew one another from Jerusalem, and were now busy catching up on news of their families and friends.

The corporal shouted, *"Sheket!"* Silence.

The nurses paid no attention.

"Sheket," I said. "Now, all of you get right into your uniforms. This minute."

"Where are we supposed to hang our clothes?" Raquela asked. She looked at the arched iron walls.

"Stick them in your duffel bags."

"And what do we do with the duffel bag?"

"You roll that up every morning and put it at the head of your bed—for inspection."

The nurses changed into uniform.

"Crazy. Absolutely crazy," a surgical nurse complained. "Experienced nurses like us taking orders from that kid."

"She looks like my twelve-year-old sister," a nurse from Neurology griped. "I'd like to hit her across the mouth."

"Get cracking," Miriam commanded.

A tall pediatric nurse talked up to the little corporal. "Who do you think you're talking to? We've been serving our country since before Israel became a state. What are you giving us this nonsense for?"

Miriam pulled herself up to her full five feet. She

addressed the whole room: "You will all report in six minutes to the parade ground!"

On the parade ground the nurses were ordered into formation, the twenty-five from Hadassah and the fifty from other hospitals around the country.

The nurses were volunteers; lining up beside them were eighteen-year-old women who'd been drafted. Raquela looked at them as they marched uncertainly to their places.

It's a new Israel, she thought, *a mosaic of fair-skinned, olive-skinned, black-skinned young women.*

"Look at these kids," she whispered to Naomi. "I feel like ancient history. At twenty-five I'm probably the oldest rookie in the whole army."

"Sheket!" Miriam commanded.

She walked through the three-deep lines of formation, pushing bodies into alignment. "Straighten your lines. Pull in your gut!"

Raquela stiffened her back and faced forward.

In front of the parade ground was a small wooden platform with three flags—the flag of Israel, the flag of the army, and the flag of CHEN. CHEN was an acronym for *Chail ha-Nashim*,—the Women's Army—and a play on the word "charm."

A mature woman colonel, flanked on each side by a captain, marched down the parade ground, climbed the small platform, and saluted.

A lieutenant standing below the platform addressed her: "Company ready for inspection."

The colonel and her two captains descended the platform; accompanied by the lieutenant, they moved through the ranks, inspecting the rigid lines.

Raquela recognized the colonel from Jerusalem; she had served in the ATS in Egypt during World War II. The colonel gave no sign that she recognized Raquela or any of the Jerusalem nurses. Her back straight, her face controlled, her inspection completed, she returned with her junior officers to the platform. "At ease!" the lieutenant blared out. Up and down the ranks the young recruits and the seventy-five nurses placed their hands behind their backs and waited.

The colonel's voice rang across the parade ground. "Welcome! You have just become part of CHEN. You are now soldiers in the Army of Israel. We know you will make us proud of you."

Soon the brief speech was over. The colonel saluted smartly and left the parade ground.

Miriam corralled her unit of twenty-five nurses and marched them back to the warehouse to pick up sheets and blankets.

In the barracks, the young corporal shouted, "Attention! I'm going to show you nurses how to prepare an army cot for morning inspection."

One of the nurses snickered, "Listen, kid, you're wasting time. We can make beds in our sleep."

"You'll make beds our way." The young woman turned red. "Now, watch me." She demonstrated tightening the sheets under the army mattress. She took a coin and bounced it on the taut sheet. She glared at the nurses.

They watched her in frozen silence.

"Now, for the blanket. It'll take two of you to fold blankets the army way." She handed one end of a blanket to a nurse and, with a complicated series of stretching and folding, produced a small square. She placed it at the head of a cot, picked up a duffel bag and set it on top of the folded blanket.

"Forget everything you've learned in your hospitals. This is the way *I* want the beds to look."

"Are you for real? Are you running some kind of a kindergarten here?" one of the nurses grumbled.

The corporal shot back, "You've got seven minutes to make these cots. Then you will be outside in front of the barracks with your mess kits, ready for lunch."

She turned on her heels and marched out.

One by one the nurses straggled out of the barracks, holding their aluminum kits. The noon sun beat down upon the rows of barracks and the dirt paths.

"Who needs lunch?" said the last nurse to emerge, mopping her forehead. "I'd like to flop down on my tight army sheet and go to sleep. I've been up since the crack of dawn. It's enough already."

Miriam looked at her wristwatch. "You call this seven minutes? You're three minutes late!" She barked between clenched teeth, "All of you run around the parade ground. You will do it in seven minutes. Then you'll know when I say seven minutes, I mean seven minutes!"

The nurses paced themselves as they trotted around the

parade ground. Finally, panting and exhausted, they entered the mess hall. Then, standing in line, they held out their mess kits. Young soldiers shoveled in mashed potatoes, peas, chicken floating in gravy, and a thick slice of rye bread. The nurses sat down at the two tables assigned to them. The eighteen-year-olds filled another area of the mess hall.

Miriam approached. "You'll find sinks behind this building. After each meal you wash your mess kits, and they'd better shine like new. Now you've got one hour to rest. At fourteen hundred hours, mess kits and beds will be inspected."

At the stroke of two the young corporal returned to the barracks. She headed for Raquela's bed. "A potato sack has more shape," she said, glaring at Raquela.

She began walking up and down the center aisle. "Okay. Looks as if you're learning. Outside now. Into formation."

She marched them across the compound to a lecture hall. They sank down on the floor with the eighteen-year-old recruits.

A scholarly-looking woman in her mid-thirties, the three gold bars of a captain prominently displayed on her shoulders, addressed them. Her brown hair was parted in the middle, with broad streaks of gray on each side.

On the wall behind her hung a huge color map of Israel. She lifted a pointer from a table, turned to the map, and pointed to the states surrounding Israel. "Here is Egypt, on our west and south; on the east, Jordan; on the north, Lebanon and Syria. You see how close they are to us. These are the countries that declared war on us and were defeated. Now they're licking their wounds; how soon they will feel ready to attack again, I cannot say. All I can say is, we have to be prepared. If we want to survive, we have to be prepared for any attack."

She stopped, letting her words sink in.

"Now, look at our borders." Her pointer traced the narrow elongated contour of Israel. "We have 594 miles of border to be defended. And here, right in the center, we're just ten miles across. We've got the smallest waistline in the world. Like an hourglass figure." A few recruits laughed. She acknowledged the laughter and went on. "It's our most heavily populated area. Within a few hours, an invading army could slice us in half. Like this." She ripped her pointer across the center of the map.

The nurses and recruits followed her pointer, absorbing her words.

"If we could have a regular standing army—like most countries—we'd be in good shape. But we can't afford it. That's why we have universal conscription. That's why every boy and girl of eighteen is drafted. That's why you're here."

Raquela looked again at the mosaic of young women emerging from adolescence and innocence to face the brutal reality of survival.

The nurses, she thought, were older, more mature; many had been in the War of Independence. They had lived with violence and the ravages of war. She had stopped listening for a few minutes. Now she forced her mind back to the captain who was looking directly at the eighteen-year-olds.

"You recruits will begin your eighteen-month tour of duty with three months' basic training. Then you'll be assigned according to your ability. Some of you will go into communications, as radio and wireless operators. Some into meteorology, some to work at radar stations. You can pack parachutes or you can become paratroopers. You can be secretaries and clerks in military installations. Some of you will teach newcomers who have not yet learned to speak Hebrew. And some will make officer-candidate school."

She paused. "Now we have a special group among us." She looked down at the seventy-five nurses sitting together.

"You nurses will do three weeks of basic training. You'll become second lieutenants and begin work in the military hospitals immediately. You're probably wondering why you need any kind of basic training, since you're already nurses."

They nodded vigorously.

"It's to give you even greater stamina, endurance, and discipline." She smiled at them. "You'll be hearing these words a lot during the next weeks. It's to teach you the *army* way."

She lay her pointer on a table.

"We don't expect women to serve in the front lines—if war comes. But even in peace, every soldier must learn how to use a gun. Tomorrow you'll be issued rifles."

They returned to the barracks, and by the end of the first day they collapsed in silence in their beds.

At five-thirty the next morning the sound of reveille over the loud-speaker shattered the dawn silence of the campground.

The nurses crawled out of bed, dressed, and marched outside. Miriam was waiting. "Setting-up exercises," she shouted.

They stretched, touched their toes, did deep knee bends. They breakfasted at six, and at seven stood at attention for bed inspection. At seven-thirty they assembled on the parade ground for inspection of their uniforms.

A top sergeant reviewed the nurses and recruits.

"You there." She singled out Raquela's friend, Naomi. "Where's your beret?"

Naomi lowered her blue eyes. "Sorry. I forgot it in my bunk."

"Forgot it! You do five laps around the parade ground."

Embarrassed, Naomi circled the field, her head down. The morning was still cool.

The sergeant counted off the laps. "Now get your beret, and make sure your hair is properly tucked in."

At eight classes began. At ten Miriam issued the rifles.

In the next days Raquela and Naomi, accustomed to shooting needles into arms and buttocks, learned to shoot rifles into cardboard figures.

A week passed. At daybreak Miriam marched her nurses, carrying their packs and rifles, out of the campground. Behind them came a unit of eighteen-year-olds led by their noncom.

All morning they hiked across the fields surrounding Tel Nof. They crawled on their stomachs. Their feet blistered. Their joints creaked. Their muscles cramped. Insect bites inflamed their faces and bare legs.

A noon Miriam called a halt.

"Twenty minutes to eat, rest, and relieve yourselves," she commanded. "Find your own bush."

Raquela and Naomi dropped their heavy packs and rifles.

The twenty minutes evaporated; the nurses and recruits gulped their food and took long drafts of water from their canteens.

"On your feet, everybody," Miriam shouted to her nurses.

The march continued. The sun rode the sky and set slowly. Still they marched. It was nine o'clock and pitch dark when they bivouacked in an orange grove. They drew lots for sentry duty. Raquela and Naomi stood guard the first four hours while the others slept.

At one in the morning they woke the second shift of sentries. Raquela unrolled her blanket and in seconds was fast asleep.

At dawn Miriam prodded them awake. They ate their field rations, marched all day, and late in the afternoon, straggled back limply, mindlessly, to Camp Tel Nof.

Raquela tore off her crumpled uniform and showered away the dirt and sand and sweat.

The nurses ate dinner in the mess hall and then fell into their cots.

Raquela could not sleep.

Overtired, her mind played tricks; she was back in the Yellin Seminar, terrified, listening to the stories of the Arabs' murdering in Motza, in Hebron; it was snowing, and she was entering the nursing school, caring for Henrietta Szold; now Athlit, Cyprus, Hadassah A, Beersheeba, began to spin in her brain. She was running again . . . the desert . . . Arik.

Why had she left him? Why had she demanded that their love be on her terms, not his?

Her limbs ached, and in the cocoon of the iron hut, surrounded by the other exhausted nurses, even her mind seemed to ache as she painfully recalled the past week.

Again she was back in Beersheba, lying in bed in the nurses' cottage, trying to understand Arik, asking herself, *Why doesn't he trust me? How can he even imagine I would look at another man now that we've slept together?*

Somewhere in the darkened hut, someone sighed. She could hear a few women turning on their cots, breathing heavily. She lay uncovered; night brought no respite from the June heat.

She closed her eyes.

Arik was beside her in the army hut; she felt him caressing her sore limbs, healing her.

Arik the doctor. Arik the healer. Arik the lover.

She saw his face. *I know the army needs nurses like you. But so do we . . . and so do I.*

She could feel his body against hers. Her heart pounded. What was she doing here? Why wasn't she in Beersheba, holding him close, listening to him tell her, "You're the most desirable creature in the universe."

She sat up suddenly in bed. *The things I love in you are the things I fear.* Is it possible he sees me as so desirable he can't believe I'm ready to stay with him forever? He, of all people—so secure as a doctor, so sure of himself as a man. How can he be so insecure about me?

Loss.

That's what he's afraid of. Afraid of losing something he loves.

The end of the second week, Raquela, felled by a stomach virus, was sent to the infirmary.

She woke in the afternoon and found Miriam sitting beside the hospital bed. She looked at her in surprise. "You've come to visit me?" she asked the young corporal.

"Why not?"

"We seem unable to do anything right in your eyes."

"You nurses were pretty arrogant."

"So you tried to break us. Was that it?"

"That's my job."

"But why? We're all in here for the same reason. You seemed to be tougher on us than the other noncoms."

"I had my reasons. You nurses acted so superior. Our army takes all of us—no matter what our background, no matter what our education, no matter what countries we came from—and makes us all equal."

Raquela studied Miriam's earnest face.

"Do you know what the army did for me? Do you know where I come from, Raquela?"

Raquela sat up. It was the first time Miriam had called her by name.

"I don't know anything about you. I'd like to know."

"I was born in the Atlas Mountains, north of the Sahara Desert, in Morocco. We lived in a cave—my parents, my twelve brothers and sisters, and I. We came here during the War of Independence. I was seventeen. I had never been to school. I went to school and in one year had learned enough so I could join the army. Now, here I am, nineteen, only two years in Israel, and I'm a corporal. And I can give orders. . . . Where are you from, Raquela?"

"Jerusalem."

"A Sabra?"

Raquela nodded.

Miriam was thoughtful. "I often wonder if a Sabra like you can understand where I come from, what it means. You and I would never have met; it's the army that brings us together. You're as strange to me as I am to you. I don't know what your life was like in Jerusalem any more than you can know what it was like to live lower than the lowest Arab in an Arab land."

"But I think I do understand," Raquela protested. "I've delivered the babies not only of Arabs but also of Jewish women from Arab countries."

"But did you ever march and eat and sleep with girls from Morocco the way you did the nights we've bivouacked? Did you ever live so closely with girls from Tunis? From Algeria? From Libya? From Yemen? From Ethiopia and Afghanistan and Cochin, India?"

Raquela shook her head.

"This is what it means to be in the Israeli army. This is what our army does. They took my brothers, all illiterate, and taught them to read and gave them each a vocation they can use when they get out. They took Jews like the Yemenites, who weren't allowed to ride camels because their heads would be higher than an Arab's. They took Jewish girls like me who weren't even second- or third- or fourth-class citizens and made us first-class citizens."

For the first time Raquela felt close to Miriam; they belonged together—she and the young corporal. The army was bringing them together.

Miriam's huge eyes focused on Raquela. "Now maybe you'll understand why I act the way I do. I want to be the best soldier in CHEN. Someday I hope to have children. Because of what the army did for me, I'll be able to give them everything I learned here—and more. The things my father could never have given me if we had stayed in Morocco."

A week later, the course was over. Miriam stood proudly as her nurses received their second lieutenant's bars.

"Good-bye, Raquela." Miriam looked up at Raquela's face. "May a corporal kiss a second lieutenant?" she asked.

Raquela and Naomi strolled through Tel Hashomer's hospital complex outside Tel Aviv. Soldiers in hospital robes sat in wheelchairs lined up in front of an iron Nissen hut. Between the hospital huts, men hobbled on crutches; some walked with canes; others struggled painfully with new limbs. A group of young men, sitting together, lifted their sightless eyes to let in the morning sun.

Dressed in khaki uniforms with the gold bar of a second lieutenant on their shoulders, Raquela and Naomi made their way toward the administration building to report for duty. They were assigned to Rehabilitation.

They changed into white uniforms and entered the ward. Soldiers lay on beds, legs up in traction, arms swathed in bandages.

A soldier whistled. "Wow! Look at these two new birds."

Every soldier who could move sat up. Long low whistles sang through the room.

"Life's looking a lot better," a soldier called out. "Pinch me. Am I dreaming?"

"Okay, guys," Raquela said, smiling broadly. Pregnant mothers had never greeted her this way. "You're not dreaming."

Naomi looked around. "How you doing, fellows?"

Two young men in traction answered, together, "Great, since you came."

"You both sound pretty cheerful." Naomi walked between the two beds; wire pulleys elevated the soldiers' legs encased in white plaster.

"We'd better be cheerful," one of the young men answered. "We want to get out of here fast." He pointed to a calendar on his nightstand. "By the time I've torn off thirty more pages, I'll be home." The calendar page read JULY 1, 1950.

Naomi turned to the second soldier in traction.

"You've got a whole art gallery pasted on your wall." She looked at the posters, cartoons, photos. "Who did these drawings?"

"My three-year-old daughter. My wife brings her every day."

Naomi fixed his sheet. "I can imagine that homecoming."

Raquela was walking through the ward, exchanging

pleasantries, when a young man deliberately turned his face away from her. She read his name on the chart at the foot of his bed. He was a quadriplegic.

"Can I do something for you, Aviad?" she asked.

"Nobody can."

In the next days Raquela sought ways to make Aviad comfortable, gently lifting the paralyzed arms and legs as she changed his sheets and pajamas. He lay silent, a dead weight, neither thanking her nor protesting.

His mother came to help the nurses; she spoon-fed him, her eyes red-rimmed. She tried to talk to him, but he rarely answered.

One morning he called out, "Nurse, will you come here, please."

"Yes, Aviad?" Raquela asked.

"My girlfriend is coming this afternoon for the first time. I want to be dressed."

"Avi—" Raquela began, then cut herself short. "Of course I'll dress you."

She left the ward and returned with a new white t-shirt and khaki pants. His mother helped her draw the clothes on his wasted limbs.

Excitement flushed his pale face. "Do you think I could sit up in a wheelchair?" he asked.

"Let's try."

Raquela brought in a wheelchair and lifted him into it. But his head—the only part of his body that moved—collapsed on his chest.

"I'll get a neck brace," Raquela said matter-of-factly, trying to control the quiver in her voice.

She whispered to his mother, "Keep holding his head up. I'll be right back."

She raced through the hospital compound to the supply room, found a high leather collar, and began fitting it around Aviad's neck. His mother turned her head to hide her tears.

Aviad looked at the soldiers watching him in the ward.

"Hi, fellows. How do I look?"

Raquela, still arranging the neck brace, heard a familiar voice say, "You look just fine."

Her heart stopped beating. She clutched the back of the wheelchair to steady herself.

She looked toward the door. It was Arik.

* * *

They walked through the hospital grounds.

"You were right, Raquela, to leave me. It made me realize that whatever years I have, I want to spend with you."

"No more fears? No more doubts?"

"I want to marry you, Raquela."

She walked beside him in silence.

"You're not saying anything. Have you—have you met someone else in these past weeks?"

"For Heaven's sake, Arik. Where? In boot camp? In the rehab ward?"

Arik put his arms around her. "Don't be angry if an old man still can't believe you could be in love with him."

"Arik, I've missed you terribly."

"Then let's get married. Let's not wait."

"I can't now, Arik. I'm committed to the army."

"How long do you think the army will need you?"

"I have no idea."

"You know, the shortage at Hadassah is worse than ever. Especially in your department. With thousands of refugees still coming in and with war babies, your maternity ward is exploding."

They found a shaded bench and sat down. "Did you know," he said, "that the Knesset has just passed the 'Law of the Return'? Any Jew from any country in the world is free to come to Israel to live, whether he is strong or maimed, blind or sighted, rich or poor. So, you see, these new citizens need you, too."

He stopped suddenly. "Maybe Hadassah could convince the army to release you, convince them we need your skill as a midwife."

"Does Hadassah have that much influence with the army?"

"We can ask."

He took her in his arms. "If we succeed in getting you transferred, will you marry me?"

She put her head on his shoulder and whispered, "Yes, Arik."

She looked up at his face; he seemed to her the essence of goodness, a *mensch,* a warm, decent, honest human being.

"Oh, Arik, I love you so. I'm the happiest woman in the world."

He held her face in his hands. "My darling," he whispered.

She returned his kiss, oblivious of the soldiers watching them embrace.

-->‡ Chapter Twenty-four ‡<--

August 1950

Turning on her stockinged feet, Raquela examined herself
in the long mirror, carefully buttoning the white linen suit
softened with a pretty eyelet-embroidered collar and cuffs.
She stepped into white low-heeled pumps, and then, holding the gossamer bridal veil as though it were a fragile
newborn, she draped it over her head and shoulders.

She moved closer to the mirror; even through the veil,
she could see her lips parted with anticipation, her eyes radiant.

Then she stepped away from the mirror and glanced
around the unfamiliar bedroom, the home of Sophia and
Leon Lustig, Arik's childhood friends from Poland. Rather
than a huge wedding in Jerusalem, she and Arik had
agreed on a small intimate ceremony the moment the
army, acquiescing to Hadassah's request, had released her.
A few days later the Lustigs had offered their cottage in
the picturesque seacoast town of Nahariya, on the
northernmost border of Israel.

Sophia Lustig, a small vivacious woman with wide green
eyes, entered the bedroom. "For the beautiful bride." She
handed Raquela a corsage of pink roses she had picked
from her bushes and tied with white satin ribbon.

Raquela lifted the veil and pressed her face into the
bouquet. She inhaled the fragrance. "It's so good," she
said. "It's got to be good. It's the twenty-ninth. Twenty-
nine is my lucky number."

"Any day would be a lucky day, marrying Arik," Sophia said. "I've loved him since I was a little girl. But I've
never seen him like he is today. You've made him very
happy, Raquela. And for this, I too will always love you."

She stood on her toes to kiss Raquela. "Now, come,
they're waiting."

Raquela walked through the living room into the garden, her heart pounding. She saw four men holding wooden poles, raising a velvet canopy under the noon sky—her three brothers, Jacob, Yair, and her adopted brother Itzhak; the fourth man was their host, Leon Lustig. And waiting for them under the canopy, dressed in a black robe with a white prayer shawl, was the rabbi, who had come, like most of the people in Nahariya, from Hitler's Germany.

She saw Arik, standing with his mother and father and sister, his face transfigured with joy and fervor. She hoped he could see her through the veil, see her own joy. Even her throat seemed to be throbbing.

The ceremony began.

Arik walked down the garden path, escorted by his mother and father, to the border of the canopy.

Raquela came next, walking between Mama and Papa, her eyes fixed on Arik. He stepped forward and led her under the canopy, facing the rabbi.

The garden smelled of pomegranates and figs and mandarins, their heavily laden branches shading the canopy and the little circle of sixteen wedding guests. Birds darted through the trees. Raquela breathed in the perfumed air. *My whole life*, she thought, *has led to this day*.

She stood at Arik's side, listening to the rabbi intone, "May He Who is supreme power, blessing and glory, bless this bridegroom and bride."

The rabbi sanctified the wine and handed the glass to Arik, who drank a few drops. Arik lifted Raquela's veil and put the glass to her lips, and she sipped one or two drops. She wanted to listen, to drink in the meaning and the poetry of the ceremony. The rabbi continued: "The sanctification of all great moments in Jewish life is symbolized by the drinking of the wine. As you share the wine of this cup, may you share all things from this day on with love and understanding."

Raquela nodded. For the rest of her life she would give Arik all her understanding, and love such as she had never felt, never given anyone before.

Arik was slipping the gold ring on her finger. "By this ring you are consecrated to me as my wife in accordance with the law of Moses and the people, Israel."

Her hand trembled; the ring belonged. Now, gently, she

placed the gold band on his finger, "a symbol that you are my husband and a sign of my love and devotion."

From the Song of Songs, she quoted, looking at his face, suffused with love, "I am to my beloved and my beloved is to me."

The rabbi held up a scrolled *k'tuba*, the marriage certificate. "This is to certify that on this day, August twenty-ninth, 1950, Aron Brzezinski and Raquela Levy have entered the holy covenant of marriage."

Arik repeated after him, "Be thou my wife according to the law of Moses. I faithfully promise that I will be a true husband unto thee and I will honor and cherish thee."

"And I," Raquela promised, her eyes shining, "plight my troth unto thee in affection and in sincerity."

Once more the rabbi gave them the wine he had sanctified. "I pronounce you husband and wife. May the Lord bless you and keep you and cause His countenance to shine upon you and bring you peace."

The rabbi now placed the empty wineglass on the grass. Arik crushed it under his heel. It was a symbol. The breaking of the glass was to remind them, even on this day of greatest joy, of the destruction of the temple in Jerusalem in the year 70 A.D.

"*Mazal tov! Mazal tov!*" the wedding party shouted.

Under the canopy, Arik kissed his bride. Mama and Papa and Arik's parents kissed the bride and groom.

Jacob embraced her. "My baby sister," he said, and smiled.

By six in the evening the wedding guests had departed. Raquela and Arik were driven inland past Nazareth to Megiddo, overlooking the Jezreel Valley. They checked into a small hotel with a bedroom overlooking a green fertile field.

Arik opened the windows. The night air carried the sweet smell of orchards. He sat in a chair watching Raquela slip a blue-silk nightgown over her head; the pale-blue straps and ecru lace bodice made her skin glow.

He spoke softly. "I want to remember this night as long as I live."

"We both will, Arik. All our lives. Forever."

He kissed her shoulders, drew aside the blue-silk straps, and kissed her throat. He led her into bed and kissed her face, her body.

"My husband, my love."

They drew together.

The room, the hotel, the world dropped away. She was somewhere, beyond gravity, in space, whirling among the stars.

The next afternoon, they climbed the mound of Megiddo, exploring the site where archaeologists had uncovered twenty layers of civilization, of a people who had lived here from 4000 to 400 B.C. Megiddo was the famous battlefield across which ancient armies had fought for this land, the doorway to the fertile soil of the great Jezreel Valley.

The late-afternoon sun turned the ruins fiery red as they circled Megiddo's protective dirt walls, prowling around the palace, the Canaanite temple, the royal stables where King Solomon had built a garrison for hundreds of horses and chariots. They looked down into waterproof silos within whose walls of rock the people had stored their grain. But in the end it was the water tunnel that fascinated them the most. They descended countless circular steps to a pool of water; ancient engineers had built a sophisticated tunnel into the hill and brought water from a spring in the plains to the garrison.

"Everything they did," Arik said, "was in preparation for defending themselves, for holding out in case they were besieged by their enemies."

"Like us," she said, looking down at the dark water, but thinking of Jerusalem.

Arik nodded. "It's as if our whole history were laid out before us on a table. The armies marching, war after war, the endless battles for this land. I guess that's why the New Testament changed the name Har Megiddo to Armageddon."

"Even the name sounds terrifying—'*Armageddon.*' " She repeated the word slowly. "I know some people believe the world will end here and all who survive will come to live in Jerusalem, right on Mount Zion."

"Well, I'm sure, darling," he laughed, "if it happens, you'll be there in Jerusalem to greet them."

They climbed back up the circular stairs to the perimeter of the huge excavation. The sun was setting as they started back to the hotel.

"Looking at four thousand years of our history," Arik

said softly, as though he were thinking aloud, "makes you realize how short, how frighteningly short, our life is."

He picked up a loose stone, shook off the dirt, and put it in his pocket.

"I've such a sense of urgency, Raquela. Today especially. Megiddo, our Jewish past, our own lives, compressed—one day in history."

He put his arm around her waist. "I want to make every minute with you count. And I want a house full of children."

She laughed. "How many do you see, my prophet? A dozen?"

"I'm serious. I'll die before you."

"Arik, why always thinking of death? You're in the prime of life. Even a twenty-year-old lover could take lessons from you."

He kissed her. "Thank you, my love. From this day on, at your service, madam, night or day."

They moved into a three-room apartment at 18 Palmach Street in Jerusalem. It was a quiet hilly street not far from the jewel-like Monastery of the Cross, built on the ancient site where the tree that supplied the wood for the cross was said to have stood. It was surrounded by olive groves in a lovely garden.

Hadassah had made the sunny apartment available to them; their neighbors were mostly other doctors married to nurses. Raquela furnished the apartment simply, following her own strong sense of color and warmth. There was little furniture in the shops, but she soon found a sofa bed and a table and chairs for the living-dining room. She hung white curtains in the bedroom and covered the bed with a multicolored knitted afghan she had made.

After their week's honeymoon in Megiddo, they both resumed their work in Hadassah. Each Tuesday, they drove down to the rapidly expanding Hadassah hospital in the desert. Every Jerusalem specialist gave time to the new immigrants and Bedouin Arabs in the Beersheba Hospital; the most difficult gynecological cases were saved for Arik's weekly visits.

For Raquela, it was a time of fusing her life with his. They were partners, sharing everything, mutually respecting each other's strengths and skills, happiest when they were together, resenting the hours that separated them.

They left for work together in the morning, took a bus to the hospital on the Street of the Prophets, looked in on each other whenever they could; at lunchtime, if they were free, they crossed the street to eat a rationed lunch at the Patt Bakery, and late in the afternoon they went home together to a light supper of rationed vegetables, two eggs a week, and bread.

Food was as scarce as it had been during the War of Independence. The two-year-old country, faced with the dilemma of more immigrants or more food, had opted for immigrants.

Tzena was the answer: rigid, planned, uncompromising austerity.

The new immigrants rushed home to Israel through the open doors, and the populace shared its meager rations with them. They stood in long queues with ration cards, and, in time-honored fashion, they made jokes out of hunger and adversity.

Carp became Raquela's staple. All over the country, farmers were digging and stocking live-carp ponds, especially in the kibbutzim and in the Huleh Valley, in the Galilee. Raquela learned to cook carp, bake it, fry it, steam it, broil it. She never knew, when she visited friends, whether she would see a live carp swimming in the bathtub, waiting to be beheaded and chopped up for Friday night's delicacy—*gefilte fish*.

Carp was nutritious, and carp was filling. Even with austerity and pangs of hunger, one could survive. *More immigrants or more food*.

The telephone rang in Arik's office in Beersheba.

Raquela answered the phone. A frightened voice spoke.

"This is Revivim."

"What?" she shouted into the phone. "Speak up. I can't hear you."

"I'm calling from Kibbutz Revivim. Do you hear me now?"

"Yes. Speak up, please."

The voice was urgent. "One of our pregnant women is very sick. She's in the sixth month. We have no doctor here."

Raquela put Arik on the phone.

"What are her symptoms?" he asked.

"Her body is shaking all over; her lips are blue. We think she's having convulsions."

"What kind of transportation do you have?"

"A farm truck."

"Get her in the truck and start toward the hospital. I'll leave this minute and meet you along the road. Watch for us; we'll be in a white ambulance."

Raquela jumped into the ambulance with Arik and the driver. The wheels churned up a cloud of sand and dust on the dirt highway. Kibbutz Revivim lay thirty miles south of Beersheba. Midway, they spotted the truck coming toward them. The truck and the ambulance pulled over to the side of the road.

The men lifted an unconscious young woman out of the truck, placed her on a stretcher, and carried her into the ambulance. They set off immediately for the hospital. The husband, a handsome young Yemenite, followed in the truck.

Inside the ambulance Arik examined the pregnant woman. His face was grave.

"It's eclampsia," he whispered to Raquela.

Eclampsia: the dread toxemia of pregnancy.

At the hospital the young woman was wheeled up the ramp.

Arik telephoned Hadassah Hospital in Jerusalem to consult the renowned gynecologist Dr. Bernhard Zondek. They decided only an operation could save her life. Arik operated.

Raquela went to the waiting room and found the young husband hunched over with anxiety.

"How is my wife? Can I see her now?"

"I'm sorry. Not yet. She's very ill."

"And my baby?"

Raquela put her hand out to comfort him. "The baby is dead."

His face was contorted with grief. "My baby—dead?"

Tears welled in his eyes. "Will my wife be all right?"

"If anyone can save her, it's Dr. Brzezinski. You have the best gynecologist in the country."

"Can I telephone her mother from here?"

"Of course. I'll take you to the doctor's office; you can use his phone."

Raquela heard him ask the operator, "I'd like to call

Jerusalem. The Ministry of Labor. I want to speak to Mrs. Golda Meir."

Raquela hurried out of the office—to give the young man privacy, and to tell Arik the young woman was Golda Meir's only daughter, Sarah.

Two hours later Raquela was called to the waiting room. Golda Meir had rushed down from Jerusalem.

"How is my daughter?"

Raquela's eyes fixed on the strong, commanding face she had last seen in Cyprus. Now it was the face of a distraught mother. Her son-in-law, Zecharia Rehabi, stood beside her.

"Tell me the truth. Will she live?"

"It's touch and go, Mrs. Meir. Dr. Brzezinski is with her. He hasn't left since the operation."

"Can I see her?"

"No one can see her. She's too critically ill."

Golda dropped into a chair in the waiting room and lit a cigarette.

"Would you like to rest, Mrs. Meir? Would you like to use one of the nurses' rooms. There's no hotel in Beersheba."

"Thank you. I'm all right here. When can I see Dr. Brzezinski?"

"I'll tell him you're here."

Arik entered the waiting room.

"How is she, Doctor?"

Arik's eyes were bloodshot with fatigue; his compassionate face was lined. "Mrs. Meir, you have a very sick daughter. We're doing everything we can to save her."

"What are Sarele's chances?"

"We won't know for a while."

"Please, doctor—don't give me double-talk."

His face grew solemn. "Her chances are not very good."

She turned to her son-in-law, sitting beside her. "I'm going to wait up all night."

"We will wait together, Mother," he said.

Raquela telephoned Hadassah in Jerusalem to cancel Arik's and her schedules. All night Golda sat, smoking cigarettes, keeping vigil. At intervals Arik and Raquela came to report. No change.

In the morning Raquela took Golda and Zechariah across the street to the staff dining room for breakfast. The desert air was transparent, the sky immaculately blue.

In the hospital courtyard Raquela suggested they sit on a bench in the morning sun. Golda sat on a stone bench, watching a Bedouin family encamped with their children and some goats, but her eyes kept returning to the small yellow stucco building where her daughter lay unconscious, hovering between life and death.

The reports continued. No change.

The second day passed. No change.

Golda's face was pinched with worry. She clung to any shred of hope Raquela could bring from her daughter's room.

The third day. The fourth. Golda hardly moved from the bench, weeping unashamedly.

The fifth day.

Still no change. Neither she nor Zechariah was allowed to see Sarah.

On the seventh day Sarah moved her eyelids, opened her eyes. "Where am I?" she asked.

"You're going to be all right," Arik said. "You're in the hospital in Beersheba. And you're going to be fine."

Raquela raced into the courtyard to tell Golda and Zechariah.

Back in Jerusalem, Raquela saw the hospital filling up again with victims of Arab terrorist attacks.

Infiltrators crossed the borders, laid mines on the roads, planted explosives, tossed hand grenades. Schools were a favorite target.

Prime Minister David Ben-Gurion announced that he was ready to sit down, face-to-face, anytime, anyplace, to talk peace with the Arabs.

They refused. The Arab states openly prepared for a second round.

Only King Abdullah of Jordan dared to talk peace.

And for this he paid with his life. On July 20, 1951, as he was leaving the silver-domed el-Aksa Mosque, in the Old City, with his young grandson, Prince Hussein, he was shot down by a relative of his hated rival, the former mufti of Jerusalem.

February 1951

Raquela hurried through Hadassah A to Arik's office.
He jumped up as she entered, his eyes wide, searching.

She smiled. "I came straight from the lab. I watched
them do the rabbit test."

"Tell me. Tell me." He looked at her. "No . . . you
don't have to tell me. I see it in your face." He held her
tightly.

"Two months," she said wonderingly. "Two months
pregnant. Can you believe it?"

"Believe it? I've been dreaming it." He moved away
from her for a moment. "But you—how do you feel?"

"So excited you'd think this was the first baby ever born
in the world."

He led her to a chair. "Now, Raquela, you'll have to
start taking care of yourself. We ought to decide right now
how long you should work." He stopped. "Maybe you
should think of giving up—"

"Come on, Arik." She bounded out of the chair. "I've
never felt healthier in my life. I'm going to go on delivering babies until I'm too fat to stand in front of the delivery table."

Through the next months Raquela watched the changes
in her body, as aware as if she were seeing it on film: the
tiny embryo taking shape inside her, with legs that kicked
her gently, a life making its presence known unconcerned
whether she was lying in bed or marketing or sitting with
Arik in the movies or helping another baby into the world.

"Rest, Raquela," Arik pleaded. They had just finished
dinner. "Go lie down on the sofa."

Raquela scoffed. "Stop wrapping me in cotton batting,
Arik. How many babies have we delivered between us?"

He led her to the divan in the living room, made her
stretch out, and covered her with an afghan. "Now you
rest. Eighth month, and you still insist on delivering babies
and waiting in those queues for rations."

"We're lucky. I got everything you like; they had frozen
carp today, and eggplant."

Arik beamed. "I'll fix you a banquet."

She heard him bustling around the kitchen. Her mind

was on the calendar she had hung on the kitchen wall.
With red crayon she had circled September 29, 1951. Four
more weeks. *Our baby* must *be born on the twenty-ninth.*

On the morning of the twenty-ninth, her pains began.
For the first time, she was the patient, experiencing what
her patients had experienced: pain, anticipation, more
pain, relief.

They taxied to Hadassah A. Arik alerted Miriam Op-
penheimer, the midwife who was closest to Raquela.
Raquela went through the familiar routine, surprised at
her own excitement and mounting tension.

The midwife prepped her. The bag of water had burst.

Arik sat at her side as the pains grew closer. Resting on
her pillow after a sharp contraction, she turned her head.

"Arik, you look petrified. The greatest gynecologist and
obstetrician in the country"—she laughed—"acting like
any nervous father."

He bent down and kissed her tenderly. He mopped the
perspiration on her forehead.

Another pain convulsed her body. She breathed into it,
telling herself, as she had told countless mothers, "Breathe.
Relax. Breathe. Relax."

An hour passed. Two. Three.

At last she was ready.

Arik helped wheel her into the delivery room and onto
the white delivery table.

"Push down," she heard the midwife commanding.

Every muscle pushed with her.

"Good. Now relax."

She filled her lungs with air.

She was wide awake. Aware. Aware of Arik, standing at
her side. Aware of her baby, pushing its way out of her
body into the world.

She heard Arik shout, "It's a boy. Oh, God, Raquela.
We have a son."

--*Chapter Twenty-five*--

April 1952

The El Al plane lifted off from Lydda airfield.

Raquela, holding seven-month-old Amnon in her arms, looked out the window. Tel Aviv lay below—a patchwork of little cement houses and red roofs sewn together with white roads like surgical tape laid on the April-green earth.

Soon they were over the white beach that curved like a scimitar around Jaffa, and now they were flying over the Mediterranean itself, its waters reaching westward, somewhere on the horizon, to Egypt's still-hostile shores. But the sea, blue-green, looked unbelievably, surrealistically peaceful.

Raquela put her hand in Arik's. He closed the medical journal he was reading and leaned over to kiss her cheek.

They were on sabbatical; they had both taken leave from their jobs so Arik could work in Beth Israel Hospital in New York, with the world-famous gynecologist Dr. Henry Falk.

Arik took Amnon in his lap, rumpled his curly golden hair, and kissed his forehead. *How alike they are*, Raquela thought. *Father and son. Unruffled, composed, easy to live with. Born to give happiness to those they love.*

She looked out as the plane climbed into a featherbed of clouds. She was euphoric. They would have a whole year away from pressure. Time to be together. Time for Arik to enjoy his baby son.

New York was a wonderland. From their apartment on Manhattan's Upper West Side, Raquela explored the city, wheeling Amnon in a large black baby carriage. She stared at the shop windows on Broadway, devouring the dresses; feasted her eyes on pyramids of fresh fruit; entered butcher shops still pinching herself that there was no austerity and she could buy meat; prowled happily through drugstores to fill her lungs with the old familiar odors; scouted for little toys for Amnon in the five-and-ten.

After a few months they bought a secondhand Chevrolet; Raquela took lessons, became a passionate driver, and knew that for the rest of her life she would have a love affair with automobiles. She drove Arik to medical centers in Boston, Cleveland, and Chicago, so he could bring back to Israel America's newest techniques in performing hysterectomies and caesarean sections.

While he worked, she visited museums and art galleries; Amnon was walking now, and he held her hand patiently as she moved through the galleries to find the paintings of the French Impressionists she'd discovered in New York.

Saturdays and Sundays, they picnicked in Central Park. She spread a red checkered cloth on the grass, unwrapped the sandwiches, and, after lunch, lay back while Arik, never without a volume of Sholom Aleichem, read her stories of America.

Amnon was at the pond, watching the children sail their toy boats. Arik was reading his favorite story, of Mottel, the cantor's son. Mottel had left Kasrilovka, sailed the Atlantic, and was about to put both feet on the shores of America. Arik, pretending to be Mottel's friend, Pinney, read:

> " 'How do you do, Columbus!'
> " 'Greetings to you, land of the free—golden, happy land!' "

Raquela smiled, looking up at the majestic Fifth Avenue buildings cutting the summer sky.

Golden, happy land. . . .

Once again Arik was Pinney, this time cursing the enemies, the anti-Semitic tyrants from whose land they had escaped:

> " 'Listen, you asses, brutes, drunken sots! Listen, you hooligans, you murderers! We have to thank you for having reached this haven, this refuge, this great and blessed land, the land of the free. If not for you who persecuted us with your evil edicts and your po-

groms, to this very day we wouldn't get to know Columbus, and Columbus wouldn't get to know us.' "

She closed her eyes, no longer listening. She was back at training camp. She saw Miriam, the young corporal from Morocco . . . the parade ground . . . the young women who had fled from tyranny and pogroms . . . from Morocco . . . Tunis . . . Egypt . . . Poland . . . Russia . . . Yemen . . . Iraq . . .

Listen, you hooligans . . . thank you for having reached this . . . great and blessed land . . . the land of the free. . . .

Israel . . . America . . . the lands of the free.

She heard Arik's voice, reading:

" 'Try not to love such a country!' "

Back again in Jerusalem in April 1953, Raquela was prevailed upon to teach midwifery in Hadassah.

Each morning, leaving Amnon with her housekeeper, she drove the Chevrolet they had brought back from America and parked it on the street near the hospital. She kissed Arik good-bye, watched him enter Hadassah A, and crossed the Street of the Prophets to the green barracks where she taught student nurses. The moment her classes were over, she raced back to her car, drove home to give Amnon lunch, and rested while he napped. Then she dressed him, took him to visit Mama and Papa, played with him in Independence Park, or went marketing.

Austerity was ending. Agriculture was flourishing; there was fresh food in the markets, and even meat. Industries were opening in the little development towns. Israel Bonds were floated in America and Europe to establish the new industries and to build highways, museums, and high-rise houses for new immigrants. Money from German reparations flowed into the state, to people who had been robbed by the Nazis of everything they owned, and to the survivors of concentration and slave-labor camps.

The German government, under Chancellor Konrad Adenauer, was trying, in part, to expiate its guilt for the Holocaust.

West Germany became a friend. France, under President Charles de Gaulle, was friendly.

The United States continued its friendship and patronage of the five-year-old democratic state.

The people yearned for peace.

But terrorists continued to infiltrate, and the Arab states continued their threats of war.

"Listen to this," Arik said one afternoon, hurrying into the apartment, his newspaper under his arm.

"What is it? You're white as a ghost."

He handed her the paper. "It's the king of Saudi Arabia this time," he said. "You read it."

He bent to pick up Amnon as she wiped her hands on her apron, took the paper to the sofa and read: " 'Israel, to the Arab world, is like a cancer to the human body. The only remedy is to uproot it, just like a cancer. Why don't we sacrifice ten million of our number to live in pride and self-respect?' "

She was stunned. *"Ten million!* Willing to sacrifice ten million human beings to defeat us!"

"They won't defeat us," Arik said. "But they're preparing for it. Like those armies in Megiddo."

He walked around the living room with Amnon in his arms. He spoke softly. "If only there will be peace by the time Amnon grows up."

A few months later, Raquela was pregnant again.

Arik was overjoyed; his dream of a house full of babies was being realized.

But, unlike her easy first pregnancy, this time she contracted *herpes zoster:* shingles, a stripe of blisters ran along the right side of her abdomen where the nerve endings had become inflamed. She stopped teaching; the rashes itched and burned and ached; she was tormented mercilessly.

But worse than the pain was her fear. Raquela knew the *herpes zoster* virus might penetrate the placenta and infect the fetus. It could damage the unborn baby's brain. Its heart. Its kidneys or its liver.

Would her baby be normal?

Raquela blocked the possibilities out of her mind. She forced herself to keep house and take care of Amnon; she tried to hide some of her misery from Arik. But each day, she saw the lines around his mouth grow deeper, his eyes sunken with worry. They tried to spare each other, and both failed dismally.

Somehow the interminable months were coming to an
end. The baby was due in late January 1955.

January was a bleak month, anyway. It was in January
1952 that her oldest brother, Jacob, just thirty-three, had
come home from his mission with the Israel Army in Paris
to die of Hodgkin's disease.

On this third anniversary of his death, Raquela and
Arik drove Mama and Papa to Jacob's grave. Papa's face
was mournful as he intoned the prayer for the dead. "A
son should say Kaddish for his father," he said sadly, "not
a father for his son."

Mama kneeled on the ground, weeping. "Why didn't
God take me instead of Jacob? Why didn't God take me
first?"

Raquela, her body swollen, tried to lift Mama.

Dear God, Raquela prayed, *let my child be normal.
And don't ever let one of my children die before me.*

Driving home with Arik, she said, "If only the baby
comes on the twenty-ninth, everything will be all right."

Arik patted her hand. "It will be all right, my darling."

But he could not control the twitching in his cheek.

January 29 arrived. No labor pains.

Raquela fixed a steaming-hot bath. She soaked her
body. No pains. She dressed and jogged around the apartment. No pains.

She took another bath, hotter than before. Without
asking Arik, she took a big dose of castor oil. No contractions. No pains.

The twenty-ninth passed.

The next morning, labor began.

Arik rushed her to Hadassah A. This time she was to be
delivered by a gynecologist, Arik's friend Dr. Sadowsky.

Labor was fast. Soon she was on the delivery table;
Arik stood at her side, holding her hand, while Dr. Sadowsky moved swiftly, easing the baby out of her body.

"It's a boy," Arik called out. "Raquela, we have another
son."

"Is he normal?"

"As beautiful as Amnon."

"Is he really all right?"

"He'll be all right."

She heard a note of caution in his voice. "Let me see
him," she said. "I want to see him right away."

"You will, you will," Dr. Sadowsky said cheerfully.

"Here, I'm putting him on your stomach. You can feel him. Count his fingers and his toes."

She pushed her head up to look at the baby lying on her abdomen.

"Oh, my God, Arik. He's jaundiced. His skin is yellow." Her head collapsed back on the delivery table.

"Raquela, honey, he'll be all right."

"Of course he'll be all right," Dr. Sadowsky echoed. He was examining the placenta on a white table beside him.

She waited to hear the words *mazal tov*, words she used when the afterbirth had come out whole.

At last she heard the doctor say, "*Mazal tov.*"

She relaxed a little; that hurdle was over.

Dr. Sadowsky placed the baby, wrapped in a sterile blanket, in her arms. She held the frail body tenderly, stroking the tiny jaundiced cheeks, her eyes filled with fear.

"Arik," she said, "we've got to keep him alive."

"We'll keep him alive, my darling. Haven't we named him Rafael—'Healed by God'? Now you rest."

He leaned over and kissed her.

She let them take their newborn son from her. Tears rolled down her cheeks.

But she could not rest. She knew too well what had caused her baby to jaundice even as he swam inside her body. The *herpes zoster* virus had penetrated her placenta. It had circulated through the fetus and then localized in the liver, inflaming many of the liver cells and destroying some as well.

She knew exactly what must have happened next. The swelling of the inflamed liver had created an obstruction of the liver tubules—the slender elongated channel through which the bile flowed to the intestines. Her baby's bile, jammed up and absorbed into his bloodstream, had caused the jaundice.

She knew liver cells could regenerate. Would her baby hold out? Could he survive long enough until the liver healed?

Slowly, Raquela regained enough strength to sit beside her baby's crib. He could hold no food. She watched the glucose drip nourishment into a tiny vein in his hand. He lay pale and listless.

Mama had taken Amnon to her house. And Arik, desperately trying, with pediatricians and pediatric nurses, to save his child's life, saw Raquela withdrawing inside herself.

"Raquela, there's nothing more you can do for our baby—for Rafi." He said the name slowly. "You must come home for a while and sleep."

"Leave me alone, Arik. I can't sleep."

"You have to keep your strength. Amnon needs you, too."

"Amnon is all right. Mama can handle him. But if anything happens to Rafi—"

He put his arms around her. "You're so pale, darling. And so thin. I'm worried about you, too, Raquela."

"It's my fault. I did it to Rafi. I caught the *herpes zoster*. I damaged his liver."

"Raquela, that's not like you. You know better. Anybody can catch a virus."

Her eyes were glazed. His words hardly penetrated the dark cloud of her depression.

Her mind was numb. Her only feeling was guilt. She refused to leave the hospital. Day and night, she sat beside Rafi's crib.

"I feel that as long as I'm close to him," she told Arik, "he'll live."

Arik watched her anxiously.

Days passed. Weeks. Rafi showed little improvement.

Raquela lost awareness of the world outside. Only Rafi existed. Only she could hold him magically to life.

Arik brought her food; she took it listlessly, vaguely aware she had to take sustenance to keep Rafi alive.

Arik sought out their friends. "Please go sit with Raquela at the hospital." He urged them to fill the hours when he was operating or on call.

"If she wants to talk, let her talk. If she wants to be silent, just sit with her and be silent, too. She's basically strong and healthy. We've just got to support her during these terrible weeks. And wait."

Friends came. Judith Steiner. Shula Patt. Her brothers, Yair and Itzhak, came with their wives. Mama and Papa came and brought Amnon.

They sat with her. But no one, not even Amnon, whom she adored, could comfort her.

At last Rafi's body began to respond; the liver cells were regenerating. The glucose was no longer fed into his body. Raquela fed him his milk formula in a bottle, a few drops at a time. Then, gradually, solid food. He began to put on weight.

Rafi was winning his battle.

Arik and Raquela took him home, to Palmach Street. She extended her leave of absence; her life had only one purpose now: to nurse Rafi until he was fully well, and to take care of four-year-old Amnon.

The days were tolerable, but the nights were filled with dread. Every few hours, Raquela woke from sleep and jumped out of bed to check the crib and make sure Rafi was alive. She let Arik hold her in his arms, but she was too exhausted to make love.

Two months later, Rafi was back in the hospital. His liver was inflamed again. He vomited. He screamed with excruciating pain.

Drawn with anxiety, Raquela helped the nurse insert the intravenous needle into his hand. Arik and the pediatricians worked around the clock to save him.

Raquela tormented herself with new guilt. "I didn't take good enough care of him."

Arik tried to comfort her. "It's a natural reaction for a mother to put all the blame on herself. But listen to me, honey, it's not your fault. Give yourself the luxury of believing you're a good mother. You are!"

She tried to listen and believe.

After a few weeks, the inflammation subsided, and the liver cells began their process of regeneration.

Raquela brought him home, and soon the apartment on Palmach Street, once again bright and cheerful, hummed with the sounds of her little boys, and of Arik's baritone voice, singing them to sleep each night.

They were sitting in the kitchen, sipping coffee; the children were sound asleep. "How was your day today, Arik?" Raquela asked.

"Two caesareans—an Arab woman and a Jewish woman, both with beautiful, healthy babies."

Raquela leaned toward him, her eyes sparkling. "And the women—beautiful, too?"

"Of course. I saved them for their husbands."

He stood up, bent over to kiss her, and led her tenderly into the bedroom.

Terror!

The year 1955 was a year of terror. The long-tenuous

borders were penetrated by terrorist gangs called *fedayeen,* Arabs recruited largely from Gaza, with bases in Egypt, Jordan, and Syria. The border settlements suffered most: children losing limbs by stepping on mines; men and women and babies indiscriminately killed by hand grenades and bullets; six children and their teacher murdered in Shafir, a southern farming village; a wedding party ambushed and murdered in Patish, west of Beersheba.

Each evening Arik turned on the radio for the latest news of infiltration.

The IDF—Israel Defense Forces—retaliated. Regular-army units attacked the bases from which the *fedayeen* infiltrated.

The United Nations took note of the terrorist activities but reacted severely whenever Israel retaliated, censuring her for "atrocities."

From Radio Cairo, beamed to Jerusalem, Arik heard the voice of Gamal Abdel Nasser, threatening war. "Burn, murder, and destroy," Nasser proclaimed to the Arab world. "Prepare for the great battle ahead."

Nasser had once been the hope for a democratic Egypt. In 1949, during the War of Independence, when he and his troops were surrounded by the Israel Army in the Negev, Nasser had convinced the Israelis that he, together with other idealistic officers, would overthrow the corrupt King Farouk and bring a friendly democratic state into being on the Nile. He had overthrown Farouk, but instead of democracy he had created dictatorship; instead of friendship he had created enmity.

The Russians found him an eager ally. For years they had sought to gain a foothold in the Middle East. Now, in exchange for Egypt's cotton, the Russians supplied Nasser with artillery and tanks, with submarines and MIGs, knowing full well they were to be used in the coming war against Israel.

In June 1956, turning against England and France, Nasser nationalized the Suez Canal, their lifeline to their markets in Africa and the Orient. And he barred Israel's ships from sailing through the Canal.

Next, he placed a battery of naval guns on the shore of the Straits of Tiran, blockaded the Gulf of Aqaba, and cut off Israel's southern port of Eilat, her window to Africa and Asia.

On the borders he stepped up the daily raids of terror,

extolling the *fedayeen:* "You have proved that you are heroes upon whom our entire country can depend. The spirit with which you enter the land of the enemy must be spread."

Visiting a colleague in the former Turkish harem that now housed the men's ward of Hadassah, Arik saw orderlies wheeling in stretchers.

"A new *fedayeen* attack!" the ambulance driver explained. "A group of archaeologists working on a dig in Ramat Rachel was attacked. Four are already dead. We're bringing in more wounded."

Arik walked toward one of the wounded men. "One of my friends was on that dig." He stopped. Only a few days before he and Raquela had met the quiet, gentle scholar whose daughter Aya had just married Golda Meir's son Menachem.

Now, Arik learned, his friend the scholar was one of the dead.

October 22, 1956, Nasser concluded a military alliance with Syria and Jordon; the three armies were placed under Egyptian command. Their troops were amassed at Israel's borders.

Israel built air-raid shelters in Jerusalem and Tel Aviv, in the towns and kibbutzim. The border settlements were fortified. Older men and women were recruited and trained for civil defense.

October 29, Israel dropped paratroopers inside the Sinai Peninsula. Under the command of General Moshe Dayan, the well-trained soldiers of the regular army pushed across the desert in tanks, armored vehicles, jeeps, ice-cream trucks, taxis, trucks, buses, and private cars.

In one hundred hours, taking the world by surprise, they slashed into the Sinai, demolishing the *fedayeen* nests, knocking out Nasser's Sinai army, one third of his total army of 150,000 men, capturing all the Russian hardware in Sinai and Gaza—millions of dollars' worth of Stalin tanks, machine guns, artillery, and untold rounds of ammunition. More than thirty thousand Egyptian soldiers were found wandering in the desert, abandoned by their officers. Five thousand were taken prisoner. Many were found with Arabic translations of Hitler's *Mein Kampf* in their knapsacks.

One hundred seventy-two Israelis were killed, eight hundred wounded. Egypt took one Israeli prisoner, a pilot whose plane was shot down and who bailed out over Egyptian territory. He was exchanged for many of the five thousand Egyptian prisoners.

Hadassah's hospital in Beersheba became the receiving hospital for many of the wounded, some of them maimed for life.

Britain and France were to have attacked the Canal Zone and invaded Egypt from the west at the same time that Israel's troops crossed the desert from the east. But they waited too long. Two days late, they finally bombarded Egyptian airfields rimming the Canal. Dragging their feet, they succeeded in putting troops into the Canal Zone.

Immediately the UN, led by the U.S. and the USSR, demanded that all British and French troops be withdrawn from the Sinai Peninsula and the Gaza Strip.

Israel tried in vain at the UN to point out that this was the time to negotiate a genuine peace treaty with Nasser. But the Russians threatened rocket attacks. They sent Israel an ultimatum: if she did not withdraw, they would destroy her.

Secretary of State John Foster Dulles sent another ultimatum, demanding withdrawal lest the U.S. support sanctions against her.

With a heavy heart, Israel withdrew from the Canal Zone and the Sinai, but she refused to withdraw from the Straits of Tiran and the Gaza Strip without guarantees of security.

During four and a half months of fruitless and frustrating debates at the UN, Israel tried to convince the world that without secure borders, her very existence was imperiled.

Finally President Dwight D. Eisenhower gave Ben-Gurion his personal guarantee: the UN would station forces in Gaza so there would be no enemy troops amassed at Israel's border and no *fedayeen* attacks. And the United States itself would guarantee Israel's free access to the waterways.

Conventional warfare dictated that after his defeat on the battlefield, Nasser would be forced to sit down, face to face, with his victor and sign a peace treaty.

Instead the UN allowed Nasser to turn his military defeat into a diplomatic victory. He was not required to sit down with Israel. He was not required to make peace.

Ben-Gurion, accepting the guarantees, ordered his troops to withdraw. "This is the blackest day of my life," he said.

He knew—as Arik and Raquela knew—as all of Israel knew—this would not be the last war for survival.

--⊷⊰ Chapter Twenty-six ⊱⊶--

August 1960

Raquela and Arik walked under the trees of the world-famous Weizmann Institute of Science, in Rehovoth, a massive lovely enclave of research buildings, homes, and beautiful gardens that lay between Jerusalem and Tel Aviv.

They chatted with African ministers of government in tribal robes and velvet headdresses. They sipped cold drinks with leaders of Asia's emerging nations—Burma, Nepal, Singapore. They shook hands with women in the exquisite gowns of Thailand and the Philippines. And when dinner was served, they dined at round tables with Nobel laureates who had come from Europe and the Americas to attend the first International Conference on Science in the Advancement of New States.

Arik, his hair gray now, had entered his middle years with grace. He walked through the semitropical garden with the serene, composed look of a doctor at the height of his career.

He held Raquela's arm possessively, nodding to friends, smiling as he watched heads turn to look at his wife. At thirty-six, Raquela had learned the art of using clothes and color to set off her regal figure and to accent the beauty of her face—the uncanny mix of Eastern and Western Jewry that gave her face its strength and vulnerability. Wherever they walked, her presence was felt at the conference.

Some one hundred twenty political leaders from forty countries on five continents had come to Rehovoth to meet Israel's doctors, midwives, scientists, economists, farmers, educators—and to learn how Israel had solved the problems of new nationhood.

Arik and Raquela had been asked to host some of the

delegates who had come looking for ways to wipe out mother and child mortality.

The Reverend Solomon B. Caulker, of Sierra Leone, was their first visitor. Brought to Arik's office in Hadassah A, he was introduced to Arik and Raquela as vice-principal of the Furah Bay College, in Freetown, the oldest university south of the Sahara Desert. The handsome young black educator was also head of the department of philosophy, dean of the faculty of arts, and warden of students. He extended his hand majestically. His English was excellent.

"I've come to you, Dr. and Mrs. Brzezinski," he said, because I need help. In Sierra Leone, eight out of every ten infants die before they are one year old. I'd like to know what suggestions you have for saving our babies. I cannot believe that nature, God—call it what you like—loves English children, or American children or Israeli children any more than African children." He paused. His voice was edged with emotion. "Just the ordinary maintenance of health—that is what I need to learn from you and from Israel. I was born in a jungle village. Our average life expectancy is in the low thirties. Yours has gone up to the sixties and seventies. And most of our people die of leprosy, malaria, or, worst of all, undernourishment."

Raquela listened intently as the young leader unburdened himself. It seemed to her that his was the voice of Africa pleading for help from Israel for the crushing problems decimating his people.

"Dr. Caúlker, we're here, ready to help you," Arik assured him. "We'll send our doctors and midwives to you in Sierra Leone. And we'll take the young people you send us and train them to become doctors and nurses."

The African leader nodded. "Yes. That's what we need. Our people still believe in magic and in witch doctors. How do we get rid of superstition? Is typhoid caused by someone who has bewitched you, or by drinking dirty water? Are your babies dying because someone who hates you has put sickness on them, or because you are not feeding them properly? I know that you, too, have suffered from colonialism and tyranny. And you had to struggle and shed blood for your freedom."

Struggle.

Raquela thought of the thousands of immigrants breaking their way through the British blockade. Captured. Deported. Imprisoned in Athlit and Cyprus.

And shed blood for your freedom.

Two wars: 1948, 1956. More than six thousand young men and women dead. Raquela saw Aviad, the quadriplegic soldier in Tel Hashomer. The wasted limbs. The broken lives.

Dr. Caulker was talking with urgency, with passion. "I think that's why we feel such ties with you. We know you will help us because of your humanity. We are afraid of the big rich countries. We are not afraid of you. We know Israel will not exploit us."

"For sure," Arik said. "There is a brotherhood in suffering."

They spent the next hour showing Dr. Caulker the delivery room and the maternity wards. He lingered longest in the nursery, walking from crib to crib, gently patting the tiny hands of Jewish and Arab babies.

He looked at Raquela. "Someday we will have nurseries and sparkling delivery rooms like these. I want to give our children who now die like flies the chance to grow up like yours—without hunger, without disease. There's a holy impatience in us."

Early the next morning Raquela and Arik returned to the International Conference at Rehovoth. As she moved through the lounge of the handsome Wix Auditorium, it seemed to her the lounge had come alive. Surely this was one of the most memorable events in Israel's brief and hectic twelve-year history—this meeting of Africans and Asians in native garb, Israelis in shirtsleeves like Arik's and summer dresses like hers, internationally famous scientists in Bermuda shorts.

She felt a camaraderie, a friendship, in the air. And the excitement of creation—as if some powerful midwife were delivering not babies but new nations into the world.

On the grounds Raquela greeted some of the young African women studying midwifery in the nursing school on the Street of the Prophets. They were highly motivated, determined to go back to their native villages in the jungles of Africa and teach what they had learned.

The student nurses were part of Israel's AID program, which sent more than five thousand experts into the developing countries and gave scholarships to more than five thousand trainees from the Third World who were now attending Israel's universities, institutes, and medical schools.

Midmorning, the formal discussions resumed. They covered the whole range of nationhood from birth through survival: hunger; medicine; the population explosion; water; inflation; radiation; politics; science; and, perhaps most important of all, international cooperation.

Delegates stood up and recounted how Israelis had come with their families, lived among them and taught them how to farm their land. How to irrigate their fields. How to raise chickens and process fish. How to wipe out diseases, reclaim their deserts, build kindergartens and schools, hospitals and hotels, shipping lines and airports.

A tall African described how Professor Isaac C. Michaelson, Hadassah's chief of ophthamology, had established the first eye hospital in Liberia's capital city, Monrovia.

"Do you know what it means," he said, "to be cured of blindness? To have your children healed of trachoma? People came not only from all over Liberia, but from Sierra Leone, Guinea, the Ivory Coast as well. No one was turned away."

Other countries, Raquela thought, *buy friendship by giving guns and tanks and war planes. We give of our people and of ourselves.*

The conference was drawing to a close. The last speaker was the young Reverend Solomon Caulker:

> I came to this conference not really knowing whether there was any contribution Sierra Leone could make or how much I should be able to learn to take home. But I want to state now that these days we have spent here in Israel have become such great days in my life that I am quite sure I will never be the same person again when I return home.

Raquela sat forward in her seat; he was the spokesman for all young nations, asking for help "to liberate the human spirit and to make us all stand up with pride and believe that we are members of the human race."

Applause filled the hall.

Dr. Caulker was summing up: "When I came here ten days ago, it was night, it was dark, one couldn't see far ahead. One was lonely.

"When I leave here, it will be light.

"Not only physically, but metaphorically, for I go home no longer feeling that we are isolated in our problems . . . we belong to a great program.

"I say to all of you that when the new day dawns, as I see it dawning beyond the horizon, we shall be standing beside you to greet that dawn."*

June 1961

It was David Ben-Gurion who selected the site for the Hadassah–Hebrew University Medical Center, soon to open in Ein Karem, in the Hills of Judea.

Standing on a mountain plateau overlooking the valley of Sorek, where once Delilah had won Samson's heart, Ben-Gurion looked at the craggy mountains bowling around him. He saw miles of empty land.

"Magnificent!" he said. "Build here. Jerusalem will grow toward the hospital."

Now the center was finished—a huge complex of buildings of honey-hued Jerusalem stone and red and white brick. The four-hundred-twenty-bed hospital was a semicircular fortress. In case of war, three floors were built underground with connecting tunnels, equipped to be converted instantly into emergency units.

The Hadassah–Hebrew University Medical Center, unique in the Middle East, held the hospital, the medical school, the nursing school, the dental school—and later there would be the Institute of Oncology for cancer treatment and research.

As his gift to the people of Israel, Marc Chagall created twelve stained-glass windows, one for each of the twelve tribes of Israel, to be installed in the hospital synagogue.

Moving day to Ein Karem was June 6, 1961.

Raquela and Arik drove to Hadassah A, to help transfer the maternity patients. Young women soldiers carried out the infants.

The convoy with doctors, nurses, and three hundred patients set off from downtown Jerusalem to the fortress hospital in the Hills of Judea south and west of Jerusalem.

Twenty army ambulances flew blue satin pennants with

_____
* On his way home from the conference Dr. Caulker was killed in an airplane crash near Dakar.

gold letters bearing the names of Hadassah chapters in America that had raised extra money for this historic day.

Behind the ambulances, Raquela drove Arik in their car. Like a joyous, triumphant parade, the convoy moved down Jaffa Road with people waving and shouting on the streets. Then they turned into the broad expanse of Herzl Boulevard in Bet Hakerem, and snaked up and down the mountains along the newly built Henrietta Szold Road.

Raquela drove in silence. Dr. Yassky and the ill-fated convoy to Mount Scopus flooded her mind as the convoy approached the hospital that would replace Scopus. Would Ein Karem be safe?

At the hospital she helped move the patients into flower-decked wards, while around her the radial corridors and huge elevators filled up as 254 doctors, 514 nurses, and the staff of 1,352 moved into their offices.

Late in the afternoon, she stood with Arik in the broad courtyard in front of the hospital, watching the sun change the colors of the mountains blue, then pink and mauve.

"It's so peaceful here," she said. "This whole panorama."

He put his arms around her and kissed her.

"This is my dream," he said. "That you and our boys will have a long life. That we can work in this new center. We've got the tools we need. If only—if only there will be no more war."

She stayed in his arms, resting her head against his shoulder.

Then she lifted her head. Her eyes were glistening. "We have so much to live for."

She looked at the majestic hills, darkening as the sun disappeared behind them. "Dear God, let there be peace."

Arik pushed open the apartment door. They had moved to a spacious third-floor apartment on Hameyasdim Street in Bet Hakerem. "Raquela, the grant has come through!"

She hurried toward him as he handed her the letter. She leaned against the door, her face glowing with pleasure. The National Institute of Health of the U.S. government was happy to inform Dr. Brzezinski he had been awarded a grant for a five-year project to study the problems of toxemia in pregnancy.

Under the controlled, scientific conditions in Israel, and with his long experience, his study could provide inestimably valuable information not only for saving lives in Israel but also for saving lives in the United States and in the rest of the world.

"I knew," she said. "I knew some day you'd be famous. It's recognition you deserve."

He put his hands on her shoulder.

"I want you to help me set up the program. Together we can get this project off the ground."

"I will, Arik. I want to work with you on this."

It was a good time to begin their five-year study, for the borders of Israel were relatively peaceful in 1962.

Nasser was preoccupied. He was busy waging unsuccessful warfare in Yemen, siding with the rebels against the ruling monarch, the Imam of Yemen.

He had had a number of failures after his defeat in Sinai. In 1958 he had joined with Syria to form the United Arab Republic, using the guns and arms his Russian patrons had given him—to replace the hardware he had lost to Israel. He was embarking on adventures in the Arab world.

First he sought to overthrow the regimes of Saudi Arabia, Lebanon, and Jordan.

President Eisenhower, outraged by Nasser, whose head he had saved after Suez, now ordered U.S. Marines into Lebanon. The United States saved Lebanon.

Next Nasser turned against King Hussein, grandson of Jordan's King Abdullah, who had been assassinated for having begun peace negotiations with Israel. Ridiculing Hussein as "the Hashemite harlot . . . the treacherous dwarf," Nasser instigated subversive acts in Jordan so threatening that Great Britain sent in troops, and the United States rushed supplies with permission from Israel to use her air space. This time three nations—England, the United States, and Israel—saved Jordan.

With most of his army stalemated in Yemen, Nasser waged a war of words against Israel. Evenings, Raquela and Arik, working on their study at home, stopped to listen to Radio Cairo, beamed specially to Jerusalem: *"The birth of Israel is the greatest crime in history . . . Israel is a shame . . . a disgrace . . . a bleeding wound . . . a cancer."*

"At least he's not threatening all-out war against us this time," Raquela said. "Remember, before 1957, the way he used to rant: 'Weep, oh Israel, the day of extermination draws near. . . .' "

Arik shook his head. "Hitler taught us never to underestimate a dictator's threats. Every time Nasser speaks, I hear Hitler's voice."

"Now he's just calling us names. We can live with that," Raquela said, bending over to work on the papers they had spread out on the dining-room table.

The scope of the study had broadened. While eclampsia, the toxemia of pregnancy, was their central interest, they were also studying premature births, stillbirths, and the deaths of live-born infants before they were one year old.

Jerusalem was an ideal laboratory. It was a city of mass immigration, a population of divergent ethnic groups—native-born Sabras and babies of families from some eighty countries.

More than 5,500 babies were born in Jerusalem in 1962 and again in 1963. Raquela and Arik studied the infant-mortality rate—22.7 for Jews, and a frightening 51.6 for Moslems and Christians. They were trying to pinpoint all infant deaths, to find out in which socioeconomic and ethnic groups morbidity was highest. Then they could plan preventive health-care services for all their pregnant women and their newborn children, Jewish, Christian, and Moslem.

"Arik," Raquela said, "you look so tired. With your patients at the hospital, your private patients, and this study, you're working too hard."

He paid no attention. He was making notes on an outline map of Jerusalem, the Old City, and Mount Scopus.

"Someday," he said, "maybe we'll be able to study infant mortality and infant morbidity in all of Jerusalem, not just in this truncated area on the map."

He looked up. "And how is our new house coming along?"

"It's speeding along. I can't wait for us to move in."

It was to be Arik's dream house. Papa had given them the land next to his cottage inside the garden. Now it was taking shape—long low lines, split level, Arik's office and their bedroom on the lower level, the boys' rooms on the upper level, and a spacious sunken living room whose French doors opened out to the tropical trees and calla lilies Papa had planted.

The house was scheduled to be ready at the end of August 1963.

Thursday, August 15.

Arik slowly climbed the three flights of stairs to the apartment they were soon to leave.

"Arik!" Raquela ran to his side. He was hunched over with pain.

"I'm afraid it's my gallbladder. I'll get into bed."

"Can I get you something?" Her heart pounded.

"Do we have Demerol in the house?"

"I'll look." She opened the medicine cabinet in the bathroom. "None. I'll run down and pick some up at the pharmacy."

She raced down the stairs, grateful that this was the day her housekeeper stayed a few hours longer.

She returned within a few minutes. Her housekeeper let her in. "While you were out," she said, "Dr. Brzezinski asked me to bring a box from one of the drawers."

"What drawer?"

She pointed to a dark chest in the foyer. The top drawer was open.

Raquela paled. It was where Arik kept his most precious photos. Pictures of his parents, both of whom had died in the last few years. Their wedding pictures. Snapshots of Amnon and Rafi. Pictures of their stay in New York.

Why did he want those pictures now?

She hurried into the bedroom.

The pictures lay on the bed, but Arik was gasping for breath. His forehead was beaded with perspiration, his body contorted with pain.

Raquela handed him the Demerol with a glass of water. "Arik—let me call a doctor."

"There's nothing a doctor can do. You know I've had these attacks before. They always pass. The Demerol should give me some relief. If I'm not better in the morning, we'll call somebody."

Raquela wiped his forehead. "Let me call a doctor now, Arik. Why should you suffer so?"

"You go into the living room. I'll be all right after a while."

Raquela fixed the sheet on his body and bent over to kiss his forehead. He was shivering in the August heat. His eyes were glazed, his face drained of color. Fear lashed her heart.

She called the children into the living room. Amnon, now a sturdy twelve-year-old, came toward her quietly. She felt a new surge of anguish; even his walk was like Arik's, the slight, almost imperceptible stoop, his head inclined forward. Surely Amnon was cut out to be a doctor. Rafi, eight and a half, robust, burst into the room. She saw herself in Rafi—her mouth, her eyes, her smile, her eagerness for life.

"Children." She controlled her voice. "Daddy is sick. He needs a lot of quiet and rest. I'd like you to spend the night at Grandma's house."

Amnon looked frightened. "Will Daddy be all right?"

"Of course he'll be all right. It's his gallbladder. He probably ate something greasy at that luncheon he went to."

Rafi ran into her arms. "I'm scared, Mommy."

"He's going to be fine. Now, both of you—get your pajamas. And take along your white shirts and khaki shorts so you'll be all set for Friday night and Shabbat."

She kissed her two sons and watched them descend the three flights to the street. Then she walked to the front window. The boys looked up, saw her, and waved. "*Shalom, Ima*," they called out.

"*Shalom*," she answered, watching them disappear down the hill toward Mama's house.

She returned to the bedroom. Arik was dozing; the Demerol had taken effect.

She tiptoed to the balcony door, stepped out, and stared up at Mount Herzl, where Israel's soldier-heroes lay buried.

Her eyes blurred. "Don't let anything happen to my husband," she whispered.

All night she lay beside him, watching, curbing her fears.

He slept fitfully, waking intermittently, confessing pain. "It's in my back and right side . . . as if my back wanted to come right through my skin."

Finally, morning came.

Arik got out of bed. "I'll try to walk," he said. "That may shake up the gallstones."

She held his arm as they walked slowly around the

apartment. "Let one of the doctors examine you, Arik. This is the worst attack you've had."

By noon he could no longer tolerate the pain. "All right, Raquela. Call."

The doctor arrived within minutes. Raquela led him into the bedroom, then stepped out as he examined Arik.

She paced the living room, squeezing her fingers until they were white.

"Yes, Doctor?" she saw the look of anxiety on his face.

"It's not his gallbladder. It's his heart."

He telephoned for an ambulance.

Raquela walked behind the attendants carrying Arik down the stairs on a stretcher. In the ambulance, she sat next to him, stroking his hand as the siren shrieked through Bet Hakerem up the hills to the valley of Sorek and Ein Karem.

Arik was rushed into the emergency room.

Raquela sat in the nurses' station. The nurses—old friends—helped to make her comfortable. They brought her coffee, tried to divert her thoughts.

But nothing could divert her. *Why did I listen to him last night? Why didn't I call a doctor myself? I knew—something in me knew—it was more than his gallbladder. Why does a nurse always take orders from a doctor? I'm not his nurse. I'm his wife. Why didn't I follow my own instincts? Arik . . . stay alive . . .*

A team of doctors came out of the emergency room. "It's a coronary, Raquela. We can't tell yet how severe it is."

Vaguely, she was aware that her friends were urging her. "Have some more coffee, Raquela . . . would you like a sandwich . . . is there anything we can get you . . . you really should eat something . . ."

"No, thank you. I just want to wait right here—until I can go in to see him."

All afternoon the doctors worked, barely leaving the room. Just before sundown, Raquela called Mama.

Mama spoke comfortingly. "Tell Arik how beautiful the boys look in their white Shabbat shirts. Now I'm going to light my Friday-night candles and pray. . . . Tell Arik."

Tell Arik.

The hours dragged. At midnight the corridors were empty. Raquela waited.

At last the special-duty nurse appeared. "Dr. Brzezinski wants to see you. Just stay a few minutes . . . please."

Raquela sped to his bedside. "I'm here, darling."

She pressed his hand.

"Ra—Raquela," he gasped. "How—how—are the boys?"

"They're fine. Mama wants you to know how beautiful they look for Shabbat."

"And you, my dearest, take . . . good care . . ."

His voice faded. His face turned grayish blue.

The nurse caught the erratic movement on the heart monitor. Raquela saw it.

"Save him," she cried out. "He's having another heart attack."

"Please step outside, Mrs. Brzezinski," the nurse said brusquely. Doctors and nurses hurried in and out of his room.

Raquela paced the empty corridor. *Don't die, Arik . . . we need you . . . Amnon and Rafi . . . and I . . . you were so happy . . . the grant . . . the house . . . the children . . . I love you, Arik; stay alive; please stay alive.*

It was one A.M., Saturday, August 17.

The doctors and nurses filed sadly out of Arik's room.

Raquela screamed.

A doctor helped her into a chair. She sat, her face stony, her eyes dry.

Sunday morning, thousands of people filled the cemetery in the Jerusalem hills as the rabbi intoned the Kaddish. "Magnified and sanctified by God's great name . . ."

Raquela held Amnon's and Rafi's hands. Arik's body was lowered into the earth.

"Good-bye, my love," she whispered. But she could not weep.

The *shiva*—the seven days of mourning—began. Sunday afternoon hundreds of people streamed into the apartment to sit with the widow and the children.

Women patients Raquela had never seen came to tell her how Arik had saved their lives.

And still she could not weep.

Monday morning, a woman appeared at the door in a threadbare black dress, a tattered black handkerchief on her head, black cotton stockings covering her legs.

"I know one should come in the afternoon or evening

for the *shiva*," she said apologetically. "But I was ashamed to be seen by all the people who will come. Please forgive me if I disturb you in the morning."

"Come in," Raquela said quietly. "Come sit over here." She led her to the sofa and poured coffee for the stranger.

"I live in Mea Shearim," she said.

Raquela nodded. The religious quarter—where Zayda and Bubba Levinrad had lived.

The woman went on. "I was pregnant, and I began to bleed. My husband knew Dr. Brzezinski was the greatest woman's doctor in Israel. He went to your husband."

She stopped to look at Raquela's face. "Your husband said he never makes house calls. But when my husband told him about me, and where we lived, and that we had no money to pay him, he came. He took care of me right away. And he told me when my time would come, he himself would deliver my baby."

Raquela was silent. So many women adored Arik.

The stranger wiped her eyes with her hands. "When he left our house, he put money in my husband's pocket and he said, 'Go right out and buy food for your wife.'"

Raquela wept.

For the remaining days of the *shiva*, she wept.

--⊷ Chapter Twenty-seven ⊷--

September 1963

Dr. Moshe Prywes, associate dean of the Hebrew University–Hadassah Medical School, stood up as Raquela entered. He walked around his desk in the former Bible House of the Anglican Church and offered her a chair.

"How are you, Raquela?" He scanned her face. "Getting some rest, finally? Isa and I worry about you."

She took hold of his hand. "You both have been wonderful to us."

It was the end of the *shloshim*—the thirty days since Arik's death; now she could return to work. She had moved into the new house, trying to pick up the pieces of their lives.

Amnon and Rafi filled up their days with school, with Scouts, with good friends. But the nights were endless. Raquela sat with them at their bedside, her throat tight as she tried to help them cope with hot anger: how could our daddy leave us, abandon us, without any warning? Anger turned to despair, then tears; she held them in her arms until at last they fell asleep.

She herself hardly slept; and when she did lose consciousness for a few hours, she woke in a freezing sweat.

Thirty-nine. A widow. Trying to fill her sons' needs. Trying to be both mother and father. Careful not to demand too much of the boys. Wary lest Amnon—thoughtful, caring, like Arik—try to become man of the house overnight. Forfeit his childhood. And Rafi—who followed her around the house, openly adoring—she worried that Rafi was clinging to her too much.

For the anxiety, the fears, the sleeplessness, work was the answer. This morning, after another endless night, she had looked at herself in the mirror and decided what she must do.

Now she was discussing it with Dr. Prywes. "Moshe, I want to continue Arik's project. It's his memorial. It's too important. I don't want it to—just to die."

She concentrated on his face as she leaned across the desk.

He and Arik had come from the same background. Both were born in Poland, though Moshe was three years younger than Arik. Both had gone to medical school in Paris. Both had the authoritative air of doctors, of medical men accustomed to facing crises. Raquela knew the way these doctors functioned; she could almost see the wheels turning in Moshe's head.

He tilted back in his desk chair. She was concentrating now on his mouth—his well-formed, sensual, aristocratic lips—which would tell her whether what she wanted was realistic and feasible or some wild fantasy.

At last he spoke. "I don't know whether we can do this, Raquela."

"Why not?" She suppressed the instant despair.

"Look here—you're a very skilled nurse. And a gifted midwife. But America would never let a nurse head up a major research project like this."

"Even though nobody worked closer with Arik than—?"

Moshe's heavy black eyebrows raised above his brown penetrating eyes. "Facts of life, my dear Raquela. Governments give grants to academicians, doctors, epidemiologists—"

She interrupted. "Moshe, couldn't you find someone? I could work with him, the way I worked with Arik."

Prywes stood up. His lithe, sinewy body seemed always in motion. She watched him looking out at the Municipal Garden toward the City Hall.

Surely he would find a solution. Brilliant. Urbane. A world traveler. Member of the World Health Organization. French Legion of Honor. Medical adviser to countries as far apart as Guatemala, Singapore, Argentina. Arik, his best friend, had called him the most creative medical educator in Israel.

It was that friendship that Raquela was relying upon now. For twelve years, their two families had been close; they had spent vacations and summer weekends together at the little beach house Arik and Raquela had built at Bet Yannai, north of Netanya.

Watching him searching for a way to help her, Raquela

thought of the evenings on the beach when Moshe had regaled them with stories of the war. Somehow he had always managed, with incredible ingenuity, to land on his feet.

He had been one of the very few Jewish doctors working in the university hospital in Warsaw when World War II began. The hospital was evacuated eastward; Warsaw was burning. The doctors were mobilized; Moshe became a captain.

A few days later the Nazi-Soviet Pact partitioned Poland; the Polish army commander gave the doctors in uniform a choice: "You can go west and join the Nazis, or you can go east and become a Soviet prisoner of war."

As a youngster, Moshe had been a member of Betar, a Zionist youth movement; the leader of his group had been a young man named Menachem Begin. Moshe, well-known as a Zionist, knew the Nazis would kill him as a Jew; the Russians would imprison him as a Zionist. He chose the lesser of the evils. He went east.

The Russians rounded up all the officers—Poles and Jews. Many were taken to Katyn near Smolensk, where ten thousand were massacred. Moshe was saved by a Communist whom he had once treated as a patient: "For the Russians, better to be a simple soldier—not an officer. Russians distrust all officers except their own."

Before the roundup, he ripped off his captain's bars and buttons. Then he folded his medical diploma into a tiny square and hid it inside the heel of his leather boot. Finally he burned all the papers that might identify him as a member of the famous and wealthy Prywes family of Warsaw.*

Now an obscure private, he was sentenced to fifteen years as a "socially dangerous enemy" and exiled to an Arctic slave-labor camp along the Pechora River, near the Ural Mountains.

Every morning, awakened at four o'clock, he was marched, with political prisoners, criminals, and prostitutes, four or five hours into the forests. All day, in temperatures that fell to sixty below zero, he chopped trees. Then, exhausted and frozen, the prisoners were marched another four or five hours back to the barracks.

* It is the Prywes family whom Isaac Bashevis Singer fictionalized in his novel *The Family Moskat*.

Moshe had spent a year and a half in the prison camp when the Nazis attacked Russia in a blitz on June 21, 1941. A few days later, all Russian doctors and nurses in the country, including all the medical staffs in the NKVD secret-police prison camps, were mobilized into the Red Army.

The twenty-eight thousand prisoners in Moshe's camp were now without a single doctor, without any kind of professional help. The camp officials began to search among the prisoners.

"Does anyone have any skills in medicine?"

Moshe decided to reveal who he was. By now he weighed less than one hundred pounds. He was dirty, emaciated, weak from malnutrition and diarrhea; he felt he had nothing to lose; he was one step away from death.

He entered the room of the NKVD commandant, a long hall with a huge T-shaped table at the end of which was a desk, and behind the desk, sitting like God, was Colonel Prokuratoff, in the khaki green uniform and red and gold pips of the NKVD.

Colonel Prokuratoff glanced up. Moshe was trembling as he walked through the long cold room; he stopped midway, afraid to approach closer.

"What do you want?" The NKVD commandant stared at the bedraggled figure.

"You are asking for medical people," Moshe said humbly, his voice little more than a whisper. "I—I am a doctor."

Colonel Prokuratoff's stainless-steel teeth glistened as he roared with laughter. "You—a doctor!"

"Yes. I am."

He pulled off his once-elegant leather boot, cut open the heel, and drew out the carefully folded diploma.

The commandant examined the document.

"*Bozhe moy!* My God. I'm going to put you in charge of medicine for all the prison camps along the Pechora River."

Moshe was given a house, a horse, and a white coat. He traveled about the heavily forested region, country-doctor-style, for five years, operating on prisoners, delivering babies, treating all the illnesses—cancer, typhus, dysentery, malnutrition, madness, and concentration-camp depression.

With prison labor he built a three-hundred-fifty-bed hospital to treat prisoners.

He survived the war and returned to bombed-out Warsaw. His wife, Isabella, a dentist, had also miraculously survived. She had worked as a nurse in a prison-camp hospital. But of the six hundred members of the Prywes family, only twenty remained alive. He and Isa left Poland; Moshe worked for the American Joint Distribution Committee in Paris until he was invited in 1951 to become Organizing Dean of the Medical School in Jerusalem. A week later, Arik invited him to Amnon's *Brith Milah*—his circumcision ceremony—and the two families became friends.

"I want to help you, Raquela," Moshe said, returning to his desk. "I'm going to call Dr. Michael Davies. He's head of the department of medical ecology at the medical school."

She listened closely as he spoke into the phone. Her heart pounded.

"Fine, Michael. I'll write the NIH in Washington immediately and ask them to transfer the project and funds to you."

He smiled at her as he continued. "I'll assure them that in my judgment you are the most qualified person in Israel to continue the work. But I have one condition—that Raquela Brzezinski work with you."

Raquela leaned forward hopefully.

"Then you admire her, too. . . . Yes, with all her other talents, she is also a fantastic organizer. Efficient. Highly responsible. Agreed, then, Michael?"

He hung up.

Approval arrived from Washington. Apprehensive, determined, Raquela honed herself to succeed.

The study involved the life and death of babies. On the basis of the material, doctors could provide better preventive-health services and keep more mothers and babies alive.

Raquela began working in the department of medical ecology of the medical school; her office was in the Bible House, one floor above Moshe's. She felt new energy unleash in her body; she threw herself into every aspect of the project.

Fascinated, she rediscovered the neighborhoods of Jerusalem as the researchers programmed the computer to produce statistical tables so they could correlate the origin of the mother's birth, the neighborhood she lived in, and her age with the rate of infant mortality, eclampsia, still-births, and congenital malformation.

Through the project, nurses were coming into their own. The survey teams were all nurses. And every Jewish, Christian, and Moslem pregnant woman in Jerusalem, and in the Arab and Jewish settlements in the Jerusalem corridor, was interviewed.

Mornings, Raquela jumped into her car and drove about the city, visiting each hospital and clinic and the vast network of mother and child care centers that Hadassah had started long ago and named *Tipat Halav*—drop of milk. (In the early days, milk for the Jewish and Arab babies in the centers had been delivered by donkey express.) From her office, Raquela could drive home in twenty minutes to be with Amnon and Rafi. And when she was not home, Mama fed them, baked their favorite cookies, kept a bag of chocolates especially for Rafi, and, whenever they liked, let them sleep in the cottage in Raquela's old bedroom. Papa, tall, scholarly, adoring grandfather, became their surrogate father.

Meanwhile, Raquela was pulling herself together, finding nourishment in her work and in raising her sons.

Her old friend Judith Steiner, who had become director of the nursing school, dropped in one afternoon for tea. She sat in the sunken living room, eating Raquela's home-baked fruit pie. Amnon and Rafi were at Mama's.

"We go back a long way," Judith said. "Will you forgive me if I try to give you some advice?"

"What kind of advice?" Raquela straightened her skirt. She dressed now like an executive, in handsome wool suits and silk blouses.

"You should start going out more." Judith bit into the pie, waiting for a reaction.

There was none.

"You're a beautiful woman, Raquela. I don't think you realize that a lot of eligible men would like to marry you."

Raquela put down her teacup. "I'm not ready, Judith. I can't do this to my boys. I can't bring a stranger into the house, into their lives. The boat's steady now. I don't want to rock it."

"The boys will grow up, and you'll be alone."

"I'm not afraid of loneliness. Someday, maybe when the boys are older, through their adolescence, I might consider marrying again. But not now. Now Amnon and Rafi need me."

She stood up and walked to the French doors. Papa's trees and plants were a tropical jungle outside, framing the doorway.

"I need time to mourn," she said.

Her best friends were Moshe and Isabella Prywes. They phoned often, constantly inviting her and the boys to dinner with their two daughters in their apartment at 19 Balfour Street, near Wingate Circle.

For Raquela, Isa was a role model, an extraordinary woman with extraordinary courage. Warm, highly intelligent, quintessential wife and mother, Isa sought to heal Raquela's wounds. But it was Isa who needed healing.

Isa was dying of cancer. She was forty-nine.

Moshe had kept her alive for eleven years. Whatever was new he tried. Every new drug. Every new treatment. He learned that in Chicago, Dr. Charles Huggins, who later became a Nobel laureate, was having some success reducing prostate cancer in men by injecting them with female hormones.

Moshe flew to Chicago. He brought Dr. Huggins slides of Isa's metastasized body. Would his treatment work for a woman? Could he help Isa?

Dr. Huggins had been to Jerusalem years before: he had met Isa, and admired her. He prepared concentrates of female hormones, and every few weeks drove to the airport in Chicago and sent them to Moshe "air express and with a prayer."

The hormones worked for a whole year. Isa had a miraculous remission.

But no longer. Even the massive doses of drugs could not halt the wildly reproducing cancer cells.

Moshe took Isa to the Hadassah hospital at Ein Karem. His office was now in the medical school on the main floor of the huge semicircular medical center.

Every hour he raced up the stairs to see her. Still fighting, she ate only when he came to feed her. Even her breakfast waited until his arrival; each morning he stopped off at a bakery to bring her freshly baked rolls and bread.

Jenny, their eighteen-year-old daughter, was serving with the army; her noncom gave her time off to visit her mother. Vivian, fourteen, came every day after school.

Raquela visited briefly each day, hoping to bring even a few minutes of distraction. She tried not to weep, marveling how Isa, racked with unbearable pain, continued to fight.

She died in November 1965.

Jenny was transferred to Jerusalem to be closer to home, and each evening she and Vivian tried to comfort their grief-stricken father. Jenny read chapters of the Bible aloud. One evening, she read from Exodus. Jethro, the father-in-law of Moses (Moshe), was addressing him in the desert: "Why sittest thou thyself alone?"

Jenny put down the book. She looked up at her father. "Daddy, you too are alone—like Moshe in the Bible. Alone too much. Someday soon I will marry. Vivi will marry. You're a young man, Daddy. Only fifty-one. You should get married."

It was the last day of December 1965.

Friends telephoned Moshe. "We're giving a New Year's Eve Party. Please come."

"I can't," he said. "I'm really not good company."

They insisted. "It will do you good. Just come to toast the New Year."

Raquela, too, was invited.

The party swirled around her; she tried to make small talk, but the evening dragged. She wondered why she had come.

Moshe, finding the gay atmosphere intolerable, took two doctors into a small room and soon involved them in a heated discussion of the medical school.

Midnight. The lights went out. Husbands and wives kissed each other.

Raquela was alone.

The lights went on. Moshe approached her. "Let's get out of here, Raquela. This is no place for either you or me tonight."

"Sure."

In the street, Moshe said, "Let me drive you home."

"I brought my car. What will I do with it?"

"I'll bring it to you tomorrow."

He opened the door of his car and helped her in.

He drove toward Herzl Boulevard, entered Bet Hakerem. She saw him pass her house and without a word continue along the highway around the Hills of Judea toward Ein Karem.

They drove in silence. Raquela could see the lights in the windows of the hospital rising up from the dark mountains.

"Let's turn around and go home," she said after a while.

"Why?" he asked, disappointed.

"It's very late."

He shifted gears and without another word turned the car around and brought her home.

The next morning Raquela found her car standing in front of the house. Why had Moshe not even rung her bell? Probably busy—the busiest man in the medical school.

Three days later he telephoned. "Raquela, I'm building a house in Ashkelon. The contractor is coming tomorrow. You've just built a house. You know so much more about this sort of thing than I do. Would you come along with me and talk to the contractor?"

"Why not?"

She sat beside him in the car, drinking in the Jerusalem air as they began the descent down the Hills of Judea. The once-barren stubbled hills with huge white boulders were now green, terraced with trees. Little settlements of Jews from Yemen, Cochin, India, Afghanistan, from Europe and from Arab lands, peopled the biblical hills and valley.

Just before Latrun, the Arab-held salient that blocked the highway, they turned south.

Raquela looked around. How often she had driven this road with Arik on her way to Beersheba. She relaxed. At last she could think of Arik without a stab of pain.

They were in the northern Negev, approaching the land around biblical Gath. The poignant words of David, lamenting the death of Saul and Jonathan, sang in her head: "Tell it not in Gath, publish it not in the streets of Ashkelon . . . lest the daughters of the Philistines rejoice . . ."

The terrain, fertile and green, became bony with bare-backed mountains. The Arab frontier closed in upon them everywhere. East of them, the Hebron Hills, in Jordan's hands, were a hotbed for the renewed Arab infiltration. Gaza, in Egypt's hands, lay south and west. The road itself was called the "Security Road," though it was far from secure and there were constant military forays upon it from both Jordan and Egypt.

Moshe stopped for gas in Kiryat Gath, the administrative center for the whole Lachish area. Lachish was the focal point of the largest and most dramatic regional scheme in the country, a kind of human TVA project that stretched from the Gaza Strip to the Hebron Hills, two hundred thousand acres of desert inside the explosive borders between Egypt and Jordan.

"I wish we had time to drive around this village," Moshe said, stretching his arm out of the car window. Kiryat Gath rose—starkly simple buildings filling up the sand dunes, as in a Dali landscape, against a gray endless hinterland of sand.

"This is where the people from the surrounding villages get together. They've got everything here—schools, factories, cotton gins, community centers. It's a fascinating experiment. Our sociologists and psychologists have worked out a new technique of absorption. We've discovered that the old pressure-cooker technique we used when the state was born—mixing all the newcomers, putting Poles and Iraqis, Rumanians and Moroccans, in one village—didn't work. We've learned that even Moroccans from the big cities like Casablanca and Rabat don't mix well with Moroccans who've lived in the caves of the Atlas Mountains."

"But it worked in Beersheba," Raquela said. "We had new immigrants from one hundred countries living together."

"It seems to work in bigger towns where you have plenty of jobs, plenty of housing, and good schools. It doesn't work in small villages, especially when you have unemployment. But the real integration will come with the children."

Raquela looked out the car window at a new village. Little yellow wooden houses stood, in a security-planned arch, on the hills and yellow sand. She saw women in colorful striped robes and men in black pantaloons, planting vegetables in their backyards.

"They're from the island of Djerba, in Tunis," Moshe said. "What we're doing now is keeping the people intact. Putting the people from one area together in single villages. Then the villages are like homogeneous satellites radiating around Kiryat Gath, which is the heterogeneous center."

"These little villages look so vulnerable." Raquela was

seeing her own country as if it were a new landscape.
"They look like little islands—so isolated."

"They're not as isolated as they seem. They're part of
our whole network of defense."

They drove on. The sand had almost disappeared. From
the main highway, Raquela saw desert land blooming.
Desert land grown fertile. Rows and rows of lush vibrant
cotton and corn marching like proud soldiers straight
toward the horizon.

"One word made all of this possible," Moshe said.

"Water!" She said it as if it were magic.

Moshe turned from the wheel to look at her. "Right. It's
a sacred word. We nearly went to war over it this year."

Nearly went to war. Raquela shuddered.

Israel had just finished the great National Water Car-
rier. Giant hydraulic engines lifted the Jordan River's
water from the Sea of Galilee; pipelines conducted it over
steep mountains; open sluiceways sped it down valleys. In
the center of the country it linked with the huge sixty-six-
inch Yarkon-Negev pipeline, which brought the water
from Tel Aviv's Yarkon River to Lachish.

The north, blessed with water, was now irrigating the
south; the once-barren desert was a harvest of crops and
flowers.

The Arabs, watching across the borders, were outraged.
Water was politics. Water was life. Water must *not* be allowed to make the Israeli desert bloom.

Syria corralled the Arab states, demanding they declare
war on Israel.

But the Arab states were not yet ready to go to war,
fearing a third defeat. In an Arab summit conference in
January 1964 they decided, instead of war, to try to divert
the headwaters of the Jordan River that ran through Syria.

War had failed to destroy Israel; diverting life-giving
water might succeed.

Israel regarded her right to the Jordan running through
her land as inalienable, as vital to her existence as the
waterways of the Straits of Tiran and the Gulf of Aqaba.

There were now constant clashes on both sides of the
biblical Jordan.

Would they go to war over water? Raquela wondered.
Would Amnon and Rafi grow up—to be alive?

But war seemed remote. The Syrians had thus far failed
to divert the headwaters. The clashes had temporarily

ended. Peace seemed in the air as they drove along the highway, smelling the fresh salt air of the Mediterranean.

Moshe drove into Ashdod. Like the empty desert Israel was now irrigating, so ten years ago had Ashdod, on the sea, been nothing but sand dunes and biblical history. Now it was Israel's second largest port, a completely manmade deep-water harbor. Raquela had driven through it with Arik when it was started—a raw frontier town with tin shacks and wooden houses. Now there were sunny garden apartments, ships flying flags of all nations in the harbor, and a pipeline bringing crude oil from Eilat.

Fifteen miles down the coast, they entered Ashkelon. One of the five great Philistine cities, it lay just six miles north of the Gaza Strip. The broad avenue was lined with date palms, flower beds, and ancient marble pillars.

"Read this." Moshe stopped the car. They walked to a historical marker to read the dedication to the prophet Zephania:

AND THE COAST SHALL BE FOR THE REMNANT OF THE HOUSE OF JUDAH; THEY SHALL FEED THEREUPON; IN THE HOUSES OF ASHKELON SHALL THEY LIE DOWN IN THE EVENING; FOR JEHOVAH THEIR GOD WILL VISIT THEM AND BRING BACK THEIR CAPTIVITY.

" 'Bring back their captivity,' " she repeated. "Look at all the people who've returned from their captivity and discovered Ashkelon."

The streets were filled with newcomers. Raquela watched them as Moshe drove down the main square, with its "Afridar" (South African) cultural center, its handsome clock tower scraping the blue sky. Hundreds of tourists ambled along; Israel had become an important tourist center. Americans, Germans, French, Swiss, Africans, Asians, and Englishmen wandered through the country, now flourishing with agriculture and industry. Ashkelon, charming and rich with biblical history, lay on the tourist route.

Moshe turned toward the beach and drove past small hotels until he reached his unfinished cottage. The contractor and his men were inside, plastering the walls.

Raquela took over. Moshe stood aside, smiling, while she examined the *balatas,* the Israeli tiles, pointed out that the floor was uneven, and discussed the way the doors

should be installed and where to put the outlets for the
stove and sink and refrigerator. The contractor began with
an argument and ended with total, if reluctant, capitulation.

They left the cottage to lunch on the side of a hill overlooking the Mediterranean. This was Samson country, and
the restaurant was named "Delilah."

They ordered a fish dinner. The breeze from the Mediterranean swept the restaurant. Through the window,
Raquela could see the sand stretching for miles, bleached
white against the turquoise Mediterranean.

Her lips curled with pleasure. She felt good. Everything
was good. The beautiful day. Ashkelon. The sea. Even the
discussion with the contractor.

The waiter brought the broiled sea bass, and the fish—
like everything else—was good.

But Moshe looked glum.

"Isn't your sea bass good? Mine's delicious. Here, try a
bite."

"It's not the fish," he snapped. "It's you."

Her mouth dropped. "What have I done?"

"If you want to know the truth, I'm hurt. You seem to
be more interested in those *balatas* than you are in me."

Raquela suppressed a laugh. "You brought me here to
talk to your contractor about the *balatas*. Now you're
complaining."

"You didn't have to enjoy it so much."

"You'd never have seen how crookedly he was laying
those *balatas* if I hadn't come along."

A few nights later they were guests at a dinner party
given by Arik's successor as chief of gynecology, Dr. Ze'ev
Polishuk. He had taken an apartment in the building next
to Moshe's, on Balfour Street.

When the party had ended, Moshe led her down the
stairs.

"Raquela," he whispered. "Leave your car here tonight.
Let's start walking around the block so nobody will see us.
I'll drive you home in my car."

"Okay." Her eyes crinkled. She had heard rumors
floating around the hospital and the university linking her
with Moshe. She had brushed them off. Ridiculous gossip.

She looked up the staircase. Sonya, one of the women
guests, was calling her. She waited. Sonya, tall, raven hair

braided around her head, hurried down, took her arm, and walked with her toward her car. "I forgot to ask you how your boys are, Raquela."

"They're fine."

"They must be big. Let's see—the older one must be almost ready for Gadna."

Gadna was pre-military training for fifteen to seventeen year olds.

"Amnon's in Gadna right now," Raquela said evenly. "In fact"—she offered more information; maybe Sonya was really interested—"he's near Eilat with his whole Gadna unit; they're in Beer Ora planting hydroponic vegetables. Well, here's my car."

She shook hands, said good-bye, opened the car door, drove a few yards away and stopped. She watched Sonya walk toward Moshe's apartment house on Balfour Street. Moshe was standing in front of the building, looking at the silver-blue sky, enjoying the serenity and beauty of the Jerusalem night, waiting to join Raquela.

Sonya chatted awhile with Moshe; Raquela watched her shake his hand and saw Moshe disappear inside the gate. Sonya walked away.

A few minutes later, Moshe knocked on Raquela's car window. She opened the door and slid over. He took the driver's seat, parked her car behind his, returned her keys, and helped her into his car.

"We're like a couple of teenagers," Raquela said, giggling.

Moshe steered the car down the Jerusalem mountains. "Here we are—the beautiful young widow with two kids, the eligible widower also with two kids—fooling a gossipy neighbor. God only knows what orgies she's picturing we're up to. . . ."

"But she's such a good friend—to both of us. She was so kind to me when Arik died."

Soon they were on the road to Tel Aviv. Moshe was humming a tune—maybe something from Poland, she thought.

She tried to look at her watch. Surely it was past midnight. Tomorrow was a working day. She had to be up at six to give Amnon and Rafi their breakfast, get them off to school, and get to her office before eight. She had a full day of meetings with nurses to discuss their findings. She had promised Dr. Davies a statistical report. She had never thought statistics could be so fascinating.

Each day the study seemed to grow more meaningful. Dr. Davies was planning a book on toxemia in pregnancy, and Moshe was to be its editor.

"We'd better turn back," she said.

Moshe stopped humming, screeched his brakes, made a desperate U-turn, stepped on the gas, and sped back to Jerusalem. He neither hummed nor spoke.

Probably tired, Raquela thought. *Or he's got a million things on his mind.* She was silent. *Better not to break his concentration.*

At her door, he let her out of the car. "Have your brother Itzhak pick up your car tomorrow morning. I'm going to be busy."

He drove away.

She unlocked the door, tiptoed to the boys' bedrooms, assured herself they were sleeping peacefully, and hurried to her room. *I won't get much sleep for tomorrow—that's for sure,* she told herself. Yet she undressed slowly and stood for a long time in front of the mirror, putting cold cream on her face. *Wonder what's bothering Moshe? He's been a widower for only two months. Grief makes people act in strange ways. Maybe this is the only way he's able to cope with Isa's death.*

The next days were hectic; a group of doctors from Washington arrived, and Raquela was delegated to chauffeur them to the hospitals and the Arab and Jewish settlements in the Jerusalem corridor. They met with the pregnant mothers, talked with the nurses. Then, late in the afternoon, Raquela took them to Musrara, a poor working-class neighborhood on the northwestern frontier of Jerusalem.

They climbed to the roof of Notre-Dame-de-France; the stone walls were pocked with bullets and gaping holes.

The Old City spread before them, its turrets and domes luminous, molten gold in the setting sun. Raquela felt a stab of pain; memories of the Old City swept over her.

A Jordanian soldier, patrolling the crenellated wall, pointed his rifle at them. Raquela could look right down the muzzle.

"Get back!" she commanded.

The doctors huddled against the wall inside.

Ten minutes later, Raquela led them out again. The soldier had disappeared. "On that hill up there," she said, "northeast of us, is Mount Scopus." They could see cars on the road, Arabs walking in long gowns. They could make out a vague cluster of buildings on Mount Scopus.

"What a frustration it must be," one of the doctors observed, "to have those great facilities lying idle, wasted. And so close."

"I know," she said. "It's awful that Jerusalem should be truncated! That we can't use the hospital and the school. That we can't get to the Western Wall and our ancient synagogues in the Old City. That Christians can't get to their holy places, though they're just a few yards away. But someday"—she paused—"someday Jerusalem will be reunited. I hope I will be alive to see it."

The next day, Raquela drove the group of doctors to Tel Aviv. She took them to museums and art galleries, let them browse in the bookshops.

"Seems there's a bookshop on every block," one of the doctors commented, filling his arms with books to take home.

They walked along the beach at Hayarkon Street, lunched in an outdoor fish restaurant in Jaffa, and cruised, bumper to bumper, down Dizengoff Street and Allenby Road.

"Traffic here's as bad as in Washington, D.C.," the bearded doctor said.

"It's not only our traffic that's like America," she said, laughing, remembering the sabbatical with Arik and Amnon in New York. "Our whole country has Yankee ways. My children buy American milkshakes in the Brooklyn Ice Cream bar. I take our linens to a self-service laundry and wash them in American washing machines. Our roads are full of American cars; our streets are full of American tourists; and my sons are growing up learning the facts of life from Hollywood."

"I tried to see a movie last night," a portly doctor said. "But I gave up. The line went all around the block."

"You know who the favorite character of our children is?" she asked. "Mickey Mouse. But we call him 'Mickey Mahoo,' which means 'Mickey What Is He?'

"After a year in New York," she went on, "I sometimes think Israel is the east coast of the United States."

* * *

For more than two weeks, heavy rainstorms swept the country.

The telephone rang in Raquela's bedroom. It was Moshe.

"I'm worried about what this rain is doing to your beach house. I'm free tomorrow. Can you take the day off? I'll drive you out there and we can see whether the rains have done any damage."

"Great idea, Moshe. I'll get to my office at seven, show my secretary what to do, and I'll be ready about eight o'clock."

"Leave your car near the last traffic light on Jaffa Road. I'll pick you up in mine."

"I'll bring sandwiches."

The rain had ended, but the day was raw.

Moshe was humming again as they drove on the coastal road along the Mediterranean past Netanya. A few miles north and they were at the summer colony in Bet Yannai. It looked cold and deserted. They walked up a sandy embankment to the beach house. The waves lashed the shore.

"First thing I'm going to do is to make us some hot coffee." Raquela's teeth were chattering. Moshe sat in the kitchen, rubbing his hands to warm them, watching her. They munched on sandwiches and nutcake and warmed themselves with Turkish coffee.

"Now, let's look around the house," Moshe said.

They examined the kitchen and the small living room.

"So far, so good," he said. "Now let's see the bedroom."

He followed her into the bedroom.

"Take off your shoes, Raquela."

She kicked off her pumps.

"Now stand up on the bed!"

Slowly she climbed up on the mattress and tried to steady herself. Moshe stood at the edge of the bed, reached up, and put his arms around her waist.

"I think I love you, Raquela."

A smile seemed to rise from inside her body. For the first time since Arik's death she felt desired.

"I want to remember you like this for the rest of my life—standing this way, on the bed, in your green suede suit."

She stepped down and looked up at his face. "I think I love you, too, Moshe."

Each morning at six, Raquela was awakened by Moshe's telephone call telling her how he loved her. And each night, after the children in both their houses were asleep, she telephoned him.

Somehow that act—asking her to take off her shoes, more intimate than asking her to take off her clothes—had ignited her.

In the next weeks he came to her late at night, parked his car a block away, and slipped into her house. Other nights, when Jenny and Vivian were away, she drove to Balfour Street, left her car up the hill on Wingate Circle, and went up to his apartment.

It seemed her whole life had led to this joyous mature love. The man beside her, recognized all over the world, was like a young lover. She could lie back, struck by his beauty, his manhood; they connected on every level. They discussed her work and his; they laughed like children. They took drives through the Jerusalem they loved, finding no need for words in the luminous air of the biblical land from which they drew their strength.

"I'm a lucky woman," Raquela said one night. She lay happily in his arms in her bedroom. Amnon and Rafi were away on an overnight hike. "Some women go through life without knowing even one great passion." Her fingertips caressed his cheek. "I've known two."

Moshe drew her closer. "We've both known love before. We both loved our mates. I think that's why we're so good together." He covered her face and throat with kisses. "I don't want to be alone anymore, Raquela. I want you at my side. All the time: in Jerusalem and when I travel. I want to marry you."

"Not yet, Moshe." She closed her eyes. "Not yet. I'm not ready for marriage."

"But we're in love."

"I need time, Moshe."

"For God's sake, why?"

"Don't ask me. I just know it. Why can't we go on like this?"

He rose from the bed and dressed.

Raquela drew her robe around her in bed.

"I can't go on this way, Raquela. I see it clearly now. We must make a decision. Either we get married or we stop seeing each other altogether."

She sat up straight. "Why? We love each other. What else matters?"

"Many things matter. For one thing, you're a young woman. You should be married. And people are talking."

"People will talk whether we sleep together or not."

"No. I want us to live together as man and wife—I, to be the father to your children; you, the mother to mine."

"Gossip doesn't disturb me. We're free people, Moshe."

"You amaze me." He sat down on the side of her bed. "I'm supposed to be the worldly one. I used to think you—this girl from Bet Hakerem and I—the big-city man from Paris. Now the tables are turned. You're the one who doesn't care how people talk."

"Let them talk, Moshe. I'm in love with you. We don't owe these gossips anything. The only ones I'm concerned about are our children."

"So am I. That's the very reason we ought to get married."

"I don't think the children are ready. I'm sure my boys aren't; frankly, I don't think your girls are, either."

"Nonsense, Raquela. We'd be doing our kids a favor by marrying. My girls hang around the house too much; they're always worrying about me. In fact, Jenny's forever telling me I'm alone too much, that I should get married."

The cold Jerusalem night filled the bedroom, but Raquela's hands were hot and damp.

"Moshe," she said. "I'm afraid Amnon and Rafi would hate any man who would try to take Arik's place. Even if it's subconscious—they could feel such anger, at the same time such guilt and conflict—they could make our lives miserable."

"We could overcome that, Raquela. I love your boys, and I think they love me. They're now, what—fifteen and ten? They need a father figure. You know there's a danger in boys' growing up with only a strong mother. You want them to be real men, don't you?"

"Of course, Moshe."

"And as for my daughters, if we marry, it would free them to begin living their own lives."

He stood up and looked down at her. "I'm sick of sneaking around. I can't keep crawling out of here late at night. I hate it when you have to drive home from my house. Those games we played—sure, they were fun for a while. But it's enough. We have to make a decision."

She lay back on her pillow. "I'm happy with what we have, Moshe. I can give you what you need—this way—if you let me."

His lips were drawn tight.

"We have to make a decision, Raquela. Tonight."

"Yes?" She hid her hands under the blanket lest he see them tremble.

"Let's have a trial separation."

Pain gripped her stomach.

He was pacing the bedroom. "Jerusalem is a very small city. Like a fish tank. Everybody knows what's going on. Let's not meet for three or four months."

"If that's what you want."

"I want it. I want to see if we can live without each other. It's no good this way."

He kissed her. "Don't get up. I'll close the door on my way out."

She heard his footsteps go down the hall, then the door—cautiously locked. She put her head in the pillow and wept.

Sometime in the middle of the night she finally fell asleep, dreaming the phone was ringing. She jumped up, reaching for the telephone. There was only a buzz.

At six, she waited for his morning call. None came.

At seven, unable to eat breakfast, she drove to her office on the campus, and somehow managed to get through the morning hours.

By noon, she thought she was going mad. In the late afternoon her associates left. She stayed on alone, trying to concentrate on the papers and huge record books spread out neatly on her desk. Over and over she read the words: *"Table 1. Jerusalem district population, sex, ethnic origin, fertility rates."* The words danced in front of her. She gave up and drove home.

Suppertime. She fed Amnon and Rafi; they went to their rooms to do their homework. They kissed her goodnight. She sat on the sofa in the sunken living room, looking through the French doors at Papa's tropical, jungle-green plants.

The phone was silent. Why had he decided on this trial by separation? Why was a man as sophisticated as Moshe concerned about what people said or thought? Didn't they have a right to be happy? Hadn't they both suffered enough? He was entitled to happiness. Why was he so sensitive to the evil-minded, foul-mouthed gossips? They were both adults. What, for God's sake, was wrong with two mature people's living together until they were *both* absolutely sure they wanted marriage?

Raquela stood up restlessly. She took out her knitting bag and began a soft, wooly green and white sweater for a friend's baby.

Had she lost him forever? Would some other woman grab him? Marry him the minute he asked? With his looks, his charm, his position of power, he could probably have any woman he wanted—in any land. He exuded sex appeal. He had touched parts of her that had been dead, reawakened her to the joys of being a woman.

She was filled with despair. Loneliness swept over her.

The telephone rang. "Raquela, I'm coming over to get you and bring you to my apartment."

She flew to the bathroom, showered, and dressed in the green suede suit. He brought her to his apartment on Balfour Street.

He helped her into a chair in the living room. The lights were low. He poured wine, and they sat, drinking it slowly.

"Isn't this nice?" he said, as though nothing had happened.

"Very nice," she agreed.

"Let's make a promise," he said. "We'll never have such a long separation again, for the rest of our lives—like these twenty-four hours."

They spent their honeymoon traveling for two months.

Moshe, vice-president of the Hebrew University, was invited to be the guest speaker at conferences and banquets, to describe Israel's work in aiding developing countries.

They went to Teheran, New Delhi, Bangkok, Tokyo, Kyoto, Honolulu, San Francisco, New York, and back to Jerusalem.

It was January 1967.

-✦ Chapter Twenty-eight ✦-

April 1967

"I've called you together to give out assignments. We've got to prepare."

Dr. Kalman Jacob Mann, the Jerusalem-born director general of the Hadassah–Hebrew University Medical Center, stood before the entire staff. His smooth-shaved face was agitated. The hospital light seemed to bounce off his troubled eyes.

"Kibbutz Gadot has just been attacked by the Syrians. We've had word the Syrians have already lobbed in some three hundred fifty shells. They're using powerful Soviet cannons. The crops are burning; homes have been destroyed. The kindergarten and two of the children's nurseries have been reduced to rubble."

"Casualties?" Moshe interrupted. He sat in the front row, facing Dr. Mann, Raquela beside him.

Dr. Mann turned to Moshe. "With the first sound of fire, all the people—there are eighty adults and eighty children—jumped into the trenches and raced down to the bomb-proof shelters. So far we've heard that only one person was injured, a Christian tourist from Switzerland who received a minor injury in his foot."

He paused. "Let me read you this dispatch I just received from army headquarters.

" 'Syrians have shelled two more kibbutzim on the Sea of Galilee—Ein Gev and Tel Katzir. Israel Air Force silenced Syrian guns. Russian MIGs attacked our planes. We shot down six MIGs. Syrians retreated.' "

The hall filled with whispers. Many had relatives and friends in these kibbutzim. Raquela could see Ein Gev, one of the most beautiful kibbutzim in Israel, with pomegranates and apple blossoms and tropical flowers; each year she had attended the music festival in Ein Gev, had

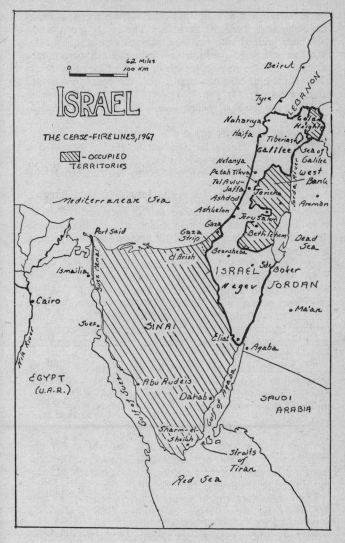

62 Miles
100 KM

ISRAEL

THE CEASE-FIRE LINES, 1967

▨ – OCCUPIED
  TERRITORIES

Mediterranean Sea

Beirut

Tyre

LEBANON

Nahariya

Haifa   Tiberias
            Galilee   Sea of
                         Galilee
Netanya

Petah Tikva
Tel Aviv–
Jaffa   Jericho   Golan
Ashdod   Heights
Ashkelon   West
            Jerusalem   Bank
Gaza   Amman
Gaza   Bethlehem
Strip   Dead
Beersheba   Sea

el Arish

Port Said

Ismailia   ISRAEL   Sde
                               Boker
Cairo   Negev   JORDAN

Suez   SINAI   Ma'an

Nile River

                    Eliat
SUEZ   Aqaba
EGYPT   Abu Rudeis
(U.A.R.)   Dahab   SAUDI
                            ARABIA

            Sharm-el-
            Sheikh
                        Straits
                        of
                        Tiran
        Red Sea

heard Israeli and visiting musicians—Isaac Stern, Alexander Schneider, Leonard Bernstein. The lovely green lawns had been gouged with trenches, like scars on a man's face. She had watched air-raid drills. Little children were taught to jump into the nearest trench or descend into the closest shelter calmly, without panic, the moment an air-raid alarm went off.

"Do you think it means war?" Raquela whispered to Moshe.

"He's preparing us anyway."

Like all of Israel's large hospitals, Hadassah served a dual purpose—civilian and military. Even Tel Hashomer, where Raquela had served as an army nurse, treated both soldiers and civilians.

Dr. Mann was now assigning specific duties to members of the staff. Raquela watched as the energetic, fifty-five-year-old kind-faced physician called out familiar names. She had known Dr. Mann and his attractive wife, Sylvia, a well-known writer, from the day he became Hadassah's sixth director, in 1951. She had delivered their fourth son.

Dr. Mann was now talking to Moshe. "As my deputy," he said, "your duties will include maintaining constant and direct contact with the front. Get information such as number of wounded, types of injuries. Pass it on to our medical teams immediately, so the moment the casualties are flown in here by helicopter they can go right to the proper departments."

"And Raquela"—he turned his full gaze on her—"I want you to organize five satellite hospitals that will be under the Army-Hadassah command. As soon as this meeting ends, the army will contact you to help you select the best locations."

The assignments continued. But Raquela was already planning possible sites. An hour later she was in her car with an army captain, driving around Jerusalem. They entered hotels, studying the facilities; they visited schools and institutions and college dormitories.

The hotels were almost empty; tourists, sensing the tension in the air, were fleeing the country. Others, afraid to enter, canceled their reservations.

Raquela selected the King's Hotel and the President, in the center of town, and the Holy Land Hotel on the outskirts—a hilltop garden spot.

The fourth satellite was a dormitory on the campus of

the Hebrew University. The fifth, which she made her headquarters, was a convalescent home in Motza, in the Hills of Judea, the scene of the 1929 massacre.

In early May, Israel seemed listless and vulnerable. The country was deep in an economic depression, euphemistically called a "slowdown." Morale was low. Unemployment was mounting.

Israel's nineteenth birthday was celebrated on May 15, 1967. Amnon and Rafi marched with the other eleven- and sixteen-year-olds in the annual Independence Day parade. Raquela and Moshe stood on the street as the soldiers marched and the leaders of the government took the salute. Because Israel was not eager to create new furor in the Arab capitals, there were no planes maneuvering overhead, no tanks rumbling down the streets.

At dusk, Prime Minister Levi Eshkol was called to the telephone. "Egyptian troops in vast numbers are moving through Cairo. Some have already reached the Sinai Peninsula."

Eshkol was caught by surprise. His advisers had assured him Egypt would not be ready for aggression before 1970.

They based their estimates on Nasser's own words—that he was not yet ready for all-out war. He was facing defeat in Yemen, where his armies were busy attempting to overthrow the Imam. German scientists, many of them former Nazis, were building rockets outside Cairo that could penetrate Israel within minutes. But the rocket program was still not completed. Egypt's population was exploding. There was starvation in the land. Nasser's charisma was wearing thin. What made him choose Israel's Independence Day to flaunt his troop movements?

Driving to her headquarters in Motza, Raquela listened to Nasser's voice on Radio Cairo: "*All Egypt is now prepared to plunge into total war which will put an end to Israel.*"

Did Nasser believe his own rhetoric?

The next day, Eshkol ordered a limited mobilization.

Nasser was moving fast.

On May 18, 1967, he demanded that U Thant, secretary general of the UN, remove UNEF (United Nations Emergency Force) troops from the Egyptian-Israeli border—from Gaza to Eilat.

Before U Thant even replied, Nasser sent Egyptian troops to reoccupy Sharm el Sheikh.

U Thant capitulated to the ultimatum and withdrew the UNEF troops. The Palestine Liberation Army instantly moved into the vacated positions in the Gaza Strip.

On May 22 Nasser addressed his pilots at the air-force base of Abu Suweir: "The Gulf of Aqaba is closed to Israelis." He imposed a total blockade of all Israeli ships, and stopped all foreign vessels carrying matériel to Israel.

Setting up the satellite hospital in the Holy Land Hotel, Raquela discussed Nasser's latest moves with an army medic, a young red-haired kibbutznik from the desert.

"It means war," the medic said. "Closing our waterways is an overt act of war."

"But there's still hope for peace," she said, to calm her own fears. "Eban's running around the world right now. Talking to all the leaders. Seventeen countries—in addition to the UN—guaranteed our right to sail into and out of the Red Sea. England, France, the United States, even Russia, guaranteed our survival. Surely they'll stand by their commitments."

Eban began his shuttle.

In Paris, President Charles de Gaulle, once Israel's great friend, told Eban the days of their cooperation were over. France, now out of Algeria, had turned to the Arabs. Even the arms which Israel had ordered and paid for were not to be delivered, de Gaulle said, "to prevent Israel from starting a war."

Eban flew across the Channel to London.

Prime Minister Harold Wilson acknowledged England's commitment. He recommended patience and restraint. His foreign minister, George Brown, flew to Moscow and proposed to Alexei Kosygin that the Big Four convince the UN to return UNEF to the borders and to get Nasser to withdraw his troops from Sharm el Sheikh. "Do you want a second Suez?" Kosygin demanded.

Eban flew to Washington.

President Lyndon Johnson agreed that Nasser must be stopped; the blockade must be lifted; Israel's survival was at stake. Johnson had a brilliant idea. He would ask all the nations who guaranteed Israel's integrity to send ships to the Red Sea. An international flotilla would sail through the Straits of Tiran, flying their flags, escorting an Israeli vessel.

Not one country sent even a rowboat.

Amnon and Rafi, their schools closed, filled sandbags.
In teams of teenage boys and girls, they dug bomb-proof shelters in gardens and parks in Jerusalem.

They helped run the post office and delivered the mail.

Women drove the milk trucks, and bakers worked around the clock; at least there would be milk and bread—if war came.

The army prepared coffins which could hold bodies for a year in case there was no time for burial. Hassidim in black silk caftans joined bare-legged youngsters digging graves in the parks. Tel Aviv was prepared for forty thousand deaths.

The men and women of Haga—the civil defense—patrolled the cities' streets, carrying white gas masks made, of all places, in Germany. Intelligence warned that the Egyptians, who had already used poison gas in Yemen, were planning to use gas in Israel.

Kol Israel told women throughout the country how to prepare for enemy bombers:

> —Tape your windows, to prevent them from splintering.
> —Get blackout material. Black out at least one room, so you can have a light in one room in your apartment.
> —Fill your sandbags, and pile them at the entrances of your house.
> —Inside your apartment, put sandbags around the butane-gas metal tanks near your stoves. If tanks get a direct hit, they will ignite.
> —Get first-aid materials. Every pharmacy has kits already made up.
> —Disconnect electrical appliances whenever possible.
> —Keep a small bag of clothing ready to take into an air-raid shelter.
> —Prepare water in cans and in the bathtub, so you have enough water for each member of the household.
> —Stock up with a week's supply of food.

Raquela, apprehensive, tried to calm her own fears. She blacked out the windows in the house and in the satellite hospitals, put sandbags at the entrances, kept small bags of clothing ready, filled the bathtub with water, stocked the pantry.

In the little frontier towns where the Jewish immigrants from Arab lands had put down roots, women were bewildered. Their sons and husbands in the army were somewhere in the desert or the mountains. The government sent the women money; at least there was food in the house to feed the children. But they had lived through so much—fleeing the Arabs back home, the strange land, the new tongue, the children going to school, learning all these new ways—and now this: tape your windows! It was almost too much to absorb.

During the last weeks of May, bells began ringing in people's homes. Messengers scurried about the country, bringing sealed envelopes. Notices were slipped under doors or handed to people in factories, in universities, in hospitals, and in the fields.

Some dashed home for their uniforms; others telephoned their homes or offices—"This is it!"—and rushed to join their groups. Red-lettered notices were posted on doors. It was total mobilization.

Every able-bodied man—teacher, taxicab driver, doctor, bartender, banker, street cleaner—up to the age of forty-nine was called up. They had been practicing for years; the whole army could be mobilized within twenty-four hours and placed in the field twenty-four hours later. Enlisted men, long after their regular stint in the army, had been serving a month each year; officers, five or six weeks a year.

Normally, married women with childen were not expected to be called up; but some of the married women with certain essential skills—doctors, nurses, computer and radio operators, intelligence officers—were mobilized before their husbands, and the telephone wires in Colonel Stella Levy's office at the headquarters of CHEN were hot with angry husbands demanding to know why they weren't called up first. Why should their wives be given this privilege? What kind of reverse sex discrimination was this?

Survival was the imperative—survival against the Arabs, as once it had been survival against the Germans. This time there was a land in which to fight, and an army to do the fighting. This time there were planes and armor and men superbly skilled in mobility and flexibility. The people turned to the army to save them, and in this army of reservists—who made up eighty percent of the total forces—the army was the people.

On May 30, Raquela and Moshe, listening to the radio at home in Bet Hakerem, heard Kol Israel: *"Jordan has joined forces with Egypt and Syria. King Hussein, of Jordan, announced the military alliance was '. . . so that we can tread the proper road leading to the erasure of our shame and the liberation of Palestine.'"*

They turned to the Arab stations: *"We will gouge out Dayan's other eye . . . we must fight with the maximum of violence . . . not a single Jew will survive."*

Raquela looked at Moshe's face, his eyes raw with fatigue. He had been working day and night, preparing the medical center. Nearly all the civilian patients had been discharged to free beds for the casualities; Hadassah had set up an additional fifteen hundred beds in the hallways and wards.

On June 3, General Moshe Dayan, called back into the cabinet to become minister of defense, held a press conference. "I do not expect and do not want anyone else to fight for us. Whatever can be done in the diplomatic way I would welcome and encourage, but if somehow it comes to real fighting, I would not like American or British boys to get killed here, and I do not think we need them."

No American or British boys. Good. But every single Israeli was ready.

Time had no meaning, save that it was running out.

Death and annihilation hung in the air. The Arabs were marching. Arab states thousands of miles away—Saudi Arabia, Kuwait, Sudan—were joining Egypt, Syria, Jordan, and Iraq, racing to the slaughter.

Would this be a new holocaust? Had Israel been born in 1948 only to be destroyed in 1976? Had the great "ingathering of all the peoples" brought them into one tiny land, the more easily to be massacred?

These were the darkest days the people had known since Auschwitz.

June 5, 1967

Raquela turned on the radio in the kitchen for the eight-A.M. news.

"This is Kol Israel broadcasting from Jerusalem. The military spokesman announces the Egyptians this morning launched a land-and-air attack."

"My God!" She gripped the arms of her chair.

"Israel's forces went into action to repel them."

Could they break out of the iron ring? Throw back the armies amassed on all their borders?

The telephone rang. It was Moshe.

"You've heard the news?" He was breathless.

"Oh, Moshe. After all the tension, I feel like one of those springs children play with. The coils are out. Can you believe—I feel something strange, almost like relief."

"Where are the children?"

"Jenny's at the university. Vivi, Amnon, and Rafi are out somewhere filling sandbags."

"Try to get them together back in the house. To be with your parents close to the shelter. The war's all in the Negev so far. We're hoping Jerusalem will be spared."

"I'll get the children right away. Then I'll go right up to the hospital in Motza. If you get any news, call me there."

"Promise me you'll drive carefully." His voice dropped. "I could not live if—"

"And you, Moshe . . ." She clutched the telephone. Would she ever hear his voice again?

She found the children near the house, brought them to Mama and Papa. "Keep the radio on," she told them. "Follow instructions to the letter."

She kissed them and drove through the city. The streets were almost empty. Would Jerusalem remain open, like Paris and Rome during World War II? She turned on the news in her car.

The radio was like a symbol of the world they lived in—in the very center of the dial was Kol Israel, surrounded on both ends by Arab stations. She tuned in Cairo Radio. The Egyptian commentator was exhorting, *"Arise! Go forth into battle! The hour of glory is here."*

A twist of the dial. Now it was Damascus Radio: *"The*

time has come! Silence the enemy! Destroy him! Liberate Palestine!"

Back to the center of the world, Kol Israel: music. Then the announcer: *"Be calm. The next newscast will be at nine A.M."*

Raquela made swift stops at the satellite hospitals in the hotels and the campus dormitory. They were all fully staffed, every nurse at her station. The hospital beds with white hospital sheets were ready.

"Keep in touch with me at our headquarters in Motza," she told the staffs, and raced back to her car.

Again the radio dial; still no news on Kol Israel. She was growing frantic. Only music. *"Be calm. Next newscast ten A.M."* The quiet voice of General Chaim Herzog, the military commentator for Kol Israel, entered the car. *"A new chapter in the wars of Israel has been opened."*

His voice stilled the pulse beating in her head. He was explaining Israel's blackout of news.

"It is not always advisable to report on battles, for at times the enemy is interested to learn the facts of the situation no less than we are. Under the circumstances of unprecedented hysteria on the part of the Arabs, their false reporting and utter instability, it is advisable that they continue to believe their own false stories, up to a point. The fog of war hinders the enemy, and so let us leave him with it rather than dispel it."

The fog of war.

It was a hard lesson learned from the Sinai Campaign. In 1956, while Nasser was broadcasting "glorious victories" against Israel, his leaders were tuned into Kol Israel to learn the truth of his defeat. In 1967 Arab leaders would know only the fog of war.

The broadcast went on. *"The young people . . . the farm boys, the Yeshiva students, the members of the youth movements, the boys of the immigrant townships, all are at this moment shoulder to shoulder fighting in the air, on the land, and on the sea for our right simply to live."*

Our right simply to live. . . . That's all we ask. . . .

She heard a jolting explosion. Sirens shrieked. People raced off the streets into air-raid shelters and hallways. She heard shells exploding. She sped her car up the Hills of Judea toward Motza.

Kol Israel at last was crackling with news. *"Jordanians have opened fire on Jerusalem. Prime Minister Eshkol ear-*

lier sent a message to King Hussein through United Nations' General Odd Bull. Eshkol's message said: 'We shall not initiate any action whatsoever against Jordan. However, should Jordan open hostilities, we shall react with all our might. And Hussein will have to bear the full responsibilities for all the consequences.' "

The commentator paused for a brief second. *"Jordanian shells have hit the Hadassah hospital."*

Raquela clamped her hand over her mouth. Not the hospital! Dear God, keep Moshe safe.

She pressed her foot on the gas. At the convalescent home, she jumped out of the car and dashed inside. She picked up the phone. The lines were open. She reached Moshe. "Are you all right?"

"We're all okay." Moshe's voice had never been so welcome. "Most of the shells miraculously fell in the courtyard."

"Anyone hurt?"

"Nobody."

She breathed relief. "The Chagall windows?"

"Just a few tiny holes. Nothing serious. Where are you?" he asked anxiously. "Are you at Motza?"

"Of course. But don't worry about me."

"Listen, Raquela. I *am* worried. Promise me you won't go out on the road like a cowboy before the 'all clear' sounds."

"You know I've got better sense than that."

"We'll keep in touch all day."

Wherever the fighting, the war was only a telephone call away.

Before noon, the whole length of Jerusalem was under Jordanian fire. The Arab Legionnaires were attacking the city and the Israeli towns along the West Bank with 25-pounders, 120mm mortars, and 155mm "Long Toms."

Two-twenty-five P.M. General Uzi Narkiss, short, slight and unmilitary looking, counterattacked.

The hospitals began filling up with wounded—the medical center at Ein Karem, the hospitals downtown, Raquela's headquarters at Motza. Every few hours Moshe called her with news. The Israel Museum and several public buildings had been slightly damaged. The Knesset fortunately was not hit.

In Haifa, Syrian planes attacked the bay area. Natanya was bombed by Iraqi war planes. At nine-fifteen P.M. Tel

Aviv was hit; the long-range guns of the Arab Legion shelled Masaryk Square.

Raquela spent the night at Motza. Every hour on the hour she turned on Kol Israel. Music. Still no news. She switched to the Arab stations. Nasser's commanders were reporting fantastic victories. The Arabs were winning on every front. At the United Nations an emergency session at ten-twenty P.M. New York time was adjourned at ten-twenty-five P.M. The Soviet Union was silent. With the reports of the Arabs' spectacular triumphs, no one pressed for a cease-fire.

More wounded arrived at Motza. Raquela, assisting the doctors and nurses, helped admit paratroopers caught by Jordanian mortars.

"I never saw such fighting," one of the soldiers told her. "We had to break through five fences of barbed wire. The Jordanians had underground tunnels kilometers long. Trenches. Hundreds of bunkers and gun emplacements everywhere. Some of our tanks were set on fire. The crews burned alive."

One-thirty A.M. News at last on Kol Israel. Raquela, snatching a few moments of rest, sat up. General Yitzhak Rabin, chief of staff, was holding a press conference. Kol Israel was carrying it live. *"The Israel Air Force has destroyed three hundred seventy-four enemy planes with a loss of only nineteen of our own. In eighty minutes Israel has destroyed Egypt's entire air force. Our armor and troops have captured Khan Yunis, in the Gaza Strip; El Arish and Rafiah, along the Mediterranean, have fallen. Gaza is encircled."*

Raquela telephoned the hospital. "Moshe, Moshe! We're winning! All the Arab broadcasts today were lies."

"Marvelous, Raquela!" His voice still had the edge of sleep. "I had my radio on but I guess I was exhausted and dozing. What a day—to end like this."

The fog of battle had lifted.

The next morning, Tuesday, June 6, Nasser and Hussein talked on the telephone; the call was monitored by the Israelis:

Nasser: "We are fighting with all strength and we have battles going on on every front all night . . . God is with us . . . I will make an announcement and you will make an announcement and we will see to it that the Syrians

make an announcement that American and British air-
planes are taking part against us from aircraft carriers."

Hussein: "Good. All right."

Nasser: "A thousand thanks. Do not give up. We are
with you with all our heart and we are flying our planes
over Israel today; our planes are striking at Israel's airfields since morning."

Nasser had concocted the story to vindicate his air
force's defeat. Israel alone could not possibly have inflicted
such deadly damage; the United States and Britain must
be helping. Hussein agreed to the myth-making.

For Hussein's own Arab Legion was being thrown back.
Israeli paratroopers captured the Sheikh Jarrah quarter
that for nineteen years had blocked the road to Mount
Scopus. Now the paratroopers began circling the hills
north of the Old City. They were young soldiers who had
never seen the Western Wall, never walked the laby-
rinthine streets of old Jerusalem. Yet they knew the Old
City. They knew it from their books, and their parents'
stories, and their Bible studies.

Advancing toward the Old City, they fought in trenches,
in rooms, on roofs, in cellars. Some of the Jordanians retreating from the front line took cover inside the buildings,
and there was house-to-house fighting. There were heavy
casualties everywhere.

The Arab Legionnaires stationed on the parapets of the
Old City wall, mowed down civilians. More than five
hundred wounded and dying men, women, and children
were rushed to the hospitals. Some nine hundred homes
and apartments were damaged.

In the wards at Motza, Raquela moved among the
wounded, bringing them news of the battles for Jerusalem.

A young officer, his chest heavily bandaged, called out
to her. "Nurse, how soon can I get out of here?"

"You've got a bullet lodged near your heart, Captain."

"It's only a little hole. I've got to join my boys. I've got
to be with them when we liberate the Old City."

Raquela spoke brusquely. "You're staying right in this
bed. You have been seriously wounded."

That night, after the captain fell asleep, Raquela removed his uniform and boots from the footlocker near his
bed. She hid them in her office.

Early Wednesday morning she made her rounds. The
captain's bed was empty.

"Where is he?" she asked the private in the next bed.

"He's back at the front by now. He borrowed somebody else's uniform. Look, nurse, don't look so upset. We'd all do the same if we could."

After forty-eight hours, Raquela decided to drive to Ein Karem to see Moshe, then return home to be with the children and collapse for a few hours in her own bed.

Nearing the semicircular hospital, she saw army helicopters landing in the hospital courtyard. Attendants rushed the wounded inside.

She found Moshe in his office, on the telephone, talking to a doctor in the field. He finished his conversation, stood up, and embraced her. "What are you doing, driving here with all the shelling?"

She clung to him, drawing strength from his body.

"Don't scold me. I drove carefully. But I had to see you."

"How can I scold you." He kissed her. "But I'm not going to let you stay long. You've got to get some sleep."

"I'm heading straight home; first I had to convince myself you were all right."

Shrieks reverberated through the corridors. Raquela heard the words: "Mount Scopus! It's freed!"

"Moshe!" she screamed. "Scopus! We have Mount Scopus again!"

Her mind was latticed with memories. Tears of joy rolled down her cheeks. Moshe held her shaking body; his own tears wet her hair.

The vast entrance hall of the medical center began filling with people. They joined the throngs of doctors and nurses, laughing, weeping, repeating the words: *Scopus . . . Scopus is freed*. They locked arms and danced the hora; world-famous surgeons danced with porters; medical students from Africa and Asia who had refused to go home in the weeks of tension danced with their teachers.

Doctors who had survived the concentration camps, nurses with Auschwitz numbers on their forearms, embraced Raquela; the hora grew faster and faster. Some of the older physicians dropped out of the circle, laughing, catching their breath, but Raquela kept on.

Scopus was freed.

Colonel Motta Gur, a brawny soldier who wrote children's books at night when he relaxed, rode up front in a half track, leading his paratroopers. He pushed the enemy until his column stood in the square outside the parapeted walls of the Old City.

The Israel High Command had given orders to the troops not to damage any of the buildings or sites holy to the three religions. Many Jewish soldiers would lose their lives that buildings might live.

Colonel Gur ordered his brigade to attack. They swept the crenellated wall and not a shot hit a single holy place.

The heaviest casualties were among the commanders, who shouted to their men, "Follow me." They were racing to see who would get into the Old City first. No one could stop the momentum now.

The paratroopers broke their way into narrow streets that wound into blind alleys. They ran, crouching against the sides of deserted houses and shuttered kiosks.

They reached the Western Wall.

A soldier scrambled to the top of the Wall and raised the flag of Israel. Chief Rabbi Shlomo Goren blew the *shofar*—the ram's horn—and the eerie notes *te-kee-ya* pierced the ears of the soldiers.

Shortly after noon, all the generals and all the commanders who had fought for Jerusalem—Dayan, Rabin, Narkiss, Motta Gur—and hundreds of their soldiers came together at the Wall.

All day and through the night the paratroopers, dirty, tired, their uniforms dusty and bloodstained, kept coming to the Wall, touching it, caressing it, kissing it, weeping. The Wall and their tears blended together.

On Mount Zion the commander of another paratroop unit stopped his half track on the little plaza in front of the home of an elderly couple from South Africa, Albert and Pauline Rose.

"We're going into the Old City from this direction," the commander told Mrs. Rose. "We've been selected. We're to put the flag of Israel on the Tower of David. But we haven't got a flag."

Pauline Rose climbed the stairs to her bedroom, pulled a sheet out of her cupboard, opened a tube of blue paint, and painted a star of David on the sheet. Then she hurried down to her garden, found a long stick, and attached the sheet to it.

The paratroopers drove off, waving her flag. At the Citadel of David, they scaled the stone rampart and planted the homemade flag of Israel.

The mystery of the Wall seemed to touch all the wounded; Raquela felt a new spirit in the satellite hospitals. In the wards she could hear soldiers humming "Jerusalem, the Golden." It had become the anthem of the war. Jerusalem was reunited.

On the southern front the desert was ablaze. Israeli tanks and Soviet tanks, shelled from the ground, were blistering. The battle whipped up the sand, turning it into a blinding sea. The air was pierced with the noise of ammunition trucks' exploding. Helicopters chugged above the desert, landing just long enough to pick up the wounded. Parachutists dropped out of the sky, bringing water and more ammunition. The temperature climbed to one hundred five degrees.

Standing in the half track with General Yeshayahu Gavish were his aides and liaison officers in constant radio communication with the units they represented: air force, armor, infantry, paratroops, artillery, engineer corps, medical corps, communications—all flying or plowing across the desert.

Buses carrying the troops trekked through the desert, followed by private cars, taxis, station wagons, milk wagons, and delivery wagons. There had been no time to paint them with army colors. Children had been given the job of splashing them with mud, "not for camouflage," General Arik Sharon explained, "but to make them look a little military." It was just as well the mud didn't stick. Looking down, the Israeli pilots could tell their troops from the Egyptians' when they saw ice-cream trucks, hot-dog vans, and laundry wagons navigating the desert.

The Israel Air Force flew a cover over the three brigades that were now reversing the course Moses had taken to lead the children of Israel out of Egypt.

Their goal was the Suez Canal.

In the northern Sinai, Brigadier General Israel Tal, the fiercely loved builder of Israel's armored corps, rushed his troops along the Mediterranean.

In the center of the peninsula, Brigadier General Avraham Yoffe, the stout conservationist called back to duty from his job as director of national parks, sped his tanks across the sand dunes toward the Mitla Pass, the strategic gateway through the desert to the Canal.

In the south Arik Sharon's troops were fighting toward Nakhl, from which they were also wedging their way through the pass to the Canal.

On the sea, a small Israeli naval assault force with helicopter cover sailed from Eilat to capture the Straits of Tiran. To their disgust, they found the Straits empty: the Egyptians had fled.

Two A.M. Friday morning, June 9, Yoffe's forces reached the Canal.

Less than five days after the Egyptian threat to fight a holy war had exploded in the Gaza Strip, the Egyptian army was in flight across the desert. The great Soviet fleet of tanks lay burned or captured.

In New York, Mohammed Awad el-Kony, Egypt's suave ambassador to the United Nations, handed a message to U Thant. It was apparent that el-Kony found the message too agonizing to read himself. U Thant read it to the Security Council. The Egyptian government agreed to a UN cease-fire. The war in Sinai and in Jerusalem and the West Bank was over. It was not yet over in Israel.

Of all the Arabs who encircled Israel, the Syrians were the most vicious.

From the day the war broke out, they directed an almost ceaseless barrage of artillery fire at the northern kibbutzim and the new little development towns. People were killed, houses demolished, livestock destroyed, orchards and fields of cotton and grain decimated. Women and little children lived in the shelters underground. The northern villages knew the war as no other part of Israel knew it; for six full days they took its brunt.

At seven A.M. on Friday morning, General David Elazar, known affectionately as Dado—a Youth Aliyah graduate who had escaped from Hitler as a child—gave the command.

From all the kibbutzim and settlements that had endured Syrian fire for nineteen terror-filled years, the army now moved with trucks and half tracks and jeeps, with infantry and tanks, and with the Israel Air Force.

They moved up the cliffs, some of which had never been scaled by men.

In Kibbutz Dan, Major Mottel, watching through binoculars, saw the first Israeli tanks burst into flames, blown apart by Syrian mines and antitank fire. He saw men leap out of turrets to pull the wounded out of the burning tractors and tanks. Under searing fire, they raced to climb into other vehicles. The tanks lumbered up the Golan Heights like prehistoric monsters.

The men in the kibbutzim below the cliffs saw the slaughter. Each time a tank exploded, they knew three men were trapped in it.

Leading a unit up a hill was Lieutenant Colonel Moshe Klein, an infantry battalion commander who had come from Hungary. The Syrians destroyed his half track; Colonel Klein escaped from his burning vehicle and with his soldiers climbed the rest of the hill on foot—running, crouching, taking cover wherever they could find it. He saw two groups of his soldiers moving up the hill separately, and, fearing they might mistake one another for the enemy, he stood up to coordinate the two groups. The Syrians killed him.

Behind him, his deputy, Major Zohar, took over. A Syrian bullet pierced his neck; the medics carried him down the hill past the troops racing forward. Thirty-year-old Major Alexander Krinsky, who had come with Youth Aliyah from Poland, was rushed in; he led the men up to the top of the hill, and there he was killed.

Without officers, even without orders, the soldiers continued to advance.

The hills were blocked by fences of barbed wire protecting the Syrian trenches and the fantastic underground network of Soviet-built concrete bunkers from which the Syrians could blast every vehicle scaling the Heights.

All Friday afternoon the Israelis fought along the Golan Heights, racing down roads, encircling camps and villages. The Heights and the valley were blazing with smoke and fire.

At dawn on Saturday, with heavy air support, the Golani Brigade, made up of crack infantry, burst into the village of Baniyas, the fortified area where the Syrians had sought to divert the headwaters of the Jordan River.

Another force raced over tough mountain terrain, knocked out antitank emplacements, and pushed on toward Kuneitra, the largest city on the Golan plateau.

The Syrian army was collapsing, retreating as fast as it could to Damascus, forty-five miles away.

One day after the first breakthrough into Syrian territory, the battle for the Golan Heights was over.

The casualties were heavy: one hundred fifteen Israelis killed and thirty wounded; one thousand Syrians dead—no one knew how many wounded—and six hundred taken prisoner. Eighty thousand Syrian soldiers and civilians had fled.

The Syrians lost the Golan Heights, the cliffs from which they had harassed and killed for nineteen years.

On Saturday afternoon silence fell on the kibbutzim. The children climbed out of the shelters and were blinded by the sunlight. To Major Mottel in Kibbutz Dan the silence was that of a roaring ocean that had suddenly grown still.

Islands of light glittered in all the hills and valleys of the north. The people were told, "Turn on your lights—even your searchlights. No more blackouts. The Heights of Golan are ours."

That Saturday afternoon, Raquela and Moshe entered the Old City of Jerusalem on foot.

They walked through the narrow streets. Señora Vavá had lived here, and before her, for more than three hundred years, the family had walked on these stones, had lived and borne children and died here.

They reached the Western Wall. Raquela pressed her head against the Wall. Moshe and their four children had come through the war alive.

A few days later, Raquela opened the French doors and walked through the garden to the patio of Mama's cottage. Voices floated to her, a strange voice she could not recognize. She hurried through the little foyer to the living room.

A tall woman in a black Bedouin gown stood talking animatedly, towering over Mama. Could it be? The mysterious smell of musk and incense filled the room.

"Aisha!"

The Arab woman flushed with pleasure. "Can this beautiful woman be my little Raquela?"

The two tall women embraced. Then Raquela stood

back, for a moment a little girl again, watching Mama and
Aisha, drawn to each other by some strange bond, their
hair a web of gray laced with black, their faces creased
with nearly seventy years of living.

"I will get us coffee," Mama said in the tones she had
spoken each morning on the patio before Jerusalem had
been torn in half.

Raquela and Aisha sat together on the sofa, holding
hands, euphoric.

The truncated city had become whole again. The ugly
barbed-wire fences and the corrugated tin walls were torn
down. Jerusalem was one city.

There had been dire predictions of bloodshed. Jews
would be massacred if they entered the Old City; Arabs
would be massacred if they walked down Zion Square. But
the warnings were groundless.

The moment the barriers came down, Raquela had
joined the thousands of Jews swarming through the Old
City, revisiting her favorite little shops, welcomed again by
friendly Arab merchants eager to sell their wares.

On Zion Square, Arab men in long gowns and *keffiyehs*
and women in beautifully embroidered Bedouin dresses
entered the clothing stores to study the western fashions
and pushed shopping carts through the wondrous aisles of
the supermarket.

Aisha and Raquela caught up with each other's lives. In
1948 Aisha and her family had gone to live with relatives
in East Jerusalem. She was a grandmother many times
over.

Mama entered carrying a tray with demitasse cups of
Turkish coffee.

"And how is the boy?" Aisha asked. "Jacob, who used
to fill my basket with pine twigs from your garden?"

Mama's hand trembled; the cups shook.

Raquela spoke mutedly. "Jacob is dead. He was very
ill."

"Ah," Aisha sighed. "I loved him like my own son."

Mama, in control again, handed her the little cup of
coffee.

"Do you remember," Aisha asked, "I always brought
you eggs so fresh—the minute the chickens laid them."

"I remember," Mama said. "You never fooled me."

Raquela watched the two women in silence. Would this
euphoria last?

She stood up. "Aisha, I must leave for work. Please come again soon."

"I will come, Raquela. I will bring you eggs and figs. It will be as if nothing had happened—between then and now."

-•⟨ Chapter Twenty-nine ⟩•-

July 1967

Raquela spent the next days talking, feeling, looking, listening, exploring, walking—walking endlessly—through the Old City.

Then, one morning, driving her car to work, she felt an overwhelming urge to return to Scopus.

She was glad no one was with her. She wanted to be alone, her emotions deflected by no one. She drove through the city toward East Jerusalem. The hideous fences and barbed wire were still there, but torn down and shoved aside.

It was 1943 again and she was a nineteen-year-old girl on Bus 9 riding through a snow storm. She steered her car through the broad streets around the crenellated walls of the Old City. Now the road began to wind. Her hands gripped the wheel in a spasm of fear. She was in Sheikh Jarrah: *Dr. Yassky . . . the convoy . . . the seventy-seven doctors and nurses massacred.*

Through the windshield she saw Arab men sitting on little stools in front of their coffeehouses, smoking hubble-bubble pipes. The mufti's villa and the Nashashibi houses stood, surrounded by trees, untouched by the war.

Above the Arab houses she saw the white flags of surrender fluttering in the mountain breeze. Her hands relaxed on the wheel.

Now she was traveling up the Mount of Olives with its crown—Mount Scopus. She drove slowly, apprehensive, beginning to fear what nineteen years and three wars had done to its "monumental serenity."

She left the car on the road. Hesitantly she approached the hospital. The white marblelike tiles were discolored and broken, like ancient ruins. The garden was a jungle of weeds and rubble. She picked her way through the dirt and stones and entered the main hall. It looked haunted. Cobwebs spun a gray filigree around the rusted pipes; the marble floor was carpeted in dust and fallen plaster.

The rest of the world was blocked out. Memories spilled over. Her graduation. The student nurses sitting on the marble steps in blue and white uniforms, like cornflowers. The speaker's table . . . *Raquela Levy*—Shulamit Cantor's voice echoed through the empty hall—*will you please come forward. . . . You have been selected outstanding student in your class . . .*"

She left the hospital and made her way through the overgrown foliage to the nursing school. The glass entrance door was shattered. Through the yawning hall, she entered the once-luxurious living room. Empty. Desolate. The droppings of birds mingled with the rubble.

She closed her eyes. She saw Carmi. His British uniform. His movie-star smile. Carmi was singing: *Raquela . . . Raquela . . . Raquela . . . it's the most beautiful name in the world.*

At the United Nations the Arabs and the Soviets sought, as in 1956, to achieve in diplomacy what they had failed to achieve by blockade and war.

Prime Minister Alexei Kosygin himself flew to New York to address a special session of the General Assembly in June 1967. He accused Israel of "treacherous" aggression. President Lyndon B. Johnson, supporting Israel, called for face-to-face negotiations, freedom of the waterways, and a just settlement of the problems of refugees.

The Arabs refused. The special session ended in shambles. Meeting in a summit in Khartoum in September 1967, the Arabs adopted three "nos": no recognition; no negotiations; no peace.

The next month, October 1967, the Security Council, undaunted by the three nos, adopted what would later become famous as "Resolution 242." It called for "a just and lasting peace . . . withdrawal from occupied territories [though by no means withdrawal from *all* the occupied territories] . . . the renunciation of all forms of belligerency, blockade or organized warfare . . . freedom of navigation through international waterways . . . the right to live in peace within secure and recognized boundaries . . . a just settlement of the refugee problem."

The refugee problem! Arthur Goldberg, the United

States ambassador to the United Nations, who drafted much of Resolution 242, explained that settling "the refugee problem" meant settling it for all refugees, Jewish refugees as well as Arab refugees.

The victory of the Six Day War opened the borders that had been closed since 1948, and a million Arabs, some in refugee camps, others living in towns and villages or on the land as farmers, came under Israeli military government.

In July 1967, Yasir Arafat, head of the PLO (Palestine Liberation Organization), set up headquarters in the casbah in Nablus on the reoccupied West Bank. The PLO had been created in 1964 as an umbrella for Arab terrorist groups. Its covenant was simple: DESTROY ISRAEL.

In the months following the Six Day War, Arafat, constantly moving his headquarters, organized saboteurs and terrorists to whip up the Arabs on the West Bank and in Gaza, to terrorize not only the Jews but also the Israeli Arabs who had remained loyal to Israel throughout the war.

The August morning was mountain cool. Moshe and Raquela drove south of Jerusalem through Bethlehem on their way to visit an Arab refugee camp outside Hebron. Hundreds of Arabs in white *keffiyehs* and white cotton pantaloons were doing road work with primitive picks.

"Machines could do in a few hours what will take these Arab workers weeks or months," Moshe said. "But government policy is to give Arabs the same work relief we give new immigrant Jews, with the same pay."

Outside Hebron, they drove through barren hills to the refugee camp. *Would it look like Athlit or Cyprus?* Raquela wondered. All these years she had seen devastating pictures of Arab-refugee camps. Tents and muddy roads. Listless, weary men. Overburdened women. Half-naked children.

A United Nations sign, inscribed in English and in Arabic, told them they had reached the Fawwar Refugee Camp run by UNRWA (United Nations Relief and Works Agency).

They entered the camp on foot. Raquela walked through the grounds unbelieving. No tents. No iron huts. No barbed wire. Nearly a thousand one-family houses in pastel pinks and grays ran in narrow streets up and down the small hills.

"This is like no camp I've ever been in!" she exclaimed. "It's like a modern town."

Dozens of children followed them to the clinic. They introduced themselves to the camp nurse and a visiting UNRWA doctor and spent the next hour discussing the problems of the pregnant women and newborn babies.

They left the clinic and followed a line of people entering a warehouse. Inside, they watched curiously as each adult showed a ration card to a young Arab in white shirtsleeves standing behind a counter.

He checked the card, counted the names listed, and then handed out large cans of cooking oil, bags of lentils, and fifty-pound white muslin sacks of flour.

Raquela moved closer, reading the English legend on the flour bags:

BREAD FLOUR
Enriched, unbleached
"Fortified with calcium"
DONATED BY THE PEOPLE
of the
UNITED STATES OF AMERICA
Not to be sold or exchanged

Driving home on the unfamiliar road, Moshe seemed lost in thought. Finally he said, "To be a refugee living in a camp is tragic. But to be used as a political pawn for nineteen years—God only knows what happens inside the psyches of children who grow up in an atmosphere of hate."

Raquela was trying to sort out her emotions.

"When I think of how we took care of our refugees— especially the Jews who came from Arab lands . . ." She looked off into the horizon. "Keeping any people in a camp—even one like this, which looks like a suburb—does terrible things to them."

"The Arab countries could have absorbed them easily," Moshe said, "the way thirty-five to forty million refugees from World War Two were absorbed. Instead, the Arab states kept them in camps to fester, and contributed little or nothing to take care of them. Do you know who footed most of the bill—the American taxpayers!"

"I hate camps—all camps," Raquela said bitterly. Memories of Athlit and Cyprus made her shudder. "I wish we could liquidate them, outlaw them all."

"Hm," Moshe grunted. "That would be Utopia."

"They're evil!" Raquela exploded.

"Sure they're evil. Even the best camps are evil. People deteriorate in them. Become demoralized. It's a scandal. Take those ration cards we saw. Every person listed gets a monthly supply of food and clothes. Sometimes there are ten names on one card. The names never get crossed off. People die and their deaths go unreported. Young men leave the camps for Kuwait and other oil countries. They earn a fortune, but their names stay on the cards." He chuckled. "The other day Prime Minister Eshkol joked, at a meeting I went to, 'When I'm reincarnated, I want to be an Arab refugee. You get everything for nothing and you never die.'"

A few days later, another scandal was revealed; the refugees had been selling their rations to buy guns and ammunition. American food—*not to be sold or exchanged*—had been exchanged for guns to kill Israelis.

Then the biggest scandal of all surfaced: the United Nations camps had become the proving grounds for terrorists.

In October 1969, the week Prime Minister Levi Eshkol died and Golda Meir was sworn in as interim Prime Minister, terrorists blew up a supermarket, tossed grenades into a bank, and bombed the cafeteria of the Hebrew University, where many of the students were Arabs as well as Jews.

Terror was on the streets, in the busy marketplaces. And still Yasir Arafat's *fedayeen* failed to disrupt daily life in Israel. His fighting arm, El Fatah, turned to a new form of terror; skyjacking.

The first plane to be hijacked was an El Al jet flying from Rome to Tel Aviv on July 22, 1968. The terrorists forced the pilot to land in Algeria. Most of the world condemned the terrorists, and also Algeria, for granting them asylum, but aside from this, the world did nothing.

A year later, on August 28, 1969, a TWA plane en route from Rome to Tel Aviv was hijacked and forced to land in Syria. Among the passengers was Shlomo Samueloff, professor of physiology at the Hebrew University, and husband of Raquela's friend, from training camp,

Naomi Samueloff. He was held prisoner in Damascus for one hundred days.

Terrorism became a way of life. Israel retaliated with massive bombings of the Fatah strongholds. And still the terrorists failed to paralyze the country.

Jerusalem boomed. Mayor Teddy Kollek was now responsible for East as well as West Jerusalem. Born in Vienna in 1911, Teddy had come to Palestine as a pioneer in 1934 and helped found Kibbutz Ein Gev, on the Sea of Galilee. During World War II he was in Europe, in charge of contacts with the Jewish underground. He returned to become part of David Ben-Gurion's inner circle of idealistic men and women fighting for the birth of Israel. After the state was born, Teddy served as minister plenipotentiary in Washington, then returned to Jerusalem as director general of the prime minister's office.

Now, as mayor, he drew upon his vast experience to rebuild a united city. He drove his car at all hours of the day and night through the city streets. His office door was always open. Hadassah had taken a vow to return to Scopus; he gave them support. New apartment houses were rising on the hills all around the city; he helped choose the sites and the architecture. He extended the city's services—water, electricity, garbage collection—to the Arab sectors of East Jerusalem; he set up additional mother-and-child-care centers in Arab and Jewish neighborhoods; he met with the leaders of the three religions—Judaism, Christianity, and Islam—to help the three communities coexist in a united city.

Each day thousands of visitors from America and Europe flew into Israel and headed straight for Jerusalem. Christians and Jews entered the Old City to worship in churches and synagogues that had been closed to them during the years of Jordan's occupation.

A new exodus began. Russia finally opened a crack in the Iron Curtain and allowed thousands of Jews to leave. They were scientists, engineers, doctors, nurses, artists, musicians. A new ingredient in the pressure cooker.

The cities were burgeoning; the population, with births and new immigrants, reached three million.

On the West Bank, Israel taught the Arab farmers how to farm their land with twentieth-century tools, and allowed them to truck their produce across the "Open Bridges" to Jordan. The West Bank grew prosperous. Israel helped the Arabs market their roses to Europe, their strawberries to England, where the Queen dined on them for breakfast even in winter.

Across the Open Bridges, Israel permitted tens of thousands of Arabs from Kuwait, Saudi Arabia, and other Arab lands to come from Jordan, to take their sick to Hadassah and other hospitals, to visit relatives and travel freely about the Jewish state.

These were pieces of the peace. But "a just and lasting peace" was still a dream. The Arabs kept repeating, No recognition, no negotiation, no peace.

In November 1969, Amnon, now eighteen, began his three-year army service.

Raquela balanced her life with work and the family. The U.S. government renewed its grant to the research team. They were to continue the study of all infants and pregnant women in Jerusalem, recognized more and more as the ideal city for the controlled study of pregnancy, its diseases and cures. The team under Dr. Davies and Raquela published its first scientific paper, "The Jerusalem Perinatal Study," in the *Israel Journal of Medical Sciences.*

In the summer of 1971 Raquela filled the house with Papa's lilies. Jenny, Moshe's firstborn, was marrying Yaakov Navot, a dark-haired young man with luminous dark eyes, the oldest son of nine children born in Morocco.

Only Papa was missing. Papa—strong, loving, Papa, who had been father to Amnon and Rafi after Arik's death, who had planted the trees under which the ceremony was now held—was dead.

As a wedding present to the young couple, Moshe and Raquela sent them to England, where Yaakov enrolled in the London School of Economics while Jenny worked in the Israeli embassy.

Soon after the wedding, Raquela and Moshe took Rafi with them to Duke University, in Durham, North Carolina, where Moshe taught medical education. While Rafi attended public school, Raquela, free of responsibilities for the first time in years, relaxed in the social life of academe and took trips with Moshe and Rafi into the gently rolling countryside.

In February 1972, Raquela returned to her work in Jerusalem, rested and happy, but Moshe was restless. The Kupat Holim (the Sick Fund of the Histadrut Labor Federation) had come to him, as professor of medical education, and asked him to work out a program for a community-oriented medical school.

There were now three medical schools in Israel—in Jerusalem, Tel Aviv and Haifa. Sitting in his study at home one evening, Moshe listed on a long yellow pad the things he felt were wrong in all three medical schools, including his own, in Jerusalem.

Intrigued by his list, he then set down what he would do if he could start all over again. It was he who had molded the first medical school in Israel in 1951.

Long past midnight, Raquela entered the den. She put her hand on his shoulder. "Coming to bed, Moshe?"

His face was flushed with excitement. "Look at this." He handed her the pad.

Raquela studied his notes. "Moshe, this material is fantastic! This whole idea of yours—it's the human side of medicine, not only the scientific. You've got to fight to promote it. It could revolutionize medicine."

"That's it exactly. I want to see medical education and medical care combined. You have to work with both hands. I'd like to see medical students go out into the community the very day they start medical school. I want every student involved with patients—with human beings—in their homes, where they live. All that our students see now is the bed in the hospital. But ninety percent of medicine happens *outside* the hospital. In homes. In places like your mother-and-child-care centers. These are never seen by students. I can see this happening on a regional basis; the best place might be the Negev frontier in that young university in Beersheba, the University of the Negev."

Moshe organized his recommendations into a position paper. The Kupat Holim and the University of the Negev, enthusiastic about the proposal, submitted his paper to the National Council of Higher Education for approval.

Before the council could act, the University of the Negev offered Moshe the post of president. He tried hard to explain that although he was greatly honored, his interest lay not in the presidency but in the creation of a new, revolutionary community-medical school.

In November 1972, Yigal Allon, then minister of education and culture, called Moshe to his office. "This new university in the Negev needs a president with your skills and experience."

"But my interest," Moshe protested, "is in the medical school."

Allon smiled. "Your taking the presidency may be helpful in promoting it."

While Moshe still hesitated, Allon added, "Mrs. Meir would like it very much."

Moshe agreed to take the presidency until the medical school could be created. But heated debates raged. Why did a little country like Israel need four medical schools? What was wrong with the ones they had? And why more doctors? Israel already had more doctors per capita than any country in the world. In his years of innovation Moshe had won strong friends and powerful enemies.

He won the battle.

He estimated it would take him a year to assemble a faculty and students and get the school off the ground. Meanwhile, he would become president of the university, whose name he would soon change to the Ben-Gurion University of the Negev, to honor the modern-day prophet whose dream had been to open the vast empty desert frontier.

On the afternoon of December 7, 1972, Raquela sat in the front row of the university hall in Beersheba. Mama and the children sat beside her. On the podium, Moshe was being sworn in as president.

She looked around; the hall was filled with dignitaries from Israel, from Europe, and from America.

Outside the window of the modern concrete building, she could see cars roaring down the road. Crowds of people moved swiftly. The dusty Wild West one-horse town she had come to live in with Arik twenty-three years ago was now a metropolis of one hundred thousand people.

Industries sent their smoke into the air; thousands of children were in elementary and secondary schools; Russian violinists and cellists sitting beside Sabras and musicians from other lands filled the seats of the Beersheba

Symphony Orchestra; artists exhibited their painting and sculpture in the new Beersheba Museum; Arabs and Jews sipped coffee together in countless cafés and restaurants and rubbed shoulders in department stores and shopping centers.

Beersheba, she thought—*this is the living absorption center for new immigrants. No refugee camps—not even good ones like Fawwar. No tents. No iron huts.* Beersheba had shown how refugees could be absorbed into a country's life.

She looked at Moshe on the dais, his handsome face and graying temples set off by his dark suit. He was talking of his plans for this new university—how it would serve new immigrants, how it would reach Arabs and Jews.

He can be anything he wants, she thought. *Dynamic. Original. He can speak a dozen languages as if he were born to each one. His fame is spreading. He could be Israel's ambassador anywhere.*

But no, she thought, continuing the dialogue with herself. *Politics is not what Moshe wants. He wants to educate young men and women. He wants to improve our whole nation's health. He wants his students to have seeing eyes and feeling hearts.*

She saw this day as a rehearsal for her next decade. She was forty-nine; more than ever before, she would have to divide her life. She would spend half the week in Beersheba as Moshe's wife, hostess to his faculty, his students, and the myriad guests and visitors from home and overseas. They would live in the ranch house the university provided its president in Omer, the growing suburb of Beersheba—its horizons, the mysteriously beautiful desert. She had already given the house her own touch, with exotic memorabilia from their trips abroad and, on the walls, her own needlework tapestries in the vibrant reds and yellows and turquoise blues she loved.

The second half of the week belonged to her life in Jerusalem: mother to Amnon and Rafi, stepmother to Jenny and Vivian, daughter to Mama, who lived alone in the little cottage Papa had built, and who now leaned on her for protection and love in the last years of her life.

Feminine, aware of her beauty, aware of her face, her statuesque body, and her deeply sensual needs. A working woman. Always she would define herself as a working woman. Sharing the language and destiny of all women of Israel. Women had to work. Women had to stand with their men, carrying on their backs the burden of life in a besieged land. Surrounded by hostility. Isolated. Nearly half the country's still-meager resources spent on defense. On survival.

She sat up tall in her chair in the university hall. Yes, she could handle her life, balance it all.

She looked at Moshe on the podium; he was concluding his speech, painting his picture of the future, how his university would help open the desert for future, for life itself.

A smile moved her lips apart. She was in love. The passionate love of a mature woman. And she was happy. Fulfilled.

Once again she filled the house with Papa's calla lilies.

Vivian was marrying a popular and handsome young captain in the Tank Corps. His name was Gideon Weiler, and both were twenty-two.

Vivian, soft and radiantly beautiful with Moshe's patrician features, stood beneath the velvet canopy under the Jerusalem sky. Gideon fixed his eyes on her, openly, passionately, oblivious of everyone else in the garden.

In the weeks and months of the young couple's courtship Raquela had grown to know Gideon well. He had come from South Africa as an eight-year-old child, with his four brothers, his sister, and their parents. His father, Rabbi Moses Cyrus Weiler, once the leading progressive rabbi in South Africa, was now chairman of the board of Progressive Rabbis in Israel.

"I have given all my children a military education," Rabbi Weiler had told an audience in a Shabbat service attended by Raquela and Moshe in a crowded little synagogue in Jerusalem. "I dedicated my children to the defense of Israel. My Judaism follows the prophets and sages of Israel, whose wisdom encompasses the universe. I believe in justice and righteousness as the great ideals of the Jewish people. But this is not in conflict with our dedication to the State of Israel, the greatest experiment in Jewish life in the last two thousand years."

Raquela had listened to the sermon, holding back the lump in her throat. He had already given one son to Israel.

Adam, Gideon's older brother, a brilliant student at Sussex University, in England, had rushed out of class in June 1967, forced his way on an El Al plane without passport or ticket, to fight with the Armored Corps in the Six Day War. He had survived that war—young Major Weiler— only to be killed in 1970, twenty-five years old, in the northern sector of the Suez Canal. It was Nasser's War of Attrition, his undeclared war to destroy Israel economically through blockade, through terrorism, and by killing her soldiers guarding the Canal.

Gideon had followed in Adam's footsteps: a graduate of the military academy at Haifa, an officer in the Armored Corps, a born leader; single-minded; fearless; a career army man who adored his men and his tanks.

Gideon was Rafi's idol.

An army chaplain, standing before the bridal couple under the *chupah,* sanctified the wine and handed the glass to Gideon and Vivian to sip.

Raquela's heart pounded against her chest. She saw Rabbi Weiler's light-blue eyes blur with tears. Was he thinking of Adam?

What did it mean to be a mother and a father in Israel? she thought. Gideon was being married in his captain's uniform. Amnon, though he had finished his three-year army stint and entered first year of medical school, was on active reserve duty as a lieutenant. She turned her eyes to Amnon, quiet, dependable, a reservoir of inner strength.

Rafi stood next to Amnon. Rafi. She could feel his warmth and laughter filling the garden even as his guitar flooded the house each evening with his music. Rafi, the humanist, writing poetry, devouring books of philosophy and classical literature, prowling through the bookstores, buying books as his treat to himself, inscribing them TO RAFI. FROM RAFI. Raffi, who could court five or six beautiful girls, totally unconcerned that each one knew about the others.

Rafi, who had nearly died from her virus, was just turning eighteen. He would finish his last term at high school and in August enter the army for his three-year service. Rafi had already told her, "I'm going into the Tank Corps. I want to be with Gideon."

The chaplain was intoning, "I pronounce you man and wife. May the Lord bless you and keep you . . ."

Gideon stamped on the glass.

"*Mazal tov. Mazal tov.*"

The words of joy rang through Papa's garden.

On Saturday, October 6, 1973, the synagogues of Israel were filled. It was the holiest day of the year—Shabbat and Yom Kippur, the Day of Atonement.

In Israel, as all over the world, men and women and their children were intoning the prophetic words: "*On Yom Kippur, it is sealed, who shall live and who shall die . . .*"

The Arabs struck.

Young and middle-aged Israelis, many with their prayer shawls still on their shoulders, raced out of the synagogues to join their units.

To the survivors of Hitler's death camps, this was a grim reminder. The Nazis had always chosen the Jewish holy days for an *Aktion*—systematically rounding up and murdering Europe's Jews. Yom Kippur was a favorite day for terror. It was to catch the Jews unprepared. It was to break their spirit.

Now it was not the Nazis; Egypt and Syria had launched the surprise attack. And Russia had given them the tools of war.

In the south the Egyptians flung pontoon bridges across the Canal. They sent waves of Russian tanks across the bridges. Thousands of soldiers forded the Canal in rubber dinghies. The Israelis had built a line of fortresses along the Canal—the Bar-Lev Line. The Egyptians surprised the soldiers in their bunkers; some were killed in their underwear before they could even reach for their guns.

In the north, one hundred Soviet MIGs streaked through the sky, strafing and bombing Israeli positions in the Golan Heights. Beneath the MIGs, seven hundred Syrian tanks attacked. They broke through the 1967 cease-fire lines, and, in a wall of fire, hurtled through the Golan into kibbutzim. They were headed for the heartland of Israel.

Amnon burst into the house and grabbed his uniform and gun.

Raquela bit her lip. He must not see her fear.

Rafi was already in training camp. Gideon was somewhere in the Golan with the Tank Corps. Now Amnon was leaving.

She dared not weep.

She looked at her serious-faced firstborn. What does one say to one's son? Are there words in any language?

She searched her mind. Are there special words to send your son into battle?

He came toward her. "Good-bye, Mother," he said.

"Good-bye, Amnon." She held him tightly.

Then she kissed him and let him go.

A deep depression spread across the land.

The people were stunned. How could their leaders have been so taken by surprise? How could their invincible army have been caught literally sleeping?

There had been signs, if they had only read them, that President Anwar el-Sadat was planning a new war.

In 1972, General Saad el-Shazli, Egypt's chief of staff, beating his drums, had made the grizzly prediction, "We will chop the Israelis up in a meat-grinder war."

Sadat himself, in March 1973, had told an American journalist, "Everything in this country is now being mobilized in earnest for the resumption of battle, which is now inevitable. . . . Everyone has fallen asleep over the Middle East crisis, but they will soon wake up."

On Friday, October 5, 1973, the Russian advisors in Syria packed, pulled up their families, and flew home. Prime Minister Golda Meir waited for more signals.

Then, at dawn on Yom Kippur, the signals came. Egyptians were massing men and tanks along the Canal. This was no military exercise. Golda's chief of staff, General Dado Elazar, pleaded for total mobilization and a preemptive strike. But Moshe Dayan, her minister of defense, disagreed. The United States had warned them against taking a preemptive strike.

It was a tragic dilemma.

Whoever strikes first in the Middle East has all the advantages. The lives of hundreds of soldiers would be saved; the war would be swift. But weighed against that strategic advantage was the threat of losing U.S. aid.

In the end, Golda agreed with Dayan. No total mobilization. No preemptive strike.

Not only Israel but the rest of the world as well, even U.S. Intelligence, was caught by surprise. And suddenly, throughout America and Europe, millions of people, Christians and Jews, galvanized themselves into action, expressing tangibly, emotionally, their ties with the beleaguered country.

In New York the associate dean of the Catholic Fordham University, Joseph Mulholland, sent a letter to the United Jewish Appeal: "We have already made a financial contribution," he wrote of himself and his wife. "We are willing to help in any other way you feel possible—to answer phones or lick stamps. I would be willing to go to Israel to relieve a man for other duties. You know, the world stood silent while the Six Million went into the gas chambers, but I do not intend to remain silent while millions of the survivors are flushed down an oil well."

Raquela, returning to work in the hospital, found a whole cadre of American, Canadian, and South African orthopedists, surgeons, burn specialists, and nurses who had rushed over to help.

The Israel Air Force was being decimated. Its planes were disintegrating in midair, destroyed by Russian-built SAM-6s. On Yom Kippur, ten Phantom jets and thirty Skyhawks were burned in the air. Most of the pilots' bodies were pulverized before the men could even open their parachutes.

The Israel Army, fighting on two fronts, realized its first thrust must be against the Syrians. The heartland of Israel was in mortal danger. The Sinai could wait.

Raquela's boys were in the north, on the Syrian front.

Gideon was with the Armored Corps somewhere in the Golan Heights.

Amnon was with an infantry unit.

Rafi, buck private, drove back and forth in a half track, ferrying bombs to the north, where the nights had begun to freeze and Mount Hermon was draped with snow. Jenny and Yaakov were still in London, desperately trying to board a plane to Israel.

The television set was an altar; each evening, exhausted after work, Raquela sat with Vivian and Mama in front of the little screen. Moshe was in Beersheba supervising emergency procedures for wounded soldiers. On the television screen, black-and-white fire streaked through the sky. The war was in their living room. They sat anguished, watching the terrible beauty of tracers and shells lighting up the sky.

Tanks exploded on the screen. Was Gideon in one of them? Where was Amnon? Was Rafi safe?

Vivian was seven months pregnant.

They kept the telephone open. Maybe one of the boys would be near a field phone and could call them.

The telephone did not ring. Not the first night or the second.

On the third night, Rafi called. No news of Gideon. But Amnon was okay and he was exhilarated. The Syrians were being pushed back!

On the fourth night, Raquela threw her arms around Vivi. The Syrians were in total retreat. The surprise attack in the north had failed. Maybe the boys were all safe.

With the counterattack in the north in full momentum, the army could now turn to the war in the Sinai.

Once again the family watched the screen as the desert exploded in flames and heat and blood.

Vivian was not sleeping nights. There was still no word from Gideon.

The battles were taking ferocious losses in lives and matériel. Russia swiftly resupplied the Arabs; in the course of one day alone, Friday, October 12, Soviet cargo planes made sixty flights to Cairo and Damascus, ferrying in new military hardware.

Prime Minister Golda Meir turned to the United States. She had resisted the temptation of a preemptive strike, thereby suffering the tragic and dangerous losses of troops and planes and ammunition. She appealed to President Richard Nixon—not for men but to balance the aid the Russians were giving their Arab clients.

A few days passed; then President Nixon ordered a rescue airlift of giant C-56 Galaxies. A wave of gratitude lifted the depression and anguish in the country. The United States had not forgotten its commitment. Israel was not alone.

On Sunday, October 14, the first of the C-56 Galaxies landed at Lydda Airport. Then, dropping onto the tarmac every fifteen or twenty minutes, the massive planes unloaded their welcome cargo—tanks, ammunition, air-to-air rockets, medical supplies, even winter underwear and woolen helmets for the soldiers in the north. Phantom Jets were flown in, to replace the fighters destroyed by Russian missiles.

In the hospitals Israeli and foreign doctors and nurses worked without rest, using the blood plasma and the medicines to save lives. The air over the Hadassah–Hebrew

University Medical Center was shattered by the whirling blades of army helicopters landing in the courtyard, bringing in soldiers with limbs torn off, faces mutilated, bodies hideously burned.

Thus far there had been no reports of the number of soldiers killed.

On the day the airlift started, the army lifted the curtain on the terrible losses of men.

Vivian, listening to the radio, rushed to the phone to call Moshe in the hospital in Beersheba. The university itself was closed; most of the students and faculty were at the front.

"Daddy"—Vivian's voice was choked—"the chief of staff has just given out the figures. Six hundred fifty-six soldiers killed so far."

"Six hundred fifty-six," Moshe shuddered.

"Daddy, General Elazar said all the families of the dead soldiers have been informed. It must mean Gideon's alive."

"Of course, Vivi. That's what it means."

"But it's more than a week since I've had any word. I can't understand how Gideon can't find some way to tell me he's all right. Amnon called us; Rafi calls every chance he gets. But not Gideon. Surely by now he could send me a message; somebody must be coming to Jerusalem from the north. Some friend of his could have phoned me that they saw him somewhere." Her voice broke. "I just don't know what to think, Daddy."

Moshe tried to reassure her. "Vivi," he said softly into the phone, "he must be alive. The army would have sent someone to inform you otherwise."

The next day, there was a knock on Vivian's door. It was Gideon's driver.

Sitting in the living room, he told her how, on the day the war broke out, Gideon had been promoted in the field to the rank of major—at twenty-three, deputy commander of a tank regiment.

Earlier, Major General Albert Mandler* tried to dissuade him from front-line duty because he had lost his brother. One death was enough for any family to endure. But Gideon had refused and gone right into battle.

Leading his tanks to the front lines, he had stopped on

---

* Major General Mandler was killed in action on the Canal on the eighth day of the war.

the highway to lay tires across the road, to save it from the heavy tread of his tanks.

Major General Dan Laner, responsible for the southern area of the Golan Heights, pulled up in his staff car. "Gideon, Gideon," he said. "This is war. What are you worried about a road for?"

"I'm not worried, sir. But other vehicles will have to use it, to bring up reinforcements and supplies. We've got to leave it undamaged."

Gideon and his men drove their tanks along the narrow ledge of the Golan. As Yom Kippur drew to a close, the Golan was strewn with burned-out tanks and the bodies of dead men.

Gideon and his tank crews fought without rest, outnumbered, ten tanks to one.

All through Sunday night and Monday, the tank battles raged. Nearly every tank in Gideon's unit was destroyed.

He had not slept for nearly seventy-two hours. In a brief lull he pulled a yellow gasoline coupon out of his pocket and wrote on the back:

> My sweet darling, I am writing these few words in the middle of a battle in the night. Only a few seconds ago, we destroyed five tanks. If, God forbid, something happens to me, know that I love you unto death and that I admire you always. I am thinking of our baby.

Three hours later, at two A.M. on Tuesday morning, a Russian-made bazooka hit his tank. Gideon, standing up in the turret, was ejected about thirty yards into the flaming sky. His men in the turret were burned to death.

Only his driver survived. It was he who found Gideon's body, broken but intact, with the note to Vivian.

What does it mean to be a woman in Israel? Raquela thought, looking at Vivi's pale strained face and swollen body, widowed at twenty-three.

How does one comfort a young woman whose body must hunger for her husband? How does one help her mourn? How does one comfort the wives and mothers and children of dead soldiers?

Once again, Israel defeated her enemies. The war, which had begun in disaster, ended in stunning victory, the most spectacular of all the four wars. Israel's soldiers stood twenty-five miles from Damascus, sixty miles from Cairo.

But a whole generation of young men, twenty-six hundred, had been wiped out.

And in the hospitals, Raquela again moved among the burned and crippled men who filled the wards to overflowing.

On Christmas eve, Vivian gave birth to Gideon's daughter, and named her Gal—the Hebrew word for "wave."

The next year, 1974, Moshe opened the medical school of the Ben-Gurion University of the Negev. He turned the presidency of the university over to Yosef Tekoah, the former Israeli permanent delegate to the United Nations, and assumed the challenge he had given himself.

Moshe was given full control of the three agencies concerned with health in the Negev—the Ministry of Health, the Kupat Holim—the Sick Fund of the Histadrut Labor Federation—and the medical school. He was in effect the medical chief of the frontier.

Raquela, at fifty-one, more beautiful than ever, began to spend more time in Beersheba, as Moshe led young medical students into the villages and the Bedouin settlements in the Negev, into the baby clinics, the mother-and-child-care centers, the old-age homes and the hospitals, to become involved, from the first day at school, in the work of saving lives.

It was 1976. Amnon was in his fourth year of medical school and Rafi was ending his three-year army stint. Rafi had followed in Gideon's footsteps; he was a lieutenant in the Tank Corps.

On a warm morning in August, he came home to Jerusalem. "Mother," he said, "I'm scheduled to leave the army on Tisha B'Av*—on the fifth of August. My commanding officer has asked me to stay on, to volunteer for another year."

Raquela's heart began to pound. "I thought you were all set to go to the university to study philosophy and literature."

"I know. But Mother, they've invested so much in me. They've trained me. . . . What do you think?"

* A solemn day of mourning for the destruction of the Temple in Jerusalem.

Raquela put her arm on Rafi's shoulder. Her fingers rested on his lieutenant's bars.

Tears choked in her throat. "As a mother, Rafi, I want you to come home. I want you to go to the university. I want you to start your life. Begin your career . . ." She swallowed hard. "But as an Israeli, I can't tell you to come home. Rafi, only you can make this decision."

She saw his face tighten. "I'm convinced I cannot say no."

On Tisha B'Av, he telephoned early in the morning. "I'm signing up for another year, Mother. I'll try to get home this weekend. . . ."

When would there be an end to this war? There had not been a single day of peace. . . .

She drove to the Hadassah hospital on Mount Scopus. It had been completely restored and reopened in October 1975. Three thousand Hadassah pilgrims had come, with joy and thanksgiving, to rededicate it.

She was restless. She jumped into her car and drove to her office in an old Arab house on Cremieux Street, in the quarter known as the German Colony. She opened the huge book for 1976. Each year had its own book, its own record, its own insights into how to save the lives of babies and their mothers.

She closed the book and got back into her car. Something impelled her to drive to the medical center on the hill in Ein Karem. She entered the delivery room. One of her friends was delivering a baby. She stood, watching. Tears welled in her eyes as she helped deliver a beautiful boy. *Like Israel,* she thought, *born in travail and blood.*

She drove home. The warm August sun dappled the road. She entered the house and began fixing dinner. Moshe was coming up from Beersheba in the late afternoon.

She walked through the French doors into the garden and stood under the tall tree Papa had planted for her. The garden was scented with roses. She walked down the small path to Mama's cottage. Mama was smiling. "I bought a big bag of chocolates, biscuits, and sweets for Rafi when he comes home today."

"Mama, he's not coming today. He's signing up for another year."

Mama nodded. "The country needs him. Such a boy.

One shouldn't say it, but he's my favorite. Kisses my cheeks, my head, my whole face, every time he comes home."

"We'll see him Saturday, I hope. He's going to try to get leave."

Raquela returned to the house.

At six-thirty in the morning the doorbell rang. Moshe went to the door.

Raquela heard him scream, "Rafi, Rafi, Rafi!"

She rushed out of the bedroom. "Moshe, what is it?"

She looked toward the door. Two officers and two young women in uniform stood in the doorway.

She steadied herself against the wall.

One of the officers was speaking. "We regret to inform you that your son, Lieutenant Rafael Brzezinski, died last night in the line of duty."

Moshe held her close.

Raquela, dressed in a black shirtwaist and skirt, stood before the iron gate leading to the Soldiers' Cemetery on Mount Herzl. Here thousands of men and women killed in the four wars lay buried in neat rows.

As each mourner approached her, Raquela extended her hand in mute recognition. Her face was pale and drawn; her eyes were dry; her mouth was fixed in the familiar Mona Lisa curve. Beside her, Moshe and Amnon, Jenny and Vivi, stood protectively. Moshe's face was ashen. Amnon's body seemed hunched with grief.

Mama wept openly. "If *I* don't die now," she cried, "there is no death."

An army van pulled up; soldiers lifted out the simple army coffin draped with the flag of Israel. Rafi was carried by his closest friends through the crowded rows of graves strewn with plants and flowers.

The procession followed to a freshly dug grave. Rafi was being accorded a hero's funeral, laid to rest next to General Dado Elazar, former chief of staff, hero of the Northern Command in the Six Day War, and Yoni Natanyahu, the brilliant young commander of the Entebbe raid who was killed in the rescue of the hostages from Uganda.

Raquela listened as the army chaplain intoned the Kaddish:

Magnified and sanctified by God's great name
In this world of His creation.

Then Rafi's commanding officer spoke in a soft voice;
he was flanked by dozens of Rafi's friends and comrades,
young men and women in uniform.

"We will always remember you, Rafi. Your sweet per-
sonality, how you played the guitar for us the long nights
in camp, how you loved to read poetry and share it with
us. You were a gifted officer and teacher in the Tank
Corps. You taught your men what a tank is—how to drive
it, how to take care of it, and what it means to be part of
this army. You taught them what Israel means to you.
They loved you, Rafi."

The healing sun shone down upon Raquela. Her throat
was choked; she was unable to speak.

"*Rafi. Rafi.*" She repeated his name over and over to
herself. "*My son, Rafael—Healed by God.*"

Around her the people stood in the noon brilliance.
From somewhere behind her in the cemetery she heard the
quiet weeping of women kneeling upon the graves of their
husbands and sons.

The brief ceremony was over. Raquela lifted a small
stone and placed it on the grave. "Rafi, my beloved Rafi,"
she whispered.

Each morning during the seven days of the *shiva*,
Raquela left the house as soon as there was light in the
sky and drove up the hill to Mount Herzl. She put fresh
flowers from Papa's garden on Rafi's grave. Then she returned home and composed herself to receive the daily
stream of visitors.

It was the ancient wisdom of the *shiva* that brought
friends from the whole country to the house, to sit with
Raquela and Moshe, with Amnon and Mama, with Jenny
and Vivi, to comfort them, to talk to them of Rafi.
Hundreds of soldiers came each day. They sat silently in
the kitchen, in the dining room, upstairs in Rafi's bedroom, neat and untouched, filled with Rafi's books of poetry, its ceiling a collage of maps he had cut from the
National Geographic.

Raquela sat among her circle of friends; photos of
Rafi's smiling face were on the coffee table; neighbors

brought cakes and sweets and poured coffee for the visitors.

Late one morning, a hush fell on the people in the sunken living room. Golda Meir had come to comfort Raquela and Moshe, straight from the Hadassah Hospital in Ein Karem, where she had been undergoing a regular checkup.

She sat on the sofa, beside Raquela; for the first few minutes all the guests—neighbors, Hadassah nurses, soldiers—withdrew into themselves in awe. Naomi, Raquela's Kurdish housekeeper, stood frozen, balancing a tray of coffee cups.

Golda was reminiscing; she had known Rafi since he was born. "Our children," she said simply, "our soldiers. We mothers and fathers"—she spoke the words on everyone's mind—"we nurture our children like precious flowers. Then they grow up . . . and go to war. . . ."

The whole atmosphere changed. The neighbors began chatting with Golda, as if a member of the family had entered, as if their own mother or grandmother were talking to them, affectionately, informally. Naomi, no longer frozen, moved closer into the circle.

In the evening, a long black limousine pulled up in front of the house. Soon everyone on Bet Hakerem Street knew that the president of Israel, Ephraim Katzir, and his wife, Nina, had come to pay their respects to Raquela and Moshe.

It was President Katzir who had served with Jacob in the Haganah, whose reminiscences brought the first healing laughter to the house. Walking to the French doors opening on to Papa's garden, he turned to his wife. "Over there"—he pointed beyond the garden—"is Bialik Street. Nina, do you remember when you and Jacob were students together at the Yellin Seminar and you lived in a room there on Bialik Street?"

Nina smiled. "How could I forget?"

"And you remember how I used to come evenings to visit you?"

Mama interrupted. "And do *you* remember, Ephraim"—her eyes were sparkling mischievously—"how you used to jump out of Nina's window at night?"

President Katzir's round face broke into a smile. "I didn't want to disturb the landlady."

*   *   *

The period of mourning came to an end. Raquela arose, dressed carefully, arranged her hair and returned to work.

Once again she spent half the week in Jerusalem in the mother-and-child-care clinics, and the other half in Beersheba, in the hospital, visiting the Bedouin Arabs in their tents and houses and the new immigrants in their modest homes.

She plunged into work. Work was the road to recovery. Her projects multiplied—projects to keep newborn babies alive.

In Beersheba, she created a new study—to find the causes and a cure for the dangerous hepatitis rampant among newborn babies from Arab lands.

Her days were crowded; friends and family came each evening, surrounding her with warmth and compassion. She was coping. Again she was the gracious hostess, pouring coffee, serving the cakes and pies she had baked. She knew herself; she knew her own feelings, and all day she could control them, though hardly a moment passed that she did not think of Rafi.

It was only at night that the loneliness, the loss, the pain and grief, refused to be controlled.

In bed, with Moshe holding her tightly, she wept.

"How much longer, Moshe? How many more sons must die before peace comes? What can we do, Moshe?"

"We go on living," he said.

—❧ Acknowledgments ❧—

For their help in the researching and writing of this book, I thank the following:

Benjamin Adin; Ike Aronowicz; Nina Ashkenazy; Shaul Avigour; Lea Avni; Ruth Berman; Rafi Blumenfeld; Rivka Burg; Shulamit Cantor; Dr. Eli Davis; Emma Ehrlich; General Rafael Eytan; George Fox; Estelle Gould; Paul Gould; Miriam Granott; Yossi Har-el; Dr. Avraham Harman; Zena Harman; Lucien Harris; Henia Heiman-Elkind; Esther Herlitz; Shlomo Hillel; Temima Hillel; Joseph Jacobson; Lenore Kahn; Dr. Jack Karpas; Jesse Karpas; Ephraim Katzir; Dr. Pearl Ketcher; Teddy Kollek; Morris Laub; Pnina Leibner; Sophia Lustig; Dr. Kalman J. Mann; Golda Meir; Dr. Isaac C. Michaelson; Oro Michaelson; Dr. Emmanuel Margolis; Evelyn Musher; Shulamit Nardi; Eliahu Nawi; Meir Noy; Shimon Peres; Dr. Moshe Prywes; Dr. Younis Abu Rabia; Yitzhak Rabin; Dr. Hanoch Rinott; Gershon Rivlin; Moshe Rivlin; Meir Rosenne; Beatrice Rosner; Naomi Samueloff; Dr. David Schaary; Dr. Tehila Schapira; David Shallon; Aharon Shashar; Eliezer Shmueli; Hannah Simonson; Betty Sobel; Dr. Samuel Hillel Sobel; Judith Steiner-Freud; Shmuel Toledano; Shula Patt Toledano; Dov Volotzky; Sarah Volotzky; Zev Vilnay; Rabbi Moses Cyrus Weiler; Raanan Weitz; Fanny Yassky; Moshe Yuvel.

—✦ About the Author ✦—

For two decades Ruth Gruber served as a correspondent in Israel for the New York *Herald Tribune*. She has made thirty in-depth trips to Israel and spent nine months traveling there with Raquela Prywes and interviewing almost all the people who appear in RAQUELA: A WOMAN OF ISRAEL. Ms. Gruber is the author of eleven books, several of which are about the Middle East.

Recommended Reading from SIGNET

☐ **A GARDEN OF SAND** by Earl Thompson. (#E8039—$2.50)

☐ **TATTOO** by Earl Thompson. (#E8989—$2.95)

☐ **CALDO LARGO** by Earl Thompson. (#E7737—$2.25)

☐ **THE WORLD FROM ROUGH STONES** by Malcolm Macdonald. (#E8601—$2.50)

☐ **THE RICH ARE WITH YOU ALWAYS** by Malcolm Macdonald. (#E7682—$2.25)

☐ **SONS OF FORTUNE** by Malcolm Macdonald. (#E8595—$2.75)*

☐ **THE EBONY TOWER** by John Fowles. (#E8254—$2.50)

☐ **DANIEL MARTIN** by John Fowles. (#E8249—$2.25)†

☐ **THE FRENCH LIEUTENANT'S WOMAN** by John Fowles. (#E9003—$2.95)

☐ **LOVE, LAUGHTER AND TEARS** by Adela Rogers St. Johns. (#E8752—$2.50)*

☐ **SOME ARE BORN GREAT** by Adela Rogers St. Johns. (#J6707—$1.95)

☐ **THE HONEYCOMB** by Adela Rogers St. Johns. (#E7605—$2.25)

☐ **THE YEAR OF THE INTERN** by Robin Cook. (#E7674—$1.75)

☐ **COMA** by Robin Cook. (#E8202—$2.50)

☐ **SOME KIND OF HERO** by James Kirkwood. (#E8497—$2.25)

☐ **KINFLICKS** by Lisa Alther. (#E8984—$2.75)

* Price slightly higher in Canada
† Not available in Canada

Buy them at your local

bookstore or use coupon

on next page of ordering.

Books You'll Want to Read from SIGNET

- [ ] **ALADALE** by Shaun Herron. (#E8882—$2.50)*
- [ ] **THE MOSSAD** by Dennis Eisenberg, Uri Dan and Eli Landau. (#E8883—$2.50)*
- [ ] **CHILDREN'S FEARS** by Dr. Benjamin Wolman. (#E8885—$2.25)
- [ ] **THE SAVAGE** by Tom Ryan. (#E8887—$2.25)*
- [ ] **SO WONDROUS FREE** by Maryhelen Clague. (#E9047—$2.25)*
- [ ] **FALL GUY** by Jay Cronley. (#J8890—$1.95)
- [ ] **THE BLOOD OF OCTOBER** by David Lippincott. (#J7785—$1.95)
- [ ] **VOICE OF ARMAGEDDON** by David Lippincott. (#E6949—$1.75)
- [ ] **SAVAGE RANSOM** by David Lippincott. (#E8749—$2.25)*
- [ ] **TWINS** by Bari Wood and Jack Geasland. (#E9094—$2.75)
- [ ] **THE KILLING GIFT** by Bari Wood. (#J7350—$1.95)
- [ ] **FURY'S SUN, PASSION'S MOON** by Gimone Hall. (#E8748—$2.50)*
- [ ] **RAPTURE'S MISTRESS** by Gimone Hall. (#E8422—$2.25)*
- [ ] **THE DHARMA BUMS** by Jack Kerouac. (#J9138—$1.95)
- [ ] **FLICKERS** by Phillip Rock. (#E8839—$2.25)*

* Price slightly higher in Canada

Buy them at your local bookstore or use this convenient coupon for ordering.

THE NEW AMERICAN LIBRARY, INC.,
P.O. Box 999, Bergenfield, New Jersey 07621

Please send me the SIGNET BOOKS I have checked above. I am enclosing
$_____ (please add 50¢ to this order to cover postage and handling).
Send check or money order—no cash or C.O.D.'s. Prices and numbers are
subject to change without notice.

Name _____

Address _____

City_____ State_____ Zip Code_____

Allow 4-6 weeks for delivery.
This offer is subject to withdrawal without notice.

More Bestsellers from SIGNET

☐ **LORD OF RAVENSLEY** by Constance Heaven.
(#E8460—$2.25)†

☐ **THE PLACE OF STONES** by Constance Heaven.
(#W7046—$1.50)†

☐ **HARVEST OF DESIRE** by Rochelle Larkin. (#E8771—$2.25)

☐ **TORCHES OF DESIRE** by Rochelle Larkin. (#E8511—$2.25)*

☐ **MISTRESS OF DESIRE** by Rochelle Larkin. (#E7964—$2.25)*

☐ **THE DOCTORS ON EDEN PLACE** by Elizabeth Seifert.
(#E8852—$1.75)*

☐ **THE DOCTOR'S DESPERATE HOURS** by Elizabeth Seifert.
(#W7787—$1.50)

☐ **THE STORY OF ANDREA FIELDS** by Elizabeth Seifert.
(#Y6535—$1.25)

☐ **TWO DOCTORS AND A GIRL** by Elizabeth Seifert.
(#W8118—$1.50)

☐ **FEAR OF FLYING** by Erica Jong. (#E8677—$2.50)

☐ **HOW TO SAVE YOUR OWN LIFE** by Erica Jong.
(#E7959—$2.50)*

☐ **SONG OF SOLOMON** by Toni Morrison. (#E8340—$2.50)*

☐ **ALOHA TO LOVE** by Mary Ann Taylor. (#E8765—$1.75)*

☐ **SWEETWATER SAGA** by Roxanne Dent. (#E8850—$2.25)*

☐ **MOMENTS OF MEANING** by Charlotte Vale Allen.
(#J8817—$1.95)*

* Price slightly higher in Canada
† Not available in Canada

Buy them at your local

bookstore or use coupon

on next page for ordering.

SIGNET Books You'll Enjoy

☐ **COME LIVE MY LIFE** by Robert H. Rimmer. (#E7421—$2.25)
☐ **LOVE ME TOMORROW** by Robert H. Rimmer.
(#E8385—$2.50)*
☐ **PREMAR EXPERIMENTS** by Robert H. Rimmer.
(#J7515—$1.95)
☐ **PROPOSITION 31** by Robert H. Rimmer.   (#J7514—$1.95)
☐ **MANHOOD CEREMONY** by Ross Berliner.   (#E8509—$2.25)*
☐ **FLAME OF THE SOUTH** by Constance Gluyas.
(#E8648—$2.50)
☐ **WOMAN OF FURY** by Constance Gluyas.   (#E8075—$2.25)*
☐ **ROGUE'S MISTRESS** by Constance Gluyas. (#E8339—$2.25)
☐ **SAVAGE EDEN** by Constance Gluyas.   (#E8338—$2.25)
☐ **CITY OF WHISPERING STONE** by George Chesbro.
(#J8812—$1.95)*
☐ **SHADOW OF A BROKEN MAN** by George Chesbro.
(#J8114—$1.95)*
☐ **BEDFORD ROW** by Claire Rayner.   (#E8819—$2.50)†
☐ **JUST LIKE HUMPHREY BOGART** by Adam Kennedy.
(#J8820—$1.95)*
☐ **THE SWARM** by Arthur Herzog.   (#E8079—$2.25)
☐ **EARTHSOUND** by Arthur Herzog.   (#E7255—$1.75)

* Price slightly higher in Canada
† Not available in Canada

Buy them at your local bookstore or use this convenient coupon for ordering.

THE NEW AMERICAN LIBRARY, INC.,
P.O. Box 999, Bergenfield, New Jersey 07621

Please send me the SIGNET BOOKS I have checked above. I am enclosing
$_____ (please add 50¢ to this order to cover postage and handling).
Send check or money order—no cash or C.O.D.'s. Prices and numbers are
subject to change without notice.

Name _____

Address _____

City_____ State_____ Zip Code_____
Allow 4-6 weeks for delivery.
This offer is subject to withdrawal without notice.